The Sociology of
Political Crisis

ALSO AVAILABLE FROM BLOOMSBURY

On Resistance, Howard Caygill

The Sociology of Political Crisis

A Theory of Fluid Conjunctures

Michel Dobry

Translated by Brian Jenkins

BLOOMSBURY ACADEMIC
LONDON • NEW YORK • OXFORD • NEW DELHI • SYDNEY

BLOOMSBURY ACADEMIC
Bloomsbury Publishing Plc
50 Bedford Square, London, WC1B 3DP, UK
1385 Broadway, New York, NY 10018, USA
29 Earlsfort Terrace, Dublin 2, Ireland

BLOOMSBURY, BLOOMSBURY ACADEMIC and the Diana logo are trademarks of Bloomsbury Publishing Plc

First published in Great Britain 2025

First published in French by Sciences Po Press, 2009

Copyright © Michel Dobry, 2025

Michel Dobry has asserted his right under the Copyright, Designs and Patents Act, 1988, to be identified as Author of this work.

For legal purposes the Acknowledgments on p. ix constitute an extension of this copyright page.

Cover design: Ben Anslow
Cover image: *The Burning of the Houses of Parliament* (1835), J. W. M. Turner
(Contributor: Artefact / Alamy Stock Photo)

All rights reserved. No part of this publication may be reproduced or transmitted in any form or by any means, electronic or mechanical, including photocopying, recording, or any information storage or retrieval system, without prior permission in writing from the publishers.

Bloomsbury Publishing Plc does not have any control over, or responsibility for, any third-party websites referred to or in this book. All internet addresses given in this book were correct at the time of going to press. The author and publisher regret any inconvenience caused if addresses have changed or sites have ceased to exist, but can accept no responsibility for any such changes.

A catalogue record for this book is available from the British Library.

A catalog record for this book is available from the Library of Congress.

ISBN: HB: 978-1-3503-7335-8
PB: 978-1-3503-7331-0
ePDF: 978-1-3503-7332-7
eBook: 978-1-3503-7333-4

Typeset by Deanta Global Publishing Services, Chennai, India
Printed and bound in Great Britain

To find out more about our authors and books visit www.bloomsbury.com and sign up for our newsletters.

For Françoise

Contents

Acknowledgments ix
Preface to the English Edition x

1 The Continuity Hypothesis 1
A Clausewitzian Perspective 1
Departing from Objectivism 4
Mobilizations and Moves 7
What Is Wrong with the Instrumental View of Mobilizations 16
Crises As Transformations of "Structures" 19
A Comparative Design 22

2 Three Illusions in the Study of Political Crises 25
The Etiological Illusion 26
The Natural History Illusion 33
The Heroic Illusion 46

3 Mapping Complexity 57
How Sectoral Logics Do Work 58
The Capture of Sectoral Calculations 60
The Objectification of Sectoral Relations 62
Sectoral Autonomy 65
Collusive Transactions and Consolidation Effects 67
Sectors and Arenas 69

4 Fluid Conjunctures and the Plasticity of Structures 73

Desectorization 74
Structural Uncertainty 80
Processes of De-Objectification 85
Elements of Discussion 88

5 Extended Interdependence 99

An Imperfect Tight Game 100
Marks, Moves, and Symbolic Politics 108
Competitions for the Definition of Reality 114

6 Some Typical Emergent Effects 127

Institutional Solutions 127
Is There Something Like a Prevalence of the Hidden? 133
Charismatic Strategies: De Gaulle and Mendès France 139

7 Regression Toward Habitus 149

Habitus, Habit, and "Creative Effervescence" 149
Dispositions and Conjuncture 152
Logics of Position, Logics of Dispositions, and Confidence in the Habitus 155
Actors' Conjunctural Location and the Emergence of Poles of Structuration 159

8 Political Crises and Delegitimation Processes 165

The Standard Paradigm 166
Delegitimation Effects and Structural Legitimacy 170
Crises in Collusive Transactions and the Political Economy of Consent 175

Conclusion 183

Bibliography 189
Index of Authors 202
Index of Notions 207

Acknowledgments

In the long gestation of the English translation of *Sociologie des crises politiques*, I have incurred many debts. First, I want to express a deep sense of gratitude to Brian Jenkins, who brilliantly and kindly translated this book. I know it was not an easy task. I thank him as well for his enduring friendship and also for his patience in dealing with my caprices, some of which may occasionally have left their mark on the translation, in which case I alone am responsible. My warmest thanks are extended to Virgile Coujard and Carole Sigman, for their invaluable, generous, and highly efficient help in reviewing the text. Special thanks also to Rod Aya and Michaël Goudoux. At Bloomsbury, I am grateful to my publisher, Liza Thompson, for her support and her unconditional confidence in the project, and to Katrina Calsado and Giles Herman, for their exceptional commitment and professionalism. Thanks also to Ben Piggott and Peter Warren and, in the production phase, to the staff of Deanta. Lastly, though by no means least, my greatest thanks are due to Kevin Passmore, who is well aware of how decisive his role was for the publication of this translation.

Preface to the English Edition

The first edition of the present work was published in French in 1986.[1] It had been preceded, three years earlier, by an article outlining the main elements of the theory of fluid conjunctures which this book develops.[2] This theory seeks to make sense of a set of critical processes or events, such as those that in common parlance are called "revolutions," "political crises," "breakdowns," or moments of "collapse" which political systems may experience, various types of "transition" from one political regime to another, "revolts," "uprisings," and so on. One of the contentions of this book is that much may be gained by bringing perspective to bear on phenomena which everyday language categorizes as separate and opposite. Or, put another way, by resisting the temptation, omnipresent in the social sciences, automatically to assume that a multiplicity of different substantives denotes differences of substance or "nature" (which is why I often place such substantives in inverted commas). Indeed, from the very outset, this book positions itself against any form of essentialization of social relations, institutions, individuals, social groups, or, *a fortiori*, whole societies. Its approach is, as the reader will soon see, a resolutely *relational* one.

I

This English translation of *Sociologie des crises politiques* is certainly long overdue, and this has impeded the diffusion of its arguments. The truth is that,

---

[1] Michel Dobry, *Sociologie des crises politiques. La dynamique des mobilisations multisectorielles* (Paris: Presses de Sciences-po, 1986). This book was a slightly edited version of my doctoral thesis entitled "Eléments pour une théorie des conjonctures politiques fluides" (Doctoral diss. [Doctorat d"Etat], Paris: Institut d"Etudes Politiques, January 1984).

[2] See Michel Dobry, "Mobilisations multisectorielles et dynamique des crises politiques. Un point de vue heuristique," *Revue Française de Sociologie* 24, no. 3 (1983): 395–419; the article reproduces the text of a paper delivered at the Congress of the International Political Science Association in Rio de Janeiro in August 1982, which is when the theoretical schema of *Sociologie des crises politiques* found its definitive formulation.

more than twenty-five years ago now, I was forced to block the appearance of a first translation, just before its publication. It included a huge number of errors and misinterpretations, so many in fact that I eventually gave up any idea of correcting it. The present translation owes its quality, precision and elegance to the skills of the translator. It is based on the third edition of the book (2009), in which I had tried to lighten a sometimes rather arid text, and where I also corrected a few misprints and clumsy formulations that I had not spotted in the previous editions. Finally, the constraints associated with the transition from French into English have led me to make some additional adjustments and clarifications. However, none of this has affected the core arguments advanced in this book, its overall features, or indeed what I regard as its coherence.

There is at least one excellent reason for this seemingly "conservative" attitude, apart from the author's own indolence. The years that have elapsed since the book's first publication have been fortuitous in one respect: its propositions have successfully passed an impressive series of empirical "tests," some of considerable magnitude. This is not only the case, for example, of the critical processes, "transitions" or "transformations," that accompanied, or rather constituted, the collapse of "Soviet-type" regimes in Central and Eastern Europe (including the USSR itself), but also somewhat different no doubt in terms of outcome, the "revolts" or "revolutions" occurring later in the so-called Arab-Muslim world. It is, of course, far from irrelevant for my argument that these various processes often led to sharply contrasting outcomes, and took place in equally contrasting "cultural" contexts. Indeed, these features merely confirm the solidity of this book's propositions. But the most significant point perhaps lies elsewhere: the propositions it develops and its overall problematics have increasingly—unexpectedly for me—impacted works and approaches which now go well beyond the field of critical processes alone. The question of what Lakatos called "excess empirical content" has been one of the major issues in the debates about the present book in recent years.[3] I do not have the room here of coming back to this matter as it would deserve. Apart from simply noting that it urges the researcher to revisit the very manner in which the social sciences account for some pivotal topics, such as legitimacy and delegitimation processes, "charismatic" leadership, how collective action takes off and spreads, the differentiation of the social spaces (or fields) characterizing our societies, or how these societies "hold together" (when indeed they do hold), and so on. And, besides this, noting that three other traits may describe the actual impact of the book. First, works using its perspective cover a fairly diverse range of "cultural

---

[3] See in particular Myriam Aït-Aoudia and Antoine Roger, eds., *La logique du désordre. Relire la sociologie de Michel Dobry* (Paris: Presses de Sciences-po, 2015); Brigitte Gaïti and Johanna Siméant-Germanos, eds., *La consistance des crises. Autour de Michel Dobry* (Rennes: Presses Universitaires de Rennes, 2018).

areas"—in addition to those referred to above and, of course, in the book itself—including a number of countries in Latin America and, more unexpectedly, in sub-Saharan Africa. Second, they concern a broad spectrum of empirical "objects," ranging from phenomena perceived as out of the ordinary (industrial and health disasters, including the Covid-19 pandemic, ecological risks, financial crises, etc.) to many others falling within the register of the stable and the "normal" (daily institutional arrangements, electoral competition, the definition of public policies, etc.). Third, more and more works explore the implications of the books theses in dimensions far away from their initial field; they do so through time, in the historical depth of our societies—for example, to study the "Wars of religion" in Europe and the emergence of the "modern" state—or through space to think about the international system (its structuration and its forms of differentiation).

II

Nonetheless, I have absolutely no doubt that, even today, the arguments of *Sociologie des crises politiques* may surprise or even disconcert some readers, and not only Anglophone ones. The book claims to make sense of a set of historical episodes, sequences of critical "events," political "crises" or "breakdowns," "revolutions," and so on, and yet it does not offer any narration of these episodes, it neither retraces their overall chronology nor analyzes the trajectory from inception to end point. It deals with processes or phenomena often heavily laden with consequences for the fate of individuals as well as for societies as a whole, and yet it refuses to explain their outcomes, effects, and by-products, whether in the short or the long term. Worse still, it even suggests setting these outcomes and effects aside. The book openly regards these critical phenomena as being entirely historical, entirely chaotic, entirely nonnecessary, entirely the realm of *contingency*. And, despite that, it asserts the curious, and for some certainly extravagant ambition not to abdicate before this *historicity*, not to concede everything. It outlines a perspective that seeks to extract from this historicity (which it nonetheless sees as fundamental) a few fragments of knowledge of a more general kind. While recognizing the historical singularity of each "crisis," the book argues that it is possible to draw these fragments out by means of a theoretical scheme whose scope extends well beyond this singularity.

The central thesis of the book is, however, easy enough to articulate. The "political crises" and similar critical phenomena which may be observed in complex social systems—in the sense I give to this notion below—become intelligible in their basic features as long as they are conceived in terms of the dynamics of *desectorization* of social space in such systems. I analyze this desectorization as a conjunctural transformation of the state of the social systems where these "crises" occur. And it is this transformation which enabled me to identify and to account for the *plasticity of the "structures"* of these systems. The book relates the dynamics of desectorization to the competing mobilizations which may be deployed simultaneously in a number of social sectors, spheres or fields, whose differentiation, relative autonomy one from another, and the social logics specific to each of them, constitute three of the distinctive features of complex systems.[4] But while it is born in these mobilizations, the dynamics of desectorization has the crucial peculiarity of *emancipating itself* from its origins.

> This idea, to my mind, is not without some affinity with a particular aspect of the thought of a perhaps unexpected author here, Clausewitz. At least in my reading of *Vom Kriege*, the most important point he makes is not his famous dictum "war is merely the continuation of politics by other means."[5] It is rather in the combination of this somewhat trivial formula with another statement, much more stronger and far reaching, that I will formulate as follows: once the war is here, and regardless of the (political) determinants or "causes" that brought it about, its protagonists—whether they like it or not, and whatever their aims or intentions—are caught up in a particular *logic of situation* (in my wording, Clausewitz calls this "grammar" of war). The main property of that logic is to confront the war protagonists with the possibility of the "rise to the extremes" of violence. As is probably understood by now, the situational logic specifying the critical processes examined here is indeed very different.

In the perspective outlined by this book (a perspective which, for this reason in particular, may also be seen as processual), this dynamics is fundamentally conceived as *internal* to the critical processes and phenomena which this perspective addresses. This means that these processes tend to break free from the historical conditions or determinants of the genesis of the multisectoral mobilizations, to break free also from the etiology and path specific to each of

---

[4] It should be added that the perspective of *Sociology des crises politiques* in no way presupposes—as openly or more surreptitiously functionalist approaches do, for instance those of Niklas Luhmann, *The Differentiation of Society* (New York: Columbia University Press, 1982), Pierre Bourdieu, *Distinction: Social Critique of the Judgement and of Taste* (London: Routledge & Kegan Paul, 1984 [1st French ed., 1979]) or, more recently, Neil Fligstein and Doug McAdam, *A Theory of Fields* (Oxford: Oxford University Press, 2012)—that these differentiated social subspaces and their specific logics refer primarily to a functional "need," "prerequisite," or even a "central issue." This perspective sees differentiated sectors and the form of differentiation peculiar to complex systems as mere products of a much more chaotic *historicity* than such approaches would admit. In other words, it offers a resolutely nonfunctionalist conception of them; on this point, see in particular Enrique Martín-Criado, "El concepto de campo como herramienta metodológica" (The concept of field as methodological tool), *Revista Española de Investigaciones Sociológicas* 123 (2008): 11–33.

[5] Michel Dobry, "Clausewitz et l' «entre-deux», ou de quelques difficultés d'une recherche de paternité légitime," *Revue Française de Sociologie* 17, no. 4 (1976): 652–64.

these mobilizations (this is one of the bases, among others, of my criticism of what I call the *etiological illusion*). Furthermore, it also means that going back to these conditions and determinants does nothing to illuminate the specific dynamics of these critical processes and phenomena. What explains a considerable number of the trend-properties, regularities, or "facts" associated with these crises is rather the desectorization of social space and the propositions or implications that may be derived from it: in particular, the emergence of *extended configurations of interdependence* (which take over the *sectoral* ones), the de-objectification of institutionalized social relations, and structural uncertainty (a question I will return to later).[6] Many of these features had already been noted, observed, commented on by the very actors of these historical episodes or by scholars, social scientists, or historians. Others, no less numerous, had hitherto remained hidden, undetected, unsuspected, or misidentified, and they could be both brought to light and explained precisely thanks to the theoretical scheme this book is based on. The reader will discover all these regularities and properties within the book itself; this is not the purpose of this Preface. There are good reasons to think that the theses advanced by the theory of fluid conjunctures will allow many others to be identified.

III

Despite the belated appearance of this English translation, several elements of the theory of fluid conjunctures seem occasionally to have filtered down, by more or less circuitous routes, among Anglophone scholars, not exclusively specialists in French society or revolutions, and to have found some echo there. I can only rejoice at the fact. However, at the same time I must acknowledge that the diffusion of these elements has not been without problems. The absence of an English translation has thus permitted a few not so glorious practices—some poaching, or low-profile "re-appropriation," so to speak (starting, to be sure, with vulgar pilfering of the theoretical scheme of critical processes emancipating themselves from their etiology). But the major difficulty has been that, very often, these elements have not really been properly "digested"; they have only been circulated, interpreted, used, or redeployed in a partial, fragmented, unsystematic way. This has led to serious errors, confusions, or simply misunderstandings, whose operation is well worth investigating. I would like, in the rest of this Preface, to look as briefly as possible at a few examples, chosen both for the intelligibility of my main arguments and because they concern issues that are strategically

---

[6]What I mean here by trend-properties is just that these properties occur and can be observed only with varying intensities, and absolutely not that they might be absent from this kind of conjunctures.

important for the social sciences as a whole, going well beyond the empirical terrain and subject matter of the present book.

I will begin with the issue of *the plasticity of structures*. Very often I have used the word "structures" in inverted commas, sometimes adding that I was using it "whatever might be understood by this term." What I was trying to convey was not just my reluctance regarding the diverse forms of reification of social relations frequently to be found in approaches claiming to be "structural" or "structuralist." I was also trying to convey something else: the plasticity of structures, and this is perfectly explicit in *Sociologie des crises politiques*, involved a very wide spectrum of what not only social scientists but also historians call "structures," thus, for example, the routine organization, in complex societies, of the social division of political labor, their social hierarchies, their differentiation into more or less autonomous sectors, social spheres or "fields," the "webs of meaning" and categorizations specific to each of these differentiated social subspaces, the institutions, or the social distribution of "resources"—or, if preferred, of "capital," though this metaphor and a fortiori the analogy itself is not without danger—of organized violence, and so on. For me, the main point lies precisely in the diversity and, above all, the systematicity of the manifestations and effects of the internal dynamics at work in critical processes, namely desectorization. Unfortunately, some years after the publication of *Sociologie des crises politiques*, a handful of authors took the plasticity of structures as I had identified it, and applied it solely to structures deemed "symbolic," "ideational" or discursive. This mistake, which is in fact a gross misinterpretation, derives, I suspect, from a major divide in the way the social sciences conceive "the social construction of reality" or—not that this makes much difference to the scholars' actual approach—"the construction of social reality." Reducing social "structures" to language categories, discourses, or, sometimes, "ideas," for example the "language of corporations" during the French Revolution of 1789 and "the general structure of cultural representations" of a whole society (like that of Fiji Islands), amounts to reducing the "construction of social reality" to its *discursive construction*, a view that has for several decades severely hampered large sections of the social sciences.

IV

However, this reduction of the plasticity of structures to the plasticity of "symbolic structures" might in some respects appear relatively benign when compared to another error, namely the persistent failure to understand the very notion of critical or fluid conjuncture as a particular state of a social system's "structures." That is also, ultimately, the inability to grasp the idea that social systems may undergo changes of state resulting from the actors' mobilizations and that such processes may occur in the *short term*.

To illustrate this, I would highlight the way the notion of critical conjuncture is systematically equated with something radically different, namely *critical junctures*. This is a very serious mistake. What gets lost in the confusion of critical conjunctures with critical junctures is precisely the diversity of possible states of the same social system, and the possibility that its state may experience transformations.[7] In other words, the confusion effectively empties the notion of conjuncture of the very substance given it by the theory of fluid conjunctures. Let us look at the question in more detail.

The notion of critical juncture is used nowadays, as we know, to designate moments of bifurcation, or "turning points," intervening in the historical trajectories or paths of social objects as different as, for example, economic systems, diverse types of political regime, single institutions or institutional configurations (and indeed, at another level, the biographical trajectories or careers of mere individuals). Though the notion predates it, the social science perspective where it has come to be most discussed is that of *path dependence*, whether in the classic versions of this perspective, those that have been formalized in economics—in many respects still the most rigorous[8]— or in the attempts to transfer the perspective to other empirical objects and terrains, like those that concern us more directly here. But the underlying idea in all these uses of this notion is that it is these critical junctures which allow us to analyze and explain changes in these trajectories or paths, and which guide or direct them, like railway points, toward outcomes that are significantly different from those that would "normally" occur or which would "normally" have been anticipated. Note first that these critical junctures are conceived as *initial moments* for the shifts or modifications of direction in these historical paths or trajectories, in other words as moments initiating *other processes*—the latter of interest to the scholar because of the specific *outcomes* to which they have supposedly led. Note, second, that the manifold uses of the notion of critical junctures all concur in placing at the heart of their interrogation the *outcomes* of the processes which critical junctures are supposed to be the starting points. And it is these outcomes and their characteristics which will then govern every

---

[7]Here is another example of misunderstanding of the notion of critical conjuncture, which is pretty weird: whereas it is unquestionably accepted that matters may exist in different states (gaseous, liquid, or solid), many scholars find it difficult to admit that something comparable may happen with the structures of social systems. The reason is that they remain stuck in the old belief that posits a dubious equivalence between critical states of social systems and *social pathologies*. I will mention further another equally dangerous form that this exceptionalism may take.

[8]See in particular W. Brian Arthur, "Competing Technologies, Increasing Returns, and Lock-in by Historical Events," *The Economic Journal* 99, no. 394 (1989): 116–31; Paul A. David, "Path Dependance, its Critics, and the Quest for "Historical Economics'," in *Evolution and Path Dependence in Economic Ideas. Past and Present*, ed. P. Garouste and S. Ioannides (Cheltenham: Edward Elgar, 2001), 15–40.

research operation. In particular, they will allow the scholar to *identify* the critical junctures and locate them in time, or at least his approach will be driven by this belief. All this entirely conceived in retrospective mode, of course. I will return to the issue of outcomes later, from a different viewpoint, a much wider one, and involving an absolutely fundamental difficulty. For the moment, let me simply note that the confusion between critical conjunctures and critical junctures is rooted primarily in the orientation of the scholars own interest or curiosity, both theoretical and empirical. But this is not the only type of problem raised by this confusion.

Equally significant is that, in these approaches, the processes, from their starting points (critical junctures) to the outcomes, are conceived as potentially being of long duration, sometimes very long (possibly several centuries). Furthermore, these same processes are also conceived as being entirely "incremental" and barely visible from day to day, if not invisible. The difficulty is that we very frequently find this feature, in different forms, when the classic versions of path dependence are transferred from the economic to the empirical domains and objects to which I have just referred, in particular the analysis of "revolutions," "crises" and "transitions" of political regime, and so on. All these remarks point to a problem which should be of even greater concern to the scholar, namely that of knowing exactly *what is supposed to be "critical"* in critical junctures. Now, it seems evident to me that the critical juncture is termed "critical" for two main reasons. First, because of the historical importance—the critical importance—the scholar will attach to the outcome occurring at the end of the trajectory or path supposedly initiated by the "critical" juncture. Second, because, at least as regards noneconomic empirical fields like those addressed in this book, the scholar will instantly reduce the critical juncture to a *situation of decision-making*[9] or, more precisely, to a situation in which the trajectory or path leading to any given outcome will be assumed to result from *a single* deliberate choice, *a single* decision by *a single* individual actor or *a single* restricted and well-defined group of actors acting "as one," so to speak.

---

[9] See, among others, James Mahoney, "Path Dependence in Historical Sociology," *Theory and Society* 29, no. 4 (2000): 507–48; Giovanni Capoccia and R. Daniel Kelemen, "The Study of Critical Junctures: Theory, Narratives, and Counterfactuals in Historical Institutionalism," *World Politics* 59, no. 3 (2007): 341–69. see also Ruth Berins Collier and David Collier, *Shaping the Political Arena: Critical Junctures, the Labor Movement, and Regime Dynamics in Latin America* (Princeton: Princeton University Press, 1991). Note that many of the promoters of the original conceptions of path dependence are reluctant to such an outrageously decisionist vision of the critical juncture.

V

This allows us to perceive what is both the mainspring and the basis of the failure to understand the notion of critical conjuncture as a specific state of a complex social system, and as a conjunctural transformation of the "structures" of this system arising from multisectoral mobilizations. It concerns what I have called the *heroic illusion*, a fallacy which is not confined to the question of critical junctures alone,[10] and which long predates the discussions surrounding this question. For the sake of clarity, let me briefly summarize the substance of this fallacy, which is discussed more fully in the second chapter of this book. The heroic illusion is shaped by two contentions. First, periods of "stability" in political systems are supposedly subject to "normal" approaches in the social sciences, namely approaches conceived both as "structural" (relying on the identification of the "structures" of the social phenomena under consideration)—once again, irrespective of what the scholar means by "structural—and as determinist. In contrast, critical processes or "events," "revolutions," "political crises," and so on are supposedly, *by nature*, liable to quite different types of approach, framed in terms of *choice*, "decision" and calculation on the part of the actors, that is, approaches which are assumed to be nondeterminist and noncausal. This represents perhaps the most pernicious form of exceptionalism we can find in the literature on critical processes, that is, methodological exceptionalism. In large part, the present book's perspective was precisely elaborated in opposition to that way of thinking.

Undoubtedly, the heroic fallacy epitomizes a problem which persistently bedevils the social sciences, the structure/agency polarity, misconceived as one of mutual opposition.

> One of the decisive moves achieved by the theory of fluid conjunctures consisted precisely in seeing the structure/agency polarity as misleading and unproductive. On this point, the approach of *Sociologie des crises politiques* concurred with the reflections proposed by Pierre Bourdieu, albeit on quite other grounds.[11] However, while recognizing Bourdieu's fundamental contribution and partly drawing on his work, it immediately extended it in a critical way, for example by dismissing any rigid opposition or frontier between habitus or dispositions on the one hand and the actor's calculations and expectations on the other; in this sense, as other scholars have pointed out,

---

[10] Thus, for example, the heroic illusion can also occasionally lead to the absurdity of reducing contingency to, here again, a mere single decision by a single individual or collective actor.

[11] Pierre Bourdieu, *Outline of a Theory of Practice* (Cambridge: Cambridge University Press, 1977 [1st French ed., 1972]).

Sociologie des crises politiques is one of the very first works to think both "*with* and *against*" Bourdieu (this is true, for example, for his theory of fields as for his theory of the habitus).[12] It is from this point of view that, by means of a systematic reconfiguration of their concepts, the theory of fluid conjunctures has relied both on Bourdieu and, for example, on authors who at first glance are very distant from him—for instance, strategic interaction theorists such as Thomas Schelling and Erwing Goffman.[13]

It is partly for this reason (the structure/agency polarity) that the heroic illusion has such appeal for scholars.[14] However, in the case of critical processes, this fallacy has specific effects that are positively catastrophic. First, because the scholar will couple this rejection of "normal" social-science approaches with the spontaneous perception that these processes diverge from the "normal" life or workings of political systems, thus recycling, not always consciously, the old belief in the inherent "pathological" character of these phenomena. Second, and even more seriously, because the scholar—again without understanding the implications—will thus be led to ignore what happens to the "structures" in these critical processes, in particular the possible transformations that these structures may experience. And at the same time ignore the issue of how these transformations may indeed contribute to shaping the perceptions, calculations, choices, and actions of actors caught up in these critical processes.

The point is that the issue matters; it matters on a number of levels and in a number of ways. To limit myself to one example, it matters when seeking to account for *the kind of uncertainty* experienced by the protagonists of these processes. In routine conjunctures, their evaluations, calculations, and consequently their choices or decisions tend to rely systematically on materials,

---

[12]See, among others, Philippe Corcuff, *Théories sociologiques contemporaines* (Paris: Armand Colin, 2022); Cyril Lemieux, "L"hypothèse de la régression vers les habitus et ses implications. Dobry, lecteur de Bourdieu," in *La Logique du désordre. Relire la sociologie de Michel Dobry,* ed. Myriam Aït-Aoudia and Antoine Roger (Paris: Presses de Sciences-po, 2015), 71–92.

[13]Thomas Schelling, *The Strategy of Conflict* (Cambridge, MA: Harvard University Press, 1960); Erwing Goffman, *Strategic Interaction* (Oxford: Basil Blackwell, 1979).

[14]The appeal of this causal fallacy also stems from convergence with the ordinary perceptions and rationalizations, let me call them "Leninist," of twentieth-century revolutionary practitioners, who dichotomize the "objective" and "subjective" factors of revolutions (on this point too, see Chapter 2 of the present book). It is worth noting that several of the leading authors identified with "transitology" in the mid-1980s and the 1990s, and clearly trapped in the intellectual logic of the heroic illusion, make an explicit reference to such rationalizations; see, for instance, Adam Przeworski, "Problems in the Study of Transition to Democracy," in *Transitions From Authoritarian Rule. Comparative Perspectives*, ed. G. O'Donnel, P. C. Schmitter, and L. Whitehead (Baltimore: The Johns Hopkins University Press, 1986) and Guillermo O'Donnel and Philippe C. Schmitter, *Transitions from Authoritarian Rule. Tentative Conclusions about Uncertain Democraties* (Baltimore: The Johns Hopkins University Press, 1986). For a critical discussion, see Michel Dobry, "Les voies incertaines de la transitologie: choix stratégiques, séquences historiques, bifurcations et processus de *path dependence*," *Revue Française de Science Politique* 50, no. 4–5 (2000): 585–614.

definitions of situation, reference points, clues, and official as well as pragmatic "rules of the game," all specific to the differentiated social worlds or sectors where these protagonists act. Things work very differently in critical conjunctures. Under the effects of the desectorization of social space, the actors tend to be deprived of these everyday materials and supports on which they rely for their orientation, calculations, and action. This is indeed this desectorization which, for example, makes it so difficult, if not impossible, and sometimes very costly, for them to assess or anticipate the effectiveness or "value" of the resources at their disposal, to assess which moves are playable or not, or indeed what is the orientation of the other protagonists, their positions or "interests," what constitutes their own "identities," or, specifically in the case of collective actors, their very consistency. This is for the same reason—and here we come to the perspective of the theory of fluid conjunctures—that we should, in the strongest sense speak of *structural uncertainty*, an uncertainty originating in the transformation of "structures" that characterizes fluid conjunctures. Clearly all that is a far cry from the imagery that tends to be reproduced by scholars trapped in the heroic illusion, an imagery in which a "decision-maker" chooses a course of action from a well-defined set of tactical options, and is assumed to be capable of determining both the payoffs to be expected from each one, and the likely consequences of its implementation.

This has also led me to reexamine the question of the actors' rationality. For, when dealing with the calculations and expectations of actors, it is not enough to speak only of *limited* rationality or even *situated* rationality. What calls for a more radical rethinking of the actors' rationality is that this rationality becomes intelligible and explainable only if we consider it as a *socially structured rationality*. When the protagonists of fluid conjunctures experience structural uncertainty, it does not mean that they stop calculating nor that they become less rational than in routine conjunctures, that is, that they relapse into the irrationality that the proponents of mass sociology or mass psychology like to imagine. It simply means they are forced, by the very situations in which they are caught up, to calculate in a different way, and to do so under new modalities, with other supports or materials (hence, for example, in fluid conjunctures, the more important place taken in their calculations by focal points). From a more general point of view, this also means that, at least in highly differentiated social systems, the modalities and effectiveness of ordinary calculation, and even the possibility of such a calculation, that is, *ordinary calculability*, are closely related to the segmentation of social space into multiple social sectors, spheres or "fields."

VI

The theory of fluid conjunctures, as I have said, makes no claim to explaining the outcomes of the critical processes it addresses (any more than those of possible processes of path dependence mentioned above). This point requires some explanation, for it is completely at odds with the most deeply entrenched thought patterns in the social sciences. For the link between the "event," especially the critical event, and its outcome would seem to be entirely taken for granted. And it would seem entirely "natural" for the scholar, when dealing with critical processes or conjunctures, to treat the outcome to which these processes or conjunctures lead—that is, its specific features or properties, those which seem to distinguish it from other outcomes—as precisely *what needs to be explained* in such processes or conjunctures (or, to use professional jargon, as the *explicandum* of his research enterprise). The scholar's fascination with the outcome is not hard to understand: *once it has happened*, the outcome "counts"; it may weigh, often heavily, on the fate of individuals, groups, or even whole societies; it may have dramatic effects in the short term, but no less important consequences in the long term, consequences which the scholar will have no trouble dignifying with the term "structural effects." The problem is that this is only true once the outcome has occurred, and *only from that moment.* In other words, these effects and consequences in no way justify the scholar blindly accepting the premise that this outcome and its specific characteristics embody, epitomize or reflect the critical processes or conjunctures from which they emerge and that they provide their explanatory key. In fact, this premise is quite untenable. However, it is this premise that wholly defines the usual approach of the scholar, an approach widely seen as self-evident and unquestionable.

The outcome thus governs the scholar's construction of the historical intrigue or narrative, to be more precise the *découpage*—the selection—of the "facts." This *découpage* follows a very special modus operandi. Conducted in "regressive" mode, it "retraces" the path leading to the outcome and the chain of "facts" that are deemed to have determined the characteristics considered specific to this outcome as opposed to other types of outcome, progressively working backward into the historical depths of the outcome in search of its primary "causes" or "preconditions." The effect is, without the scholar being aware of it most of the time, such as to *make these "facts" converge towards this outcome* (this problem is equally present with the critical junctures mentioned above, which are identified by the scholar by exactly the same procedure). This retrospective reading of history has the fatal flaw of ruling out any comparison between the historical cases under consideration and other cases which, by bad luck, have inelegantly led to other types of outcome, and it also precludes the suspicion that very similar configurations of "facts" or "events" might lead to outcomes that are very different from one another. The intellectual logic of this kind of perspective implies that the critical processes, conjunctures, or events which led to any specific outcome (seizure of power by the fascists, democracy, military dictatorship, installation of a communist regime, civil war, etc.) must have a "nature" or "essence" and, of course, a historical trajectory or path which are no less specific, and certainly different from the "natures" and trajectories or paths attributed to critical processes, conjunctures, or events which supposedly led to other types of outcome. It is no doubt becoming clear that this is not just a methodological question, for it also relates to difficulties of a different order. These difficulties, present in any approach that analyzes critical processes on the basis of the outcomes to which they led, become particularly salient whenever the scholar seeks to establish something like a chronological sequence of steps, stages, events, or bifurcations deemed to have culminated in a given type of outcome.

These observations entirely apply to what is sometimes called "reactive sequences." It is interesting to note that in the approach outlined in the 1990s by Andrew Abbott, which became the major reference for this kind of analysis, this author, in order to clarify his argument, explicitly appeals to the intellectual tradition of "natural history," the same tradition that underpins the "natural history of revolutions" and whose shortcomings and flaws are dissected in the present book (chap. 2).[15] As Wolfgang Knöbl has aptly observed, Abbott seems in some later works to have abandoned his initial approach and to have moved closer to the perspective of the theory of fluid conjunctures.[16] Nevertheless, my critique of historicism in no way implies the rejection of all forms of historical causality or determination that Abbott now seems to suggest (but it is possible, as Knöbl thinks, that even Abbott cannot bring himself to fully accept everything such rejection implies).[17]

My concern is that the intellectual logic underpinning this kind of approach necessarily means the scholar will fail to understand what I consider decisive, namely the role that *contingency* (very frequently at least) plays in the outcomes of these processes, and will also fail to understand the fact that these outcomes

---

[15]See, for example, Andrew Abbott, "History and Sociology. The Lost Synthesis," *Social Science History* 15, no. 2 (1991): 201–38.

[16]Andrew Abbott, "Against Narrative Sociology: A Preface to Lyrical Sociology," *Sociological Theory* 25, no. 1 (2007): 67–99; for Wolfgang Knöbl's notation, see his "Politische Krisen und Prozessualität: Das Werk Michel Dobrys in der aktuellen theoritischen Debatte," paper given at the Workshop "Theoretische und methodische Problemstellungen soziologischer Prozessforschung," Bielefeld University, 2017.

[17]For a fully developed discussion of my critique of historicism, see Jean-Philippe Heurtin, "La logique des situations comme nômos du présent. La sociologie des crises politiques et le congé donné à la causalité historique," in *La logique du désordre. Relire la sociologie de Michel Dobry*, ed. Myriam Aït-Aoudia and Antoine Roger (Paris: Presses de Sciences-po, 2015), 95–123, and, for my answer, Michel Dobry, "Eléments de réponse. Principes et implications d"une perspective relationnelle," in *La logique du désordre. Relire la sociologie de Michel Dobry,* ed. Myriam Aït-Aoudia and Antoine Roger (Paris: Presses de Sciences-po, 2015), 260–331; on this issue, see also now the impressive work by Wolfgang Knöbl, *Die Soziologie vor der Geschichte. Zur Kritik der Sozialtheorie* (Berlin: Suhrkamp, 2022).

result from conjunctions or confluences—stripped of any historical (or functional) necessity—between multiple series of heterogeneous causal chains, intertwining a multiplicity of configurations of social facts or events, equally heterogeneous and more or less independent of one another. Or, expressed a bit differently, this means that an approach which involves analyzing the critical process on the basis of its outcome inevitably involves various forms—some shamefaced or embarrassed, some less so—of *historicism* (I use the term in a similar sense to Popper, although my critique of historicism relies on a different foundation from his, namely contingency). Furthermore, the role of contingency in the "march of history" means that it is beyond the scope of the social sciences to establish, let alone explain, "laws of history," that is, laws of historical development, for that is precisely what we are dealing with in the case of approaches focusing on the outcomes.

VII

To all these difficulties and impasses, the theory of fluid conjunctures proposes a remedy admittedly somewhat counterintuitive in character, but there is no alternative. The remedy, to which I briefly referred at the beginning of this Preface, involves, first of all, making the methodological decision to forget, or, if preferred, to put on ice, albeit provisionally, the outcomes that emerge from critical processes, events, or conjunctures. I willingly concede that this solution is not always easy to achieve, but the task is not insurmountable. This is indeed the reason why, for example, *Sociologie des crises politiques*, at the empirical level, favors historical materials or "sources" that are directly contemporaneous with the action as it is unfolding. The solution has another aspect, however. For the decision to parenthesize the outcomes also involves a major epistemological issue, namely to dismiss the notion that critical processes are explained by explaining their outcomes. In other words, to put it more brutally, the challenge is to give oneself a different "enigma," a different "puzzle" to solve, a different *explicandum*.

That decision, in fact, represents a radical transformation in the way the social sciences approach critical processes and phenomena. Instead of the illusory objective of explaining the outcomes of critical processes—tantamount, as I have just suggested, to constructing a social science capable of establishing "laws of history"—the theory of fluid conjunctures outlines a systematic theoretical and empirical focus on what the critical processes, events, or conjunctures *are made of*, on *what actually happens during them*, on *what* their protagonists *do*, and on what in these processes helps shape their actions. Namely, a focus on *history in the making*. This was precisely what was made possible by understanding these critical processes in terms of conjunctural transformation in the state of the "structures" of social systems impacted by multisectoral mobilizations. Thus, in the confused historical entanglement of heterogeneous chains of determination, this perspective has also made it possible to identify categories of situation or configurations of interdependence constituting different types of *situational logic*, which weigh on the actors, their perceptions, anticipations, calculations, and practices. And, at the same time, it has moved my attention to the materials, instruments, reference points, and operations on which the actors rely in order to orient themselves in the situations in which they are caught and forced to act. In doing so, the approach developed in *Sociologie des crises politiques* departed from the traditional imagery of causality and replaced it with what can be thought of as *conjunctural causality*. But a conjunctural causality in the strongest sense of the term, that is, in the sense that it also rejects the temptation, quite common nowadays, to link to the role given to contingency in the "march of history" the misleading and self-defeating idea that social sciences are doomed by the very "nature" of their objects to deal only with historical singularities.

It is through this shift in questioning that the theory of fluid conjunctures became able to account for the regularities or trend-properties that persistently characterize these processes. This constitutes the substance, and indeed the central ambition of the book whose translation follows. On the other hand, the reader will have understood that these regularities or trend-properties do not allow us to anticipate or explain the outcomes emerging from the critical processes, events or conjunctures. And, more specifically, they do not allow us to establish constant causal relations between the initial historical conditions of the critical processes and the outcomes emerging—or supposedly emerging— from them, nor indeed between the internal dynamics of these processes (a dynamics which, we must not forget, the theory of fluid conjunctures sees as having broken free, emancipated itself from its initial conditions) and these outcomes. Neither do they allow us to foresee which particular action or move will be performed by this particular actor at that particular moment. But I am far from convinced that, for the theory of fluid conjunctures or more generally for the intelligibility of critical processes, this represents any kind of handicap.

Michel Dobry
Paris, November 2023

References

Abbott, A. "History and Sociology. The Lost Synthesis." *Social Science History* 15, no. 2 (1991): 201–38.
Abbott, A. "Against Narrative Sociology: A Preface to Lyrical Sociology." *Sociological Theory* 25, no. 1 (2007): 67–99.

Aït-Aoudia, M. and A. Roger, eds. *La logique du désordre. Relire la sociologie de Michel Dobry*. Paris: Presses de Sciences-po, 2015.

Arthur, W. B. "Competing Technologies, Increasing Returns, and Lock-in by Historical Events." *The Economic Journal* 99, no. 394 (1989): 116–31.

Bourdieu, P. *Outline of a Theory of Practice*, Translated by Richard Nice. Cambridge: Cambridge University Press, 1977 [1st French ed., 1972].

Bourdieu, P. *Distinction: Social Critique of the Judgement and of Taste.*, Translated by Richard Nice. London: Routledge & Kegan Paul, 1984 [1st French ed., 1979].

Capoccia, G. and R. D. Kelemen. "The Study of Critical Junctures: Theory, Narratives, and Counterfactuals in Historical Institutionalism." *World Politics* 59, no. 3 (2007): 341–69.

Collier, R. B. and D. Collier. *Shaping the Political Arena*. Princeton: Princeton University Press, 1991.

Corcuff, P. *Théories sociologiques contemporaines*. Paris: Armand Colin, 2019.

David, P. A. "Path Dependance, its Critics, and the Quest for 'Historical Economics'." In *Evolution and Path Dependence in Economic Ideas. Past and Present*, edited by P. Garouste and S. Ioannides. Cheltenham: Edward Elgar, 2001.

Dobry, M. "Clausewitz et l' 'entre-deux', ou de quelques difficultés d'une recherche de paternité légitime." *Revue Française de Sociologie* 17, no. 4 (1976): 652–64.

Dobry, M. "Mobilisations multisectorielles et dynamique des crises politiques. Un point de vue heuristique." *Revue Française de Sociologie* 24, no. 3 (1983): 395–419.

Dobry, M. *Sociologie des crises politiques. La dynamique des mobilisations multisectorielles*. Paris: Presses de Sciences-po, 1986.

Dobry, M. "Les voies incertaines de la transitologie: choix stratégiques, séquences historiques, bifurcations et processsus de path dependence." *Revue Française de Science Politique* 50, no. 4–5 (2000): 585–614.

Dobry, M. "Eléments de réponse. Principes et implications d''une perspective relationnelle." In *La logique du désordre. Relire la sociologie de Michel Dobry*, edited by M. Aït-Aoudia and A. Roger, 260–331. Paris: Presses de Sciences-po, 2015.

Fligstein, N. and D. McAdam. *A Theory of Fields*. Oxford: Oxford University Press, 2012.

Gaïti, B. and J. Siméant-Germanos, eds. *La consistance des crises. Autour de Michel Dobry*. Rennes: Presses Universitaires de Rennes, 2018.

Goffman, E. *Strategic Interaction*. Oxford: Basil Blackwell, 1979.

Heurtin, J. P. "La logique des situations comme nômos du présent. La sociologie des crises politiques et le congé donné à la causalité historique." In *La logique du désordre. Relire la sociologie de Michel Dobry*, edited by M. Aït-Aoudia and A. Roger, 95–123. Paris: Presses de Sciences-po, 2015.

Knöbl, W. "Politische Krisen und Prozessualität: Das Werk Michel Dobrys in der aktuellen theoritischen Debatte." Paper presented at the Workshop "Theoretische und methodische Problemstellungen soziologischer Prozessforschung", Bielefeld University, 2017.

Knöbl, W. *Die Soziologie vor der Geschichte. Zur Kritik der Sozialtheorie*. Berlin: Suhrkamp, 2022.

Lakatos, I. "Falsification and the Methodology of Scientific Research Programmes." In *Criticism and the Growth of Knowledge*, edited by I. Lakatos and A. Musgrave, 91–196. Cambridge: Cambridge University Press, 1970.

Lemieux, C. "L'hypothèse de la régression vers les habitus et ses implications. Dobry, lecteur de Bourdieu." In *La logique du désordre. Relire la sociologie de Michel Dobry*, edited by M. Aït-Aoudia and A. Roger, 71–92. Paris: Presses de Sciences-po, 2015.

Luhmann, N. *The Differentiation of Society*. Translated by Stephen Holmes and Charles Larmore. New York: Columbia University Press, 1982 [most of the essays in this work were published in German in 1971].

Mahoney, J. "Path Dependence in Historical Sociology." *Theory and Society* 29, no. 4 (2000): 507–48.

Martin-Criado, E. "El concepto de campo como herramienta metodológica" (The concept of field as methodological tool). *Revista Española de Investigaciones Sociológicas* 123 (2008): 11–33.

O'Donnel, G. and P. C. Schmitter. *Transitions from Authoritarian Rule. Tentative Conclusions about Uncertain Democraties*. Baltimore: The Johns Hopkins University Press, 1986.

Przeworski, A. "Problems in the Study of Transition to Democracy." In *Transitions From Authoritarian Rule. Comparative Perspectives*, edited by G. O"Donnel, P. C. Schmitter, and L. Whitehead, 47–63. Baltimore: The Johns Hopkins University Press, 1986.

Schelling, T. *The Strategy of Conflict*. Cambridge, MA: Harvard University Press, 1960.

Chapter 1
The Continuity Hypothesis

This book is about processes of political crisis. To be more precise, it is devoted to a specific category of crises, those related to mobilizations which simultaneously affect several differentiated sectors of a given society. Its ambition is to recapture and account for the dynamics of such crises, and one of its central theses is that this can be done only by giving full consideration to the form of "structural" differentiation characterizing most contemporary societies. Taken as a whole, the analyses developed in the chapters that follow derive from certain initial choices, and these are not all pure and simple methodological decisions, far from it.

A Clausewitzian Perspective

The first of these choices might seem paradoxical. This book will focus on phenomena usually defined in terms of social processes leading to, or likely to lead to a breakdown in the operation of the political institutions—whether legitimate or not—of a given social system, and, simultaneously, appearing to threaten the "survival" of these institutions (incidentally, this standard way of conceiving political crises is acceptable as a provisional definition of these processes, but, indeed, only a very provisional one). In other words, I will be dealing here with phenomena that are perceived and analyzed, both by the actors of these crises themselves and by their "external" observers, as discontinuities interrupting the "normal" flow of political routines and exchanges. And yet, quite contrary to this representation, the first of my choices is to put forward a *hypothesis of continuity*. Thus, from the very outset, I will be rejecting the assumption that, in order to understand this type of phenomenon, we should necessarily look for factors, variables, or causal configurations which are radically different from those which historians and social scientists refer to when analyzing politics in routine situations. In this perspective, "continuity" simply means that the driving forces, the social factors of political crises, are not to be found exclusively, or even mainly, in social pathology and "disequilibrium," in discontent and frustration (however "relative"), in psychological deviances, or in "outbreaks" of irrationality—be they individual or collective. In this respect, the approach I outline here may legitimately be likened to a series of works that endorse the "resource mobilization" perspective.[1]

It also resembles them in another of its choices, which in a way represents the positive side of the point I have just made. This choice consists in systematically including, in the analysis and explanation of political crises, the *tactical activity* of their protagonists. More generally, it implies we give ourselves the means to understand the place, in the emergence and unfolding of these processes, of the mobilizations in which these protagonists engage in the course of the competitions and confrontations that frame political relationships, whether in routine conjunctures or in those which are less so.

In other words, the hypothesis of continuity clearly involves a shift of theoretical focus toward what actually "happens," toward what occurs and what is at stake *within* the crisis processes themselves, that is, within the "exchanges of moves" (*échanges de coups*)[2] of which they are constituted, rather than the "causes," "determinants," or "preconditions" of crises, which are supposed to explain everything. The hypothesis of continuity also works against another error—sometimes found in conjunction with this emphasis on "causes"—namely, the "explanation" of crisis processes by their outcomes or by-products, such as, for example, the fall of a regime, a civil war, a compromise leading to the "re-

---

[1] Among the most typical of such works, see especially: William A. Gamson, *Power and Discontent* (Homewood: Dorsey Press, 1968); Anthony Oberschall, *Social Conflict and Social Movements* (Englewood Cliffs: Prentice-Hall, 1973); John D. McCarthy and Mayer N. Zald, "Resource Mobilization and Social Movements: A Partial Theory," *American Journal of Sociology* 82, no. 6 (1977): 1212–41; Charles Tilly, *From Mobilization to Revolution* (Reading: Addison-Wesley, 1978); Mayer N. Zald and John D. McCarthy, eds., *The Dynamics of Social Movements* (Cambridge: Winthrop, 1979). Many of these works seem, apparently, without their authors being fully aware of it, to share the same inspiration as certain analyses from outside this perspective, like, for example, those of Frederick G. Bailey, *Stratagems and Spoils. A Social Anthropology of Politics* (Malden: Blackwell 1979) and of Warren F. Ilchman and Norman Thomas Uphoff, *The Political Economy of Change* (Berkeley: University of California Press, 1969). For works adopting the resource mobilization approach, Charles Perrow suggests distinguishing between two orientations—or sensibilities—which seem to me far from incompatible: one, more "political," the so-called political process model, considers mobilizations, collective actions, social movements in terms of their role and their effects in the political game; the other, more "economic," remains somewhat indifferent to the political dimension of such phenomena and focuses on how political resources, as rare commodities, are created, exchanged, and managed. The first orientation is especially interested in the factors contributing to the solidarity of social groups and in the instruments facilitating collective action, while the second orientation stresses competition for resources, the degree of substitutability of "products" (ecology and "women's liberation," for example), demand curves, and the promotion of political goods, or on the careers of "social movement entrepreneurs" and the ways in which the activity of their members is remunerated. This distinction, however interesting, has little relevance for my argument, see Perrow, "The Sixties Observed," in *The Dynamics of Social Movements,* ed. Mayer N. Zald and John D. McCarthy (Cambridge: Winthrop, 1979), 199–205.

[2] On "exchanges of moves," see also below, Footnote 20.

equilibration" of the political system, and, of course, "change," one of the most vague and sloppy catch-all categories available in the social sciences. And, as we shall see, it would be wrong to assume too hastily that these outcomes and by-products somehow encapsulate, reflect, or represent "what happens" in the actual unfolding of the crises.

Does this refocusing of interest oblige us to base our research agenda and analyzes on ordinary categories of perception, dilemmas, rationalizations, concepts, or even, so to speak, on "indigenous" theories—namely, those of the actors themselves? I don't think so. Certainly all this constitutes one of the richest sources of research material relevant to the present work. Without doubt it also represents a significant component of the very reality I shall be examining. But its role goes no further than that. Because the "enigma" to be solved or, if preferred, the specific "puzzle" addressed by this book can hardly be derived from the pragmatic or "theoretical" problems set out by the social actors in the course of their practical activity.[3] What primarily will interest us in the mobilizations is their relationships with their "structural contexts"—a term which, like "crisis," requires delicate handling. A major feature of the approach I will outline here consists in conceiving these contexts as likely to experience *short-term* transformations, which means as sensitive precisely to the mobilizations that may occur within them. In other words, it requires a move, indeed a decisive one, toward specifying *different types of conjuncture*—and, among them, critical conjunctures—as *specific states* of political systems' "structures."

These initial choices mean that the analyses and hypotheses developed in this work can be described, first, as a Clausewitzian perspective. But a Clausewitzian perspective free of any temptation to think of continuity in teleological or instrumental terms, that is, in particular, free of the virtues often attributed to the use of the "ends-means" schema.[4] And, second, as a perspective also structured around the distinction between *routine states* and *critical states* that may be experienced by one and the same society.[5]

This last point puts significant distance between the approach I am outlining here, and some of the assumptions posited by advocates of the resource

---

[3]On the "enigma" issue, see Thomas S. Kuhn, *The Structure of Scientific Revolutions* (Chicago: The University of Chicago Press, 1970 [1st ed., 1962]).

[4]Indeed, one of the main weaknesses of the astute but very often fragile interpretation of Clausewitz's *Vom Kriege* offered by Raymond Aron is that it precisely reduces the idea of continuity to this finalist schema: Raymond Aron, *Clausewitz, Philosopher of War* (Englewood Cliffs: Prentice-Hall, 1985 [1st French ed., 1976]). Aron (1985 [1st French ed., 1976]); for a critique of this watering down of Clausewitz's thought, see Dobry, "Clausewitz et l''entre-deux', ou de quelques difficultés d'une recherche de paternité légitime," 652–64.

[5]It is possible to see in this distinction a reminder of the Durkheimian point of view. However, in my perspective, in strong contrast with Durkheim, the distinction is entirely stripped of any reference either to any kind of social pathology or to sociological organicism, in all its forms.

mobilization approach. To their undeniable credit, they have "rehabilitated," as it were, the tactical dimension of the individual and collective actors' behavior in the explanation of social movements, violent internal confrontations, "revolutionary" phenomena, and, more generally, mobilization and conflict processes. But, on the other hand, they were also seriously mistaken in believing that this rehabilitation could be achieved only by disregarding any reflection about the possibility that social systems may experience different states of their "structures" and variations in these states.

Let me clarify this divergence, for it goes to the very heart of my system of hypotheses. It concerns the way in which we conceive processes which are both generators of "crises," and components of them, that is, mobilizations. In this respect, the analysis must avoid two opposing pitfalls: on the one hand that of objectivism and on the other a manipulative or instrumental vision of mobilizations and political resources. Significantly, the latter is often found in the works of authors who identify themselves with the "resource mobilization" perspective.

Departing from Objectivism

For the mainstream political science of the 1960s and the early 1970s, the notion of mobilization had few ties to the tactical activity of social actors. On the other hand, a close association was made at that time between mobilization and "modernization," or "political development," in more or less traditional societies. This was the case, for instance, with Karl Deutsch, whose topic, however, was mainly "social" mobilization. For this author, mobilization meant a "general process of change" within societies in transition from traditional to modern lifestyles. In such a process, social, economic, and psychological commitments are supposed to crumble and to collapse, thus freeing individuals from traditional allegiances and making them open to new models of socialization and types of behavior.[6]

For Deutsch, this "social" mobilization entails a series of political consequences, such as strong pressure to increase the capacities of government, enlarge political participation or transform the forms and flows of political communication. The empirical indices he uses to measure this kind of mobilization (exposure to the means of mass communication, urbanization, per capita revenue, level of literacy, etc.) clearly reveal the objectivism of his approach. In fact, they are entirely external to the tactical activity of the social actors, in particular external

---

[6]Karl W. Deutsch, "Social Mobilization and Political Development," *American Political Science Review* 55, no. 3 (1961): 493–514.

to the travail of mobilization that we can observe in the unfolding of political confrontations where the "modernization" of traditional societies may be the issue at stake.[7]

Today, such conceptions would be considered to be of purely archeological interest if it were not the fact that they have deeply marked the intellectual habits of political scientists, sociologists, and historians, and, therefore, the entire way of thinking about processes of political mobilization. An excellent illustration of this is provided by the conceptualization of Amitai Etzioni, who was, however, one of the most perceptive critics of the confusions engendered by the developmentalist school and an author to whom advocates of the resource mobilization approach refer quite systematically. It was indeed Etzioni who cut the "umbilical cord" linking mobilization to modernization.[8] Defining mobilization as the process by which a social unit acquires significant control of previously inaccessible assets,[9] this author has no difficulty establishing that the processes of mobilization and modernization are not necessarily the same. There are, for example, mobilizations that "block" modernization, and also mobilizations that are more specifically "counter-revolutionary," which are far from always being modernizing.[10] A significant point: Etzioni clearly seeks to reject the "objectivism" (the term is mine) of the developmentalist school and to focus analysis on the actual actions of the actors. More specifically, he believes he is thereby developing a "voluntaristic" conception of mobilization processes: for him, these processes involve a kind of "steering" by certain social subunits, in other words by certain collective actors such as a government, the administration of an agency, or a regional council. In Etzioni's view, therefore, it would be an error to interpret mobilizations as simple, unintentional by-products resulting from interaction between several social units or from a multitude of micro-decisions. In this view, the notion of mobilization belongs to the same family of concepts as that of *decision-making*, of social planning or of public policy. But, setting aside this last issue for the moment, it seems to me the difficulty is twofold. First, Etzioni, who comes from a developementalist tradition, still sees mobilizations as "social changes."[11] Second, the implications of his particular use of the notion of "control" are problematic: actually, Etzioni is primarily interested in changes

---

[7]With many variations and nuances, the coupling of "mobilization" and "modernization" can be found in many other works; as typical examples, see: Daniel Lerner, *The Passing of Traditional Society* (New York: The Free Press, 1958); David E. Apter, *The Politics of Modernization* (Chicago: University of Chicago Press, 1965); John P. Nettl, *Political Mobilization* (London: Faber and Faber, 1967).

[8]François Chazel, "La mobilisation politique: problèmes et dimensions," *Revue Française de Science Politique* 25, no. 3 (1975): 502–16.

[9]Amitai Etzioni, *The Active Society. A Theory of Societal and Political Processes* (New York: The Free Press 1968), 388.

[10]Etzioni, *Active Society*, 418–21.

[11]Etzioni, *Active Society*, 389–90.

in the "structure of control" of resources, which means changes that modify the "model" of resource allocation between different, hierarchically defined types of social unit.

It would be out of the question to deny the frequent link between mobilizations and social transformations or changes. The point is that, unfortunately, his conception of these changes leads Etzioni to exclude *minor* and *non-cumulative fluctuations* of the control of resources from the range of phenomena that the notion of mobilization is supposed to capture[12]; thus, day-to-day variations in the tactical activities of the protagonists within a conflict would be ignored because these activities, more often than not, do not modify the resource control "models," at least in the short term. Here, the *objectivist bias* takes a similar form to what can be observed in the works of historians who favor the long term (*la longue durée*) and pay little attention to what is at stake in the event and how it is played out by its actors. In spite of his "voluntaristic" intention, Etzioni's analysis has been sidetracked: its focus is not on what "happens" during confrontations but on their "outcomes"; and this only when these outcomes are *stabilized* in the form of durable models of resource distribution. Moreover, the very idea of "control" represents a problem when included in the definition of the processes of mobilization because it carries an image of an *action potential* on the part of the social unit or actor who acquires it, an action potential that is assumed to be equivalent to the accumulated resources. The scholar is thus led either to confuse this action potential and what he believes to be its "actualization" (the deployment of that action potential in the course of confrontations) or to abandon the issue of "actualization" and focus only on the processes of acquisition of action potentials. *De facto*, in his work, Etzioni had chosen the latter strategy.[13] In addition, the idea of control also implies the structuring of the mobilization around a "central" unit or subunit; as we shall see later, this creates even more difficulties for the analysis of mobilizations (in particular of multisectoral mobilizations) than does the supposed *downward process* of the mobilization, moving from the elite or upper levels of the social unit to the lowest, which Etzioni considers typical of all mobilization processes.

---

[12] Etzioni, *Active Society*, 389. In the same vein, let me draw attention to his exclusion of all social mechanisms of "maintenance" of the system and, more generally, the very clear boundary that Etzioni traces between what corresponds to "maintenance" and what constitutes mobilizations, in other words, in his view, change (see 390).

[13] For example, Etzioni, *Active Society*, 391, when the author comes to the issue of how to measure the mobilization. Note that Etzioni's discussion of this question is rendered excessively vague by his use of a thermodynamic analogy (392).

Mobilizations and Moves

The above invites a narrower conception of the notion of mobilization. This is one of the conditions allowing the integration of the tactical dimension of political confrontations into the analysis of the crisis processes. I shall speak of "mobilization" only when any given resources fit into a line of action, or, better, into a *move*, and moreover, only when this occurs in a conflictual context. Since this perspective is fairly unusual in contemporary political sociology, it requires clarification:

(1) It should be emphasized that, in this perspective, the function of moves becomes decisive. Indeed, it is through the move that the tactical activities of the protagonists are placed at the heart of the analysis of mobilization processes. But it is equally clear that this is where the perspective outlined here most diverges from the objectivist definitions of these processes. By the term "move" I will refer to individual and collective acts or behaviors which have the property of affecting either the expectations of the protagonists in a conflict about the behavior of the other actors or what Goffman calls their "existential situation" (in other words, the relation between these actors and their environment), or both simultaneously, since a change in this existential situation is almost always connected to a reassessment of the situation and a change in the expectations of the diverse actors.[14] Thus, to dissolve the National Assembly, to occupy the building of the *Gouvernement Général* in Algiers or that of a *sous-préfecture* in the Finistère (Bretagne), to erect barricades in the Paris Latin Quarter, to announce one's candidacy for mayor of Paris (or, of course, of New York), or to meet the French military chiefs in Baden-Baden, all of these are good examples of what I mean by "move"—despite the obvious differences between these moves in terms of the role played by norms, institutions, or coercive resources in the course of the events.[15]

---

[14] I borrow the notion of "move" from theoreticians of "strategic interaction" (or "interdependent decisions"); see in particular the seminal works of Schelling, *The Strategy of Conflict* and Goffman, *Strategic Interaction*, 90 et seq. The extended meaning that I give to this notion allows me to avoid the troublesome—and for my purposes irrelevant—problem of hidden or invisible moves. See also Katheleen Archibald, ed., *Strategic Interaction and Conflict* (Berkeley: University of California Press, 1966).

[15] It should also be stressed that, for the perspective presented here, the move is disconnected from any concern to specify a "determined solution to a game"; in other words, the core intellectual aspirations of game theory are absent. The point merits some clarification. Contrary to the widespread belief of many sociologists and political scientists, the analytical autonomization of moves—a task undertaken across diverse registers and empirical terrains by Thomas Schelling and by Erving Goffman—represents a de facto break with the "game theory" approach, at least in the latter's most accepted formulations. On a technical level, the move, as it is understood by Schelling, represents only the passage of a given game from one particular matrix of retributions to *another* "game," that is, a matrix of different retributions. Thus, regarding the categories of "moves" analyzed by Schelling—for

(2) If "mobilization is not (always) war," nonetheless, from the point of view I shall adopt here, it will always coincide with one or several "moves," that is, with tactical activity by the protagonists of a conflict. However, this activity may very well be what is usually called "symbolic," in the sense that certain acts might symbolize other forms of action that seem, for example, more "hardline." The meeting of General de Gaulle with French military chiefs in Baden-Baden (May 29, 1968)—at the peak of what was perceived as a major derailment *(dérapage)* of the "events", that is, their skidding out of control—obviously did not involve the actual deployment of French troops stationed in Germany. Nonetheless, it constituted a move, it was interpreted by the protagonists of this confrontation as a true threat, and it modified their expectations and calculations. However, the scope of this observation goes far beyond the special case of threats or even that of dissuasive tactics. For the real point here is the notion of "potential" alluded to earlier. It must not be forgotten, of course, that in their anticipations and calculations, as well as in their interpretations of the situations they face, the actors usually take into account resources that are not directly used in the conflict. Similarly, neither should it be forgotten that often the "reality" of these resources can give rise to phenomena of *misperception*[16]—in fact, it is altogether possible that in the conjunctures that interest us, "appropriate" perceptions are rather rare. All that, however, is not the most important point. Beyond the sociological platitude of opposing "action potential" and "acts" (or, similarly, "latent power" and "manifest power," or "mobilization" and "actualization," etc.),[17] the only genuinely fruitful research question concerns the *different ways of giving resources "value" or "weight."* In other words, the perspective of this book shifts attention onto the tactics through which what is supposedly "latent" or "potential" can be brought into play.[18]

---

example, the commitment, the fact of "tying one's hands"—we are talking about a change to matrixes that considerably restrain the options left to my adversary due to the disappearance of certain options that were open to me before I played my "move." This is, in the strictest sense, a question of the intervention of an element external to game theory: as a matter of fact, the introduction of "moves" reinstates the temporal dimension of conflicts, restores the diachronic character to the *exchange of moves*, and highlights the evolution of the game in terms of the actual tactics adopted by the players (here "game" no longer has the same meaning). Basically, as Anatol Rapoport noted, it restores everything which game theory sought to eliminate through the synchronic flattening-out *(mise à plat)* of the retributions in a matrix (the so-called normal form of game). See Schelling, *Strategy of Conflict*, 99), and, for the remarks of Rapoport, Archibald, *Strategic Interaction*, 165.

[16]Robert Jervis, *The Logic of Images in International Relations* (Princeton: Princeton University Press, 1970) and *Perception and Misperception in International Politics* (Princeton: Princeton University Press, 1976).

[17]This is the orientation of the definition proposed by Etzioni, *Active Society*, 388; see also, regarding "power," Raymond Aron, "Macht, power, puissance; prose démocratique ou poésie démoniaque?" in R. Aron, *Etudes politiques* (Paris: Gallimard, 1972), 171–94.

[18]See also Gamson, *Power and Discontent*, 98–9.

(3) Moreover, the exclusion of situations of pure cooperation presents no serious problems. It does, however, logically imply that when I speak of "mobilizations," I will never be dealing with purely unilateral or consensual phenomena, that is, phenomena that do not involve competing or antagonistic mobilizations. In fact, and this goes virtually without saying, the vast majority of cases confronting the analysis of political crisis processes correspond to "mixed interest," or "mixed motive" games, where cooperative and conflictual elements coexist.[19] However, I suspect that a more rigorous analysis might also replace the notions of "mixed interests" or "mixed motives" with formulations that were rather more cautious regarding the driving forces at work in this kind of situation. This is not, mainly, because the protagonists of political confrontations are frequently forced to deny their acts of cooperation, especially to their own followers (see, for example, in May 1968, the efforts of the French Communist Party [PCF] to impose a different interpretation of its—not only tacit—cooperation with the government, and this example is far from unique). Neither is it because the imputation of a particular "interest" or "motive" to an actor is always a risky operation for social scientists. The main reason is a more fundamental one, namely that, contrary to what diverse "sociologies of action" claim, far from being in every situation the driving force behind acts and "moves," in reality the motives, interests, ends, priorities, and objectives of the actors are themselves shaken, jostled, transformed, discovered, or forgotten in and through the exchange of moves itself.[20] That is, in and through a dynamics peculiar to the conflict and *autonomous* with regard to the actors' supposed motives and interests. For this reason, I prefer to use the term "mixed-dynamics conflict" rather than concede a priori so central a role to such a patently teleological representation of the actors' tactical activity and what drives it.

(4) In this perspective, there is also no reason to regard mobilizations as necessarily the doings of the "discontented," of "opponents," the "oppressed," or "challengers," nor indeed to assume that they can only be directed against the authorities that be or the existing social or political order. "Social control agencies" on the one side against mobilizations on the other, the tactical

---

[19]Schelling, *Strategy of Conflict*, 99–118.

[20]My use of the notion of "exchange of moves" is close—but not identical (because it also concerns critical conjunctures)—to that of Goffman: "Now it is possible to review the defining conditions for *strategic interaction*. Two or more parties must find themselves in a well structured situation of mutual impingement where each party must make a move and where every possible move carries fateful implications for all parties. In this situation, each player must influence his own decision by his knowing that the other players are likely to try to dope out his decision in advance, and may even appreciate that he knows this is likely. Courses of action or moves will then be made in the light of one's thoughts about the others' thoughts about oneself. An exchange of moves made on the basis of this kind of orientation to self and others can be called strategic interaction" (Goffman, *Strategic Interaction*, 100–1).

activities of the "dominant" opposed to those of the "dominated": these contrasts represent one of a series of highly questionable theoretical choices made by many of the leading authors of the resource mobilization approach. Of course, I am not suggesting that there is no disparity between the resource stocks and the action repertories of the former and the latter. Frequently, the disparities are very striking, and they can furthermore be found in most, if not all, democratic systems.[21] The disparities are often so immense that it is here, rather than in some dubious "taste," disposition, or propensity for submission, that we should look for the main source and the social logics of the consent of the dominated to what appears to them, in Barrington Moore's words, as "inevitable."[22] But we would be wrong to deduce from these disparities that there is a "difference of nature" between oppositional or protest mobilizations and the tactical activity of the agents of "social control." This would be to turn a blind eye to the similarity of the social "mechanisms" at work in the two types of processes. To see the two as opposed is all the more surprising when theorists of the resource mobilization school do not hesitate to emphasize, sometimes rather imprudently, the role of rational calculation in the behavior of actors, the weighing-up of the benefits and costs of their possible participation in a collective action.[23] Yet it would surely be absurd to think that this kind of calculation does not also impact social control agencies; and that, at least occasionally—for instance, in certain critical conjunctures—sanctions against defectors or incentives to loyalty could become as much of a crucial "problem" for these agencies as they are in the case of "social movements." Avoiding this trap leads us to identify another one close by: it is not an "essential" attribute of "social movements" to emerge only in the less-structured zones of the social space. They are just as likely to arise even *inside* agencies of social control,[24] and we will see later that the possible occurrence of mobilizations inside highly institutionalized social spheres is crucial to understanding critical conjunctures and their dynamics.

---

[21]No serious political scientist nowadays supports the idea that the existing "polyarchies"—if indeed she or he admits their existence—operate other than by often leaving large segments of society out of the game. Just as the most rigid classical economists got used to the idea of the frequent emergence of underemployment equilibria, so the most avid proponents of the polyarchic perspective finally came to accept that pluralistic systems may function with "stable under-representation"; see Robert Dahl, "Pluralism Revisted," *Comparative Politics* 10, no. 2 (January 1978): 191–203.

[22]Barrington Moore, Jr., *Injustice, The Social Bases of Obedience and Revolt* (Basingstoke: Macmillan, 1978), 191 et seq.

[23]See, for example, the "model" that Tilly's analyses lead to in *Mobilization*, especially 138–42. This is also the basis of the extension proposed by Oberschall to Mancur Olson's hypotheses on participation in collective action, see Oberschall, *Social Conflict*, 113–45.

[24]In the same lines, see Mayer N. Zald and Michael A. Berger, "Social Movements in Organizations: Coup d"Etat, Insurgency, and Mass Movements," *American Journal of Sociology* 83, no. 4, 5 (January 1978): 823–61.

(5) Finally, the narrow definition of mobilizations developed here does not take a stand on the various ways mobilizations emerge and spread. Here we touch on one of the difficulties presented by conceptions assuming that mobilizations inevitably proceed from some central point—a view which very often permeates the resource mobilization approach. These conceptions posit that mobilizations consist in the "activation," by a "center," an "authority," or a "leadership," of resources at their disposal, for instance the activation of commitments to a particular organization or patron, or that of ethnic ties, in order to achieve certain collective ends or around certain issues, all defined by this "center," "authority," or "leadership." Tilly's conceptualization illustrates the point rather well[25]: the mobilization of any given social unity, for example a social group, is produced through the operation of diverse mechanisms, amounting to a kind of call for resources by a central authority when it feels the need. Of course, this view of things *may be* relevant for the description of *some* contexts or situations. Such may be the case of mobilizations occurring in highly institutionalized contexts, and one could even maintain that the day-to-day activities of our great, modern bureaucratic organizations may owe their efficiency in part to the more or less explicit presence of social mechanisms of this type. It is along these lines that Tilly develops his analysis of loyalty in such organizations—loyalty meaning the commitment to delivery of certain resources when called upon to do so by the organizational leadership.[26] But the same may be observed in some much less-structured situations, as in the declaratory tactics whereby "moral leaders" may try to initiate mobilizations that overturn or disrupt the usual division of political labor: one such call for resources was the *"Appel aux travailleurs"* (Call to the workers) by the French Vigilance Committee of Anti-fascist Intellectuals on March 5, 1934, just after the crisis of February 1934; another was *"L'appel des 121"*, on September 6, 1960, during the Algerian War, aimed at legitimizing the insubordination in the ranks of the French army.[27]

My point is that, in spite of these empirical references, the centralist conception of the mobilization process is nothing less than a constant source of confusion and bias. First, because, on closer scrutiny, the call for resources proves to be just one particular move among many others. Neither its components—that is, its costs, risks, the resources involved, albeit symbolic ones, and so on—nor its particular effects, especially as regards the expectations and calculations of

---

[25]Tilly, *Mobilization*, 69. The understanding of the "delivery" of resources in terms of statistical probability does not in the slightest attenuate the representation of mobilizations as processes initiated by a "center."

[26]Tilly, *Mobilization*, 70 et seq.

[27]See Nicole Racine, "L'"Association des écrivains et artistes révolutionnaires (AEAR)," *Le Mouvement social*, no. 34 (January–March 1966): 44–6; Hervé Hamon and Patrick Rotman, *Les porteurs de valise. La résistance française à la guerre d"Algérie* (Paris: Albin Michel 1981), 277–81, 307–12, 393–6.

other actors, distinguish it from the other categories of tactical moves. Moreover, the call for resources, contrary to what Tilly seems to believe, most often does not benefit from any chronological antecedence in the mobilization process and in the sequence of moves, nor, a fortiori, any particular causal antecedence. But, above all, the centralist conception of mobilizations has a much more serious flaw: namely, it fails to account for the strategic dimension and the dispersed character of mobilization processes.

The Strategic Dimension of Mobilizations

The strategic dimension of mobilizations refers to the fact that the "activation of resources" is a process involving *calculations* by the social actors. This applies even to the most closed and restrictive "apparatuses." Certainly, these calculations are a far cry from the image of *homo oeconomicus* devised by classical economists, and indeed from the *homo politicus* portrayed by some leading authors of the resource mobilization approach. But this is not the point. To capture what I mean by "calculations," suffice it to say for the moment that, except in very rare social contexts, they do not operate by using the intellectual tools that economists and mathematicians forge for their own purposes. They rely, in situations susceptible to major variations, on other points of reference or landmarks, other clues, other tests, other evaluation or assessment tools, and soon, linked not only to the cultural stocks of a society, group, or sphere of activity, to the routines and rules of the game of the institutions or organizations within them, but also—and this is of vital importance for understanding political crisis processes, as we shall see later—to the very evolution of the games, that is, to the dynamics of the conflicts.[28] Because they ignore these modalities, that is, the social logics of actual calculations, most of the so-called models developed in this field of research are likely to be nothing more than formal artifacts. For this reason, as regards all the possible or actual configurations of street demonstrations or crowd formations, it is quite futile to go looking for quantitative thresholds, the crossing of which would somehow guarantee the "crystallization" or "take-off" of a movement, and, indirectly, the success of a mobilization. Not only futile, but symptomatic of the scholar's misunderstanding of the role of modelization in the scientific process.[29] Similarly, it is a gross error on the part of the historian, when trying to account for the development of the May 1968 "events" in France, not to

---

[28]In no way recognition of the strategic dimension of mobilizations means that, in the improvization or emergence of behaviors (including tactical behaviors), everything runs on "calculations" of the actors. On some social contexts that may exempt actors from explicit calculations, see Bourdieu, *Outline* and *The Logic of Practice* (Stanford: Stanford University Press, 1990 [first French ed., 1980]).

[29]Mark Granovetter, "Threshold Models of Collective Behavior," *American Journal of Sociology* 83, no. 6 (1978): 1420–43.

appreciate the significance of the number of students, "in itself" not impressive (no more that 4,000 or 5,000), who, early in the morning of May 6, that is, many hours before the "official" demonstration called for the late afternoon, occupied the streets of the Latin Quarter. She or he is equally mistaken when disregarding the significant number of participants in the "republican" demonstration in Paris on May 28, 1958 (certainly more than 200,000 people), just because knowing ex post facto that the demonstration produced no obvious result. In both cases, the numbers matter; in both cases, indeed, there are "thresholds," even quantitative ones, which the protagonists of the confrontation take into account. But these thresholds make sense to these actors and consequently have practical effects only in relation to the actors' own "cultures," to the structuration of the mobilized group or groups, and, above all, in relation to the historical process of *this* particular mobilization,[30] to its previous trajectory (especially to the process of its extension to social locations, spheres, or groups external to the sites of its initial "take off" or starting point). These real thresholds usually belong to the realm of what is arbitrary or contingent in historical and situational terms, and thus cannot be deduced from mechanistic assumptions about the actors' rationality and the aggregation of individual strategies. In short, instead of asking "how many," we should ask, "how": How do these thresholds emerge, how do they operate in real situations, how do actors identify them, how do they use them in their calculations and tactics, and also how do the actors sometimes become prisoners of these thresholds when they emerge? The strategic dimension of mobilizations is rarely more visible than when it appears in "negative" so to speak: when whole sections of certain institutions—that is, of course, the agents of these institutions—block entirely "legitimate" calls for resources with their manifest inertia or "wait and see" attitude (*attentisme*). It would seem, for example, to be this kind of phenomena that faced the Daladier cabinet on the evening of February 6, 1934, the Pflimlin cabinet during the May 1958 crisis, and, ten years later, during the May 1968 "events," the Pompidou cabinet, at least during the week of May 24 to May 30.[31] At all levels of the hierarchies constituting the "state apparatus," the calculations made by the agents of these institutions on the basis of the probable outcome of the crisis, as they perceived it *at those moments*, led huge numbers of them to decide, by various means, not to compromise themselves with governments they "knew" to be in a precarious situation.

---

[30]For example, the distribution of students between spatially dispersed faculties, their compartmentalization according to distinct disciplines or even more complex factors such as their seniority in the university curriculum, the visibility of the social homogeneity of certain departments' recruitment, and so on.

[31]Serge Berstein, *Le 6 février 1934* (Paris: Gallimard-Julliard, 1975), 199–211; Jean-Raymond Tournoux, *Secrets d'Etat* (Paris: Union générale d'éditions [1960]), 268 et seq., and 280–83) Adrien Dansette, *Mai 1968* (Paris: Plon, 1971), 291; Edouard Balladur, *L'Arbre de mai. Chronique alternée* (Paris: Jullian, 1979), 271–336.

To sum up, the approach outlined here resolutely challenges the idea according to which institutions or highly institutionalized social spheres "walk as one man." Of course, this also applies to mobilizations that are less "legitimate" or less hierarchically structured than those discussed immediately above, as evidenced by the "wait and see" attitude of many officers in Algeria during the attempted military putsch in April 1961; obviously, this attitude was one of the major causes of the coup's failure, even though most of these officers sympathized with the putsch, and many of them were committed to it.[32]

The *dispersion* of mobilizations is directly linked to this point. It is for heterogeneous reasons, motives, or interests or, better, under the effect of causal series largely independent of one other, that, in different social locations, groups, or individuals are prompted to seize mobilizations initiated by others, to give them other meanings, and, by "entering the game," to alter their historical trajectory. In other words, mobilizations do not necessarily come about because the stakes, objectives, ends, or strategic perspectives are the same for all the mobilized actors and social segments, far from it. And that is why, to reiterate a point made earlier, it is extremely unwise to attribute the mobilization process mainly to the pursuit of certain collective goals or values. We would struggle to find shared strategic perspectives—or even shared perceptions of the issues at stake—among the actors involved in the Paris riots of February 6, 1934, although any remotely sophisticated historian might be tempted to show that the different groups of rioters, be they royalists from Action Française, grass-roots activists of the Croix-de-Feu or communist sympathizers of the ARAC (Republican Association of Veterans), shared a common, but, above all, tacit interest in turning the demonstration into a riot.[33] As a matter of fact we find a similar dispersion in virtually all the *journées* which, as historians put it, "weighed heavily on the course of events." Thus, on May 13, 1958, at the Forum of Algiers, it would be futile to look for any political project common to all the protagonists of the mobilization; the local extreme-right activists, those embroiled in the diverse "plots,"[34] the military or the few supporters of de Gaulle present in Algiers

---

[32]Cf. Paul Marie de La Gorce, *La république et son armée* (Paris: Fayard, 1963), 660; Jean Planchais, *Une histoire politique de l'armée* (Paris: Seuil, 1967), vol. 2, 361; John A. Ambler, *The French Army in Politics* (Columbus: Ohio State University Press, 1966), 259–61; Joseph A. Field and Thomas C. Hudnut, *L"Algérie, de Gaulle et l'armée* (Paris: Arthaud, 1975), 177–89.

[33]Berstein, *Le 6 février 1934*, 148–50, 176–8.

[34]While they can clearly never "explain" events like, for example, the fall of the French Fourth Republic, and while scholars should beware of all conspiracy or plot-based "theories" of history, it is important to stress that plots, as a particular *mode* and *style* of action (and as representations of the action), do exist. Political science should examine them more closely, mainly because this mode of action is familiar to a whole series of social groups—not necessarily those least endowed with political resources—but also because the corresponding representations of the action may themselves have some effects on "real" political games.

found themselves immersed in an inescapable and uncontrollable situation of competitive struggle. This is also clearly the case of the Paris *journée* of May 13, 1968: while the calls to demonstrate coincided, and there was a degree of "on the ground" coordination between the demonstration organizers, the presence of the communist-led Confédération Générale du Travail (CGT, General Confederation of Labour) and the Communist Party alongside the "student movement" (itself riven by internal political rivalry) can hardly be explained by any common strategy or goal.

Although *journées* of this kind offer the scholar an almost-experimental way of observing, through synchronic cuts, the dispersion of mobilizations, the phenomenon is by no means confined to such instances. The dispersion can also be observed from a more diachronic point of view, by examining the historical path of each mobilization, in particular the successive "entries into the game" of its protagonists, for instance the major collective actors. It is at these moments that the practical problem of control of the mobilization by its initiators becomes acute—as, for example, in the "events" of May 1968, the extension or spread of the mobilizations from the "student movement" to the labor world—with the occupation of factories beginning on May 14 and 15 and then, in the days that followed, the deliberate acceleration of this extension by the unions' leadership.[35]

Furthermore, dispersion constitutes the principal source of "betrayals" (De Gaulle vis-à-vis the Algerian movement, the Communist Party vis-à-vis the student movement), as well as the source of many "derailments" (*dérapages*) in the events, and of endless quarrels between the actors as well as scholars as to the "true meaning" of these historical episodes. In fact, this very question of "meaning" has a further interest for us: it helps to understand why centralist conceptions of mobilization processes remain both appealing and relatively plausible for many social scientists. For these conceptions are not derived only from the actors' rationalizations. They are also sustained by the intellectual routines of social scientists and historians, in particular by the purely academic demand for "synthesis" in the presentation of the events. These routines tend to seek and ascribe a *single, homogenous and unifying meaning* to phenomena—in particular the kind of mobilizations constituting "crises"—whose contours, often uncertain and always fluctuating, only take shape in the unfolding of events; in other words, in the successive exchanges of moves, in their outcomes, and in their effects. And scholars all too rarely realize, when they take on the supposedly

---

[35] I should add that dispersion is not confined only to "spectacular" mobilizations like those just mentioned. Apart from this form of dispersion that we can call horizontal, mobilizations also experience vertical dispersion, where mobilization poles can be found in the lowest strata of the social units or segments concerned, or toward zones that are the least experienced in the specific work of mobilization (as clearly evidenced, to revert to spectacular examples, by the history of the extension of the French strikes in 1936, 1953, or 1968).

"theoretical" task of trying to determine the unique "historical meaning" or "sense" of a given social movement, conflict, or crisis, that this meaning also, and primarily, involves a delimitation of boundaries, a process of inclusion and exclusion. And that what is at stake here is the control of the mobilization or of its outcomes through the imposition on them of a definition which acquires the aura of legitimacy and becomes the accepted meaning, for example an "industrial strike" (*grève revendicative*) or a "political strike," "reform" or "revolution," and so on. To express this more precisely, the assignment of an unifying "meaning" or "sense" to a mobilization is, in the political games we are dealing with here, merely a particular (and particularly interesting) kind of move or, more usually, the result of an exchange of moves.[36]

What Is Wrong with the Instrumental View of Mobilizations

It now remains to examine some of the implications of the instrumental view of mobilizations. This view is rudimentary: the resources mobilized are means used by the actors to attain their ends. Its most immediate effect is seeing resources as entities that have a fixed reality apart from the contexts in which they are deployed. In other words, as "things in themselves," so that the properties of the mobilized resources are considered as quite independent of the social relationships in which they are embedded, and—even more important for my present point—independent of the conjunctural transformations that these relationships may undergo.

Highly significant in this respect is that, for example, an author such as Tilly dwells on the "intrinsic character" of mobilizable resources.[37] However, let me avoid any misunderstanding: there is no question here of denying the stable physical reality of some of these resources. Armaments and banknotes are unquestionably endowed with durable physical properties—but the same cannot be said, one suspects, of resources like legitimacy or charisma. The problem is that when we talk of the intrinsic characteristics of resources, we are forgetting that such properties only begin to interest social sciences when they are, so

---

[36] One illustration among many others regarding the French "events" of May 1968: Pierre Dubois et al., *Grèves revendicatives ou grèves politiques. Acteurs, pratiques, sens du mouvement de mai* (Paris: Anthropos, 1971). It is obvious that certain conceptual distinctions, such as those between "crisis" and "conflict—one, an expressive confrontation, and the other, more instrumental—refers to the same concern for the unique meaning and thus constitute a serious handicap for the understanding of mobilization processes (for a typical example, see Alain Touraine, *The May Movement: Revolt and Reform* (New York: Random House, 1971 [1st French ed., 1968]).

[37] Tilly, *Mobilization*, 69.

to speak, "retranslated" into certain social relationships, where they "operate" according to the logics of the relationships in which they are *embedded* (thus, to take the example of money, the logics of social contexts where a banknote is something other, something more than just printed paper, where it is accepted or even imposed for certain types of transactions, etc.).[38]

This is also, very largely, the source of the illusion that political (and other) resources operate and can be exchanged in the same way as economic goods on the market—a market, in itself somewhat idealized for the sake of the theoretical model. Failing to perceive the *relational character* of resources, many social scientists are thus led to ignore that political resources can have stable properties only in relation to particular social logics and to particular lines of action allowed or defined by these logics. For the same reason, these resources are not easily transferable or "convertible" from one social location or sphere to another.[39] It was not possible for De Gaulle's Rassemblement du Peuple Français (RPF, Rally of the French People) in 1947 to "convert" its extraordinary success in the municipal elections into effective resources at the national parliamentary level. Likewise, it was not possible for the British Communist Party to "convert" its very real and long-standing influence in the trade union movement into electoral success and political weight in the parliamentary sphere. And, provided we reject the absurd idea that the State "walks as one man," we can even discern serious problems of "conversion" in the fear that certain political parties rightly feel after they have won the elections, "taken power," and formed a government: Will they be capable of transforming the resources that they acquired in the electoral arena into effective policies; in particular, will they be able to convert these resources into effective action on the part of the various bureaucracies that make up the "state"? Besides, it is doubtful whether the idea of convertibility or transferability makes much sense at all in relation to resources like the power to dissolve a parliamentary assembly (we shall see later that the substance and significance of this power vary according to changes in the political conjuncture, as was the case in the French crisis of 1968, where it was used as an element in the tacit bargaining between government leaders and their "challengers").

---

[38]The idea of the "intrinsic character" of resources is present even in taxonomic ventures that explicitly seek to conceptualize variations in the "value" of resources. Thus, James Coleman is driven to contrast resources that are important "in themselves" (or have an "intrinsic value") with those that can engender other resources (and whose "value" depends on their combination with other resources); see James S. Coleman, "Race Relations and Social Change," in *Race and the Social Sciences*, ed. I. Katz and P. Gurin (New York: Basic Books, 1969), 275–7.

[39]The hypothesis of this convertibility is developed by S.C. Flanagan in a theoretical framework, which I shall discuss at length later (see Scott C. Flanagan, "Models and Methods of Analysis," in *Crises, Choice, and Change*, ed. G. A. Almond, S. C. Flanagan, and R. J. Mundt (Boston: Little Brown, 1973), in particular 73; see also Ilchman and Uphoff, *Political Economy*, 59 and 84–9, which associates the convertibility of resources with the postulated existence of "political currencies."

Thus, the instrumental view of mobilizations not only substantializes resources, but it also engenders a naïvely economistic, and therefore misleading conception of what constitutes the efficiency or "value" of mobilized resources. Value, according to the instrumental view, is best understood as resulting from the interplay of supply and demand on a "political market" or arena governed by mechanisms identical or similar to those operating on economic markets. Thus, it would supposedly be possible, by assessing the "market value" of the resource stocks controlled by a given political actor, to "measure" this actor's power (Ilchman and Uphoff) or the level of mobilization he could realize (Tilly).[40] Unfortunately, this conception of resources' value is a complete dead-end, for one conclusive reason: the social logics at work in most social spheres simply cannot be reduced to the logic(s) of the economic market(s). Indeed, they differ radically from the latter in several of their core features. To mention just one, the most salient of these: there is simply no equivalent, in these social logics, of what money represents for "modern" economic transactions. Even if we accept the hypothesis that it is possible to find "currencies" in other social sites besides the economic market (for instance, what Ilchman and Uphoff, drawing on Karl Deutsch's *The Nerves of Government*, call "political currencies"),[41] the specificity of economic markets nonetheless remains intact in this respect. To take the case of threats and supports (in the sense Easton gives to the latter),[42] which represent "currencies" corresponding respectively to force and to legitimacy, it is perfectly clear that these supposed "political currencies" are ill-equipped to perform the *function of value measurement*. Money, on the other hand, usually works in a way that permits it to serve as a medium of exchange and, simultaneously, to *convey information* about the value of the goods to be exchanged, even when this value is undergoing sudden wide fluctuations. Variations in the "value" of political resources—while these variations are fundamental components of political crisis conjunctures, as we shall see—do not have comparable mechanisms. The absence in other social spheres of an informational equivalent of price on economic markets is crucial. It means that the "value" and value-variations of resources, in particular those of political resources, are very unlikely to make themselves immediately apparent (i.e., through the automatic action of "natural" social mechanisms) to the actors located in these spheres.[43] In short,

---

[40]Ilchman and Uphoff, *Political Economy*, 30 and 59; Tilly, *Mobilization*, 69.

[41]Karl W. Deutsch, *The Nerves of Government: Models of Political Communication and Control* (New York: The Free Press, 1963), 117–18.

[42]See Chapter 8.

[43]Though they do not draw the necessary conclusions, Ilchman and Uphoff are clearly aware of this when they write: "A political currency is analogous in function to money in economics; it may serve as a medium of exchange, a store of value, a standard of deferred payment, a measure of value of some combination of these functions. In our model unfortunately, the last function mentioned is the least concrete" (Ilchman and Uphoff, *Political Economy*, 54). For an interesting discussion of what

the mechanisms whereby actors obtain information about the value of political resources (or gain access to this information) are very far from possessing what I would call *metric transparency*, a feature increasingly displayed, to a greater or lesser extent, by "modern" economic markets.[44] This is true of "ordinary times," but it is even more the case in critical conjunctures, as we shall see. It should be added that this elementary difference has a significant impact on the strategic behaviors of political actors, on the ways they calculate, and on the formation of their expectations and their perceptions of what is possible, probable, or inevitable. In other words, it also affects how we should think of their rationality.[45]

Crises As Transformations of "Structures"

To sum up, and in straightforward terms: it is impossible to grasp the "value" or efficiency of political resources, their "properties" (however "intrinsic" they may be), and the calculations or even the manipulations they entail, without considering their relationship to the social "contexts" in which the mobilizations take place and, above all, in the case of political crises, to the transformations that these contexts may undergo.

This is clearly where the approach I develop here dramatically diverges from the "resource mobilization" perspective. The continuity hypothesis requires us to address

---

distinguishes individual resources and collective resources as regards their "liquidity," see Dennis H. Wrong, *Power. Its Forms, Bases and Uses* (Oxford: Basil Blackwell, 1979), 130 et seq.

[44]See Arthur L. Stinchcombe, *Constructing Social Theories* (New York: Harcourt Brace and World, 1968), 165 et seq.

[45]Another major difference between the logic of a market economy and the social logics of other social spheres derives from the fact that the relationship between the "value" of political resources and the supply-and-demand functions of these resources is, in most sites, rather loose. The notion of resource supply and demand, however convenient, is simply not appropriate to describe what happens with political resources and how they operate. Let me take a borderline case which seems to embarrass the promoters of the "political economy," namely the case of coercive resources. According to Ilchman and Uphoff (who chose to measure the value of political resources in terms of "power," which in their view is the equivalent of price as it appears on the economic market): "The power conferred by possessing a certain resource is a function of the extent to which another wishes to have the resource and what it stands for; or, if the resource is negatively valued, as are violence or coercion, power is a function of the extent to which another wishes to avoid receiving the resource" (Ilchman and Uphoff, *Political Economy*, 54). The idea of resources having a negative value might appear interesting. However, it barely disguises the fact that the "supply" of coercive resources corresponds here to the actual use of these resources or, at the very least, the threat to use them. To pick up the economic metaphor again, it is rather a question of *supply without demand*. In this case, it would be difficult to localize the "demand" elsewhere than with those actors (or their allies) who "supply" these goods, and I hesitate to conclude that the "value" of the coercive resources would tend to reduce each time such a situation occurs.

what the latter perspective simply ignores, namely the task of identifying the differences between routine and critical conjunctures. What are these differences? It would undoubtedly be tempting, paraphrasing Clausewitz, to formulate the hypothesis of continuity as follows: "(political) crisis is the continuation of political relationships by other means." By "other" means? Even this is far from certain, for there is nothing to substantiate the idea that the means deployed in critical conjunctures are radically "other" or different from those operating in more stable conjunctures.

The differences—for the continuity hypothesis certainly does not mean there are no differences at all between crisis conjunctures and routine conjunctures—should be sought not in the means but elsewhere. To identify these differences, we must shift the focus of our inquiry to possible transformations affecting the "structures" of social systems under the effect of mobilizations taking place within them. The major amendment I would bring to the way the resource mobilization perspective conceives political crises is this: crises should be thought of *both* as mobilizations and as transformations of the very states of the "structures" or institutional patterns of social systems—namely, as transitions or shifts from routine to critical states of these "structures." In contrast to all forms of reification of institutions, we must constantly conceive "structures," "organizations," or "apparatuses" as being *sensitive* to the mobilizations, the exchange of moves, the tactical activity of the crisis protagonists. And this means also that we need simultaneously to identify and explain the *situational logics*, which, in such contexts, tend to constrain these actors, and to structure their perceptions, their calculations, and their behaviors.

At this juncture, let me establish a few points of terminology. I will call *complex* social systems those systems which are differentiated into multiple, autonomous, highly institutionalized social spheres, each being governed by its specific social logics. I will use the term *sectors* to refer to these autonomous spheres whose precise characteristics will be detailed later. I will call *multisectoral mobilizations* those that take place in several of these spheres at the same time and *restricted mobilizations* those located in one single sector. It will be no surprise to find that the "great" political crises (such as, for instance in recent French history, those of 1947–48, of 1958–62, or of 1968), all fall within the definition of multisectoral mobilizations. As we shall see, these are far from being the only examples.

Finally, for reasons which will, I hope, become clear later, I will call *fluid conjunctures* that particular class of critical conjunctures where complex systems experience transformations of the state of their structures under the effect of multisectoral mobilizations. In fact, these fluid conjunctures are characterized by social dynamics and structurally defined tactical games which are entirely unique, that is to say, which cannot be reduced to the binary logic of sociological common sense, the opposition between routine and political stability on the one hand and social disintegration and the reign of violence on the other. It is precisely these fluid conjunctures that constitute the focus of the system of hypotheses developed hereafter, and it is by identifying the *trend-properties* characterizing these conjunctures that it will be possible to account for a wide range of aspects of the political crisis processes that this book deals with.

To stick to the problematics outlined above means having to set aside various problems, questions, and empirical topics that "political crises" might well be thought to involve. They include the stimulating "sociology of conflict" from the late 1950s that—against the prevailing overintegrated conception of social systems attributed (not altogether wrongly) to Parsons—studied the formation of "conflict groups," the effects of crosscutting social cleavages and multiple affiliations, and the "positive functions" of conflicts.[46] They also include other issues of possible "intrinsic" interest that preoccupy social sciences today like the relation between economic and political crises, the crisis of the Welfare State or "fiscal crisis of the state," and the sudden (though rather suspect) "crisis of ungovernability" in democratic systems—all these remain outside my field of attention. And, I should add, here are just a few illustrations, and nothing like an exhaustive list.[47]

The organization of the book does not follow the logic of research or of empirical discovery. It is primarily intended to facilitate access to problems which are not always easily accessible. My first concern will be to further clarify the framework and tools of analysis implied by the approach whose main features I have outlined above. The importance of this task lies in the fact that these tools, especially the concepts, can only be given effective definition—effective in terms of generating knowledge—if geared to a specified research "program" and to a clear theoretical objective. And, moreover, only if they are used not in isolation, but in relation with one another (Chapter 3).[48] The next steps will be to identify, first, the core "structural" transformations characterizing fluid conjunctures (Chapter 4) and, second, the structures of interdependence that shape the tactical games of actors in this type of conjuncture (Chapter 5). Once this *theoretical matrix* has been achieved, I will explore and test its fertility by examining several of its empirical implications on various terrains more familiar to social scientists. Thus, alongside an exploratory reflection on the working, in critical contexts, of dispositions internalized by individuals (Chapter 7), I will address some of the classic issues of political sociology such as, on the one hand, charismatic phenomena and the mechanisms of bargaining and conflict

---

[46]For example, Lewis Coser, *The Functions of Social Conflict* (New York: The Free Press, 1956); Ralf Dahrendorf, *Society and Democracy in Germany* (London: Weidenfeld and Nicolson, 1968 [1st German ed., 1957]).

[47]It was also by *decision of method* that I chose, in this outline of a theory of fluid conjunctures, to leave aside the external factors or "pressures" which, in various ways, intervene in internal political games.

[48]Cf. Carl G. Hempel, *Fundamentals of Concept Formation in Empirical Science* (Chicago: The University of Chicago Press, 1972 [1952]), especially 47–50.

resolution (Chapter 6) and, on the other, processes of delegitimation (the so-called crises of legitimacy) observable in critical conjunctures and affecting political regimes and "authorities" (Chapter 8). As a preliminary to all this (Chapter 2) comes a discussion which the reader may choose to disregard, but which has a very specific purpose in this book, namely to return to certain of the pathways that led to the choices and the perspective outlined in this first chapter. This discussion will deal with the intellectual obstacles inherent in this book's research field—that is, to be precise, with the specific fallacies or illusions that scholars quite inevitably encounter when confronting with processes of political crisis— and which underline how difficult it is for them to apply to their own work, in practice, the principles of methodological doubt to which, in the abstract, they may well fully subscribe.

A Comparative Design

At the empirical level, the strategy of this research is twofold. First, wherever useful, I engage the critical discussion of other perspectives and conceptualizations on their own empirical terrain. This is not, however, a simple question of *fair play* for the authors discussed. Something perhaps even more serious is also at stake, namely anchoring the discussion within a defined and controlled set of distinctive (and, at least for some of them, "paradigmatic") historical cases in order to facilitate the identification of significant theoretical problems—one unexpected virtue, for instance, of the interwar Italian and German crises. Second, I further sustain this approach by drawing on French political crises of the twentieth century, in particular those of 1934, 1958, and 1968, which (because of their outcomes) slip through current taxonomies and are often described as "bizarre," and for that very reason are particularly interesting. But I must also say that this last choice is best justified by the relative ease of controlling the precise details in the unfolding of these historical episodes.

However, this should not distract us from the key point: both in its construction and in its formulation of propositions the theoretical schema outlined in the pages that follow constitutes a *comparative* framework.[49] It is, as Sartori puts it, designed "to travel."[50] This means in particular that we should expect the trend-properties of fluid conjunctures, as identified hereafter, to be observable

---

[49]On the difficulties the comparative approach may encounter in this respect, through the apparently innocuous practice of using proper names, see especially Przeworski and Teune (1970: 17–30). Adam Przeworski and Henry Teune, *The Logic of Comparative Social Inquiry* (New York: John Wiley and Sons, 1970), 17–30.

[50]Giovanni Sartori, "Concept Misformation in Comparative Politics," *American Political Science Review* 64, no. 4 (1970): 1033–6.

in the "most different" political systems[51]—as long as these do not depart too much from the "structural" features characterizing "complex" societies and are therefore subject to multisectoral mobilizations.

In other words, what this work aims to achieve in theoretical terms—and in the social sciences this is perhaps the only acceptable way to define "theoretical"—is to extract from the historicity and singularity of diverse "crises" some fragments of knowledge that have a nomological scope. Admittedly, the adoption of this kind of research posture before or at the beginning of the research itself represents something of a gamble (which is no longer necessarily the case when it happens to lead to some results—however crude—that are consistent with this objective). So it is entirely understandable that there are such frequent debates as to whether this kind of knowledge of the social world is even possible. However, I would simply add that the fashionable a priori skepticism displayed by many scholars regarding this "possibility" is probably one of the most blinkered and pernicious forms of the *self-defeating prophecy*, the impossibility of moving forward being "proved" by the absence of any attempt to do so.

Sartori, who does not belong among the "defeatists," nonetheless endorses, albeit with nuances, the idea that any gains made in terms of generalization and abstraction seem necessarily to involve losses in precision, information, and, above all, "testability."[52] The issue is an important one, and cannot be satisfactorily dealt with in a few lines. However, let me point out that the difficulty might be less serious than it appears at first sight. It all depends on the scholar's conception of "testability" and on what he expects of a theoretical schema. Many might think that a set of hypotheses should be "tested" individually, one hypothesis after the other, each independently of the previous one, or even concept after concept (but here we are verging on the absurd: How indeed can a concept be "tested"?). From this kind of perspective, it is true that the difficulties seem absolutely insurmountable.

But the situation is no longer the same if, instead of this segmented and disjointed vision of "validation," we attempt to assess the empirical and explanatory scope of a theoretical system in terms of its fertility, that is, the extent and variety of its implications, and the possibility that these implications, or some of them, may provide some opportunity for critical tests or, at least, be observable. Thus, in this second conception of "validation," not only does the supposed "contradiction" between abstraction and testability disappear (at least, of course, when the schema proves fertile), but it also allows us to

---

[51]Przeworski and Teune, *Logic*, 34 et seq.; it should be noted, however, that the similarities between these "most different" systems within "complex" societies, are not to be found at an *infra-systemic* level, unlike what is proposed in the comparative strategy ("*most different systems*" *design*) outlined by these authors.

[52]Sartori, "Concept Misformation," 1041–4.

understand why statements formulated at the macro-sociological level—especially propositions relating to the properties of fluid conjunctures—may lead to empirical observations at other levels, for example at the micro-sociological level of the individual's identity or of his tactical calculations.

As regards these problems, the research strategy I have adopted has several serious advantages over other possible strategies. First of all, it effectively neutralizes the illusion that all the crisis cases invoked below should, in every respect, be regarded as equally important, equally "decisive" for the development of a comparative approach.[53] In fact, depending on the particular problems and properties being addressed, certain cases will be more decisive, and thus more *discriminating*, than others: when seeking to account for the phenomena of delegitimation, it will be more profitable to examine the French "events" of May 1968 than those of May 1958, because in the latter case it is difficult to separate from each other the different processes of loss of legitimacy; when examining the "natural history" approach, we will see that a "negative" case like that of the "unfinished" Bolivian Revolution of 1952 has much greater demonstrative weight than all the "positive" cases that could be invoked. Second, and no less important, this research strategy allows us to avoid the overwhelming temptation to reconstitute all the temporal sequences or chains of "events" involved in individual historical cases of "crisis" or "revolution," or indeed to engage in the logical reconstruction of one such phenomenon in its entirety.

This is simply to restate, in another way, that the research orientation defined above involves setting aside much of the phenomenal richness and complexity of real social processes. In my view, however, this *selectivity* does seem unavoidable. Far from being an obstacle to the understanding of these processes, it is in fact one of its indispensable preconditions. In social sciences, and particularly in the empirical domain that I shall explore in the chapters that follow, nothing is more absurd than the *totalist* temptation—the total explanation of the whole reality of an "event" such as a political crisis—and it is only by mutilating this reality that we have any chance of adding any fresh knowledge to the stock of what social actors already know.

---

[53]Harry Eckstein, *Support for Regimes, Theories and Tests* (Princeton: Princeton University Press, 1979), 11.

Chapter 2
Three Illusions in the Study of Political Crises

The *substratum of errors*[1] at work in the sociology of political crises is no longer located where an informed reader might think to find it. To be sure, neither the ponderous schemas of sociological organicism nor the plainly ideological presuppositions have entirely disappeared from the contemporary canon.[2] But they have long been identified, and can be avoided at will. The real difficulties are of a different nature, more diffuse, subtle, resistant, arduous to drive out, and harder to overcome. The obstacles discussed below—the etiological, "natural history," and heroic illusions—concern some of the most fundamental (and often least conscious) decisions on method the scholar has to make: what exactly must be explained when he or she tries to explain political crises, and in what must the explanation consist?

The aim of this chapter is to briefly consider what particular problems have to be dealt with when the research agenda implied by the continuity hypothesis is pursued. This is why the reader should not expect to find here any general compendium of common prejudices, biases, impasses, or fallacies in the social sciences, or even any survey and evaluation of the vast literature relating to processes of political crisis, breakdown, revolution, and

---

[1] The idea refers to the epistemology of Gaston Bachelard, who shows that any serious advance in scientific knowledge can only be achieved against a "background of errors" (*fond d'erreurs*); see Gaston Bachelard, *Le Rationalisme appliqué* (Paris: PUF, 1966 [1949]), 48.

[2] Even Brinton, despite using an obvious medical metaphor, explicitly refuses to draw any analogy between society and natural organism: "We find it convenient to apply to certain changes in a given society a conceptual theme borrowed from pathology. We should find it inconvenient and misleading to extend that conceptual scheme and talk of a body politic, with a soul, a general will, heart, nerves, and so on," Crane Brinton, *The Anatomy of Revolution* (New York: Vintage Books, 1965 [1938]), 17.

so on.[3] On the other hand, through the discussion of diverse elements of the works I have selected, so to speak, for their representativeness, he will hopefully perceive that the most frequent obstacles in this field of research remain active, irrespective of the approaches, schools, or "paradigms" which these works espouse.

The Etiological Illusion

At first glance, it would seem entirely legitimate to relate crises and neighboring phenomena back to their "determinants," their "historical roots," their "origins," the "conditions of their production," in sum, to use a paramedical image, to their etiology. There can be no doubt that explaining this kind of phenomenon consists essentially in setting out its "causes." That is the initial movement—the first reflex I should say—of the scholar. It is also the prime expectation of his public.

In this respect, as far as political crises are concerned, the harvest seems exceptionally rich. Etiological hypotheses are countless, and impressive in their variety.[4] In a review article which took stock of the field long ago, in the mid-1960s, Harry Eckstein tried to put some order amid the most frequently invoked hypotheses, the results of which may be summarized as follows. Under the heading "intellectual factors," for example, Eckstein lists hypotheses on "alienation," on the "transfer of allegiance" by intellectuals, and on the "conflict of social myths" within a particular society. Under the rubric "economic factors," we find growing poverty as well as rapid economic development, along with the hypothesis of a long period of economic improvement followed by a sudden downturn. Under the heading "hypotheses underlining certain aspects of the social structure," the idea of elite closure is set against the hypothesis of excessively wide recruitment undermining elite unity; and the hypothesis of "anomie" resulting from too much social mobility is set against the "frustration" produced by too little mobility. Finally, under the rubric "political factors"—and indeed there are others— we find the estrangement of elites from the rest of society, as well as internal cleavages among those who govern, or the hypothesis of inadequate outputs by

---

[3] A few examples of such works: Rod Aya, "Theories of Revolution Reconsidered. Contrasted Models of Collective Violence," *Theory and Society* 8, no. 1 (1979): 39–99; Harry Eckstein, "Theoretical Approaches to Explaining Collective Political Violence," in *Handbook of Political Conflict, Theory and Research*, edited by T. R. Gurr (New York: The Free Press, 1980), 155–66; Jack A. Goldstone, "Theories of Revolution: The Third Generation," *World Politics* 32, no. 3 (1980): 425–53.

[4] Such an accumulation may in itself be an obstacle peculiar to this field of research, insofar as it encourages large syncretic or "synthesizing" types of theoretical enterprise; for an example, see Ekkart Zimmermann, *Political Violence, Crises and Revolution. Theories and Research* (Cambridge: Schenkman, 1983).

governments in response to the demands addressed to them, and so on.[5] The reader will find it easy enough to add to this list, for example simply by drawing on the innumerable—and often surrealistic—"explanations" of the events of May 1968 in France.

Taken individually, no doubt, none (or barely any) of the etiological hypotheses of the type referred to above (or, indeed, of those that I will discuss later) is actually absurd. What concerns me below is their claim to explain and, more precisely, what this quest leads them *not* to see. And, in this respect, it is possible to speak of a bias, or even a genuine *etiological illusion*, in the sense that the scholar's first move—to look for the "causes" of crises, to elucidate their etiology—is most often, given our *present state of knowledge*, particularly damaging, precisely because it appears to be beyond methodological suspicion.

The Etiological Posture

The problem lies mainly in the research posture to which the etiological preoccupation leads. In this perspective, the puzzle to be solved, the research objective, will be reduced to the identification of factors, variables, or phenomena located *upstream* from the phenomena or events to be explained. So that the crises and related phenomena will henceforth be regarded as transparent, devoid of mystery, in other words of no real interest for the scholar, because the main focus of attention should obviously be on the "causes." After all, do we not "know" how the Paris riots of February 6, 1934, developed, or how the clashes between students and police from May 6 to May 11, 1968, also in Paris, led to a much wider social and political confrontation? At best, surely this is a job that can be left to columnists and eyewitnesses of the events, while the scholar's true vocation is to concentrate on what is not the mere "surface" of things and which—I should point out in passing—in this perspective, is always supposed to lead us back to causes. The "invisible" is not the actions of the crisis protagonists, it is not "what happens" in the events, it is not the internal characteristics of the phenomenon to be explained, it is not what the "crisis" consists of, so to speak. On the contrary, it is supposed to be something *external* and *anterior*: the degradation of the material condition and social status of the middle classes in the 1930s, the increasingly restricted employment opportunities for students on the eve of 1968, or, as an "explanation" for the crisis of May 1958, the frustration of the French military after the Indochina war, and so on.

---

[5]Harry Eckstein, "On the Etiology of Internal Wars," *History and Theory* 4, no. 2 (1965): 133–63. In fact, Eckstein is interested in a limited category of political crises, "internal wars," which he nonetheless defines in fairly broad terms: "The term internal war denotes any resort to violence within a political order to change its constitution, rulers or policies."

However, the etiological posture does not only involve focusing theoretical interest in this particular direction. It can also assume a more insidious guise, namely a rarely conscious and explicit, but nonetheless extremely frequent, commitment to the assumption of the *fundamental heterogeneity* of causes and their supposed products, that is, crises. Here too, preconceptions are based on the immediate evidence, on what is perceived as absolutely obvious: the gap between the expectations generated—in reality very unevenly—by the university system and the state of the labor market does not belong to the same category of social facts as those they are meant to explain, namely collective violence, the use of certain openly coercive resources. Now, on a methodological level, it seems true, a priori at least, that there is nothing particularly shocking in itself about seeing determinants and their products as heterogeneous. Nothing except this: by doing so, etiological perspectives considerably restrict the range of causal relations that can be conceived as potential explanations. They thereby deprive themselves of the capacity to discern any sort of continuity between the products—namely crises—and their supposed determinants. By the same token, they also prohibit any exploration of those components which products and determinants might have in common (it is also, of course, an excellent way of not identifying some of their discontinuities). It is this feature of the etiological posture which leads to the frequent tendency to forget, among the determinants we may find upstream of political crises, precisely those factors which are "political," those which concern struggles and issues that belong most directly to the realm of politics.

Put differently, it is not unfair to confront the etiological view with obvious questions like these: Does every degradation of middle-class social status or material conditions produce events like the *journées* of February 1934? Every frustration of in the career expectations among graduates occasion a "student revolt" like May 1968? Every frustration among military men lead to a "regime crisis" such as that of May 1958? True, these objections may seem banal. But they highlight two troubles with the etiological stance. One is the difficulty of identifying (with even minimal precision) a causal connection without specifying the actual properties of the effects supposedly produced by the causes invoked. The other—no less serious than the missing theoretical bridge between these determinants and the characteristics of their results—is the exclusion from the range of imaginable hypotheses the possible *emancipation* of processes of crisis from the causes occurring before the crises, that is, their possible *autonomy* in relation to these causes.[6] In other words, an additional feature of the etiological view is its lack of any theoretical curiosity about causal chains internal to the very processes of crisis.

---

[6] This does not mean that, even if only partly, such "causes" could never feed the initial mobilizations resulting in these crises.

The Theory of the J-Curve

The effects of the etiological illusion are probably never as visible as when they tend to reduce the whole explanation of a "crisis" or related phenomenon to the motivations—conscious or unconscious—of the individuals or groups who will go into action. In this respect, James Davies's theory of the J-Curve has an unrivaled paradigmatic value.[7]

This theory, at least in principle, aims to explain revolutions. Its central proposition sets out what Davies considers to be a generalization of certain intuitions which he attributes to Tocqueville and Marx:

> Revolutions are most likely to occur when a prolonged period of objective economic and social development is followed by a short period of sharp reversal. The all important effect on the minds of people in a particular society is to produce, during the former period, an expectation of continued ability to satisfy needs—which continue to rise—and, during the latter, a mental state of anxiety and frustration when manifest reality breaks away from anticipated reality.[8]

The proposition is less trivial than it appears. It has the merit of breaking with a naïve vision of revolutionary phenomena. It is not deprivation as such, that is, "absolute" dispossession, that can explain *who* will rebel against the established social order. By placing the emphasis on the representations of the future, that is, the hopes and expectations of social actors, Davies suggests that it is not necessarily the most deprived individuals and groups that provide the active elements of the mobilizations.

However, what interests Davies is clearly located upstream from the "revolutionary" phenomena he seeks to explain. His main concern is with identifying, in advance of these phenomena, some sort of frustration linked to a discrepancy between expectations (the anticipated satisfaction of certain needs) and lived reality (the actual satisfaction of these needs). "Revolution" occurs when the gap between actors' expectations and what they get becomes "intolerable."

---

[7] James C. Davies, "Toward a Theory of Revolution," *American Sociological Review* 27, no. 1 (1962): 5–19. Davies; see also "The J-Curve of Rising and Declining Satisfactions as a Cause of Revolution and Rebellion," in *Violence in America. Historical and Comparative Perspective*, edited by H. D. Graham and T. R. Gurr (London: Sage, 1979), 415–36 and, in response to some critics, his "Comments," *American Sociological Review* 39, no. 4 (August 1974): 607–10.

[8] Davies, "Theory of Revolution," 6. While the question of what precisely the "theory of the J-Curve" owes to the conceptions of Tocqueville and Marx is not relevant here, it is perhaps worth noting that it would be difficult to find in the work of these two authors such a simplistic representation of the causality of revolutionary processes as Davies ascribes to them (see Aya, "Theories of Revolution," 54).

Davies thus focuses on a "state of mind," a "mood," "what is going on in people's heads" before they start to take action.[9] As these psychological states are not easily observed and measured, Davies proposes to track them through more tangible or "objective" indicators, especially the evolution of economic well-being (indices showing changes in income, prices, etc.), and more generally of social well-being (e.g., legal provisions regarding concrete individual liberties such as, in advance of the 1917 Russian Revolution, the expectations generated by the abolition of serfdom).

The problem is that only the actual satisfaction of needs can be derived from genuine observation. For its part, at least in Davies's own work, expected satisfaction is simply inferred from the actor's actual satisfaction. The way the author suggests "invalidating" this hypothesis is to check whether, prior to a given "revolution," there was a long-term rise in expectations followed by a sudden collapse (here is the "J" of the curve). Unsurprisingly, Davies's theory was contested mostly on this ground.

Now, what is the empirical scope of the J-Curve theory? Let me first of all note that Davies's formulation seems to be a fairly prudent one: for example, he never claims that revolutions happen "every time" the above conditions take shape in a given society. However, this prudence is purely formal. The deviant cases listed by Davies—the nonexistence of these conditions in China in 1949 or in Hungary in 1956—are explained away on the grounds of insufficient or unreliable data.[10] Furthermore, the explanatory scope of the J-Curve seems to extend well beyond "revolutions" as such. Notably, Davies suggests that the J-Curve hypothesis first emerged as an explanation during his study of the Pullman strike of 1894 in the Chicago region, and significantly he goes on to compare this strike, which was broken by the forceful intervention of federal troops, with the episode of the 1871 Paris Commune. This ubiquity, this wide-ranging deployment of the J-Curve, reveals how indifferent Davies is to the very "content" of the "revolutions" or "violent" events he seeks to explain. And it is all the more perplexing because Davies systematically evades the following difficult question: In what way are the behaviors denoted by the rubrics "revolutions" or "violent events"—to use the terminology of the behaviorist psychology he refers to—an "adequate" or "appropriate response" to the existential problems, the frustrations of the social actors subjected to the effects of the J-Curve? Is it simply an avatar of the good old "discharge of aggression," in which case should all the confrontations caused by the J-Curve of satisfactions be placed in the category of what Coser

---

[9] Davies's theory claims to be psychological and is explicitly linked to behaviorist conceptions of frustration and aggression. More specifically, Davies refers to the theory of the hierarchy of "human needs" elaborated by Abraham Maslow (Davies, "J-Curve," 417–18).

[10] Davies, "Comments," 609.

calls "nonrealistic conflicts"?[11] Or, on the contrary, are we dealing with rational responses, driven by the objective of bringing the satisfaction of needs in line with frustrated aspirations?

The causal imprecision is not only due to these missing links. For example: How exactly can we know the difference between a *tolerable* margin of dissatisfaction and an *intolerable* one, of the sort that generates revolutionary phenomena? If we follow Davies, then again we infer it, ex post, from what happened next, namely social movements expressing themselves through "violence" or "revolution." In other words, the demonstration is doomed to remain entirely *circular*. First, some "violent" event allows the scholar to decide that a *tolerable margin* between aspirations and actual satisfactions has become an *intolerable margin*. And, second, this inferred existence of an intolerable margin is taken as proof of causality; namely, it explains the observed violence. Furthermore, there is always the risk of rendering the explanation true by making the "violence" or "revolution" proof of dissatisfaction or, worse, of any dissatisfaction. The explanation thus becomes both irrefutable and trivial, since it permits an endless quest for any kind of disparity, that is, a quest for an unspecified gap between unspecified aspirations and actual satisfactions.[12] So in cases where the economic indicators prove to be manifestly irrelevant, all that needs to be done is to detect "dissatisfactions" in other spheres of social life or in other types of more or less abrupt change or reversal. Thus, for example, to explain the sudden emergence onto the American political scene of radical Black movements in the 1960s, Davies locates the gap between aspirations and actual satisfaction in the reappearance of physical violence against the Black community, this "frustration" following the extended period of improvement in life conditions (employment, education, civil rights, and physical security) underway ever since the end of the American Civil War.[13]

A Crude View of Causality

As suggested earlier, these problems are by no means unique to the J-Curve theory. In fact, they are common to nearly all etiological works that focus on phenomena like the disappointment of expectations, relative "privation" and

---

[11]Coser defines the nonrealistic conflict by the noninstrumental character of the conflict behavior of one of the protagonists (the behavior is not a means for achieving an end), Coser, *The Functions of Social Conflict*, 48–54.

[12]On this point, for some observations congruent with my own, see David Snyder and Charles Tilly, "Hardship and Collective Violence in France, 1830 to 1860," *American Sociological Review* 37, no. 5 (October 1972): 520.

[13]Davies, "J-Curve," in particular 429–34.

"deprivation," or, of course, "frustration."[14] But, perhaps more significantly, they are also at work in approaches that deploy strictly sociological variants of this kind of hypotheses, as illustrated in some of the works of authors as diametrically opposed as Raymond Boudon and Pierre Bourdieu, when dealing with the French May 1968 "events."[15] They even affect those approaches that claim to be resolutely *macro-sociological*, as in the case of the systemic perspective outlined by David Easton.[16] And it is worth noting that the same problems identified above in Davies's theory arise in Easton's conceptualization precisely at the point where the scholar confronts the question of how to move from the supposed "causes" of the crises to their supposed products, the crises themselves, that is, the question of *how* these causes might result in these products. In other words, here as elsewhere, the etiological stance leads the scholar to turn his attention away from the very *mobilizations* from which these products emerge, and which also, in a sense, constitute them.[17]

Of course, what I am questioning here is not the legitimacy of any attempt to analyze crises in terms of causality. When seeking to identify what mobilizations feed on upstream of crises, some of the factors emphasized by etiological hypotheses (especially morphological factors shaping expectations that are subsequently frustrated) may sometimes prove pertinent. However, the problem lies, I must stress again, in an overly narrow and misguided conception of causality: the idea that the determinants of a crisis can be identified by means of an intellectual coup de force or, more naively still, by statistical inference, both devoid of any attempt to understand what crises are made of. And complementary to this is the idea that the explanation of what, on closer analysis, might represent, at best, a few limited aspects of the genesis of a mobilization also explains the whole phenomenon of which this mobilization is a part of.

---

[14]See in particular, despite their more complex "causal structure," the works of Ted R. Gurr, "A Causal Model of Civil Strife," *American Political Science Review* 62, no. 4 (1968): 1104–24, and *Why Men Rebel* (Princeton: Princeton University Press, 1970).

[15]Raymond Boudon, "Mai 68: Crise ou conflit, aliénation ou anomie ?," *L"Année sociologique* 19, third series (1968): 223–42. Pierre Bourdieu, "Classement, déclassement, reclassement," *Actes de la recherche en sciences sociales*, no. 24 (November 1978): 2–22.

[16]See especially David Easton, *A Systems Analysis of Political Life* (Chicago: University of Chicago Press, 1979 [1965]); for a developed discussion of these points, see the first French edition (1986) of Dobry, *Sociologie des crises politiques*, chapter 2.

[17]In this respect, it is significant that Easton is unable to account for *"special situations"* involving a rapid transformation in the division of political labour—when demands addressed to the authorities become direct, *unmediated by the "gatekeepers"* of the political system—except by effectively abandoning his conceptualization, and using the argument, or rather the rhetoric, of the "exception" (Easton, *Systems Analysis*, 88 and 89, especially note 3).

The Natural History Illusion

However, to move forward it is not enough to simply replace the quest for "causes" with a focus on the outcomes of crisis processes. We will understand why by examining the temptation of the natural history approach, and the trap it represents. Like the first, this second recurrent fallacy of the sociology of political crises relates to a particular set of research objectives: to reconstruct the specific temporal sequence or chaining of diverse phases or stages leading to a given type of outcome—which I will call the "effect-phenomenon"—for example, a "revolution," strike wave, political scandal, collapse of authoritarian regime, or seizure of power by a fascist party. The temptation of natural history rests on a fairly simple basic belief, namely that there are certain temporal regularities in the "march of history," and that the sequential ordering of these regularities provides the historian or the social scientist with a principle of decoding reality, where other ways of organizing facts seem impotent. For this same reason, the natural history approach is indissolubly linked with a comparative intention: the will—with which one can only sympathize—to break free of another fallacy, and also much more commonplace, that is, the idea of an irreducible singularity of each "crisis" phenomenon. It is in this respect however, from this same comparative ambition, that the natural history approach should be seriously challenged, and right at the very heart of its intellectual logic.

The Comparative Study of "Great Revolutions"

The classic domain of natural history, the place where we can best see its logic at work, is the comparative study of "great revolutions." Even if Crane Brinton is not the initiator of this approach,[18] the study he has devoted to four "great revolutions" certainly remains the finest example. Brinton took as his subject the English, American, French (1789) and Russian revolutions, and sought through their comparison to bring out the "uniformities" which these historical episodes might have in common. He thought that these uniformities could be articulated in the form of successive distinct stages, which recurred in each of these episodes, and which, in his view, were characteristic of the whole phenomenon "revolution."[19]

The pattern composed of these uniformities has become familiar even to those who have never read Brinton. It is a paramedical analogy, apparently at least, which seems to organize the sequence of the different phases. The

---

[18]See especially the preface by Morris Janowitz, in Lyford P. Edwards, *The Natural History of Revolution*, IX–XII (Chicago: University of Chicago Press, 1970 [1927]).
[19]Brinton, *Anatomy*.

first moments of revolution, its gestation, will be recognized through a series of typical "preliminary signs" or "symptoms": accelerated economic growth, rising expectations resulting from this growth, acute social divisions fuelled by this same growth (Brinton refers to "class antagonisms"), transfer of allegiance of the intellectuals, a loss of self-confidence by the old ruling classes, the visible ineffectiveness of the government machinery, and, at least in three of the four cases, very serious problems with the public finances. These different features, however, only constitute early signs, the "prodromes" of the coming "fever."[20] The first stage of the revolution proper sees a seizure of power by the revolutionaries. The seizure of power occurs after a double failure: on the one hand, the failure of the mobilized social groups to achieve their demands, and on the other the failure of the authorities' attempts to repress the former by the use of physical force. But this seizure of power, Brinton points out, is achieved rather easily, without much bloodshed, and, above all, it favors the "moderate" revolutionaries. Thus, it is the groups most open to compromise, the Girondins, the Presbyterians, and the Mensheviks, who take over the reins of government.[21] However, they are not able to prevent the development of a situation of "dual power."[22] This "fever" stage is followed by the most acute phase of the revolutionary process, the phase of "crisis." In this stage, the "moderates" are ousted from power. In Brinton's perspective, this represents a slippage of the process, favored by potent "objective pressures," in particular military interventions by foreign powers threatening the new regime and, above all, by the fact that the "moderates" would be incapable—by nature, Brinton seems to think[23]—of establishing the strong centralized government "demanded" by the circumstances. Then we are faced with the "reign of the radicals" characterized by, at once, the emergence of a strong man, the monopolization of action and of government positions by relatively restricted political groups (Independents, Jacobins, Bolsheviks), as well as the organization of terror. Finally comes the last stage, "Thermidor," marked by the return to a tolerable status quo, a phase of "convalescence" for a society that has recovered a certain equilibrium after the "sickness."[24]

We should not be too quick to deride this over-schematic or naïve representation. First because, as we will see later, the intellectual logic which

---

[20] Brinton, *Anatomy*, chapter 2.

[21] Brinton, *Anatomy*, 133.

[22] Or, to be more precise, of "dual sovereignty," Brinton no doubt having in mind the model of *dvoevlastie* in the Russian Revolution of 1917 (*Anatomy*, 132–7).

[23] "The Moderates by definition are not great haters, are not endowed with the effective blindness which keeps men like Robespierre and Lenin undistracted in their rise to power(. . .) The Moderates, then do not really believe in the big words they have to use. They are all for compromise, common sense, toleration, comfort" (Brinton, *Anatomy*, 146).

[24] Brinton, *Anatomy*, 235–6.

underpins the natural history approach is at work, often somewhat disguised, in many other approaches to critical phenomena. But also because it would be absurd not to recognize that its descriptive qualities can be quite disturbing on occasions. Thus, it would be easy enough to apply it to several other cases besides those envisioned by Brinton, such as, for instance, the Iranian Revolution of 1978–79.[25] The "symptoms" of coming revolution are clearly present in Iranian society before 1978. One can certainly observe rapid economic growth, linked, in this case, to oil revenue, and the consequential widening of cleavages opposing diverse social groups takes in particular the form of an estrangement of those who enjoyed a Westernized consumerist lifestyle from the rest of the population. The other "prodromes" or "early signs" also figure here, from the transfer of allegiance by intellectuals—no doubt reinforced by the hesitant position of the American administration on human rights—to the loss of self-confidence of dominant groups who, for example, saw the regime in summer 1976 declare "war on profit." And, above all, the same goes for the other stages of the revolutionary process. The insurrection of February 9, 1979, is indeed preceded by a period of erratic choices and moves by the authorities, oscillating between concessions which will appear quite inadequate to their adversaries and the resort to repressive actions which in January 1978, and even more so in September of the same year, despite their manifest brutality, will prove quite unable to quell the mobilizations. The seizure of power by the revolutionaries will indeed take the form of a "moderate" government, that of Bazargan, which will prove impotent as the state rapidly loses any effective monopoly over the use of organized violence.[26] With the removal of Bazargan in November 1979, the movement toward a government of "radicals" will become clear, and this will coincide with an intensification of the confrontation with the "external enemy" (the occupation of the American embassy begins on November 4)[27] and will subsequently be fuelled by the war with Iraq. Finally, there is no reason not to think that someday, sooner or later, this "crisis" phase could give way to a period of "convalescence," of internal stabilization in Iran and of normalization in its international situation.

Why then should we have any misgivings about a schema which seems to work so well? In what ways might the natural history approach, which seems capable of accounting for historical episodes so distant in time, and so different in terms of the cultures of the countries where they occurred, seriously impede

---

[25] See in particular Michael M. J. Fischer, *Iran, From Religious Dispute to Revolution* (Cambridge, MA: Harvard University Press, 1980), 23.
[26] Fischer, *Iran*, 223.
[27] Fisher, *Iran*, 234 et seq.

our understanding of revolutionary processes and, more generally, of critical conjunctures?

The Logic of the "Regressive Method"

The answer to this question lies mainly with the specific modus operandi of natural history (regardless of the type of phenomenon to which this schema is applied). The intellectual logic of natural history is largely driven by a specific historical method which is almost inevitably adopted when the research objectives are like those set by Brinton, namely to identify a particular *sequence* of events, stages, uniformities, or, occasionally, preconditions, a sequence which supposedly leads to a given type of phenomena, in this case "revolutions." For the sake of clarity, it is worth focusing on the variant of natural history which claims to be the most rigorous, the variant which rests on the "regressive method." The French sociologist Arthur Bauer, one of the unsung precursors of the natural history approach, in his *Essai sur les révolutions* published in 1908, offered the most unambiguous formulation of the principles of this method:

> Revolutions are attempts to bring about change by force in the constitution of societies. That is the social fact whose causes we seek to discover. To do that, a regressive method must be used: start with the outcome, and work back to the initial causes, taking care to cover the whole series of intermediate causes on the way.[28]

Now, all this is far from being as obvious as it seems. The regressive method, coupled, as Bauer indicates, with a definition of the effect-phenomenon (revolution), is, at least in our domain of research, the source of severe difficulties.

To begin with, the selection (*découpage*) of pertinent historical "facts" that the regressive method involves is problematic twice over. First, because the classes of facts chosen in the historical depth of each case depend on the plot (*the intrigue*[29]) proper to each natural history variant—I will come back to this. Second, because the historical cases thought to be comparable are precisely those that display the features stipulated by the definition of the effect-phenomenon.

Undoubtedly the most unexpected consequence of this way of proceeding, and curiously one which is rarely understood, is that the historian (or social scientist), who, luckily, happens to be a comparativist, and follows Bauer's instructions, innocently using the "effects" or the outcomes—for example, "revolutions"—as

---

[28]Arthur Bauer, *Essai sur les révolutions* (Paris: Giard & Brière, 1908), 11.
[29]On the notion of *intrigue*, see Paul Veyne, *Writing History: Essay in Epistemology* (Manchester: Manchester University Press, 1984 [1st French ed., 1971]).

the starting point and then working back through the causal chain, will reach a veritable *impasse*. He will, in fact, be confronted by the *logical*—and above all *practical*—impossibility of detecting differences as well as similarities between the category of phenomena selected in this way, and other historical processes which actually might be very close, but which, rather inelegantly, have produced outcomes which do not match the definition of the effect-phenomenon adopted as the starting point of the analysis. Thus, the scholar, trapped in this approach, cannot expect to identify differences and similarities, except *within* the narrow set of historical cases delineated by the definition of the effect-phenomenon he has chosen (in this respect, the definition of the phenomenon "revolution" used by Bauer, because it includes *attempts* to change things by force, delineates a much broader range of phenomena than Brinton's definition, which besides is largely implicit).

In other words, any selection of historical facts which follows this same logic unavoidably represents a major obstacle to comparison. It will even impede what the natural history approach in principle aims to achieve, namely the identification of possibly unique features of the class of phenomena singled out by the scholar and, furthermore, the identification of the possible *specificity* of the historical sequences supposed to have produced the "effect" which served as the starting point of the whole analysis. One is thus unable to specify how these historical sequences might be distinguished—or not—from other processes which led to different outcomes, and were therefore left out of the field of comparison.

Furthermore, there is no reason, in this respect, for thinking that some relaxation of the regressive method, and even its abandonment in favor of an intuitive—or even "inductive"[30]—understanding of the "uniformities," would suffice to significantly modify this logic of selection. The scholar would still go on using as a starting point his definition of the effect-phenomenon, and, furthermore, would no longer have to worry about establishing causal linkages between the uniformities or stages identified.[31] The natural history approach would thereby lose in terms of its explanatory ambition and capacity, without gaining anything at all—it would be astonishing if otherwise—at the comparative level.

---

[30]Brinton was perfectly aware of this: "The popularization of Baconian ideas on induction is probably the chief source of the erroneous notion that the scientist does nothing to the facts he laboriously and virtuously digs up, except to let them fall neatly into a place they make for themselves. Facts themselves are not just 'out there' and we should be willing to accept L.J. Handerson's definition of 'fact' as an empirically verifiable *statement* about phenomena in terms of a conceptual scheme" (see *Anatomy*, 9).

[31]In addition, it is worth noting that tracing causal linkages in this way, by moving backward from effects to causes, is certainly not as easy as Bauer seems to think, especially insofar as it requires the use of a theoretical schema allowing one at least to decide which "facts" are likely to constitute such "causes."

The same is true, in my view, of the attempts that have sometimes been made to save this approach by making Brinton's sequential schema the definition of what a "revolution" is.[32] These attempts would only result in further restricting, quite explicitly this time, the number of historical cases deemed comparable to the "great revolutions" referred to above.[33]

However this impasse in the natural history approach has a second dimension, which concerns the causal relations supposedly at work in Brinton's sequence of historical phases. Take, for example, the case of the Bolivian "revolution" of 1952, that is to say, the events which are presented in contemporary historiography under that heading.[34] First, we can easily imagine how troublesome this historical episode must have been for the advocates of the natural history approach. Compared to the sequence described by Brinton, the 1952 Bolivian Revolution is characterized by its *incompleteness*, that is, the lack of the reign of the radicals and of the Thermidorian reaction. By contrast, the other stages of this episode seem to entirely coincide with the natural history schema.[35] Here let me also point out that the seizure of power by the moderates—Paz Estenssoro's Movimiento Nacionalista Revolucionario (MNR, Revolutionary Nationalist Movement)—was accompanied by the disappearance of any state monopolization of organized physical violence.[36] In the mining zones, and even in some rural areas, militias autonomous of the new central authorities emerged. And, above all, the radicals were certainly not absent from the political scene: for instance, they were conspicuously active and influential in the trade unions, especially in the tin mines.[37] And yet the "revolution" went no further; it remained dominated by the moderates, the MNR, but far from stabilized, until the intervention of the military in 1964. It remained, in the very telling phrase of its commentators, "unfinished,"

---

[32] . Georges Nadel, "The Logic of the *Anatomy of Revolution* with Reference to the Netherland Revolt," *Comparative Studies in Society and History* 2, no. 4 (1960): 473–84.

[33] As Brinton himself clearly recognized, the American case presents some very serious problems in this respect (Brinton, *Anatomy*, in particular 254).

[34] See especially James M. Malloy, *Bolivia: The Uncompleted Revolution* (Pittsburgh: University of Pittsburgh Press, 1970), and James M. Malloy and Richard S. Thorn, eds., *Beyond the Revolution: Bolivia since 1952* (Pittsburgh: University of Pittsburgh Press, 1971).

[35] On the "preliminary symptoms" of the revolution (transfer of allegiance by the intellectuals, divisions, and estrangement of the elites or sudden downturn in the economic conjuncture), and on the erratic use of force by the authorities, see in particular Malloy, *Bolivia*, 64 et seq. 71, 81, 323–4, 327–8, and 330.

[36] Malloy, *Bolivia*, 179–84.

[37] For the variable conjunctural relations between, in particular, the groups describing themselves as Marxist (the Partido de la Izquierda Revolucionaria [PIR: The Revolutionary Left Party] and the Partido Obrero Revolucionario [POR, Revolutionary Workers' Party]) and the Central Obrera Boliviana (COB, Bolivian Workers' Central Union), and, within the COB, between the "radicals" and "moderates," see Malloy, *Bolivia*, 283–90. On the very radical "Tesis de Pulacayo" adopted by the COB, see Malloy, *Bolivia*, 147, and Guillermo Lora, *A History the Bolivian Labour Movement, 1948–1971* (Cambridge: Cambridge University Press, 1977), 246–22.

"uncompleted." What, then, was the natural history approach to make of this "revolution"? Does it really deserve that name? If we were to take our lead from the natural history approach—or at least from Brinton's classic variant—then we could hardly treat the political confrontations in Bolivia as comparable with the unfolding of the "great revolutions." Unless, and here we face the causal dead end of natural history, we try to salvage some of its logic, as Huntington does, by explaining the "failure" of this "revolution"—namely, for that author as for many others, the absence of a radical phase—by its "peaceful" character. According to Huntington, violence in the revolutionary process has two distinct types of consequences. First, violence has the "function" of permitting the elimination of rival groups competing for leadership of the revolutionary process—but in this historical case such competition persisted and even increased in intensity right up until the fall of Paz Estenssoro. Second, the argument goes, violence is the source of that state of exhaustion which constitutes the mainspring of the Thermidorian restoration of order.[38] To tell the truth, Huntington's argument is quite surprising since, as the pioneers of the natural history of revolutions explicitly stressed, the initial periods of "great revolutions" are, as in the case of the Bolivian Revolution, relatively peaceful: the point is that in these cases the low level of violence certainly did not prevent the subsequent development of these historical episodes toward their "crisis" phase. In other words, the rescue operation manifestly misses its target.

We can now discern more clearly that the *découpage*, the selection problem is strongly coupled with the difficulty of keeping a minimal degree of control on the causal relations that—more or less explicitly, depending on the authors—are supposed to account for the temporal sequencing or chaining of the different stages identified by the proponents of the natural history approach. But this also means that there is no serious justification at all for accusing that approach, as some have, of neglecting the issue of causality (e.g., T. Skocpol claims that it is this interest in causal linkages that precisely represents the demarcation line between the natural history approach and her own "comparative historical analysis").[39] And, actually, wherever the natural history schema is applied, the

---

[38]Samuel P. Huntington, *Political Order in Changing Societies* (New Haven: Yale University Press, 1976 [1968]): 327–8.

[39]Theda Skocpol, *States and Social Revolutions. A Comparative Analysis of France, Russia and China* (Cambridge: Cambridge University Press, 1979). This is why the demarcation proposed by Skocpol is far less clear-cut than she suggests. Admittedly, works like that of Skocpol at least strive to check the causal sequences by confronting the selected cases (e.g., "social revolutions") with other cases with different final outcomes. But, on the other hand, we should also note that Skocpol is not particularly interested in the actual unfolding of revolutionary processes, in contrast with Brinton (of course, this must be seen as one of the liabilities of her "comparative historical analysis"). And, finally, not less serious, that these works seek their causal "uniformities" much deeper in the past of the societies concerned (for another good example of this approach, apart from the pioneering works of Barrington Moore, see Ellen K. Trimberger, *Revolution from Above. Military Bureaucrats and Development in*

relative plausibility of the uniformities identified always relies on the fact that these uniformities seem to be organized by causal linkages. This is present in Brinton's idea of the radical and moderate being different "human types," and also in his conception of the inevitable dynamics of dual power situations,[40] just as it is in Huntington's reflections on the functions of violence in revolutionary processes. In reality, the difficulty with this lies elsewhere, and relates closely to what I have already said about the comparative impasse that natural history leads into: How can we be sure that in historical episodes other than those that have been selected, the *same causes* or the same causal configurations (say, for the sake of simplicity, the defection of the intellectuals) may not produce more or less *different effects*[41] as indeed seems to be the case with the Bolivian Revolution of 1952? Here, the uncertainty about causal sequence is inseparably linked with the flaws inherent to the process of selecting historical facts according to specific types of outcomes. In this respect, it makes little difference whether these outcomes were "political" revolutions, as opposed to revolutions "from above," "coups d' État" or "social revolutions."

Natural History, Historicism, and Common Sense

I will now deal briefly with two final difficulties, admittedly quite commonplace in the field of political studies, but which go to the very heart of the natural history approach. The first concerns the whole objective of this approach, namely the identification of historical sequences supposed to be characteristic of a given type of effect-phenomenon. The problem is that this objective is inherently underpinned by a very special representation of the analyzed social processes—a representation of the "march of history" which sets the theoretical horizon for any approach of the natural history type. To fully grasp this problem, we need to have not just one effect-phenomenon in mind, but several at the same time. Hence, the natural history perspective, by and large, boils down to the simple idea that for each type or class of effect-phenomena—"revolutions," "political crises," "scandals," "revolts," "riots," "civil wars," and so on—there is a

---

Japan, Turkey, Egypt and Peru (New Brunswick: Transaction Books, 1978, in particular 19, for a comparison of the trajectories of "revolutions from above" with those of the cases described by Brinton).

[40]That is precisely the reason why we should not attach too much importance to the paramedical analogy which, according to Brinton, drives his conceptual model. None of the causal relations suggested by the supposed uniformities can be linked in any plausible sense with this analogy (the only case worth discussing, in this context, would seem to be the frustration related to the "hopes" resulting from economic growth; however, for an opposite interpretation, see Nadel, "The Logic of the *Anatomy*").

[41]See also James Rule and Charles Tilly, "1830 and the Unnatural History of Revolution," *The Journal of Social Issues* 28, no. 1 (1972): 52.

corresponding type of historical pathway, a pathway specific to a particular class of effect-phenomena, and *different* from the pathways that characterize other types of effect-phenomena or outcomes. It is in this precise sense that each type of effect-phenomena supposedly has a *specific nature*. The ultimate ambition of natural history, most often undeclared, is to show that from its very birth the analyzed process is endowed with a "substance" or "essence" which can be located in—and which achieves fulfilment in—the outcome to which it leads, and which constantly directs the process toward that particular outcome.

Thus, the historicism of the natural history approach, right from the start, goes hand in hand with its focus—decisive in the whole logic of the approach—on the *outcomes*, the results of conflict processes. Natural history does not accept that, at least in some cases, the mutation of a given phenomenon into another phenomenon of a different type (i.e., with a different outcome) might be produced only *at the margins*. It is quite reluctant to admit the idea that *small local* shifts or *low amplitude* variations may sometimes have "big effects" and may deflect or reverse powerful trends—such as, for example, "structural" or *longue durée* ones. However, what is questioned here is clearly not, broadly speaking, "methodological determinism" or "causality" in general, but indeed the specific vision of the natural history approach. The latter's focus on the outcomes of social processes signals its failure to understand the very *contingency* of these outcomes, and to grasp the fact that these outcomes result from relatively random conjunctions of multiple series of determinations, causal chains that, at least most of them, are separate and autonomous one from another.

This brings me to a further point, certainly no less serious. As may have been anticipated from what has already been said, the natural history stance seems all the more untenable because the definitions of these effect-phenomena, the boundaries supposed to separate them, and, more generally, the organization of the field of phenomena that natural history entails, are most likely to be nothing more than a duplication, a stylization or, at best, a systematization of divisions and delimitations embedded in everyday language categories (this explains the inverted commas which have sometimes adorned notions such as "revolution"). Of course, these categories—"revolution," "political crisis," "riot," "revolt," "strike wave," "political scandal," and so on—are extremely valuable *materials* for the social scientist. They *make sense* for the actors, and they structure their perceptions, their interpretations, their calculations. They often constitute the issues at stake in their political contests and conflicts, and they condition their actions and even their affects and emotions. Thereby, they are fully part of social reality itself. Nonetheless, to turn these categories into our primary research tool or framework, the principle governing the selection of "facts" and of causal chains is undoubtedly much more dangerous than has hitherto been recognized: it is not only unproductive but also counterproductive. The danger is simply that of forgetting that if "we know intuitively that this is a revolution and that a mere riot (. . .), we will not be able to say what a riot and a revolution are: we talk about them without really understanding them." But, adds Paul Veyne, we will have the "illusion of intellection."[42] Above all, we will talk about these categories using the most imprecise elements of everyday language, its blurred boundaries, its implicit schemas, its confused taxonomies, all the while under the illusion (which often serves an alibi) of having at our disposal, at very little cost, an effective "observational vocabulary." That is to say, in other words, that it is certainly not through the approach of natural history that social sciences and history are likely to identify—if there are such things, indeed—potential recurrent sequences at work in real social processes.

Tree-Shape Variants

Have the objectives and the intellectual logic of natural history been definitively rejected in the sociology of political crisis? Whatever some might have believed on occasion, nothing is less certain. However, the most important is that these objectives and logic have left their mark precisely where the scholar explicitly aimed to break free of some of the assumptions of natural history.[43] In our field of research, this is in particular the case of works a priori as different in their theoretical styles as, on the one hand, the set of studies devoted by Linz and Stepan et al. to the crises and breakdowns experienced by democratic political systems[44] and, on the other hand, the analysis developed by Poulantzas of the crises that resulted in the seizure of power by fascist parties in Italy and Germany.[45]

These works are of particular interest to my argument because they share two characteristics. First, the principle structuring their approaches, which is the quest for a sequence (or sequences) of stages deemed specific to the crisis processes that they examine.[46] Second, this quest goes hand in hand with the

---

[42]Veyne, *Writing History*.
[43]Even the theoretical schema of "added value" developed by Smelser to account for the emergence of different types of collective behavior is colored by this temptation, Neil J. Smelser, *Theory of Collective Behavior* (New York: The Free Press, 1962), see, on this point, Michel Dobry, "Éléments pour une théorie des conjonctures politiques fluides" (Doctoral diss. [Doctorat d'Etat], Institut d'Etudes Politiques de Paris, 1984), 28–35.
[44]Juan J. Linz and Alfred Stepan, eds., *The Breakdown of Democratic Regimes* (Baltimore and London: Johns Hopkins University Press, 1978), 4 volumes, volume 1 of which (Linz, *Crisis, Breakdown, and Reequilibration*) presents the overall theoretical perspective of this ambitious collective enterprise.
[45]Poulantzas, *Fascism and Dictatorship: The Third International and the Problem of Fascism* (London: Verso, 1970 [1st French ed., 1970]).
[46]For example, "can one distinguish within the general framework of political crisis, different and distinct types of crisis, each leading to forms of exceptional regime—bonapartism, military dictatorships, fascism—that are specific versions of the exceptional state?" (Poulantzas, *Fascism and Dictatorship*, 60; see also Linz, *Crisis, Breakdown, and Reequilibration*, 4.

stated intention of finding a way to deal with the *bifurcations* that may occur in such processes. This relaxation of the natural history approach seeks to evaluate the impact of the tactics deployed by the crisis protagonists in the course taken by the events.[47] The chaining of successive phases that these authors believe to have identified thus takes the form of a *tree-shape structure*, whose branches mark the diverse possible paths which, at least in some phases of the process, might have been taken by the "march of history."

Broadly speaking, Linz sees the stages of the "breakdown" process in democratic regimes as obeying the following sequence: emergence of insoluble problems/ erosion or loss of power of the authorities/ power vacuum/ transfer of power to the antidemocratic opposition or shift of the situation toward civil war.[48] For instance, in this sequence, one of the points where "branching" occurs is clearly located at the end of the loss-of-power phase. Whether the crisis develops in the direction of a "reequilibration" of the system, toward co-optation of the "disloyal" opposition—a "legal revolution"—or toward civil war, thus depends, in this perspective, on the maneuvers of the various actors, and especially on those of the pro-governmental political leaders.[49] For his part, Poulantzas, when describing the various stages of the "fascization process" in Italy and in Germany, introduces a distinction, supposedly quite clear-cut, between the period that precedes what he calls the *point of no return* of the process, that is, the period when the process still remains *reversible*, when it could still bifurcate, and the stages where the process becomes "unavoidable" and irresistible. This point of no return, according to Poulantzas, is reached at the moment the fascist party, having assumed the features of a mass party, wins the open support of the world of high finance and big industry.[50]

However, and this is my key point, this relaxation of the natural history schema does not perhaps have quite the significance that Linz and Poulantzas attach to it. More precisely, this means that even such an apparently radical modification of this schema as the introduction of this kind of "branching" fails to avoid the intellectual constraints and pitfalls involved in this approach to crisis processes.

In this respect, the overt return of tree-shape variants to the objective of identifying typical sequences of successive phases of "events" is far from being the only problematic issue. For this way of dividing up historical reality into phases, and the causal linkages it implies, clearly follows the logic of *teleological retrodiction*, analyzing processes *on the basis of their outcomes*,

---

[47]This approach is certainly not free of the more directly political intent to root out and denounce certain "historic responsibilities."
[48]Linz, *Crisis, Breakdown, and Reequilibration*, in particular 4 and 51.
[49]Linz, *Crisis, Breakdown, and Reequilibration*, 75–80. I will have occasion later (Chapter 6) to discuss in more detail certain aspects of the "legal revolution" processes.
[50]Poulantzas, *Fascism and Dictatorship*.

the selfsame logic that is at work in the natural history of revolutions. Once again we find effect-phenomena—civil war, "legal revolution," "reequilibration," seizure of power by the fascist parties—governing the regressive identification of the preceding stages and causalities. And, what is more (though harder to perceive), also governing the localization of the branching points (or "critical junctures") and of the "points of no return."

In these tree-shape variants, the specific objective of the natural history approach is expressed through a series of methodological choices and "technical" operations. These choices and operations respond to the following question: How does one identify the different "branches" of a tree-shape process? If, seen from the branching points, from the junctures, "legal revolution," "civil war," or the "reequilibration" of the democratic regime seem like possible paths that crisis processes can take, then that is only because it is highly likely that the historian or political scientist has simply based his analysis on a more or less sophisticated idea of the resemblances and contrasts between the outcomes that actually occurred in Italy and Germany between the wars, in Spain 1934–36, and in France in 1958.

The tree-shape variants certainly have an advantage over the classic versions of natural history: the gain is a comparative one, provided by the hypothesis of some kinship between processes that had significantly different outcomes. However, on the other hand, I should stress that introducing "branches" into natural history models is entirely compatible with imputing to each type of effect-phenomenon, to each type of outcome, its own specific historical path. And, as the same causes may sometimes result in the same effects, with these natural history variants the logic of regressive *découpage* based on outcomes leads to very unfortunate consequences when it comes to the issue of determining causal relationships.

One difficulty—which is a typical feature of tree-shape variants, and a good indicator of the limitations of the venerable "method of differences"—originates in the fact that, when a historian or political scientist seeks to explain different outcomes by looking for differences in the historical sequences deemed to have produced these outcomes, he will need little ingenuity to find them. Thus, for example, the imprudent (albeit quite sophisticated) attempt to account for the resort to the army's open intervention in Popular Front Spain by the *absence* of a "war generation" which might, as in Italy and Germany, have provided, along with the students, a solid activist base for the fascist movements.[51] Such an

---

[51] Linz, *Crisis, Breakdown, and Reequilibration*, 56. The historiography of contemporary France offers what might be considered the extreme, caricature example of this type of reasoning, when it ascribes the failure of the *Ligues* in the 1930s to this loose array of "causes": the political debility of the leaders of the *Ligues*, the inconsistency of their programs, the lack of any coherent strategy, or—the "cause" that lazy thinking inevitably falls back on—their distinctive "nature," so different from that of Italian or

explanation not only presupposes a somewhat manipulative view of the political game—social groups, as "dominant" as they might be, are very rarely able to choose, in that way, between different types of "solution"—but also assumes that the development of a strong fascist party would necessarily have had the effect of deterring open intervention by the military as a state institution. And that too is far from being entirely self-evident.

Unsurprisingly, causal relations in this kind of approach frequently remain extremely ambiguous. Let us return to Poulantzas, who spells out very clearly the sequence of stages which, in his eyes, constitutes the specific historical path leading to the success of fascist parties, and which distinguishes it from the trajectories of other types of political crisis.[52] Briefly, the sequence is as follows:

- A stage characterized by a series of working-class defeats following a working-class offensive
- A stage of "relative stabilization" conceived by Poulantzas in terms of a "war of position"
- A stage of bourgeois offensive, constituting, in his mind, the "process of fascization" in the strict sense

However, what is less visible is that Poulantzas, at the same time, actually avoids identifying any causal link that would account for the specificity of this trajectory. Instead, he replaces this by a mere *description* of a set of traits—or what he calls "specific characteristics"[53]—whose impressionistic accumulation leaves no room for any serious concern about what links these characteristics together, or about the "added value" they bring to the process being analyzed. For example, among the traits that are supposedly specific to the process of fascization, we find the "crisis of hegemony," the crisis of partisan representation, the emergence of a "generalized ideological crisis," or, indeed, the coincidence of the "political crisis of the bourgeoisie" with an offensive strategy by this same bourgeoisie. In other words, Poulantzas's perspective, like all tree-shape approaches, seems at this point to drift toward what Nadel, referring to the classic version of the natural

---

German fascism. One dares not imagine what this kind of "explanation," through implicit or explicit comparison, might manage in similar fashion to deduce from the success of fascisms in Italy and Germany.

[52]In particular, those leading not only to military dictatorships, to "bonapartism," but also to revolutionary situations.

[53]These "characteristics," in Poulantzas's perspective, correspond to the "pertinent effects" whereby diverse social groups, in a given conjuncture, take shape, or do not take shape, as social forces, and it is through these "pertinent effects" that the diversity of conjunctures becomes decipherable.

history of revolutions, called a "syndrome," that is, an approach aiming much more at *diagnosis* than explanation.[54]

Actually, this is probably the most that the sociology of political crises can reasonably expect from any approach wedded to the intellectual logic of natural history or, more generally, to the logic of retrodiction (even comparative) on the basis of the outcomes of conflict processes.

The Heroic Illusion

What I will call the "heroic illusion" is based on the idea that periods of political crisis differ from routine or stable conjunctures in that they belong—much more than the latter—in the realm of decision-making analysis, that is, one that focuses on the choices and, more generally, on the actions of individuals and groups. The logic of this illusion—and this is where it represents an obstacle—leads the scholar to a priori rule out any consideration of crisis processes in terms of "structures," whatever the precise substantive content given to that notion.

The Location of Choice and Decision

Thus, the heroic illusion can, above all, be recognized by the fact that, from the outset, it conceives crisis periods as moments in history when the tactical choices and decisions of actors become *the* determining factor in the course of events. Borrowing from historians a terminology that is, to say the least, colorful and revealing, it sees such moments as "nodal points" or, better still, as "moments when history hesitates."[55] Along the same line, many will invoke the Greek roots of the word "crisis," *krisis*, discrimination or decision and *krinein*, examine and decide.[56] Furthermore, it is such moments that make it possible to represent all those "lateral possibilities," all those abortive collective destinies that failed to materialize simply as a result—the explanation is readily available—of the choices made by the actors in such crises.

In the chapters that follow, we will have the opportunity to see why the heroic illusion is, in a way, well founded, in the sense that the "structure of the game" in critical conjunctures is most likely to lock actors as well as eyewitnesses into this kind of representation. But for the moment, let us just see how it works.

---

[54]Nadel, "The logic of *The Anatomy*," 476; however, Nadel applies this term to the whole historical sequence constructed by Brinton rather than to "uniformities" characterizing one particular stage.

[55]Emmanuel Le Roy Ladurie, "La crise et l'historien," *Communications*, no. 25 (1976): 29.

[56]Randolph Starn, "Historians and Crisis," *Past and Present*, no. 52 (August 1971): 3–22.

First, in its classical form. Admittedly, this form is fairly mundane, but more surprisingly it is to be found even in the most objectivist, the most macro-sociological of works, those that are, in principle, as far removed as they could possibly be from phenomenological or decisional perspectives. This is the case, to take a typical example, of the explanation of revolutionary phenomena by Chalmers Johnson, which is largely in line with the tradition of Parsonian structural functionalism.[57] Johnson may well conceive social systems in terms of "homeostatic equilibrium"; he may well conceive their disequilibriums in terms of "dysfunctions" affecting the "fundamental variables" of equilibrium (broadly speaking, the values of a society, and its division of labor), but once confronted with critical moments, this whole conceptual framework is simply set aside. From this point forward, Johnson will radically contrast the nonintentional operation of changes resulting from the homeostatic mechanisms supposedly characteristic of routine conjunctures, and *conscious, intentional* actions which, according to him, replace these mechanisms when the social system is moving out of equilibrium: "In these cases, the concern of the actor, as well as of the analyst, is not with homeostatic processes but with conscious policies and policy formation (. . .) Structure changing *policies* are needed precisely because some sudden or unfamiliar situation has exceeded the capacities of customary homeostatic practices."[58] The weight suddenly given to action, to the consciousness of actors, to their intentionality—whenever the scholar deals with critical conjunctures— no doubt raises a much broader question than the one I am addressing here. Indeed, it is easy to perceive that this greater weight is closely linked to the scholar's own conception of the "consistency," so to speak, of social "structures." To be more precise, the heroic illusion seems nearly always to go hand in hand with the opposition—Poulantzas calls it the "radical distinction"—between, on the one hand, social "structures" or "systems," and, on the other, "practices" or "action."[59] And also with the reification of these "structures," which seems inherent in all approaches of this kind.

In this respect the heroic illusion of political scientists and historians is perhaps not so very different from certain common actors' representations and rationalizations, in particular those that take the form of practical recipes or guidelines in "handbooks" of revolutionary strategy. The intellectual procedure whereby practitioners of modern revolutions conceive crises as objects of organized activity consists precisely in dividing social reality into two distinct blocs or entities: "objective factors" and "subjective factors." And the fact is that this

---

[57] Chalmers Johnson, *Revolutionary Change* (Boston: Little-Brown, 1966) and *Revolution and the Social System* (Stanford: Hoover Institution Studies, 1964).

[58] Johnson, *Revolutionary Change*, 57.

[59] Nicos Poulantzas, *Political Power and Social Classes* (London: NLB, 1968 [1st French ed., 1968]).

opposition is perfectly homologous with the academic imagery mentioned above: the objective factors correspond to the domain of "heavy social determinisms," namely what the actors cannot control, whereas the subjective factors bring us back to the activity of the revolutionary organization, to its conscious orientation, to the objectives it sets for itself, to its strategy.[60] It will come as no surprise that, on the other hand, times of crisis are straight off perceived and rationalized as moments when subjective factors acquire peculiar political efficacy.

Crises and Rational Choices

A more sophisticated form of the heroic illusion will allow me to strip down its main mechanisms. I refer to the work of a group of scholars around Gabriel Almond at Stanford who sought to account for the outbreak, unfolding and resolution of a large sample of political crises, by combining several distinct theoretical approaches deemed relevant for the analysis of this type of process.[61]

The historical paths of these crises were each divided into several distinct temporal phases. The authors applied to each of these phases a different theoretical perspective, supposed to be more "appropriate" than the others to deal with the specific theoretical problems posed by that particular phase.[62]

Phase I and Phase IV represent the political system before and after the crisis. In principle, the description of these two "phases," the preceding political system and the system resulting from the crisis, should allow us to assess the

---

[60]For example: Vladimir I. Lenin, *Marxism and Insurrection* (Moscow: Progress Publishers, 1980 [1st Russian ed., 1917]); A. Neuberg, *Armed Insurrection* (New York: St. Martin's Press, 1970 [1st French ed., 1931])—this is a "manual" edited by one group of Komintern "military" specialists, including Toukhatchevsky, Ho Chi Minh and Wollenberg; Leon Trotsky, *Problems of Civil War* (New York: Pathfinder Press, 1970 [1st Russian ed., 1924]); Emilio Lussu, *Théorie de l'insurrection* (Paris: Maspero, 1971 [1936]).

[61] . Gabriel A. Almond, Scott C. Flanagan, and Robert J. Mundt, eds., *Crisis, Choice, and Change* (Boston: Little-Brown, 1973); the historical episodes selected are as follows: the British crises of 1832 and 1931, the birth of the Third Republic in France (1870–75), the formation of the Weimar Republic, the Meiji "restoration," the Mexican (1935–40) and Indian (1964–67) "crises." The project of the Stanford group was one of two major initiatives to revise the developmentalist approach in the face of—in my opinion, decisive—criticisms formulated in the 1960s. The second of these initiatives took place under the auspices of the "Committee on Comparative Politics" of the Social Science Research Council in the United States, and also partly involved giving a major explanatory role to political crises; see Leonard Binder et al., *Crises and Sequences in Political Development* (Princeton: Princeton University Press, 1971); this work was followed by a series of case studies, in Raymond Grew, ed., *Crises of Political Development in Europe and The United States* (Princeton: Princeton University Press ,1971). On the place of the heroic illusion in this set of studies, see Dobry, *Esquisse,* 94–118.

[62] . Gabriel Almond, "Approaches to Developmental Causation," in *Crisis, Choice, and Change*, ed. Gabriel A. Almond, Scott C. Flanagan, and Robert J. Mundt (Boston: Little-Brown, 1973), 25; the initial logic of the project is outlined in Gabriel Almond, "Determinacy, Choice, Stability, Chance: Some thoughts on Contemporary Polemics in Political Theory," *Government and Opposition* 5, no. 1 (1969–70): 22–40.

degree of political change that occurred in the course of the selected historical episodes. Hence, these two phases are primarily examined through a structural-functionalist lens.[63] Initially at least, the authors expected these phases to display certain characteristic properties which would help to identify them. The most important of these properties is a state of *"synchronization"* between the structure of political demands coming from the environment in which the political system operates, and the structure of the allocation of goods, statuses, and rewards originating in the "political structure."[64] Identifying this property proved less easy than the authors expected: in certain historical cases (the emergence of the French Third Republic, for example, or that of the Weimar regime), it was not possible to open the study with a description of a situation that corresponded, even approximately, to a state of synchronization.[65]

The second phase is the one which leads to a "dyssynchronization" between demand and allocation of political goods or resources. This dyssynchronization results from exogenous changes, that is, from outside the political structure. These changes may be international as well as internal. But it could also possibly be the by-product of major modifications in the performance of the political structure.[66] The approach supposed appropriate for the special characteristics of this phase—which above all concern the relationship between changes in the environment and the structure of political demand—is that of social mobilization theory (K. Deutsch or D. Lerner).

Finally, Phase III (called the "breakthrough" phase) corresponds to the political crisis proper, to the changes that occur in the political structure itself. The crisis, a "systemic" one, is defined as

> a challenge to the authority of the constituted decision makers expressed through extralegal means of protest on a scale sufficient to threaten the incumbent ability to maintain order and continued occupancy of authority roles. In other words a crisis becomes visible when noncompliance or

---

[63]A perspective described as "system-functionalism" by Almond, who is thereby seeking to underline the relevance of systemic metaphors for the analysis of social systems. (Almond, "Approaches," 6–7).

[64]This is an adaptation of the "systemic loop" schema, a classic idea in political science ever since the works of Easton, with the term "synchronisation" being preferred to that of "equilibrium" because, according to the authors, the latter term did not correspond to anything that was empirically observable and did not lend itself to unambiguous definition; see Flanagan, "Models and Methods of Analysis," 46 and especially 47, note 3.

[65]Almond, "Approaches," 25; see also Gabriel A. Almond and Robert J. Mundt, "Some Tentative Conclusions," in *Crisis, Choice, and Change*, ed. Gabriel A. Almond, Scott C. Flanagan, and Robert J. Mundt (Boston: Little-Brown, 1973), 619–20. Note that even the British "crisis" of 1931 raised similar problems (Kavanagh, "Crisis Management and Incremental Adaptation in British Politics: The 1931 Crisis of the British Party System," in *Crisis, Choice, and Change*, ed. Gabriel A. Almond, Scott C. Flanagan, and Robert J. Mundt (Boston: Little-Brown, 1973), for example: 183).

[66]Flanagan, "Models and Methods," 52–5 and 58–67.

the imminent expectation of noncompliance to the authorized rules and procedures for processing demands and effecting change threatens the incumbents' *constitution*.[67]

The point is that here the analysis focuses on the *strategies* of the actors, the *choices* that face them at different moments in this phase, the alliances they form, and the benefits they may expect to derive from them. The theoretical thrust of the analysis is to identify several possible courses of action for each of the crisis protagonists and to break with "deterministic" conceptions of processes of political change. This is why the preferred tool for understanding Phase III, the moment of crisis in political systems, is, for the Stanford group, a particular, and ad hoc adaptation of "coalition theory"[68] (supplemented, when convenient, by a rather timid recourse to certain theories of leadership—among which, significantly, the work of Erik Erikson, *Young Man Luther* and *Gandhi's Truth*).

The main objection to this theoretical framework concerns, indeed, this shift of perspective at each phase of the processes described. The authors do seem to have vaguely sensed some of the difficulties that their methodological choices had exposed them to.[69] But the reorientation they outlined, which consists in simultaneously using all the selected approaches, is only suggested for the supposedly "stable" phases (I and IV), *but not for the others*. This, of course, indicates the limits of their methodological remorse. But, above all, it also tends to show that the crucial feature of these difficulties has not been perceived or understood, let alone dealt with. And, indeed, it is no accident that Phase III (which constitutes, as the authors explicitly acknowledge, the focus of their research) is treated from the outset as the moment *par excellence*, the "natural" temporal location of actors' *choices*, *calculations*, and *decisions*, as opposed to the other phases where, in various ways, it is the "deterministic" perspectives that are supposed to explain "what happens."

How to Distinguish the Different Phases?

The change of theoretical approach at each "phase" of the selected historical episodes makes it difficult to detect any possible discontinuities between the different phases. This is a very elementary point: these discontinuities can only appear if the whole operation, that is, the analysis of the four identified phases, is

---

[67]Flanagan, "Models and Methods," 48.
[68]Flanagan, "Models and Methods, 55–6 and 67 et seq.
[69]Almond, "Approaches," 25 and 27. Note however that the various case studies remained overwhelmingly dependent on the initial methodological choice.

embedded in the same particular approach. It is only if we give ourselves such a "fixed point" that significant differences have any chance of appearing.

Let me consider this question in a less abstract vein: if we want to apply the framework proposed by the Stanford group, we have to introduce chronological cut-off points in the historical episodes we analyze. For the periods located on either side of these chronological thresholds, we must deploy this or that theoretical perspective rather than any other. Take, for example, the temporal cut-off points which define the crisis period (Phase III) in the study which Rittberger devotes to the birth of the Weimar Republic.[70] The emergence of the crisis phase is located, broadly speaking, in July 1917, when *Burgfrieden* is definitively abandoned. The end of the crisis phase is clearly identified with the (supposedly effective) establishment of the Weimar institutions. This seems to be confirmed by the results of the elections of March–June 1920, where there is a decline in support for the majority socialists in favor of some polarization toward the two extremes. It is, therefore, in the period between these two dates, these two chronological caesura, that the analysis of the actors' behavior should adopt, as explanatory principle, a focus on their strategic calculations, in particular on their rational choices. Thus, the scholar will direct his empirical efforts toward the quantitative evaluation of: first, the stocks of different political resources available to each of the crisis protagonists; second, the fluctuating value of these stocks during this crisis phase; and, third, the distance separating the various protagonists on the salient issues of this period (armistice, constitutional reform, peace treaty). This evaluation should make it possible to identify the optimal alliances on the basis of a—revised, as I have said—version of coalition theory. This is precisely the way that the scholar will seek to explain why only three coalitions—out of a possible eight—will emerge as workable "solutions" at the end of the crisis: a "reactionary" coalition involving the state bureaucracy, the military high command, the DNVP, and the DVP along with the National Association (*Nationale Vereinigung*); a "radical" coalition integrating the Independent Socialists into the social-centrist bloc; and finally an alliance of the center parties with those institutional elites that were—as we know, very temporarily—"loyalist." It is in the same way, on the same theoretical basis, that the scholar will also attempt to explain why it was the last of these three coalitions that prevailed.[71]

However, this analysis in terms of coalition theory stops in 1920, at the cut-off point between Phase III and the following phase. Here we get to the heart of this aspect of the heroic illusion: after this chronological break, *it is no longer the*

---

[70] Volker Rittberger, "Revolution and Pseudo-Democratization: The Formation of the Weimar Republic," in *Crisis, Choice, and Change*, ed. Gabriel A. Almond, Scott C. Flanagan, and Robert J. Mundt (Boston: Little-Brown, 1973), 285–391.

[71] Rittberger, "Revolution and Pseudo-Democratization," 361–3.

same facts (or data) *that are being collected, nor the same kind of explanation that is being deployed.* The stocks of resources, the distances between actors, these fade into the background, and they no longer provide the bases for determining the most advantageous alliance strategies in order to explain why some attempts at coalition-building succeed while others fail.

Even if, though this is never really made explicit, the 1920–23 period seems sometimes to be treated as a process of adjustment, from the 1920 cut-off point onward the analysis in terms of rational choice is replaced by the description of the social, economic, and political structures of the system after the crisis, and the description of the system's relationship with the international environment.[72] This methodological shift has inevitable consequences: it becomes entirely impossible to know whether—and how—the system after 1920 (or even 1923) owes its characteristics to a stabilization in the value of the resources available to the diverse collective actors, which would be one possible way, though scarcely a convincing one, of explaining the "apparent stabilization" of the Weimar regime between 1924 and 1930, or whether it owes these characteristics to variations in the configuration of these resource stocks and in the distances between the actors.[73] The cut-off point of 1920 might indeed be significant, but how could this be verified, given that we are deprived—as a result of a methodological choice—of any information on variations in the value of resource stocks or on variations in the distance between actors for the period following 1920? Are we to assume that, after this date, the behavior of the actors no longer owes anything to the resources they have and to the perceptions they have of their mutual relations? Are we supposed to accept a priori the idea that from the 1920 caesura onward (though why on earth should this be the case?) the main, indeed the only, elements that matter are the "structural" determinisms? And that from then on the working of the Weimar regime is disconnected from the strategic calculations, decisions, and "rational" choices of the different protagonists in the political life of Germany? May be this is not what the authors always meant to say, but the approach they have used makes all of these issues truly *undecidable*. Once again, it becomes impossible to compare the periods demarcated in this

---

[72]Rittberger, "Revolution and Pseudo-Democratization," 366. To be fair to that author's otherwise very subtle study, I should point out some of the dilemmas he faced. In fact, Rittberger seems somewhat uncomfortable in the methodological straitjacket I have discussed, and he cannot avoid worrying about what happens to the stocks of resources, and to the distance between the protagonists, in the later phases of the confrontation. However, this concern does not result in his carrying out any evaluative procedures that supposedly would allow an effective use of coalition theory in these later phases. It appears only in allusive form, and seems merely to reflect something like a methodological guilty conscience on the part of the author.

[73]That is where we should no doubt look for at least a partial explanation of the "elusive" characteristics of this sequence which Dahrendorf significantly calls the period of "misleading stability" (Dahrendorf, *Society and Democracy in Germany*, 399).

way, or indeed to "measure" the differences between them—for that is the stated ambition of the Stanford group—as long as the scholar *uses a different reference tool* for each phase of the crisis.

Under these conditions, how could we even be sure that the instability in the value of resources was greater between 1917 and 1920 than it was after the 1920 cut-off point? The political confrontations of 1923, or even of the years preceding the fall of the Weimar regime, do permit some doubt on this point.[74] Finally, it should be added that these reflections concerning only one particular aspect of the demarcation of phases could easily be extended to the whole approach and that, at a more general level, the issue of the chronological thresholds reveals with great clarity how the authors of *Crisis, Choice, and Change* went about dividing up the historical episodes they studied into distinct phases. Quite clearly, they tended to do this by intuition, on the basis of some apparent traits emerging from ordinary historical narrative, especially the shifts from one particular set of institutional arrangements to another perceived as different.[75]

Indifference to the Structural Aspects of Political Crises

Furthermore, the heroic illusion not only prevents us , as I have just seen, from understanding how periods that are supposedly stable and synchronized may owe these features, at least in part, to possible fluctuations in the value of resources and to strategic calculations, in other words to the actors' decisions, but it also forbids us to pay specific attention to the political and, more generally, the social "structures" which may appear during the crisis phases proper. This criticism might seem strange: Is it not true that political crises and periods of social upheaval are precisely marked by an instability, an evanescence, a fluidity of social relationships so pronounced, that any use of

---

[74]See in particular Karl D. Bracher, *The German Dictatorship. The Origins, Structure and Consequences of National Socialism* (Hardmondworth: Penguin Books, 1978 [1st German ed., 1969]), 204–27.

[75]I leave aside here another difficulty inherent in the logic of the heroic illusion: applying a specific approach to each distinct phase of the crisis process has exposed the authors of *Crisis, Choice, and Change* to the "problem" of *converting* one approach into another. This conversion operation was supposed, despite the obstacles I have described, to establish a causal link between the different phases. However, that led to a systematic confusion between, on the one hand, the formal conversion, made by the scholar, from one theoretical approach and the variables it sets up, to another theoretical approach with its own set of variables, and, on the other hand, the actual "conversion," in reality, from one social fact to another social fact. For the reasons outlined above, the overall theoretical framework works in such a way that, paradoxically, these variables *cease to vary* when we change phase, they simply disappear from the analysis. This results in our being unable to know anything about the possible impact of these variables on the processes under consideration. For a detailed discussion of this issue, see Dobry, *Sociologie des crises politiques*, 92–5.

the term "structure" would seem out of place? Does not this term apply, at least according to most of the approaches that deal with the notion of structure, a certain repetition, recurrence, a certain stability over time in social relations from which the structural features are supposedly "extracted"? Are we not faced here with a radical antinomy between these critical situations which Siegfried Nadel, for example, has called "amorphous," and the central argument, the very core of any "structural" approach?[76] Are we not forced, therefore, each time we try to account for the logics, if there is any, of these situations, to focus our investigation not on "structures," but on the purposive actions and the decisions of the actors?

I will return at length to these issues in the rest of this book. For the moment, I will restrict myself to a few brief remarks, whose sole ambition is to chip away at the robust certainties that these questions point to, and that indeed represent one of the "theoretical" bases of the heroic illusion. First, let me take the example, familiar to political scientists and historians, of the possible emergence, in the course of certain "great" political crises, of situations of dual power, "dual sovereignty" (Brinton) or, perhaps in a slightly more satisfactory formulation, "multiple sovereignty"(Tilly). Clearly, even if over a very short period, Germany—in 1918—seems to have experienced this situation. Faced with the civil bureaucracy and the Army High Command, workers' and soldiers' councils and the institutions or organizations they developed rapidly asserted themselves as alternative "poles of power." It is more than likely that this configuration of the social space can—maybe only to a small extent—help explain the interactions, transactions, issues, conflicts, and strategies which were the very weft of events in this period. It is significant, in this respect, that among the various alternative *scenarios*, Rittberger has precisely singled out the scenario where a radical coalition around the majority socialists would have made the workers' and soldiers' councils the main locus of its agency and the defining axis of the new regime.[77] The problem is that we are dealing here, as we remember, with phase III of the process, the phase of "breakthrough," where account is taken only of the choices and decisions of the actors. And that, for precisely this reason, the theoretical framework of the Stanford group leaves no room for such "structural facts" and, a fortiori, makes any specific questioning about this kind of political "structure" simply unthinkable.

The problem becomes even more salient when we turn to comparative analysis. While the project of the Stanford group is a comparative one, the analysis is unable, given its theoretical framework, to compare this particular case of multiple sovereignty with other configurations which might have

---

[76]Siegfried F. Nadel, *The Theory of Social Structure* (London: Cohen & West, 1957).
[77]Rittberger, "Revolution and Pseudo-Democratization," 389.

something in common with it. This is the case of the 1868 crisis in Japan, known as "the Meiji restoration." The issue of multiple sovereignty is not addressed in White's study of this historical episode.[78] But, in the breakthrough phase of this "aristocratic revolution," several structural features deserve, in this respect, further exploration. Here it is not a matter so much of the apparent duality of powers which takes shape after 1862, gradually at first, between Edo, the traditional seat of power of the Tokugawa shogunate, and the imperial court at Kyoto; the point is that the interactions within this bipolar structure can only be understood in the framework of a more effective structure of multiple sovereignty made up of the principal fiefdoms (Satsuma, Choshu, Tosa, etc.), a structure within which the shogunate was becoming no more than a political unit on the same footing as at least some others.[79] And, actually, the relations between these political units could in no way be subsumed under the simple heading of "dual power": they were more like the political games played out in certain segmentary societies, excepting, however, that here they correspond to a radical crisis in a society that could only be described as "segmentary" in a very loose fashion, and that these games constitute what has sometimes—not very appropriately—been called a "revolution from above."[80] Anyway, these brief reflections allow the reader to obtain an initial insight into the value and relevance of a comparative exploration of such "crisis structures," a task which the heroic illusion forbids us even to conceive, and which would certainly do considerable harm to the classic, still prevalent, and somewhat Leninist view of duality of power.

I should add that I deliberately chose, to better illustrate my point, an example of "crisis structure" which is familiar to the political actors themselves. But other much less explored research objects or fields could well prove equally fruitful for the study of "crisis structures." Before temporarily leaving this issue, let me give another example: the possible sudden emergence, in periods of acute political crisis, and sometimes the equally sudden disappearance, of social groups, that is to say, entities with a minimal set of properties—symbols of identity, self-recognition, possession of instruments of collective action, and so on—so we can properly speak of "collective actors." Such entities, whose formation cannot easily be traced to those features which historians and sociologists routinely use to link social classes to the overall structuring of a society (status, resources,

---

[78]James White, "State Building and Modernization: The Meiji Restauration," in *Crisis, Choice, and Change*, ed. Gabriel A. Almond, Scott C. Flanagan, and Robert J. Mundt (Boston: Little-Brown, 1973), 499–559.

[79]Paul Akamatsu, *Meiji 1868. Révolution et contre-révolution au Japon* (Paris: Calmann-Lévy,1968), 191–278.

[80]For example, Trimberger, *Revolution from Above*, 16; this author has however fully acknowledged that there was, in the revolutionary process of the Meiji restoration, something like a structure of multiple sovereignty.

location in the relations of production, or domination), seem, rather, *to define themselves first and foremost in relation to events* and, perhaps even more importantly, *to be defined by them*, that is to say, by the political crisis process itself. It is from this perspective that we probably can best account for, and in the most rigorous way, the unclassifiable *sans-culotterie* of the French Revolution, the "lumpen-aristocracy" of the Meiji restoration, or indeed, though here there is still a dearth of precise knowledge, the social milieu of the Revolutionary Guards in the Iranian Revolution of 1979.[81]

All in all, the heroic illusion leads us to lose simultaneously on two counts, in our knowledge of the "structures" typical of critical conjunctures, and in our understanding of the action, the tactical moves, and the calculations of the crisis protagonists. First, it leaves us ignorant of what happens to structures in periods of crisis, of the possible transformations they may undergo, and of the possible effects of these transformations. Second, and for exactly the same reasons, because of the impossibility of identifying how far the actors' choices, decisions, or calculations in such periods are specific, or, indeed, different in comparison with "normal" periods (e.g., are we so sure that, in critical situations, the actors' calculations are much less socially conditioned or constrained than they are assumed to be in "normal" periods?).

---

[81]On the Japanese "lumpen aristocracy" case, see in particular Barrington Moore Jr., *Social Origins of Dictatorship and Democracy: Lord and Peasant in the Making of the Modern World* (Boston: Beacon Press,1966). For another example of this kind of emergence of a social group, see Marc Ferro, "La naissance du système bureaucratique en URSS," *Annales ESC* 31, no. 2 (1976): 243–67.

Chapter 3
Mapping Complexity

The feature that perhaps best characterizes most contemporary social systems is the presence within them of multiple differentiated sectors, social spheres or fields, that are, at the same time, inextricably entangled and more or less autonomous from each other.[1] To say this—even though "structural differentiation" is hardly a new idea in sociology—is to distance oneself from the metaphors, admittedly convenient but fruitlessly reductive, which many social scientists still deploy when trying to capture and describe how *politics* works in these systems. The usual distinctions between state and civil society, or between the political system and its environment, both fail to perceive what is at play *within* the multiplicity of differentiated sectors, what is at play *between* these sectors, in short what constitutes the *structural complexity* of these social systems.[2]

However my aim is not to analyze this complexity per se, but as a means to understanding the processes of political crisis occurring in such systems. This is indeed a substantive proposition, since the very components of that complexity are bound to help us to identify and understand the *plasticity* of

---

[1] On this structural feature see in particular, from different perspectives, Pierre Bourdieu, "Les modes de domination," *Actes de la Recherche en Sciences Sociales*, no. 2–3 (June 1976): 122–32; Luhmann, *The Differentiation of Society*; most of the essays in this work were published in German in 1971).

[2] The conception of complexity referred to here should obviously not be confused with the very different use made of this notion in his own particular perspective by Luhmann: "Systems can be designated as complex when they are so large that they cannot anymore link every element with every other one. (. . .) Complex systems are characterized by the fact they cannot realize the mathematically possible (. . .). Consequently, complex systems must constrain themselves to using only a fraction of mathematically possible relations." In Luhmann's perspective, the notion of complexity clearly cannot be dissociated from the issues of the selectivity of social relationships and it is precisely the reduction of this complexity which social systems and subsystems are bound to achieve, Niklas Luhmann, "Temporalization of Complexity," in *Sociocybernetics. An Actor Oriented Social Systems Approach*, ed. R. F. Geyer and J. Van Der Zouwen (Leiden: Nijhoff, 1978), 96–7.

these societies' "structures," as well as the impact of the mobilizations that can spread within them. The structural traits which are of a particular interest in the light of the research orientation outlined here—those traits which allow us to see how sectors may be *sensitive* to multisectoral mobilizations—can be split into those pertaining to the "internal" face of the sectors, and those pertaining more to their "external" face. The internal face refers to their specific social logics and how these logics exercise a hold on the actors perceptions, calculations, and actions; the external one corresponds to the autonomy that sectors enjoy in relation to one another, and to the possible consolidation effects that may result from their relationships. However, this distinction between the internal and external dimensions can be made only if we constantly keep in mind that they are interwoven in the actual "working" of the sectors and thus can be dissociated only on an analytical level.

How Sectoral Logics Do Work

The specific logics mentioned above might be a familiar feature for social scientists. A venerable sociological tradition has, over the years, more or less identified and described them. Or, to be more precise, it has forged their ideal-types, for example, the logics—or "laws"—of the economic market, of large "rational" bureaucracies, of military organizations, or of educational systems. That is kind of what Weber has in mind when he refers to the "laws" peculiar to religious institutions (as opposed to those of "worldly" institutions or spheres of life), the "laws" characterizing the modern justice system, or, of course, those that govern the free market.[3] However, these ideal-types, which relate mainly to the specialized functional activities of each sector (fighting as long as the militarized sectors are concerned, teaching activity for educational systems, etc.) tend in most cases to obscure the very social reality of the sectoral logics at work in highly differentiated societies. These logics are, in fact, shaped and transformed by a *historicity* which is much more chaotic and much less "functional" than most sociological traditions would have us believe. A simple, but significant, illustration of this point is provided by the political field in democratic systems which can work according to very different logics whether it is a parliamentary regime or a presidential one (and within each of these two categories of regime, we would have no difficulty in finding further genuine variations in these logics).

---

[3]Max Weber, *Economy and Society*, ed. Guenther Roth and Claus Wittich (Berkeley and Los Angeles: University of California Press, 1978 [1968]), vol. 1, esp. chap. 6); the German term Weber most often uses in this context is *Eigengesetzlichkeit*.

At this point, a second problem, closer to my present concerns, should also be singled out. Some authors have indeed suspected the necessity of taking into account this variety of logics when analyzing processes of political crisis. However, they have rarely avoided giving a normatively charged view of these logics. This becomes particularly evident when dealing with the question of the specific logics of militarized sectors, an issue which cannot easily be ignored in the case of crises like, for example, that of 1958 in France. Of course, the scholar is not necessarily adopting a normative stance if he or she admits that these sectors' logics and those specific to political sectors are far from identical, not only in democratic systems but also in many contemporary authoritarian systems, including those in Eastern Europe. However, this question is often confused with that of the tactical use that certain actors may, during confrontations, make of the "specificity" of their sectoral activity an *argument*, or, to be more precise, a component of a *move* (in the meaning given above to this term).[4] This was the case, for instance, in the French crisis of 1958, when large segments of the army, involved in vigorous multisectoral mobilizations, claimed to act in the name of their professional values and the particular "requirements" of their own specialized expertise.[5]

Finally, it should be noted that the variety of sectoral logics does not seem entirely incompatible with Pierre Bourdieu's hypothesis of a *structural homology* between different social fields in the societies that concern us here.[6] The problem is that this hypothesis might not be the most helpful to account for the wide variety of cleavage systems and configurations of positions which structure sectors in a great range of contemporary complex societies. It would not be useful to develop this point further here, but I would suggest that each time, in a given society, differentiated social sectors (or fields) get closer to homologous structural configurations, this becomes, in historical situations where multisectoral mobilizations emerge, a powerful factor of tacit coordination of these actors' anticipations. This is especially the case of *dualist* configurations of positions (or those which are *perceived* as such), fully exposing, in each sector, the cleavages between "dominant" and "dominated" agents. Here we most likely have one of the main driving forces behind the mobilizations constituting some of the crises that impacted East European political systems, especially the Polish crisis of 1980.[7]

---

[4] For example, Linz, *Crisis, Breakdown, and Reequilibration*, 52.

[5] See, among many others: Planchais, *Une histoire politique de l'armée*, vol. 2: 289–349. Ambler, *The French Army in Politics*, 277 and seq., and, on the doctrine of "revolutionary war" especially 308–36; Raoul Girardet, ed., *La crise militaire française, 1945–1962* (Paris: Presses de Sciences Po, 1964).

[6] Bourdieu, *Distinction*.

[7] On the more general issue of the differentiation of the social space in "Soviet-type" systems, for useful discussion elements, see in particular: Harold G. Skilling and Franklyn Griffiths, eds., *Interest Groups*

The Capture of Sectoral Calculations

However diverse, sectoral logics have in common several features that are of crucial interest for the understanding of crisis processes. The first one is the hold they exert on the calculations of actors located in various sectors (or, to be more precise, on these actors' calculations regarding the social games and activities proper to a given sector), which make these sectors *limited zones of tactical interdependence* for the actors. The anticipations, evaluations, interpretations, and, more generally, the tactical activity of these actors depend on the stakes, issues, official and pragmatic rules of the game,[8] kinds of resources and their distribution among various individual or collective actors—that is to say, by and large, among the more or less institutionalized positions these actors very often occupy—and above all, reference points, indices, and instruments for assessing, predicting, and identifying situations specific to each sector.

All this relates the notion of sector to other neighboring concepts, like that of "field" (Bourdieu), that of "system of interaction" (Baumgartner et al.) or, in the same vein as the latter, that of "action system" (Crozier and Friedberg). These diverse notions, like that of sector, seek to designate social spaces of interdependence between actors, limited zones, or areas of endo-determinism and, as Luhmann puts it, of *self-reference*. The notion of sector departs from that of "field" particularly by not being, in any way, concerned to identify the *specific function* that the field, or the sector, supposedly fulfills for various types of publics, that is, the type of special interest it might satisfy (on the other hand, also note that nothing guarantees that a given particular sector should be monofunctional). It differs from the notion of "action system" by rejecting the theoretical focus on the "problem" of the *regulation* of systems and the mechanisms that allow them to "maintain their structure"—and also by refusing to remain indifferent to the degree of institutionalization and, more generally, to the degree of objectification of the social relationships which make up such systems (this latter remark applies as well to many of the uses Bourdieu makes of the notion of field).[9]

---

in Soviet Politics (Princeton: Princeton University Press, 1971); Lenard J. Cohen and Jane P. Shapiro, eds., *Communist Systems in Comparative Perspective* (Garden City: Anchor Press-Doubleday, 1974); Thomas Lowit, "Le parti polymorphe en Europe de l'Est," *Revue Française de Science Politique* 29, no. 4–5 (1979): 812–46; Zygmunt Bauman, "Social Dissent in East European Political Systems," *Archives Européennes de Sociologie* 12, no. 1 (1971): 25–51; Stephen White, "Communist Systems and the 'Iron Law of Pluralism'," *British Journal of Political Science* 8, no. 1 (1978): 101–17; Jadwiga Staniszkis, *Poland's Self-Limiting Revolution* (Princeton: Princeton University Press, 1984 [1st French ed., 1982]).

[8]On this distinction, see Bailey, *Stratagems and Spoils*.

[9]See in particular: Pierre Bourdieu, "Genèse et structure du champ religieux," *Revue Française de Sociologie* 12, no. 3 (1971): 295–334 and "Une interprétation de la théorie de la religion selon Max

In this sense, it may be said that sectors are characterized, in routine conjunctures, by their capacity to close off the universe of reference which frames their members' calculations, or rather by their capacity *to attract* or *capture* these calculations. For instance, it is precisely such a capture of calculations, in favor of the political field, that is at work in the unfolding of most of the "ministerial crises" experienced by the French Fourth Republic: from 1947 to 1949 onward, when we can observe the emergence (or sometimes reemergence) of a set of rituals, tests of position, and procedures of control of the situation, the "political class" demonstrates a remarkable mastery of these crises, which become increasingly routinized processes, where the unpredictable is circumscribed or, so to speak, domesticated.[10] However, this capture of calculations cannot be equated with some kind of explicit or tacit *consensus* among the members of a given sector about the projects, representations, or interests of those holding the dominant sectoral positions. Neither does it reflect some shared acceptance of the internal rules of the game at work in this sector, nor even some tacit agreement against the outside, the nonmembers, nonspecialists, or laymen. If representations legitimizing the internal game frequently and powerfully reinforce it, the effectiveness of the capture of calculations is based on something else, namely the fact that—whether they like it or not—the members of a given sector have no other option, in their relevant activities, but to calculate and orient themselves on the basis of the social logic of that sector. They are, in some way, *caught up* in this logic. It is why the social mechanisms which sustain this capture could, not too imprudently, be compared to those in which Hirschmann detects the wellsprings of the loyalty often enjoyed by institutions and organizations.[11] However, this analogy is subject to the condition that capture and loyalty should not be confused. Here we are touching on one of the weak points of Hirschman's theory of loyalty: high entry rights (the severity of the initiation) and tough penalties for defection may well contribute to secure the capture of calculations, without necessarily any loyalty developing among the members, and without necessarily any affective attachment to sectoral aims, values, norms, and interests becoming apparent.

Weber," *Archives Européennes de Sociologie* 12, no. 1 (1971): 3–21; Tom Baumgartner, Walter Buckley, Tom R. Burns and Peter Schustern, "Meta-Power and the Structuring of Social Hierarchies," in *Power and Control: Social Structures and Their Transformations*, ed. T. R. Burns and W. Buckley (London: Sage, 1977), esp. 220; Michel Crozier and Ehrard Friedberg, *Actors and Systems: the Politics of Collective Action* (Chicago: The University of Chicago Press, 1980 [1st French ed., 1977]).

[10]On these "ministerial crises," see, among others, Philip Williams, *Crisis and Compromise: Politics in the Fourth Republic* (New York: Archon Books, 1964), part IV.

[11]Albert O. Hirschman, *Exit, Voice and Loyalty* (Cambridge, MA: Harvard University Press, 1970).

The Objectification of Sectoral Relations

The second issue that must be addressed here is the remarkably *high degree of objectification* that the social relationships constituting sectoral logics have commonly acquired in the contemporary period. The weight and the role, in these logics, of processes that produce and sustain the perception of sectoral relationships as *external* realities *constraining* their protagonists, along with the impersonality of these relationships, are certainly nowadays much more important than suggested by Weber's erstwhile analysis of the objectification processes at work in modern bureaucracies or in the markets characterizing monetary economies.[12] In addition to these two distinct components of objectification, I should mention a third one, which relates to what, in the social world, is perceived and dealt with as "taken for granted."[13]

First, let me pass rapidly over the impersonality of social relationships: the point is well known (though it should be emphasized that, even in societies where the objectification of sectoral relations achieves a high degree, like those focused on here, it is still easy to find *islands of personal ties and relationships*, particularly, but far from exclusively, in the political sectors or fields).[14] Second, I must point out that to understand how the constraining character of sectoral logics works as well as its effects, it is needless to resort to the canonical example of the "laws" of the economic market. Among many other illustrations, equally conclusive is the case of organizations which simultaneously operate in several differentiated sectors, for example in the political field and in that of industrial relations. Such organizations, even when it goes against their official doctrines and the self-image they seek to impose, are forced to manage their activities according to several distinct sectoral logics. Hence, a number of practical difficulties arise for their members, one of the best examples of which is provided by the delicate relationship that existed (and often still persists) between "working-class," "social-democratic," or "labor" parties and their parliamentary groups, the latter having

---

[12] Weber, *Economy and Society*; on the market, see vol.1, 635 et seq.; on modern bureaucracies, see vol. 2, 956 et seq.

[13] See in particular Peter E. Berger and Thomas Luckmann, *The Social Construction of Reality* (London: Penguin Books, 1971 [1966]).

[14] On clientelism, see, among many works, Shmuel N. Eisenstadt and René Lemarchand, eds., *Political Clientelism, Patronage and Development* (London: Sage, 1981); see also the remarks of Jean-François Médard "Le rapport de clientèle," *Revue française de science politique* 26, no. 1 (1976): esp. 123–8, and, on clientelist relations as *addenda* to institutionalized relations, Carl Landé, "The Dyadic Basis of Clientelism," in *Friends, Followers and Factions: A Reader in Political Clientelism*, ed. S. W. Schmidt et al. (Berkeley: University of California Press, 1977), 13–38.

a "natural" tendency to get caught up in the parliamentary game.[15] The third component of objectification concerns those networks or webs of *meaning*—produced mainly without the conscious and deliberate intervention of individual or, a fortiori, of collective actors—which represent the inescapable framework and cognitive material for their actions, perceptions, and interpretations.[16] One of the best ways to grasp this component is by analyzing the working of typifications, taxonomies, and operations of classification that ordinary speech reveals and conveys, and, more generally, by analyzing the resources provided by the cognitive tools of everyday life, not least in its most directly political aspects.[17] Far from being the reflection or the veil of a supposedly "deeper" social reality, these objectified meanings are directly involved in that reality through, in particular, the effects of the constraint they exert on the actors. As we will see later, this component has much greater interest for the social sciences, and especially for the analysis of critical processes, than it may appear at first sight, because on it hinges much of our understanding of the legitimation and delegitimation processes of political regimes or of authorities.

Indeed, it would be irrelevant to examine here all the issues and difficulties raised by the still fledgling exploration of objectification processes. Excepting, however, for one of them, which directly concerns my hypotheses. The idea of different degrees of objectification of social relationships has so far served to highlight, in the strictest Weberian tradition, certain features of contrasting or opposing types of social universe. That is the case, for instance, of the distinction outlined by Bourdieu between two types of modes of domination. In one, the relationships of domination are "made, unmade and made again in and through interaction between individuals," and the reproduction of these relations can only be the precarious product of a "genuine process of constant creation," requiring direct, permanent, and personal (and therefore costly) working. The other mode of domination consists in a series of objective and institutionalized mechanisms that exempts the agents from "this ceaseless and indefinite task of establishing and restoring social relationships."[18] However it is not this distinction I want to

---

[15]For this reason, much can be learned from the study of multisectoral organizations which have profited from successfully disciplining their parliamentary groups or which, more generally, have succeeded in managing this type of *multiple insertion*, as is notably the case, in France, of the communist party. The behavior of the Rassemblement du Peuple Français (RPF) members of parliament after the 1951 legislative elections suggests that these difficulties are certainly not confined to "working class" parties alone.

[16]Cf. Clifford Geertz, *The Interpretation of Cultures* (New York: Basic Books, 1973), esp. 4–30. In my view, however, to give that place to objectified representations in no way implies adopting any consensual vision of these webs of meaning (like, for instance: "community of meaning" equates "consensus").

[17]See in particular Berger and Luckmann, *Social Construction*, 85–9.

[18]Bourdieu, "Modes de domination," esp. 126.

challenge here. Only an *inverted ethnocentrism* could imply that such processes of objectification are present in the same way, to the same degree, with the same density, in contemporary societies and in those that, for convenience, are called traditional or archaic. While, of course, we find objectification quite everywhere, this point of view would turn a blind eye, taking a very elementary example, to all the differences between, on the one hand, *rudimentary technologies of objectification*, such as corporal stigmas or even uniforms (note that here objectification still involves the individual himself, that is, mainly his body), and, on the other hand, much more elaborated technologies which deal rather with the actors' *expectations* than with the *immediate visibility* of social relationships, as seen, for instance, in careers with well-defined stages of promotion up the hierarchy, retirement prospects, the "revolving door" from public administration to business (typically the French *pantouflage*), or other kinds of occupational reconversion.[19]

The point on which I must amend or at least supplement these remarks in no way prejudices the theoretical usefulness of the distinction between *several types of society* based on the degree of objectification of social relationships. My argument is that, alongside this distinction, any analysis of critical conjunctures, especially in the case of complex societies, must give its proper and decisive place to *conjunctural variations* in the objectification of sectoral relations within *one and the same society*.

For, contrary to what Max Weber sometimes seems to believe, social spheres, institutions, or organizations endowed, in his own terms, with a high level of "objectivity" (particularly modern, rational-legal bureaucracies) are not entirely "indestructible" or invulnerable.[20] One of the most interesting properties of highly objectified social relationships is that these are not entirely things. If objectification is something of a trap for the natives of any given society, the "societal illusion" par excellence, the *reification* of the effects of objectification processes by the scholar himself—especially the reification of social structures and institutions—is another one, certainly different, subject to a different logic,

---

[19] In contrast to what might be suggested by shallow evolutionism, this does not mean that these rudimentary forms have disappeared or are destined to disappear in complex societies. On a more general level, it should be noted that the assessment of the degree of objectification of social relationships within sectors raises similar problems to those that emerge in the evaluation of their degree of institutionalization, a particular form of objectification (even though, in my view, the "criteria" proposed by Huntington in this respect—the adaptability, complexity, autonomy, and coherence of procedures and organizations—are far from entirely convincing, on account in particular of the fact that Huntington's vision of institutionalization curiously excludes everything that produces objectivity or exteriority in relation to individual actors and their perceptions of the social world, as well as the resulting constraint effect; see Huntington, *Political Order*, 12–24).

[20] Weber, *Economy and Society*, vol. 2, in particular 987–9.

but no less dangerous.²¹ In fact, it is only by utterly rejecting any "realism of the structure" that social sciences can become able to identify one of the fundamental dimensions of the *transformations of the state*—that is, the *plasticity*—of highly differentiated social systems, the complex societies that interest us here.²²

Sectoral Autonomy

Even if its forms and degrees actually vary among sectors, autonomy characterizes all sectors in any routine conjuncture. At first sight, this feature of the sectors' "external" face does not require lengthy explanation, since the topic of autonomy has been much explored by social scientists. However, it is for this very reason that I must specify what sectoral autonomy means here, namely the relationships between the everyday operation of a given sector and those of the other sectors. Thus, with the major proviso of what I will say later about social groups and movements, this notion does not cover the relationship between institutions and social classes, or between political system and civil society.²³ As long as this issue is concerned, it may even be worth underlining that, when a given sector is successfully monopolized, if only in its highest positions, by a specific particularistic social group (a classic example is the aristocracy in certain institutional systems), then this may itself contribute to strengthening the autonomy of this sector.²⁴ The same, of course, is true of the presence in these positions of professional or semi-professional specialists whose interests favor

---

²¹Speaking of "societal illusion" is obviously not without risk, inasfar as it suggests an opposition between illusion and reality, whereas in the perspective I develop here, the objectification constitutes the "reality" itself, and there is no other more "authentic" reality disguised or concealed behind or within the processes of objectification and their products. It is for this same reason that this issue should be entirely detached from the old debate on "false consciousness" or "alienation" (see, however, for a contrary view, at least in places, Peter L. Berger and Stanley Pullberg, "Reification and the Sociological Critique of Consciousness," *History and Theory* 4, no. 2 (1965): 196–211.

²²The wording comes from Bachelard, who, considering the transformations that physics underwent at the beginning of the twentieth century, attached—in contrast to my use of this expression here above— a positive value to it; see Gaston Bachelard, *Le nouvel esprit scientifique* (Paris: Presses Universitaires de France, 1934), 78.

²³It is, in fact, this relationship which holds most interest, albeit with nuances, for authors as different as Huntington (*Political Order*, 20) and Poulantzas, at least on the question of the "relative autonomy" of the capitalist state (*Political Power*, in particular 278).

²⁴Needless to say, one of the classic theorists of this type of institutional technology is Montesquieu. Besides upper parliamentary houses, conservative "by vocation," other technologies with similar social roots should be mentioned, like institutions designed to "preserve change" along the lines of the "Councils of the Revolution" composed of military leaders in Portugal after the Carnation Revolution, or those composed of religious leaders in Iran during the Islamic Revolution.

a monopolization of sectoral activities and their protection against the "outside" world.[25]

Alongside this, sectoral autonomy can also be tracked through the presence, more or less pronounced, of an extremely wide range of *institutional technologies*, accumulated, perfected, and refined over a period of two centuries. As a matter of fact, numerous jurists, sometimes at the risk of idealizing them, have tried to describe these technologies by adopting the perspective of members of given sectoral institutions. It is precisely from this point of view that the various incompatibilities of functions (i.e., of institutional positions), penal or political immunities, securities of tenure and of salaries or allowances, and so on have all the common property of aiming to protect these individuals from external interference or pressure (at least as regards their relevant sectoral activities). However, other sources of autonomy have remained much less explored, even though their effectiveness is not in doubt: internal courts within sectors, esoteric language, or genuine "codes of silence" toward the outside world, and, more generally, all that we can consider as a kind of micro-physics of tracing and marking the sectors' boundaries.

The same applies, to some extent; to another factor of autonomy (to which I will need to return later), namely the specific *temporal rhythms* embedded in the routines and procedures of each sector. Actually, authors like Easton or Luhmann were right in seeing in such rhythms one of the most potent elements of the autonomy of any institutional system, even though the representation of the relationship between a given system and its environment—the latter being characterized by different social temporalities (*temps sociaux*)—in terms of *inputs* and *outputs* is hardly convincing on this point.[26] I should perhaps add that to account for sectoral autonomy in no way means that sectors are somehow self-sufficient or isolated from their environment. But the exchanges they have with this environment tend, in routine conjunctures, to be constrained by the sectors' specific logics, or, and in fact this is not incompatible, by institutionalized arrangements common to two or more sectors. It is here, perhaps, with regard to sector autonomy, that systems analysis may still keep a minimum of relevance.

---

[25]As regards "total institutions," Goffman observes that it is not necessarily in the upper strata of their personnel but rather at other levels, that we are most likely to find the most passionate defenders of the "traditions" peculiar to the various types of these institutions as regards their sectoral autonomy; see Erving Goffman, *Asylums: Essays on the Social Situation of Mental Patients and Other Inmates* (Chicago: Aldine, 1961). This remark may well have a more general relevance. In particular, we may find a less rigid attitude—one more open to external exigencies—in the higher positions of these sectors, especially when their occupants have the advantage of *multi-positionality* and enjoy institutional mechanisms promoting the "circulation of elites" between sectors (see, for example, in very different political systems, the "Nomenclatura" in the authoritarian regimes of Eastern Europe, or, in France, the *Grands corps* of senior civil servants).

[26]See Easton, *Systems Analysis*, in particular 67–9 and 443–7, and Luhmann, *Differentiation of Society*, 142–3.

Collusive Transactions and Consolidation Effects

Some of these "external" exchanges are of great interest for us, those that I call *collusive transactions*. Actually, these exchanges constitute one of the main characteristics of most contemporary political systems, especially democratic ones. In the perspective set out here, they should be analyzed as powerful intersectoral forms of domination, which may be best termed *consolidation networks*. For instance, modern "States" provide one of the best examples of how such networks operate—indeed this goes against the often monolithic and nearly always reified image ascribed to them in many contemporary conceptualizations.

Let me now further specify what these transactions consist of. Collusive transactions can certainly not be reduced to some "functional contribution" by sectors to the working of the whole system, based on complementary exchanges and relationships between differentiated social spheres with distinct specialized activities, and, at least in some functionalist approaches, supposedly necessary to the survival or reproduction of the system. However, for the analysis of critical processes in complex societies, their crucial aspect lies elsewhere. We can begin to identify what makes up collusive transactions through the pragmatic principles of *non-interference* at work in many consolidation networks. Even in societies claiming democratic values, a "responsible" politician—usually a helpful label in political contests—must know how to turn a blind eye (*fermer les yeux*) to certain activities, barely "legitimate" in terms of these values. This tends to happen when these activities are located in sectors belonging to a consolidation network, and more or less refer to how these sectors define their own legitimate internal practices (I mean here not only "sensitive" sectors, such as those of intelligence agencies or of repressive institutions, but also much more ordinary sectors like economic ones). Of course, the actors or agents of these sectors justify these activities by technical arguments, that is, the imperatives derived from the "specific nature" of their activities (here again we see the tactical uses of sectoral logics). An illustration of the respect for pragmatic rules of this kind can be found in the attitude of members of several French governments toward the military authorities when, especially in the 1956–58 period, these governments "covered"—the indigenous term is symptomatic here—a series of acts (hijacking of the plane carrying leaders of the Algerian Front de Libération Nationale [FLN, National Liberation Front], bombing of Sakhiet, etc.) which they had not "decided," an attitude that completely contradicted the ordinary, official, or legitimate perceptions of the relationship between the political sphere and the army (note also that this respect for pragmatic rules became, with increasing frequency in this period, unilateral, that is to say, inattentive to reciprocity).[27]

No doubt the reader has, at this point, understood that what is at stake in collusive transactions is, in fact, the sustainability and solidity of the definitions that sectors tend to give of themselves, whether in relation to their environments or to their own agents. Thus, the consolidation of political systems consists in *mutual recognitions*, and is, in this sense, external to each individual sector. In this regard, the more or less visible evolution of some of the most liberal democracies toward configurations resembling "societal corporatism" reflects a trend toward *maximum inclusion* of the diverse autonomous sectors in consolidation networks.[28] This also leads, by the same token, to a progressive marginalization, in terms of social importance or "weight," of sectors that are impelled to remain outside this process of mutual recognitions. Moreover, collusive transactions produce in that way a surplus, an *added value of objectification* (in the definition of this notion given above), since these recognitions take place between social entities that are already highly objectified. In these conditions, it is easy enough to understand why the historical paths or patterns of conflicts characterized by the stability of collusive relationships between sectors included in a consolidation network are likely to be very different from those where collusive relationships are eroding or breaking down. If we come back to the French example, the latter was clearly the case, in 1958, in the relationship between the political field and the militarized sectors, where, whatever the initial intentions of their respective agents, their acts manifested the collapse of mutual support. Note however that such *crises of collusive relationships* are not always as spectacular and transparent as in 1958. An equally interesting example is provided by situations where political parties, often after lengthy periods in opposition and proclaiming reformist or even radical ambitions, succeed in elections and come to power: the fragile position of the governments that are then formed, despite their apparently complete political legitimacy, is precisely due to the loosening, not so infrequent in such cases, of the consolidation routines. It would not be absurd to interpret in this way at least some aspects of the French *Front Populaire* experience in 1936

---

[27]Equally interesting in this respect is the observation of *repair rituals* which may occur—to use Goffman's terminology—when "profanations" have been perpetrated against the "territory" of a sector (here I am very freely transposing some of Goffman's analyses of reparation activities in daily face-to-face interactions); see Erving Goffman, *Relations in Public. Micro Studies of the Public Ordrer* (New York: Basic Books, 1971).

[28]On societal corporatism and what distinguishes it from state corporatism, see Philippe C. Schmitter, "Still the Century of Corporatism," *Review of Politics* 36, no. 1 (1974): 85–131; and, in order to compare with the "consociational" transactions that may occur in social systems characterized by a high degree of cultural fragmentation, see Gerhard Lehmbruch, "Consociational Democracy, Class Conflict and the New Corporatism," in *Trends Toward Corporatist Intermediation,* ed. P. C. Schmitter and G. Lehmbruch (Beverly Hills, London: Sage, 1979), 53–62.

or, more recently, the difficulties faced by the socialist government resulting from the French elections of 1981.

Sectors and Arenas

All the above and the image of complex societies this suggests require a few brief additional observations.

(1) First, if it is wise to leave aside, for the moment, the issue of the precise demarcation of all the social universes displaying the structural features examined above (since such an overall demarcation would imply in particular to grasp in detail the specific logics of institutional arrangements in different types of authoritarian political systems), I need however to underline straightaway that, in democratic systems at least, a series of highly institutionalized social sectors clearly exhibit all these features. This is not only true of sectors directly constituting what is usually called, in reifying language, the "machinery" of the state: the universes of economic firms, even during the most "Keynesian" periods, the social subspaces of university institutions, or those of trade-union (or "corporatist") representation, also very often correspond to what the notion of sector covers. The same is true, for example, when carefully scrutinized, of the organizational conglomerate around the French Communist Party (or similarly, at least in some periods, around the Gaullist movement or the SFIO, the old socialist party [Section Française de l'Internationale Ouvrière, French Section of the Workers International]). On the other hand, other social entities or subsystems may indeed depart from the definition of the notion of sector, but, to tell the truth, this does not really present a major problem. No more than having to admit that the detailed enumeration of the differentiated sectors in a given society— and here again we have to distance ourselves from the theoretical approach of most functionalisms—is a *strictly empirical* issue and cannot be achieved by some kind of deduction based on the universal "needs" or "functions" that are supposedly essential for the survival or the reproduction of every society and every political system.

(2) Second, it must be understood that what I am trying to capture with the notion of sector is not differentiated social universes or spheres as places of production of some kind of goods or of a particular form of exchange (i.e., as sites where we find *cooperative games* between their members), but rather as sites of *competition, contest, and confrontation*. This observation matters for situating the approach outlined here in relation to that of some of the pioneers of the resource mobilization perspective, who have tried to identify the processes whereby social groups, in particular those most deprived, may increase their stock of political resources. For example, it is in this way that Coleman conceives what he calls arenas as social places where the value of the resources mobilized

by a given group (*input resources*) is transformed through particular combinations of resources in "interaction," each type of arena corresponding to a typical combination or interaction of resources. The products of the operation of the arena, called *output* resources, are then usable in other acts of production.[29] It thus appears that not only, for the most part, such arenas do not fit the sectors as defined above but also that an activity of production defined as cooperative because of its results is not necessarily—we might even say it is almost never— separable from the conflicts or competitions which tend to oppose those who "cooperate" (the point is perfectly illustrated by the works of *the bureaucratic politics* approach on decision-making in large bureaucracies).[30] Furthermore, and this is often missed, Coleman views interaction as being *between resources*, whereas the notion of sector refers explicitly to interaction *between actors*, in particular, to the *interdependence* of their perceptions, evaluations, and strategic calculations, whose interplay and mediation this author entirely ignores. In addition, conceiving sectors as sites of conflict also allows us, by looking at internal cleavages and confrontations, to grasp one of the factors of the possible *extension* of mobilizations, that is, of their process of *multisectorization* through the importation of external resources, the interference of actors from other sectors, or the resort to collusive tactics, and so on.

(3) The third observation concerns another possible source of confusion, linked to the *practical categories* that structure the actors' immediate experience (and are produced by that experience). These actors are led to see their environment in terms of distinct sites of action in the same way that they are led to segment their time according to the diversity of these sites.[31] Some phenomenological-inspired approaches, sensitive to indigenous classifications and typifications, describe how the actors objectify these diverse sites (which should, more rigorously, be termed sites of *direct interaction*), by attributing to them specific

---

[29]This is no vague metaphor with a purely ornamental function: the tables devised by Coleman to record—in its strict sense—the *conversion* of certain types of resources into resources of a different type or value call to mind those developed by Leontieff to capture the relationships between diverse economic sectors. The specification of differential *conversion rates* for each arena—that is, for each combination of resources—embodies the sociometric ideal which, according to Coleman, this approach should strive to attain, Coleman, "Race Relations and Social Change," esp. 317–25.

[30]See first Graham T. Allison, *Essence of Decision, Explaining the Cuban Missile Crisis* (Boston: Little Brown, 1971); Graham T. Allison and Morton H. Halperin, "Bureaucratic Politics: A Paradigm and some Policy Implications," in *Theory and Policy in International Relations*, ed. R. Tanter and R. H. Ullman (Princeton: Princeton University Press, 1972).

[31]This is well illustrated by Goffman's analysis of what he calls "regions" and "regional behaviour" (Erving Goffman, *The Presentation of Self in Everyday Life*. [New York: Doubleday Anchor Books, 1959 (1956)]); note that Goffman distinguishes "regions" from "sites of action," a notion which he gives a very narrow technical extension, to be brief, sites of risk (E. Goffman, *Interaction Rituals: Essays on Face-to-face Behavior* [Chicago: Aldine ,1967]).

expectations about rules governing behavior, roles for oneself and for others, and action objectives and the kinds of resources operating within them.[32]

Taken in this way (and we gain by reserving the term "arena" for these sites of direct interaction), the notion of arena implies that any sector is very likely to comprise several, and even, sometimes, a large number of arenas. The number depends, of course, on the particular history of each sector, on its dimensions, on the type of resources, and, more generally, the repertory of possible lines of action that we can find in each case. With the representation of students in the university councils established in France after May 1968, there appears a series of electoral arenas which even those actors in the university system who wield the most important resources would find it hard to ignore. Nothing allows us to think that, *in itself*, this student representation (and its arenas) constitutes a sector, that is to say, in particular, that it enjoys real autonomy in relation to the rest of the university system, a capacity to capture calculations, and so on (on the other hand, it is possible that this would be different with the setting up of regional institutions or of constitutional arrangements of federal type).

(4) My final remark relates to a more delicate issue. The problem lies in the opposition, taken for granted by any freshman student, between highly institutionalized social entities (and exhibiting the external attributes of institutions) and other entities like social groups or even social movements. The point is that here too it would be wrong, without any further precaution, to turn differences of intensity or degree in the dimensions by which I have characterized social sectors into radical differences of "nature" or "kind." Groups, but also sometimes social movements, at least over short periods, *may* display quite high scores regarding their autonomy, the objectification of their "social reality," or the hold on their members of a specific social logic. Both the anti-independence movement of 1958 in Algiers city and the French student movement of 1968 constitute systems of tactical interdependence between their members, that is, universes of micro-organizations in which the perceptions, opinions, and behaviors of actors are caught up in particular collective logics.[33] The point is a consequential one: it is precisely this kind of phenomenon that a crudely

---

[32]Very close to this perspective, Bailey, for his part, reduces arenas to "situations of interaction or competition in general," which leads him to list as many arenas as there are distinct situations of competition in any social entity and in any social segment (Bailey, *Stratagems and Spoils*); thus, in the approach he proposes, there are "arenas" which correspond to ritualized competitions where the actors display restraint and appear to have a common interest in respecting the rules of the game (see, for example, Bailey's description of the battles of words, the *doladoli*, between different factions in the Indian village of Basipara), and "arenas" of a different type, involving decisive confrontations ("decisive" in the military sense), particularly interactions in which an actor may lose his key resources, for example his allies.

[33]On the Algiers movement, see especially Jean-Luc Parodi, "Le 13 mai 1958: les Algériens d'origine européenne et la politique" (Master diss., Institut d'Etudes Politiques de Paris, 1960); on the student movement, see, among others, the vivid picture of its different components drawn by two of the

shortsighted description would interpret as a "consensus" about, on one hand, what are worthy of being legitimate issues around which actors may dispute and take a stand, and of becoming the stakes of collective action, and, on the other hand, about what should be the marks or stigma of exteriority in regard to the movement. By contrast, an approach paying more attention to mobilizations, and, beyond this, to what might be termed *social tectonics*, will become able to discern in all that—and this is a great advantage—something like a process of autonomization of these universes from other social spheres or sectors.

This also means that the perspective developed here is fully compatible with taking into account of the crucial role of such entities, especially of social groups, in political games and confrontations, as well as in the emergence of the latter. As a matter of fact, this perspective does nothing more than highlight the *kinship* of processes at work in social entities which ordinary—but also, and above all, sociological—common sense tends to separate and oppose. Armies as well as social groups may experience breakups and disintegrations. Both contain arenas where conflicts tend to fashion, so to speak, their social consistency. Both, finally, are *conductive* for mobilizations that may challenge their frontiers and their social identities. In short, this perspective drives the scholar's attention to some dimensions of social groups which are only too rarely included in the analysis of these "collective beings."[34] Additionally it allows us to disregard the eternal and inconclusive debates on the "in-itself" and the "for-itself" of groups or classes and simultaneously those on the magics of sudden processes of becoming class-conscious (*prises de conscience*), namely the passage from one to the other.

Let me leave the discussion at this point. No doubt the observations, illustrations, precautions, and qualifications could be multiplied or extended. Phenomena such as the *multi-positionality* of many individuals or the location of certain arenas *in* or *between* several sectors would certainly deserve further treatment, as would a number of the methodological or even theoretical choices at work in the approach outlined in these pages, not all of which I have indicated. Such as they are, however, with regard to the objectives I have set for the present undertaking, the elements of the analytical framework elaborated and discussed above are sufficient in that they allow us to go well beyond a mere conceptual rearrangement, that is, they allow us to identify and explore the working and the impact of multisectoral mobilizations *in* and *on* the "structures" of complex societies.

---

movement leaders, Daniel Bensaïd and Henri Weber, *Mai 1968: une répétition générale* (Paris: Maspero, 1968).

[34]For the role of instruments and factors of objectification in the emergence and "success" of a social group, see in particular Luc Boltanski, *The Making of a Class: Cadres in French Society* (Cambridge: Cambridge University Press, 1987 [1st French ed., 1982]).

Chapter 4
Fluid Conjunctures and the Plasticity of Structures

Every instance of multisectoral mobilization, whatever its form and whatever the actors involved, is likely to impact and transform, in its very "structures," the routine organization of society. This basic proposition of the perspective I am developing here needs to be complemented by another one, which states that this process should be conceived differently from the dynamics which social science usually regards as typical of political crises, namely the rise in the level of violence or in the intensity of conflict (i.e., the degree of the actors' involvement or of their mutual hostility). Identifying this other dynamics means determining the theoretical and empirical significance of political fluidity. This task, or rather its first stages, is the purpose of this chapter. More precisely, its aim is to single out and specify some of the elementary properties or components that characterize this fluidity and the conjunctures in which it occurs. These properties are elementary in the sense that they are the basis, in terms of both derivation and intelligibility, of other properties, some of which will be analyzed later (this does not mean however that they are less interesting or important for the understanding of crisis processes). These elementary properties define *fluid political conjunctures*. They are not necessarily "in themselves," taken individually, characteristic only of "crisis" dynamics involving multisectoral mobilizations, and probably none of them would be present with the same intensity or force in the entire set of historical cases in which these dynamics appear—they are, as I said, *trend-properties* (see Chapter 1).[1] However, such dynamics always display all of these properties;

---

[1] In a sense, this points to a phenomenal "imperfection" in the processes these properties account for. But make no mistake about it: this is in no way an attempt, as is often the case in the social sciences, to justify, in advance, possible exceptions. In the perspective I am developing here, to speak of trend-properties present with variable intensity means exactly that we must expect their actual presence, which also entails—to say one further word about the conditions under which the theoretical scheme developed here is open to critical discussion or, if preferred, falsification—that any empirical exception

this is precisely what constitutes their distinctive feature, whatever the visible differences—often significant, as we shall see—which may separate them, and whatever the variety of phenomenal forms in which they may appear to us. And, indeed, whatever the specific causes, determinants, or origins supposed to be attached to each historical situation where this kind of dynamics has emerged.

Desectorization

Among these elementary properties, it is the *conjunctural desectorization of social space* that has the richest theoretical and empirical implications. First, it allows us to identify the main components of the changes in their state that complex social systems undergo in critical conjunctures. Second, it also gives us the means to highlight other properties that specify more precisely what the fluidity of these conjunctures is made of. In a way, this property—that is, desectorization—only encapsulates certain "structural" aspects of the dynamics originating in multisectoral mobilizations, aspects which are all related to transformations of the relationships between several routinely differentiated sectors. This mainly concerns the reduction of the autonomy of the sectors impacted by the mobilizations, the opening up of their confrontational arenas, and the process of calculations escaping, or, if one prefers, breaking free, that we can then observe.

(a) *The reduction in sectoral autonomy* derives from the actual unfolding (*la marche*) of the multisectoral mobilizations, that is, from the decompartmentalizations and the interferences of different sectoral logics, as well as from the occurrence of trans-sectoral moves, that such mobilizations are much more likely to involve than restricted ones. Reduction in autonomy is evidenced both from an overall point of view (in particular that of intersectoral relations, transactions between sectors, and their possible collusions) and when focusing on a single sector, on its specific social logic, its legitimate and pragmatic definitions, its boundaries or its social rhythms, and so on. An interesting problem arises here, in that the reduction of the autonomy of a given sector may well result in a sudden *autonomization of its subunits* or component elements. This happens frequently in highly fluid conjunctures, with—in the case of political sectors or fields—the fragmentation of political parties, or even, as noted by some observers of political crisis processes, with the conjunctural saliency, within certain institutional systems, of "organs" which, in routine

---

or anomaly is likely to become a problem, that is, to challenge it as a whole or at least in some of its particular aspects.

conjunctures, only enjoy a very limited degree of autonomy.² A typical illustration of these phenomena is offered by the prominent role suddenly assumed by the president of the French Republic in the development of the May 1958 crisis. A related example of this kind of process is the strange *emancipations* that, in authoritarian systems, may be experienced by institutions exhibiting, in ordinary times, a facade of autonomy (in which, moreover, the actors themselves most often "do not believe") when these systems experience the effects of multisectoral mobilizations. As in the case of certain judicial" or even "political" organs during the Polish crisis of 1980–81, these institutions can suddenly—in a context where the encompassing sector loses autonomy—begin to operate for a while, much to the surprise of the indigenous actors, in a way that corresponds to their official status, their autonomy thus largely losing its fictitious character.³ It is easy to see, however, that the occurrence of this type of internal autonomization of one (or several) institutional elements in no way indicates or induces the autonomization of the encompassing sector itself, indeed quite the contrary. Nonetheless, this phenomenon frequently obscures—at the empirical level—the reduction in the autonomy of sectors, and is a constant source of confusion in the interpretation of political crisis dynamics.⁴

(b) Besides this first aspect, the desectorization process is also reflected in *the opening up of confrontational spaces*, arenas, or sites of competition specific to the diverse sectors affected by multisectoral mobilizations. As we shall see later, this opening up has very important consequences for the tactics of the actors and for the effectiveness or "value" of the resources located in these sectors, as well as for the characteristics of the game itself. It also produces an effect of another kind, which is particularly compelling for the analysis of critical processes, namely the loosening of the link which, in routine conjunctures, connects, on the one hand, sectoral arenas and, on the other hand, issues and stakes peculiar to the competitions or conflicts located in those arenas. Or, so to speak, a trend toward

---

²Linz, *Crisis, Breakdown, and Reequilibration*; see also, for partially converging observations, Poulantzas, *Fascism and Dictatorship*.

³On this conjunctural emancipation of institutions like the Polish Diet and other "transmission belt" institutions, or even like the local organizations of the communist dominated PZPR (Polska Zjednoczona Partia Robotnicza, Polish United Workers' Party), see especially Staniszkis, *Poland's Self-limiting Revolution*.

⁴I will examine later the problems raised in this respect by Linz's theoretical approach. It should be noted, however, that, in his study of the Italian crisis of 1919–22, Paolo Farneti, by contrast, perfectly well understood that the processes I have just referred to are indeed components of the loss of autonomy experienced by the political field (even though, in his attempt to make this observation compatible with Linz's theoretical model, Farneti tried to identify this loss of autonomy as a particular phase in the crisis process, preceding a phase of "political vacuum"; see Paolo Farneti, "Social Conflict, Parliamentary Fragmentation, Institutional Shift, and the Rise of Fascism: Italy," in *The Breakdown of Democratic Regimes: Europe*, ed. J. J. Linz and A. Stepan (Baltimore: The Johns Hopkins University Press, 1978), 3–33.

a *despecification* of these issues. This is one of the reasons why conjunctures involving multisectoral mobilizations are at the same time conjunctures characterized by a high level of *issue mobility* or volatility, and by a difficulty for the actors to understand what and where the issues and stakes are and how to control them. This is also one of the reasons why a favorite explanatory schema of many historians, who like to ascribe a driving role, in political crises, to the issues of the confrontations and to lend these issues the capacity to dictate the behavior and tactics of the individual and collective actors, should be significantly amended.

(c) The third analytical component of desectorization is what I will call *calculations escaping process.* Let me clarify this. The loss of the hold that sectoral logics exert on the actors located in sectors impacted by multisectoral mobilizations makes itself felt in that these actors tend to give weight to a range of reference points, clues, indices, and landmarks for assessing the situation that fall largely outside the specific social logic of that sector—this at least in their relevant calculations (i.e., those that concern the activities, issues, and stakes characterizing a given sector). It is a trend which might be described in Luhmann's terminology—though solely with reference to the way actors, in making their calculations, perceive and define situations—as a *reduction in the self-referentiality* of the sectors. The escaping of calculations process is particularly salient in historical episodes where, as in the French crisis of 1958, the political sector undergoes a spectacular "sensitization" as a result of trans-sectoral moves and interferences originating in, especially, the army, and which led the members of parliament, and more generally the "political class" of the Fourth Republic, quite openly to give up their sectoral game and its rules, even those which were the most stabilized. In the case of the French crisis of 1934, although the sensitization of the political "field" occurs over a much tighter time span, the night of February 6 to 7, 1934, the same analysis is, of course, relevant. However, I must emphasize here that the escaping of calculations *is not* necessarily objectified or incarnated, as in the French 1934 and 1958 crises, in the actual *outcomes* of the confrontations. That is why, in order to identify its presence, other, apparently less direct indicators must be used, such as, and these are just examples, the perceptible dispersion— in fact the multisectorization—of the bargaining that then takes place, or the multisectoral location of the *tests of position* whereby actors seek, in this kind of conjuncture, both to situate themselves and to situate the other protagonists of the confrontation (this pertains as well to the French episodes of 1934 and 1958 as to those of 1947, 1953, and, of course, 1968).

As identified above, the trend toward conjunctural desectorization of social space invites nevertheless some further remarks which should, I hope, help to avoid some misunderstandings.

(1) First, this desectorization, in the three dimensions I have described, remains for the most part a purely *conjunctural* phenomenon. It is conjunctural

in the sense that it does not crystallize into institutions that unify or homogenize the social space in a sustainable way. For this reason, it must be distinguished from all the processes of "integration" which transform social spaces in the long term (*longue durée*), as was the case, for example, with the formation of Nation-States, or with the emergence of unified economic markets (the same observation might also apply to certain less studied processes, like the establishment of centralized trade-union organizations, or even, as can be seen in a number of political systems, the gradual alignment of local and regional political fields with cleavages prevailing in the central or national arenas). However, this question, that is, this distinction, should not lead to the mistaken conclusion that fluid conjunctures can never, in any circumstances, give birth to original institutions or institutional crystallizations which might possibly survive the resorption of the fluidity in which they initially appeared.

(2) But the risk of confusion is much greater with the temptation—and it is all too easy to see how this might happen—to overlay conjunctural desectorization with terminology and analogies drawn, often somewhat carelessly, from the laws of thermodynamics, especially the image of an "entropic" tendency constantly at work in the "life" of social systems, and which the latter must constantly seek to counteract.[5] If this type of perspective must always be tackled with great caution, this is not only because of the confusion resulting usually from the deployment of these analogies in sociology or in economics, especially over the meaning of notions like energy, entropy, disorder, or irreversibility when applied to social systems. The main reason for caution is that the use of these analogies has proved to be, at least at the moment and in the research domain of the present work, most often unproductive, and even, not infrequently, counterproductive. In a word, the fact is that these analogies, like all analogies, are of no interest and no help until the scholar has to invent and organize a set of hypotheses capable of grasping certain aspects of reality and of accounting for them. Not only is this not the case here (such an analogy would, so to speak, be arriving after the

---

[5]The idea is present in a large number of works; see, for example, to refer to an author already discussed, Etzoni, *Active Society*, esp. 14, 389–90; see also Claude Lévi-Strauss, *Tristes Tropiques* (London: Penguin, 2011 [1st French ed., 1955]). Note that the uses that the social sciences have made of the notion of entropy are extremely varied, but it is not my purpose to enter further into this debate. Two points, however. First, many of these works go beyond a simple analogical use of the thermodynamics laws, as shown, for example, by Nicholas Georgescu Roegen, *The Entropy Law and the Economic Process* (Cambridge, MA: Harvard University Press, 1971) or Richard N. Adams, *Energy and Structure. A Theory of Social Power* (Austin: University of Texas Press, 1975). Second, note that according to Luhmann, in what also seems to be an analogical use of this notion, the entropy of a social system corresponds to relationships between elements of the system that are *non-effectuated* but mathematically possible—which, I suspect, does not necessarily represent any measurement of the "disorder" or "disorganization" of a social system (quite the contrary, these noneffectuated relationships "indicate their [complex systems] real ordering activities"; see Luhmann, "Temporalization of Complexity," vol. 2, 97.

battle), but in addition this type of analogy nearly always promotes the image of a spontaneous movement of societies headed toward a social vacuum or a situation where all "structures" disappear, whereas the approach I develop here is explicitly set up *against* this kind of representation, which equates crises to the absence of any social structure—this, it will be remembered, is one of the main features of what I have called the heroic illusion.[6] Finally, in line with the above, these analogies are counterproductive because the imagery they convey tends to obstruct our understanding of a fundamental fact, namely that the changes of state political systems may experience are in no way the effects of some structural degradation occurring "naturally," and "by itself." The point is that, on the contrary, these changes are brought about by the mobilizations, by the *active* and *costly interventions* of social actors—often much more costly than what is involved in restoring or maintaining "structures." This quite simply means, if I allow myself to occasionally use the terminology drawn from thermodynamics, that critical conjunctures in political systems cannot—independently of specific circumstances and the specific history of the exchanges of moves (*échanges de coups*) peculiar to each crisis—be considered as *attractor states* toward which these systems irresistibly evolve.

(3) The third error worth pointing out straightaway concerns a more empirical issue. It relates to certain tactics, or to certain social technologies deployed in critical conjunctures and which may be analyzed as attempts to *isolate* a given sector from its social setting. A classic example concerns the organizational arrangements (*dispositifs)* or devices of "enclosure" which have long been part of the repertoire of militarized sectors[7]: these sectors tend, in critical conjunctures, to cut themselves off, often quite physically, from the rest of society, by

---

[6]This is the reason why it would be best to leave aside for the moment the case of analogies based on the recent results of the thermodynamics "third stage," which focuses on the dynamics of dissipative structures and phenomena of self-organization (see Ilya Prigogine and Isabelle Stengers, *Order out of Chaos: Man's New Dialogue with Nature* (Boulder: New Science Library, 1984 [1st French ed., 1979]); however, this remark certainly does not mean that we should subscribe to the philosophical—and sometimes even genuinely metaphysical—theses that some believe can be drawn from these results, nor indeed to superficially metaphorical transpositions that have rapidly appeared in some sectors of the social sciences and which may have the effect of discouraging any serious attempt to explore possible homologies between the so-called behaviors of dissipative structures and certain social facts).

[7]On this point, see Alain Joxe, *Le Rempart social* (Paris: Galilée, 1979). To a large extent, the issue behind recourse to such technologies and tactics is clearly the—not always easy—task of managing the multiple allegiances of the agents of militarized organization, allegiances which might possibly form the basis of multisectoral mobilizations that may affect these organizations. One of the primitive forms of institutionalized closure consists of recruiting military personnel who are perfectly *alien* to the society in which they have to operate, the Ottoman Janissaries being an interesting variant. In the same vein, regarding the use of certain "martial" ethnic groups, especially in culturally pluralistic societies, see also Cynthia H. Enloe, *Ethnic Soldiers. State Security in a Divided Society* (Harmondsworth: Penguin Books, 1980), esp. 23–49.

institutionalized procedures that insulate troops, like permanent states of alert and the restriction, or even suspension, of communications with the "outside world." Unsurprisingly, here we come back to one of the familiar preoccupations of structuralist-functionalist sociology, whereby the isolation of systems or subsystems is thought of as one of the elementary defense mechanisms of such entities in relation to their social environments.[8] This brings me to the possible objection: Is the fact that the uses of these tactics and social technologies are actually observable consistent with the propositions developed above? Is it not the case that crises are periods when sectors or organizations, so to speak, withdraw or turn inward on themselves, rather than being phenomena moved by a dynamics of desectorization of social space? To tell the truth, the objection carries little weight. Everything suggests, on the contrary, that the implementation of such technologies and tactics, when it works effectively in the course of multisectoral confrontations, can only support and strengthen the hypotheses I have outlined above. This is for one simple and decisive reason, namely that the deployment of these technologies and tactics can only be satisfactorily explained by the effective presence of a social dynamics working in the opposite direction, *against which* certain actors *react* (because they possibly may perceive some of its manifestations as a threat), by opting for this course of action. Furthermore, and this is not a negligible point on the empirical level, these technologies and tactics are far from being able, in all circumstances, to shield the sectors concerned against the dynamic of desectorization, the reduction of their autonomy and the weakening hold of their specific social logics. In other words, what matters here—that is, what represents a good indicator of the actual impact of the desectorization process—is not the success or the failure of these technologies, but their very implementation.[9]

I should add that such technologies and tactics of insulation are not specific to militarized sectors. When considering the unfolding of a number of historical

---

[8]Traces of this can be found in the way Easton criticizes approaches that see social systems in terms of equilibrium: he remarks that these systems have many ways of responding to disturbances, including indeed their insulation in relation to their environment (Easton, *Systems Analysis*, 20). For an incisive discussion of the use of this notion in the functionalist perspective, see Alvin Gouldner, "Reciprocity and Autonomy in Functional Theory," in *Symposium on Sociological Theory*, ed. L. Gross (Evanston: Row- Peterson, 1959), 241–70.

[9]Incidentally, this also means that speaking of desectorization of social space does not imply that all the actors located in sectors that are subject to this dynamics are consciously seeking and working to make it happen, far from it. For instance, some of them—but there are no general laws governing this (in particular, it is not necessarily those occupying the dominant positions in these sectors)—may well have an interest, albeit a conjunctural one, in playing the sectoral isolation card, and others may also engage in more complex tactics to bring about this isolation through the intervention of other actors located elsewhere in the social space, that is to say, by operating on a wider multisectoral register (thus, by the same token, most often unintentionally, helping to fuel the dynamics which at the local level they are trying to contain).

episodes, like for example May 1968 in France, it is easy enough to detect, alongside the deployment of insulation devices by the army, the use of similar tactics in other social sites, such as the attempt by the CGT, relatively successful it would seem, to compartmentalize the industrial strikes, and "protect" them from outside interferences, especially from the student movement.[10] As I will show later, defensive tactics do not all necessarily involve the same forms of physical separation from the sector's environment. But, in every case, the external "performance" of the sectors—the *outputs* they can generate—seem to depend heavily, during critical conjunctures, on their capacity to escape, at least partially, the dynamics of desectorization of social space.

Structural Uncertainty

The second major property of fluid conjunctures, structural uncertainty, is closely linked to what I have just examined. Strictly speaking, it derives from it. As a matter of fact, its principal driving forces are the disappearance or blurring of reference points, clues, and indices, and the loss or reduced efficiency of assessment tools, that is, of the sectoral logics components that serve in routine conjunctures as supports and materials for actor's interpretations, expectations, definitions of situations and, more generally, calculations. These are all direct by-products of the desectorization process.

Structural uncertainty—as we shall verify below and in later chapters—allows us not only to account for a considerable number of "facts," empirical regularities, as well as of the crisis actors' feelings, personal experiences, or even, sometimes, rationalizations, but also to discover other features. Let me start with one of these regularities, which will allow me to tackle a far from negligible methodological issue. Structural uncertainty is the key to understanding an

---

[10]See, for example, the account of the reception accorded to the student "marches" on the Renault factories at Boulogne-Billancourt in Bensaïd and Weber, *Mai 1968*, 150–8. The success of the closure tactics, though impossible to measure with any accuracy, can nonetheless be deduced from the fact that—*at least during the "upward" period* of the crisis and with the exception of the very special case of the Loire-Atlantique district (*département*)—the student movement was visibly not able to win support from any working-class "bastion" that might have acted as a symbolic counterweight to the CGT's control of the strike. It is also, of course, very difficult to assess the weight, in the emergence of this success, an important one no doubt, of the *social distance* between students and industrial workers, which the CGT evidently played on in its tactics (on this point, see Gérard Adam et al., *L'Ouvrier français en 1970* (Paris: Presses de Sciences Po, 1970), esp. 223–5; see also Pierre Dubois, "Les pratiques de mobilisation et d'opposition," in *Grèves revendicatives ou grèves politiques. Acteurs, pratiques, sens du mouvement de mai*, ed. P. Dubois et al. (Paris: Anthropos, 1971), 370, which from a "sample" of 182 enterprises in the North and Pas-de-Calais district, register about 6.5 percent of cases where discussions with students were organized, a proportion whose significance is not easy to ascertain.

empirical observation or regularity, of which we have already had a glimpse in this book, and which runs parallel with the impressions sometimes experienced very intensely by the actors in numerous crisis episodes—impressions which have been noted in at least some of the literature on revolutions and political crises. As I have suggested, it could be formulated the following way: in critical periods or conjunctures, the effectiveness or "value" of the political resources (or, if one prefers, assets or kinds of capital) available to the protagonists of such events are subject to significant, and sometimes quite sudden, fluctuations. While this formulation is certainly convenient (and for this reason I will be using it again), it is not entirely satisfactory and needs to be somewhat qualified. For the scholar who encounters such fluctuations, there is a significant risk of falling into the admittedly rather common trap of what Marion Levy has nicely dubbed *the fallacy of useless measurement*.[11] Except that here the measurement is not so much useless as seriously *misleading*. To clarify this point, let me return for a moment to the theoretical model of the authors of the Stanford group discussed in Chapter 2.[12] This model set itself the task of reconstructing the calculations of the actors involved in the "crisis" phases of the selected historical episodes, calculations which supposedly led them to their choices of tactics and alliances. The trap here consists in embarking on a quest for some kind of miracle formula which will make it possible to *measure* the changing effectiveness or "value" of the actors' resources, that is to say, to *assign precise values* to these resources. I believe this quest to be a hopeless one. Because we are simply unable to register any "natural" measurements of the effectiveness or "value" of these resources (like prices on an economic market), we run into a "solution" which is disastrous in every respect. Overlooking or forgetting that we are substituting, *after the event*, our own evaluations for those of the actors, we erase or discard precisely what is the most interesting and illuminating for the analysis of critical conjunctures, namely the effects of fluctuations in the effectiveness or "value" of resources occurring in these situations.[13] To be more precise, we thereby discard,

---

[11]Marion J. Levy, "Does it Matter if he is Naked? Bawled the Child," in *Contending Approaches to International Politics*, ed. K. Knorr and N. Rosenau (Princeton: Princeton University Press, 1969), 98.

[12]Almond, Flanagan, and Mundt, *Crisis, Choice, and Change*.

[13]The reasons that led the authors of the Stanford group to this methodological choice are directly related to the *heroic illusion* which shapes their entire approach: the reader probably remembers that in order to grasp the phases of genuine "crisis" in the historical episodes they considered these authors in fact believed that "structural" approaches were not appropriate and that only approaches focusing on the actors' choices or decisions were pertinent. And the reader also should remember that, to simplify, Almond and Flanagan tried to show that the coalitions which supposedly brought these "crises" to an end came about thanks, mainly, to the *rational choices* of the actors; and in order to account for these rational choices, it simply seemed obvious to them—and absolutely nonproblematic—to assign, *ex post factum*, through their own assessments, quantified "values" to

without realizing it, some of the most determining properties of the ways the actors calculate in critical conjunctures: we blindly brush away much of what constitutes the *uncertainty* that these actors confront, thereby simultaneously losing the means of understanding this uncertainty and of understanding the effects the uncertainty has on the calculations and interpretations of the actors.

As the reader has no doubt anticipated from everything that has been said so far, in such critical contexts the actors' calculations are characteristically affected by the very serious difficulties they encounter when trying to evaluate the effectiveness and "value" not only of their own resources but also of those of the other protagonists. This is due to the fact that the efficiency of the assessment tools available to the actors—in other words, ordinary *calculability* itself—is heavily dependent on the stability of sectoral logics and the persistence of sectoral autonomy. Of course, political actors make calculations in crisis conjunctures. But my point is that the "value" of resources as information that may be used by the protagonists in this kind of situation has little chance of emerging "naturally." In short, if we need to confront the issue of conjunctural fluctuations in the resources' effectiveness or "value," it is only by locating these fluctuations in contexts experiencing more or less sudden transformations—which must then be rendered intelligible—that it becomes possible to outline a satisfactory answer (I will return to this in more detail later).

Actually, the difficulties facing the actors go well beyond the issue of the effectiveness or "value" of resources. In conjunctures of political fluidity, these difficulties become particularly significant, both in terms of the capacity of these actors to anticipate the probable lines of action or moves of their adversaries (or, indeed, of their partners or allies) and in terms of their capacity to identify or define the situation in which they find themselves. In such contexts, there is a high probability that multiple and noncongruent definitions of the situation will emerge. *The collapse of routine definitions*, which the crisis protagonists are confronting, frequently contributes, along with all the other factors just mentioned, to give birth to a sort of situational *inhibition* of the actors' tactical activity (this also may be fed by some other factors which will be discussed later). Finally, it should be stressed that these contexts tend to make access to information very *costly*, and, on the other hand, that the anticipation of the costs of information itself is subject to the same components of uncertainty I have examined above.

These various features may be observed almost in "laboratory conditions" during *moments of derailment (dérapage)* occurring in the course of "great" political crises. Actually, such moments are quite easy to identify, for we can rely directly on the perceptions of the actors themselves and, especially, on their

---

the political resources at the disposal of the protagonists (as regards more precisely this issue, see Dobry, *Sociologie des crises politiques*, 128–40).

sense of having lost control of events, of having lost the capacity to interpret the situation. It is worth pointing out that these derailments tend to occur especially in contexts where certain actors endowed with important resources have tried to stabilize a situation which seemed to be escaping their control, and where, indeed, they had grounds to believe (like most of the conflict protagonists) that they had been successful. This means that, just before these derailments, they had succeeded in building, enforcing, or negotiating a socially plausible interpretation of the situation, and in identifying lines of action or strategic orientations that seemed "appropriate" to the situation as they perceived it. This is the case, for example, with the sudden derailment of the French May 1968 "events," between May 27 and May 30, following the rejection of the Grenelle agreements by the strikers at Renault's Boulogne-Billancourt factories (in the minds of their promoters, these agreements were expected to allow the industrial conflict to be *disconnected* from the other elements of the confrontation, that is, in the perspective and the terms of this book, to help the mobilizations and the conflict as a whole be *re-sectorized*).[14] Indeed, it was a similar configuration which produced the derailment of the June 1936 strikes in France, immediately after the Matignon agreements, a derailment of events which surprised or worried (often both) most of the actors, trade-union leaders and members of the government included—this is the precise moment of communist leader Maurice Thorez's famous "One should know when to end a strike" *(Il faut savoir terminer une grève)*.[15] And we find again, albeit in a different form, the failure of

---

[14]The interpretation suggested by some authors like Stanley Hoffmann, *Decline or renewal? France since the 1930's* (New York: Viking Press, 1974), which in this respect resembles the versions sometimes put out, ex post, by the leaders of the CGT and those among their adversaries who were most eager to adopt a conspiratorial vision of history, whereby the rejection of the Grenelle agreements was a tactical maneuver organized and directed by the leadership of the CGT itself, never seems to have had the slightest plausible foundation. Georges Ross, from whom Hoffmann's interpretation is derived, seems indeed to have entirely abandoned it; cf. Georges Ross, *Workers and Communists in France. From Popular Front to Eurocommunism* (Berkeley: University of California Press, 1982), 200–3. The most likely explanation of the most confusing aspects of this episode refers to the haste with which the leaders of the CGT and PCF improvised a response to the charismatic initiatives of Mendès France, which were then emerging, by trying to reach an early agreement which would provide a "drop-off point" *(point de chute)*, as Roger Garaudy, a member of the Communist Party leadership, later put it, namely a way out of the strikes which otherwise risked having uncontrollable consequences; for the point of view of the CGT leadership, see Georges Séguy, *Le mai de la CGT* (Paris: Julliard, 1972), 117, and the more cautious account by Jacques Frémontier, *Renault: la forteresse ouvrière* (Paris: Seuil, 1975), 368–70.

[15]The signing of the accord in the night of 7–8 June was followed by a new upsurge of strikes, despite the CGT's instructions for a return to work (at least in places where the employers had accepted the signature of specific contracts and the principle of collective bargaining). This strike upsurge would culminate in the signature, late in the evening of June 12, of an accord in the metal-working industries, the strikers delegates having set a deadline of 6 p.m. that day for reaching agreement, threatening that otherwise they would demand "the nationalisation of the factories on strike and of those working for the state. This agreement would lead to the decline of the movement; see especially Georges Lefranc, *Juin 1936* (Paris: Julliard, 1966), 164–74; see also Antoine Prost, "Les grèves de juin 1936. Essai

a more or less negotiated solution just upstream the derailment of the French crisis of 1958, with the situation created by the "landings" in Corsica on May 24, a move which marked the definitive and transparent failure of the bargaining for a legalistic definition of relations between the government and the military in Algeria, which the prime minister had been attempting to promote since 13 May.[16] Significantly, in all these cases, the derailment of events tends to occur not only when the multisectorization of the conflict is at its height but also at the moment when numerous protagonists make the uncomfortable, and sometimes tragic, discovery that the collective actors are not necessarily all marching "as one man," or in step, and are subject to what may be qualified as processes of de-objectification, a point I will return to shortly.

Of course, structural uncertainty is not always as intense, far from it, as in derailments of this kind, but this does not present any particular difficulties, except perhaps for one somewhat marginal point, which nonetheless merits some clarification. We have just seen that individual actors—but also, in other ways, groups—perceive and experience this uncertainty, and it could be admitted that structural uncertainty necessarily impinges on the psychological state of individual actors. However, from the perspective developed here, that of the theory of fluid political conjunctures, the fundamental dimension of the uncertainty is first and foremost a *relational* one. This means that uncertainty stems from a conjunctural transformation of the relationships between sectors and of the internal logics of sectors; it corresponds to a *particular state of the structures and social relations*. That is why this uncertainty, while it may legitimately be compared to some contiguous notions—like, in particular the uncertainty, also dubbed "structural," that Steinbruner analyzes in his study of decision-making processes—is far from coinciding with them. In Steinbruner's approach, the "structural" aspect of the uncertainty refers to the impossibility, in certain situations, of specifying both the full range of possible outcomes of a particular line of action *and* the probability attached to the occurrence of each of these outcomes. From this author's point of view, uncertainty and its "structural" aspect are conceived in terms of game theory, and thus the relevant situations

---

d'interprétation," in *Léon Blum, chef de gouvernement, 1936–1937*, ed. P. Renouvin and R. Rémond (Paris: Presses de Sciences Po, 1967).

[16]Faced with the May 13 events in Algiers, Félix Gaillard, having resigned, delegated civil and military powers in Algeria to General Salan. This would be the basis of a curious deal, the Pflimlin government having accepted this tactical option, even though it would subsequently restrict the scope of this delegation of power; see, for a record of the discussions of the Pflimlin government, Tournoux, *Secrets d'Etat*, 1962 [1st ed., 1960], 242–4 and 250–5. Everything points to the "Corsican" operation having been conceived in General de Gaulle's immediate entourage; cf. Pierre Viansson-Ponté, *Histoire de la République gaullienne* (Paris: Fayard, 1970), vol. 1: 57, which rests on the testimony of Pascal Arrighi at the trial of General Salan in 1961; a tendentious, sometimes incorrect, but nonethess lively description of this operation can be found in Alain de Sérigny, *La Révolution du 13 mai* (Paris: Plon, 1958), 115–23.

are those that could be called "unstructured."[17] Therefore, it should be clear that this particular "structural" aspect of the uncertainty *does not* correspond to the meaning I have given it above (a particular state of the structures). Note however that the state of social structures we find in fluid conjunctures may indeed very well have the additional effect of placing the protagonists of the confrontation in contexts characterized by the "impossibility" Steinbruner refers to.[18]

Processes of De-objectification

Processes of de-objectification certainly represent one of the most interesting vulnerabilities of societies whose structural configurations approximate those of what I earlier called complex systems. To fully grasp the scope of this third major defining property of fluid conjunctures, we need to remember that such systems are characterized, on the one hand, by a high degree of objectification of sectoral relationships and, on the other, by the consolidation of this objectification originating in the intersectoral collusive transactions we can observe between the differentiated sectors constituting these systems. It is precisely these two structural features which are impacted by the emergence and development of multisectoral mobilizations. More specifically, this hypothesis—which clearly runs against the conceptions reifying social structures and institutions that inform the most influential approaches in contemporary social sciences—concerns all of the three dimensions I have used to define objectification processes, namely the exteriority of social relationships, their impersonality, and their perception by the social actors as taken for granted. In these three respects, complex systems or societies are exposed, when experiencing multisectoral mobilizations, to sudden collapses of objectification in sectoral relationships. Or, put another way, I could say that the objectification of social relationships within sectors, or within intersectoral exchanges, is not independent of or impervious to what the

---

[17]John D. Steinbruner, *The Cybernetic Theory of Decision* (Princeton: Princeton University Press, 1974), 17–18.

[18]By contrast, though on a quite different scale from the crises I have discussed hitherto, it is indeed a situation of uncertainty that more or less fits my own definition of structural uncertainty that Bailey refers to when describing the "moral crisis" which opposed members of the impure—"untouchable"— Pans caste to members of higher castes in the Indian village of Bissipara. The Pans, who wanted to climb the caste ladder, rather than playing by the *internal* rules of the game and ascending slowly by gradually converting wealth into status, opted instead, at least the more militant among them did, to resort to *external* resources, that is, the administration, the politicians, the police of the state of Orissa and federal laws forbidding discrimination against untouchables. The courses of action chosen by the Pans had the immediate effect of calling into question and depreciating the value of all the traditional resources and lines of action of the village arena and, notes Bailey, constituted a potent factor of uncertainty and tactical disarray for the protagonists of the confrontation, especially the members of the higher castes (Bailey, *Stratagems and Spoils*).

protagonists of confrontations do, that is, to their mobilizations and moves.[19] Reaching this point, I will readily concede that a precise measurement of these objectification collapses is not always unproblematic.[20] But at the same time I should emphasize that the phenomena corresponding to this particular property of fluid conjunctures are nonetheless easily *observable*, whether directly or through their effects. At the risk of unveiling some of the developments which will appear later in this book, let me point out that it is this property which best explains the *moments of madness* or, in the words of Durkheim, of "creative effervescence" which witnesses and analysts like to depict in the unfolding of the "great" political crises, with the "events" of May 1968 in France serving as the complete archetype.[21] Much has been written about the images of "carnival" or, for some authors, of "psychodrama" that these "great" crises afford, about their atmosphere of "freeing speech," the sense of "liberation" experienced by their actors, the moments when it seemed to them that "everything is possible," about the transgressions of social distances and frontiers, or on the desecration or the taboo-breaking episodes[22]—and there is little to add, except perhaps to stress that these phenomena are in no way specific to the May 1968 "events," or even to French "political culture" or French society.[23] And, above all, that not every process of de-objectification is as colorful or has the same appearance as those just mentioned. This is particularly true of the fluctuations which, in

---

[19]The *conjunctural* collapses of objectification in social relationships must not be confused with the disinstitutionalization processes (in fact, extremely relative) experienced, in our time, by several domains of everyday life (mostly aspects concerning "private life," family and sexual relationships, etc.); these processes, which represent *long-term developments*, have led some authors, somewhat hastily to say the least, to discern, in modern societies, social spheres that they assume to be much less institutionalized—or even de-institutionalizing—in comparison with those found in traditional societies; for example, Arnold Gehlen, *Man in the Age of Technology* (New York: Columbia University Press, 1980); see also the reflections on this author by Peter L. Berger and Hansfried Kellner, "Arnold Gehlen and the Theory of Institutions," *Social Research* 32, no. 1 (1965), 110 et seq.

[20]However, it is possible to see each of these three dimensions as a particular source or matrix of empirical indicators, which, some of them at least, seem capable of being "operationalized." A familiar example of this, which I will return to later, and which relates to the impersonality of social relationships, can be found in the perfectly observable occurrence, for instance, of face-to-face relationships, which do not conform with institutional (especially hierarchical) arrangements producing distance and impersonality and often designed to do so, or even in the possible emergence of a continuous and socially extended bargaining about "keeping up the appearances" of an institutionally defined relationship.

[21]For example, Aristide R. Zolberg, "Moments of Madness," *Politics and Society* 2, no. 2 (winter 1972): 183–207.

[22]In an abundant (and very "literary," which is romanticized and, often, fictionalized) literature devoted to these aspects, see in particular Michel de Certeau, *La prise de parole. Pour une nouvelle culture* (Paris: Desclée de Brouwer, 1968) and, in many of its passages, Edgar Morin, Claude Lefort, and Jean-Marc Coudray [Cornelius Castoriadis], *Mai 1968: la brèche* (Paris: Fayard, 1968).

[23]See, in particular, on some aspects of the widespread processes of de-objectification experienced by Polish society in the year following the summer of 1980, Staniszkis, *Poland's Self-limiting Revolution*, 133 et seq.

critical conjunctures and in the short term, often affect the stocks of legitimacy or "diffuse support" which political authorities or regimes may enjoy in routine periods. Among these processes of delegitimization, special attention should be paid to *crises of collusive relationships* inside what I have called intersectoral consolidation networks (e.g., in the case of France, the crisis of May 1958 or, over a very short period, that of February 1934), for this is where these processes are most likely to have the greatest political impact. As will be shown later on (see Chapter 8), this perspective inevitably leads us to challenge the role that social sciences usually attach to the loss of legitimacy in processes of political crisis.

The particular attention devoted here to the most patently political processes may however lead to a misunderstanding: it should not obscure the close kinship between these phenomena and much smaller-scale processes of de-objectification, like those, for example, that can be seen at work when we examine what might be described as the *art of de-objectification*, that is, a set of micro-technologies or micro-tactics whose efficiency can only become intelligible by considering the interferences of the differentiated social logics that are the principles of these micro-technologies operation. Two contrasting illustrations will convey the flavor. The first consists of *bureaucratic technologies of "de-blocking,"* thought to bring about adaptation to change in bureaucratic organizations (or even, as in Michel Crozier's initial—and very fragile—formulation of that idea, in French society as a whole, and in its different subsystems), which, according to the promoters of these technologies, are unable of correcting their mistakes, and have also transformed their "dysfunctions" into elements of "internal equilibrium." Now, these technologies, and this is the interesting point, involve the intervention within these organizations of "agents of change," whose task it is to manage and resolve these crises of adaptation, that is to say, essentially, to *throw into crisis* the internal social relationships of the organization, these agents being themselves defined by their *exteriority* to the organizations in which they intervene. As Crozier rightly observes, these agents, for example the members of *Grands Corps* in the French administrative system, constitute isolated "castes" by virtue of their recruitment, their training, and their career aspirations, and are thus insulated against all the pressures that might come from within the organization they have to deal with.[24] The second illustration concerns what is described in the indigenous jargon as "provocation-repression-solidarity cycles" or acts of "creating situations" designed to reveal the "contradictions in the system"; in fact, these *acts of rupture*, to use Alain Touraine's phrase, also consist of the intervention, within a sector endowed with its own specific social

---

[24]Michel Crozier, *The Bureaucratic Phenomenon* (Chicago: The University of Chicago Press, 1964 [1st French ed., 1963]).

logic, of resources, lines of action, or moves obeying other social logics, external to this target-sector.[25]

None of this should however encourage the reader to see sectoral institutions and logics as being as fragile and precarious as it is suggested by some formulations of sociologists linked to the neo-phenomenological tradition (who nonetheless do have the merit of having recognized the operation of this kind of process, albeit mainly in very different research domains such as the representation of oneself or "subjective identity").[26] For a significant collapse of objectification in social relationships to occur in highly objectified social spheres—and here the reader will excuse me just this once for using an imagery I explicitly rejected earlier—a considerable "expenditure of energy" is sometimes required. It is in this way that we can best account for certain observations by classical theorists of revolution, observations taken up by their more recent successors who, like Skocpol, have insisted on the links between the emergence of this type of phenomenon (visible in particular in the weakening or, sometimes, collapse of state machineries) and severe military defeats or heavy pressures originating in international confrontations.[27] It will have been understood, however, that one of the central theses of the present work is that there is no need to look to "energies" at such a high level as those stemming from the interstate scene in order to witness significant downfalls in the objectification of sectoral or intersectoral relationships.

Elements of Discussion

Let me dwell for a moment on the properties discussed just above, in order to try and define some of their contours more precisely. As a matter of fact, these properties share the characteristics of being both selective and observable.

---

[25]About May 1968, see Touraine, *The May Movement*; and for some accounts of the use of these tactics, Philippe Labro, *Ce n'est qu'un début* (Paris: Éditions et publications premières, 1968), 43–58; Daniel Cohn-Bendit, *Le Grand Bazar* (Paris: Denoël-Gonthier, 1978 [1975]), 58. See also, for a genuine recipe-book of such tactical ploys, Saul Alinsky, *Rules for Radicals* (New York: Random House, 1971).

[26]Cf. Berger and Pullberg, "Reification and the Sociological Critique of Consciousness," 196–211, and, for an analysis of what these authors call *anomic terrors*, Berger and Luckmann, *Social Construction*, 119–21.

[27]See, among others, Skocpol, *States and Social Revolutions*, 23, 31–2, 60–4, 73, and 94–6, as regards political crises related to "social" revolutions in France, China, and Russia; see also the works mentioned above (in Chapter 2) by the proponents of the natural history of revolutions. Skocpol is perfectly aware that external pressures are most frequently relayed or, better, retranslated into internal conflicts and into the mobilizations of which these are made of.

Selectivity

They are, first, selective properties. When we decide to focus on the boundaries of a given sector impacted by multisectoral mobilizations, when we choose to observe what happens in these contexts to the diverse elements of that sector's specific logic, or when we set ourselves to understand how the actors' calculations, evaluations, and anticipations then operate, each time new light is shed on reality. Put another way, these properties represent only points of view from slightly different angles on the same real processes. The list of properties could very easily be extended, and this would be far more than a purely formal exercise every time it would allow us to see phenomena that had hitherto been perceived wrongly or not at all, or it would allow us to explain them better. Here are three illustrations of this approach, which also open up exciting research pathways.

(a) *Simplification of social space*. Let me thus raise the question of what happens, in conjunctures associated with multisectoral mobilizations, to the diversity of the sectoral social logics that characterizes complex societies. The answer consists of a somewhat counterintuitive proposition: we must conclude that a sort of underlying simplification of social space comes into operation, an issue that will not be further discussed in the present work. Note however that one of the advantages of identifying this could be to stimulate further reflection on the relationship that may be observed between social contexts of structural complexity and the ways actors calculate, or even the very possibility of their calculations.

(b) *Unidimensionalization of personal identity*. I have so far given only marginal attention to the impact that the dynamics of multisectoral mobilizations might have on the social personality of the individual actors themselves. One of the best means of exploring this issue more thoroughly is provided by starting from the *multiple insertion*, which individual actors experience in complex societies, because of the sectoral differentiation of the latter. This matters of course as regards how we think of the individual's socialization process and its dispositional outcomes. But it matters also, here is my point, in another way: the actors experience this in particular as regards the definition of their personal identity (this is of course widely recognized in contemporary sociology). This identity is forged through the multiplicity of "roles" or social facets that are available, albeit unequally and with highly differentiated profiles, to all the individual actors. That is why social dynamics which disrupt precisely what I will term the *social substratum* of this multidimensional personal identity should be of major interest to the social sciences. And indeed, we can observe that the individual actors—again unequally—often experience serious difficulties, during "great" political crises, in preserving this multidimensionality. In a way that quite resembles the processes whereby, as Goffman has shown, total institutions deprive recluses of the multiple roles they claim in the outside world,[28] so critical conjunctures tend to reduce identity, ultimately, to a single dimension serving as a practical clue to or sign of the person's identity in interactions that are usually—that is, in routine contexts—fairly differentiated. Unidimensionalization of identity may appear in its pure state, so to speak, in "revolutionary" conjunctures: the qualification "aristocrat," "worker," "true believer," or "patriot" then becomes a *universal identity marker*, that is, it tends to be effective across the entire social space.[29] Let me add that, just as the multiplicity of "roles" does not necessarily cause serious existential problems most of the time, neither does its collapse necessarily result in an identity crisis.[30] But that too is a discussion I will avoid pursuing any further here.

(c) *Extended tactical interdependence*. This will not be, however, the case of my third example, which concerns one of the empirical topics I will pursue in the next chapter and which in reality constitutes its very mainspring. The example deals with a property which directly affects the tactics of the actors, and (though this term has its dangers) the "constraints" which impinge on these tactics. This property may be

---

[28] Goffman, *Asylums*. I owe the idea for this comparison to a remark by Vincent Merle.

[29] For some partly congruent observations on the disappearance of multidimensional personal identity in "disaster" situations—for example, natural catastrophes—see Lewis M. Killian, "The Significance of Multiple-Group Membership in Disaster," in *Group Dynamics*, ed. D. Cartwright and A. Zander (Evanston: Row-Peterson, 1953), 249–56; see also, on critical situations, Niklas Luhmann, *Funktion und Folgen formaler Organisation* (Berlin: Duncker und Humblot, 1964); Boltanski, *The Making of a Class*.

[30] This may be one of the missing links in the explanation of the close relationship, brought to light by Emile Durkheim, *Suicide* (Glencoe: The Free Press, 1951 [1st French ed., 1897])—and since discussed by numerous sociologists and political scientists, for example Maurice Halbwachs, *The Causes of Suicide* (London: Routledge and Paul Kegan, 1978 [1st French ed., 1930]); Seymour M. Lipset, *Political Man* (Garden City: Doubleday, 1960), who seems to know Durkheim's work only through Halbwachs—between the occurrence of political crises and the very observable decrease in the suicide rate; the explanation for this phenomenon usually wavers between a first hypothesis, that of an increased social cohesion or integration supposedly derived either from a "collective euphoria" characterizing crisis situations or from the interest in what is happening generated by decisive political struggles, and a second hypothesis outlined by Halbwachs, who observes that "in such circumstances *life gets simpler*" (emphasis by *M.D.*). Though these two hypotheses do not appear entirely incompatible, the second clearly has a close affinity with the unidimensionalization of identity occurring in this kind of critical conjuncture.

analyzed as a tendency, a trend toward the emergence of a growing interdependence between the tactical activities of actors located in different sites across the social space. This may be rephrased more rigorously as the passage from a routine-driven and, above all, local form of interdependence between actors within a given sector (an interdependence where the effectiveness or "value" of the resources and lines of action available to the various actors is guaranteed by the relative compartmentalization of the sectors in relation to one another) to an extended form of interdependence which tends to bring the various, hitherto compartmentalized, resources and lines of action directly into confrontation with one another, and to determine their effectiveness or "value" in that confrontation. The crucial significance of this property is due in particular to the fact that it brings us back to the problem of how to account for the sudden fluctuations affecting the effectiveness or the "value" of political resources in critical conjunctures. My argument is that it is in the way outlined here that this problem has some real prospects, probably the only ones, of being tackled effectively by social scientists. Furthermore, as we shall see, extended tactical interdependence plays an important role in considerably reducing the control the actors exercise over the effects of their actions and on the meanings that are attached to them in the course of the confrontation (this is evidently not irrelevant to the frequent emergence of the tactical inhibition I pointed out earlier).

Observation and Refutability

The second series of remarks concerns the question of "checking" or "testing" the propositions set out above against *observable* phenomena, and this is not quite the same question as the issue of their acceptability or persuasiveness. Here I must very briefly return to what I said in that respect at the very beginning of this book. Contrary to what is commonly believed, a systematic set of theoretical propositions cannot be "validated" by "proving" each of its propositions *one by one*, by means of some scattered data thought to be specific and suited to each single proposition (we should note in passing that very often, in this kind of supposedly "empirical" approach, this single proposition is designed ad hoc precisely to account for that isolated set of data).[31] As a matter of fact, a systematic set of propositions, deliberately built up by the scholar, and deliberately articulating each proposition with the others, derives most of its demonstrative

---

[31] On the impasses of this kind of approach, which Popper calls "adhocism," and on its links with the intellectual logic of inductive procedures, see Karl R. Popper, *Objective Knowledge: An Evolutionary Approach* (London: Oxford University Press, 1972).

power and explanatory value from the richness and diversity of its implications. Moreover, these, like the contents of the propositions that generated them, may well not all be immediately and directly observable. It is toward this kind of "validation," as the reader probably remembers, that the approach outlined here is oriented right from the outset. Thus, the way this approach confronts its theoretical propositions with the empirical departs significantly from the popular image of crude *fact-gathering*, which, despite the claims of its numerous proponents, is nothing more than a naive, impressionistic, and, finally, sterile factualism. Alongside what I have just mentioned—the demonstrative power of the richness and diversity of their implications or consequences—the kind of "checking" or, indeed, refuting that this approach favors is to achieve it through *critical* or *decisive tests*, of which I will later give one or two good illustrations. However, I should add here that all this is not entirely incompatible with the use of other modes of confronting empirical reality, modes which are no doubt less powerful, less rigorous, less demanding, and also less convincing, but which address that reality more immediately.

On this basis it should be emphasized that the properties examined in this chapter, as I have already suggested, include many aspects that are easily and *directly* observable. And, precisely for that reason, we can use them as indicators of the presence, the operation, and, sometimes, the scale of the dynamics which these properties describe—of course, without this necessarily constituting a critical test. But we should do this only with extreme caution, since we are always tempted to forget, first, the *relational* character of the "facts" we are dealing with, and, second, that the demonstrative significance or weight of an indicator may well extend beyond the "validation" of a single proposition—for the reasons I mentioned above—and affect the whole, or a large part, of the theoretical scheme under discussion (it can affect that scheme not only negatively but also positively: when it works, an indicator is often much richer, especially from the heuristic point of view, than some methodology handbooks might lead their readers or users to believe).

A fairly simple illustration may help to clarify still further these somewhat abstract reflections. Let me return to the issue of *sectoral rhythms* or *temporalities*. These rhythms, as we have seen, constitute important elements of the specific social logics in the diverse differentiated sectors, and contribute significantly to the autonomy of the latter. At least in highly institutionalized sectors, like, for example, the political sectors in complex contemporary societies, they often acquire a high level of social visibility (and besides, it is easy enough to see that social actors use these rhythms as practical pointers for their assessments and calculations). For these two reasons, sectoral rhythms should be regarded as good indicators with regard to the purposes of the theoretical scheme developed here, insofar as each time we may suspect that a dynamics such as I have identified earlier (that of desectorization) is at work in a social system, we should expect to find it reflected in what happens to the sectoral rhythms.

To pursue that point further, I should first note that some scholars have been aware that the temporal dimension of crises is vital for understanding these processes.[32] But what seems to represent one crucial empirical observation about sectoral rhythms is the one recalled, with some other authors, by Pierre Bourdieu: "great" political crises seem to have the property of "synchronizing" the rhythms or "structural temporalities" peculiar to the different social spheres of the societies affected by these crises.[33] This observation is all the more interesting in that it is directed mainly, in Bourdieu's works, at the rhythms of certain social fields that are secondary or peripheral, at least in relation to the social sites or sectors from which the mobilizations are drawing most of their resources. Bourdieu refers to the fields of cultural production (literary, artistic, etc.) into which burst, during "great crises" or "revolutions," events and groups which, as he puts it, "make their mark," draw clear cut-offs or breaks with the past and which, so to speak, align or harmonize the temporalities of these fields with the events, and in particular with the changes of rhythm occurring in other social spheres that might be seen as more central. It is hardly necessary to stress that, from the perspective outlined here, the extension of this so-called synchronization to sectors that are so peripheral is in itself an excellent indicator of the scale of a dynamics of conjunctural desectorization. And it goes without saying, of course, that there is no difficulty for this perspective if such an extension—to peripheral sectors, as in the French May 1968 episode— should not be expected to appear in every case of multisectoral mobilization.

To sum up, at first sight at least, the idea of a sectoral rhythms "synchronization" is overwhelmingly consistent with the implications derivable from the theoretical scheme of the present book. However, things are not quite so simple. We shall see that this "synchronization," as conceived by Bourdieu, is far from being entirely free of ambiguity and is not pertinent for the analysis of fluid conjunctures without some serious amendments. The point is that the very idea of rhythms "synchronization" is *highly misleading* and that here again we have to deal with the difficulties inherent in any direct observation, any constitution of certain facts as empirical indicators. First of all, we must question the relevance of the notion of "synchronization" itself, a notion which inevitably evokes the image of

---

[32]For example, Juan J. Linz, "Time and Regime Change," paper given at the Edinburgh Congress of the IPSA, August 1976.

[33]For a sketchy but explicit presentation, Pierre Bourdieu, "La production de la croyance: contribution à une économie des biens symboliques," *Actes de la Recherche en Sciences Sociales* 13 (1977): 40. For similar observations, before Bourdieu, see, for example, André Béjin, "Crises des valeurs, crises de mesures," *Communications* 25 (1976): 41. See also Alain Gras, *Sociologie des ruptures* (Paris: PUF, 1979), 165.

multiple sectoral rhythms entering into phase with one another (or even merging into one single rhythm). Now, far from an alignment of phases, is it not more a case, in critical conjunctures, of a tendency toward a *co-occurrence* (or, if we nethertheless want to use the term, a "synchronization") of *breaks* or *ruptures* in sectoral rhythms? Rather than a harmonization of the rhythms, are we not dealing with the appearance, more or less simultaneous, or at least within a relatively short period of time, of *discontinuities* taking the form of events which, in the routine autonomous working of the sectors, in line with their specific social logics, would not have happened precisely when they did? It is only in this way, if we focus especially on social spheres whose temporalities are explicitly institutionalized (like, as I have said, the political sectors) that, "by themselves," relatively anodyne events may be interpreted as indicators, among others indicators, of the "synchronization" of the political sectors' rhythms with the transformations or ruptures of temporalities that have occurred in other sectors affected by the multisectoral mobilizations. It is the case, to take a few familiar illustrations concerning French political crises, of the resignation of the Chautemps government followed by that of the Daladier government in January–February 1934, the investiture of General de Gaulle in 1958, or the dissolution of the National Assembly (Assemblée Nationale) in May 1968. And here we can also see how dangerous it would be to interpret indicators like temporal rhythms in isolation from the social relationships they are embedded in. Moreover, it is remarkable that, in highly fluid contexts, these ruptures in sectoral rhythms become, at least temporarily, *central issues* for competing mobilizations, whatever the initial issues or stakes of the confrontations and the specific objectives of their different protagonists.

This phenomenon may sometimes become fully transparent for the actors, as was notably the case with the entirely *intentional* "synchronization" of the demonstrations outside the Chamber of Deputies and the investiture debates within it during the *journées* of both February 6, 1934, and May 13, 1958. In fact, this touches on an essential point: the so-called synchronization of sectoral rhythms should never be considered from an exclusively or primarily *objectivist* perspective, that is to say, in isolation from the actual mobilizations, the tactical games and moves of the confrontation protagonists.[34] In the approach I have

---

[34] We may, indeed, wonder whether there is not an inevitable tendency toward an *objectivist stance* in any attempt to grasp the so-called synchronization of sectoral rhythms (and these rhythms themselves) on the basis, as Bourdieu seems to do, of cleavages which, for example in the field of cultural production, set against each other works of art, styles, positions, and "schools," and which could quite well be simply the *products* of the crises. Or, put another way, on the basis of the traces these crises leave on the routine structure of a given field. I must add that the discussion of this whole question would gain nothing by taking on the objectivist "achievements" of the *Annales* historical school, achievements which are, at least in that domain, very questionable because—with the distinctions between "event history" (*histoire événementielle*), "conjunctural history," and "structural history"

defined here, if we are to talk of something like "synchronization" between the diverse sectors impacted by multisectoral mobilizations, it is only on condition that we see this as the *emergence of a particular issue* (the possible ruptures in sectoral rhythms), an issue produced by the confrontation, by the exchange of moves, and which imposes itself on the diverse actors, whether they like it or not. This also means that the latter, in this situation, have no option but to define their moves, their tactical activities, their alliances, the objectives of their action on the basis of this issue. This is clearly true of the aforementioned episodes of 1934 and 1958, but it is equally true of the French 1947–48 crisis, even though in the end the recently formed Gaullist party, the RPF, failed in its attempt, following its spectacular success in the municipal elections, to obtain the dissolution of the *Assemblée Nationale* (in an ideal-typical way, one of the *locking* mechanisms of the political field involved a manipulation of its own specific time rhythms, notably through the decision in September 1948 *to postpone* the cantonal elections). Similarly, in the under-explored episode of the French "wildcat" strikes of August 1953, "synchronization" became the central stake of the confrontation, with the rupture in the specific sectoral rhythms of the political field being held in check by the successful tactics deployed by certain actors — notably the parliamentary group of the Christian-democratic MRP (Mouvement Républicain Populaire, Popular Republican Movement) — which *disconnected* the parliamentary arena from the "professional" conflict.[35]

Beyond the systematic character of the relationship between what happens to the autonomy of sectors and what happens to their internal rhythms, these remarks also help us to discern one of the by-products of the intentional organization, within a particular sector, of differences, or of *time lags*, among its principal institutionalized temporalities (here we have another illustration of how an indicator can go beyond the role of simply "validating" one or more propositions).

(a "long term"—*longue durée*—or "immobile" history)—they mix up the historian's own approach, in particular, the temporal demarcations he constructs, with the real social temporalities as they impose themselves on social actors; see, for example: Fernand Braudel, "Histoire et sociologie," in *Traité de sociologie*, ed. Georges Gurvitch (Paris: PUF, 1960), vol. 1, 92–4, and "Histoire et sciences sociales: la longue durée," *Annales ESC* 13, no. 4 (October–December 1958): 725–53.

[35]The socialist (and then communist) demand for convening an extraordinary session of Parliament was thwarted, despite attracting the support of first 224 and then 211 deputies, a little more than the number required by Article 12 of the Constitution (a third of the membership of the Assemblée Nationale, which is 209), by the deliberate refusal of the Assemblée bureau to follow the constitutional rules of the game. The MRP justified its position in this way: "The convening of Parliament is meaningless as long as its sole objective is, in the midst of the social disturbances, to precipitate a new political crisis which could only be resolved by an immediate enlargement of the parliamentary majority, something the last national congress of the MRP expressly hoped, but which does not yet have the necessary support" (*Communiqué du Bureau national*, August 25). The relative speed with which major concessions were made to the trade-unions organizations — described by commentators as a "near total success" for the strikers — seems related to the success of the disconnection mentioned above (on all this episode, see in particular *L'Année politique 1953*, 60–7 and 171–6).

As can be seen, for example, in the case of a fact well known to jurists, namely the unequal length of the mandates of different types of specialized officials, this kind of technology is often found in political sectors (in the strict sense), where these differences in the rhythms of replacement and renewal concern positions that the constitutional arrangements render interdependent (or, to use Montesquieu's terminology, "linked," *liées*) in terms of their "functions." Certainly the idea of *splitting the political risks*—not putting all your eggs in one basket, not to play all one's cards at the same time—is likely to be one motive, among others, for establishing such institutional technologies. However, it is equally well founded to see the latter—whether this has been intended or not matters little— as one of the major factors which may increase the resilience of the political sectors in conjunctures where they risk facing pressures, from both without and within, to fall into step with external events or transformations.

Lastly, these observations help shed new light on the *thresholds* that mark and structure critical processes as well as the mobilizations that constitute them. Far from coinciding with the quantitative boundaries mentioned above (Chapter 1) or, a fortiori, with those mysterious points or zones of rupture in social systems which followers of structural-functionalist or systemic approaches like, often tautologically, to imagine,[36] these thresholds are most frequently related to certain elements in sectoral logics—such as, precisely, their rhythms, their specific institutionalized temporalities—which the peculiar history of a given confrontation in some way promoted to a position of saliency or prominence. The following illustration should help make the point. It concerns the curious episode of the clashes during the French "events" of May 1968 over the issue of whether the date of the university exams should be deferred or maintained.[37] This episode occurred at the moment when, from May 14 on, the "movement" rapidly spread beyond the sphere of higher education and achieved a (literally) unprecedented breadth in French society. The observer of this episode is often tempted, if indeed he should find the matter worthy of mention at all, either to smile at the disproportion between the scale of the event and the trifling preoccupations of the actors or to be irritated by it. Wrongly so, because the proximity of the final exams constituted an obstacle—a very real threshold—for the student movement, an obstacle which could well have broken the movement's dynamism and, for the two are linked, its collective "being," something that many of its adversaries and competitors were perfectly aware of (hence the violence, the extension, and the duration of the confrontations that marked this episode). Above all, however, the crossing of this barrier was the key factor in the radical, albeit conjunctural, transformation of

---

[36] For more developed discussion of this point, see Dobry, *Sociologie des crises politiques*, 56–60.
[37] Alain Schnapp and Pierre Vidal-Naquet, *Journal de la commune étudiante* (Paris: Seuil, 1969), 663–73; Bensaïd and Weber, *Mai 1968*, 159–60.

the relationship these actors, especially the students, had with the social logics of the sector in which they were immersed. For them, this *breakdown of sectoral rhythms* marked the collapse of this social logic's hold, thereby affecting their calculations—such as the ordering and ranking of their "priorities"—as well as their perceptions of *what was probable* and *what was possible*. And also—as an effect of the breakdown, and not, in any way, as its "precondition"—the collapse of their adherence to the "naturalness" of the sectoral rules of the game. It is worth adding that, during the short period of these "May events," some other sectors, for example the militarized sectors, did not experience similar phenomena of rupture or threshold-crossing and that this is one of the fundamental features that shaped the singular historical profile of this crisis.

Clearly then, one of the most effective ways of checking the actual presence of the properties that characterize fluid political conjunctures is to seek it in the *actual activity* of social actors, in what they do and in what they perceive: it would thus be possible to state that these properties are at work in reality if it can be observed that the crisis protagonists are dealing with them (*font avec*), that is, if these properties impose themselves on the political actors, their perceptions, and their activities, as constraining and unavoidable issues. Or if these properties can be detected in the features of the political technologies deployed by the actors—until now an almost-unexplored research field.

That is why, for the theory of fluid political conjunctures, special attention should be paid to *institutional technologies of crisis control (technologies institutionnelles de maîtrise des crises)*. These technologies belong to a larger family of practical recipes, devices or *savoir-faire* to draw on in crisis situations, which political actors often use effectively without ever needing to ask themselves why such formulae work . . . at least when they do work. Now, the mainsprings of these technologies take us straight to the properties described above. First, in their most visible aspect: the transformation of the *social division of political labor* which, in diverse ways, these technologies tend to bring about.[38] Beyond their juridical variety, the transfers of competence that they institutionalize—without necessarily ever matching the true utopia provided by Article 16 of the French Constitution of

---

[38]See especially: Clinton Rossiter, *Constitutional Dictatorship. Crisis Government in the Modern Democracies* (New York: Harcourt Brace and World, 1963 [1948]); Geneviève Camus, *L'état de nécessité en démocratie* (Paris: LGDJ, 1965); Paul Leroy, *L'organisation constitutionnelle et les crises* (Paris: LGDJ, 1966). All these works stress the differences between the juridical regimes within which these technologies are implemented and therefore tend to ignore the ways they work, that is, the ways they may contribute to a possible "normalization" of the situation. On the remarkable similarity of these technologies of crisis manipulation in the most dissimilar political systems, see the observations of Joyotirindra Das Gopta, "A Season of Caesars: Emergency Regimes and Development Politics in Asia," *Asian Survey* 18, no. 4 (1978): 17. Of course, this last remark applies particularly to authoritarian systems, including those of Eastern Europe (take, for example, the case of Poland after the December 1981 coup d'Etat).

1958[39]—all attempt to unify and homogenize a large range of activities which, in routine contexts, are governed by heterogeneous social logics, each one specific to a more or less autonomous sector. Whatever rationalizations and legitimations concur with their institutionalization, one of the main principles on which these technologies operate lies always in the simplification of social games and in the more or less expanded substitution of a single social logic for the multiplicity of logics described above. In short, its principle consists in a movement tending to carry out a *suspension of the complexity of society*. Quite remarkably, this suspension, in the first place, affects the machinery of the state. It involves, so to speak, the working of the state on itself, especially by manipulating the social logics of its diverse constituent sectors (thus, of the twenty-five decisions taken in 1961 under the auspices of Article 16, twenty directly concerned the internal sectoral logics of the army, the police, and the judiciary, particularly the professional status of their agents). As for the orientation of these transfers of competences, they usually tend to benefit the militarized sectors. This statement would be little more than a banality if I did not simultaneously emphasize that these sectors are characterized, in addition to their "external functions" (the use of organized violence), by their institutional capacity to *isolate* themselves, and to preserve a high level of objectification in their internal social relations. They owe this second feature to their particular hierarchical structuration and disciplinary organization, and to a much less-known mechanism, the constant verification of the state of their internal relations through the medium of highly visible routine tests—for instance, the refusal to salute provides instant information. By placing these *hardened* sectors at the heart of their *modus operandi*, technologies of crisis control tend to operate on *differentials of objectification*: curfews, night raids, the threat of instant severe penalties without any rights of appeal, and so on have the advantage of weighing heavily on the calculations of those they are aimed at, by putting them, so to speak, in *Olsonian situations* (situations where strategies of *free-riding* are irresistibly and widely appealing to individuals, and thus affect the very "being" of collective actors, or the hold they exercise on individuals).[40] In such cases, the observable reduction in structural uncertainty—when the technology works, indeed—does not amount to the return of routine configurations of intersectoral relationships.

---

[39]See particularly Michèle Voisset, *L'article 16 de la Constitution du 4 octobre 1958* (Paris: LGDJ, 1969), 105–10, 124–6, 133–6.
[40]This phrasing refers of course to Mancur Olson, *The Logic of Collective Action* (Cambridge, MA: Harvard University Press, 1965).

Chapter 5
Extended Interdependence

Far from resulting from any supposed "intrinsic" characteristics of mobilized resources, or indeed being the by-products of their supply and demand interplay, the fluctuations in the "value" or effectiveness of the resources and lines of action deployed in critical conjunctures can only be understood by referring to the varying configurations or contexts of the actors' interdependence. We have already seen how these context variations occur and are related, as their effects, to multisectoral mobilizations: with the conjunctural desectorization of the social space and the opening up of the confrontation sites, an extended form of interdependence emerges, which substitutes itself for more local, more compartmentalized, more segmented forms which are strongly shaped by the specific "contents" of the different sectoral logics. The analyses that follow are based on the hypothesis of such an emergence. That means that the key to understanding many of the "problems" or "dilemmas" that social actors confront in critical conjunctures is located precisely in the properties of the extended interdependence contexts. These properties also constitute the theoretical tool giving us access to the strictly tactical features of the *situational logics* characterizing these conjunctures.

"Situational logics" refers here to the constraints (not an altogether unambiguous term, but I will use it *faute de mieux*) which in such contexts weigh upon the perceptions, evaluations, and calculations and upon the actions of the confrontation protagonists. Of course, these constraints concern the aims, the goals, or the purposes that individuals set for themselves, or at least those ascribed to them by the researcher. However, even though we have already encountered some of these aims—in connection with the issues which impose themselves on the actors, whether they like it or not, as products of the conjunctural desectorization of the social space—there is no good reason to limit ourselves solely to this type of research objective. Actually, when attempting to understand situational logics, social sciences have nothing to gain by adopting Popper's somewhat crude approach, that of "objective knowledge."

This approach, which seeks to avoid overstating psychological factors in the explanation of behavior, mainly consists of trying to show, in Popper's own terms, how the actions of individuals are "objectively appropriate" to the situations in which they are operating. Quite apart from the difficult problems raised by any idea of "appropriateness" or "adequacy" between individual actions and contexts of action, the extension I shall give to the notion of situational logic will allow us to avoid having to burden ourselves with the fallouts from the long-standing debate—far less fruitful, perhaps, than is sometimes claimed—between "methodological individualism" and "holism." My point is that most often this debate, on both sides, evades the essential issue, namely that the fundamental "technical" operation, which is the necessary condition of any deductive demonstration in terms of the aims, interests, and calculations of individuals, involves a description, far from individual, of the properties of an action context or institutional system. That is to say, it involves the description of the "rules of the game" peculiar to a given market, a given political arena, or even to those competitions where, as in the "game of chicken," the players are compelled—on pain of losing face—to launch their vehicles on collision course against each other, and to avoid bailing out too soon. In other words, even when the research objective is to reconstruct "objective" individual goals, the decisive hypotheses for the explanation, its key elements, relate first and foremost to the properties of the action contexts.[1]

An Imperfect Tight Game

To move forward, I will use a rather rudimentary tool—which the reader may find excessively simplistic. It is a conceptual construction devised by Erving Goffman in order to account for processes of strategic interaction.[2] I will use it only as a guideline in the analysis, trying to show how the contexts of extended

---

[1] See especially: Karl R. Popper, "The Logic of the Social Sciences," in *The Positivist Dispute in German Sociology*, ed. T. W. Adorno (London: Heinemann, 1976 [1st German ed., 1969]), 102–3; see also the interesting discussion on this aspect of Popper's conception of situational logics by Fred H. Eidlin, *The Logic of "Normalization." The Soviet Intervention in Czechoslovakia of 21 August 1968 and the Czechoslovak Response* (New York: Columbia University Press, 1980), especially 17–22. On the links usually taken for granted between the notion of situational logic and methodological individualism, see, among many others, Joseph Agassi, "Methodological individualism," in *Modes of Individualism and Collectivism*, ed. J. O"Neil (London: Heinemann, 1973), 185–212; Raymond Boudon, *The Unintended Consequences of Social Action* (London: Palgrave Macmillan, 1982 [1st French ed., 1977]); Pierre Favre, "Nécessaire mais non suffisante: la sociologie des effets pervers de Raymond Boudon," *Revue Française de Science Politique* 30, no. 6 (1980): 1229–71.

[2] Goffman, *Strategic Interaction*, 85–145.

tactical interdependence differ, in many quite distinctive features, from other configurations of interdependence, the very ones that Goffman himself describes.

Tight Game and Loose Game

The basis of Goffman's conceptual construction is the distinction he draws between two categories of "moves," which I will call, for convenience sake, *direct* moves and indirect or *mediated* moves. The principle behind this distinction is very simple. Direct moves are lines of action which, by themselves, merely by their occurrence, change the situation of the protagonists in a given interaction — and Goffman conceives their situation in strictly physical terms. The examples he offers are limited to face-to-face contexts between two protagonists or to contexts where a single actor confronts his physical, nonhuman environment (i.e., games against nature).[3] Because of this limitation, I need here to introduce one *extension*, which will represent a significant change, first in scale, but also, as we shall see later, in the very structure of the game. Thus, when on May 13, 1958, demonstrators seized the government building in Algiers, or when strikers in an aeronautical factory at Bougenais near Nantes on May 14, 1968, sequestered several members of the firm's senior management, or when protesting columns of war veterans and demonstrators from the *Ligues* converged on the Chamber of Deputies in Paris on the evening of February 6, 1934, and confronted the defending police cordon, we are dealing, in the broad sense of the notion of direct moves I outlined above, with acceptable approximations of this kind of situation, which tend, in these historical examples, to be defined principally in physical terms. The point is this is only true at a *local* level, and that has some crucial implications.

In the case of indirect or *mediated moves*, between the move and its outcome, the filter of an "enforcement agency" intervenes, which retranslates and re-evaluates — according to what may be analyzed as this agency's own specific logic — the move whereby the actor has sought to modify the situation to his own advantage. If I go to court and, through the medium of my lawyer, entrust it with certain items that are important for my case, there will be, between my move and the outcome I obtain, a process of transformation very largely independent of the materiality of my move, of its physical consistency, and at least under ordinary circumstances, beyond my capacity to directly influence it. In this operation of an enforcement agency, we clearly find again some elements of sectoral logics. But,

---

[3]Clearly, only the first type of situation involves the emergence of strategic interaction, the reciprocal assessment which the protagonists in the interaction carry out on the basis of their own anticipations concerning perceptions, calculations, and anticipations of their opponent(s); cf. Goffman, *Strategic Interaction*, 99.

for the moment, this point only interests us in one much narrower aspect: what characterizes the mediated move is the fact that the relationship between the move and the outcome *loosens*—the term Goffman uses—each time the filter of an enforcement agency comes into play.[4] The effectiveness of the move, its "weight," its "value," its effects on the other protagonists in the game tend then to depend on the internal routines, timetables, procedures, rules of the game, interests and power relations of the enforcement agency.

Following Goffman's terminology, I will call *tight game* any interaction context where moves and counter-moves—coupled with various elements of the immediate physical context of the interaction—directly determine the changes in the protagonists' situation, and *loose game* any contexts where enforcement agencies intervene between the moves and their eventual outcomes. It is therefore the relationship between the move and its outcome—or rather the outcome resulting from the exchange of moves—which constitutes the distinguishing feature between the two types of game. What discriminates them is their enforcement systems, i.e. the processes which produce the outcomes of the exchange of moves and which indeed structure such exchanges. In one case, the moves themselves, by their very physical characteristics, represent a large part of the enforcement system; in the other, the "enforcement" is separated from the move, and located in the autonomous working of an institution.[5]

By means of this *ideal-type* distinction between tight game and loose game, Goffman is above all seeking to show how strategic interaction, as a specific category of interaction, must be distinguished from the exchange of information, that is communication (even tacit communication), between the protagonists in the interaction. In this respect, Goffman's argument is convincing: if we accept that strategic interaction is characterized by this sequence [assessment by the protagonists of their situation, decision (choice of a course of action), initiation of this course of action, followed by pay-off (outcome)][6], then we must acknowledge that none of these elements is fundamentally made of communication. The assessment made by each protagonist does indeed depend on what he believes the other's assessment to be, but this involves nothing more than observing the

---

[4] Goffman, *Strategic Interaction*, 115.

[5] In addition to the protagonists' physical environment, other elements are at work in the enforcement system characterizing the tight game, such as the constraint to play (nonaction thus becoming a tactical option), the "structured" form of the game (a limited number of discrete and clearly differentiated tactical options), and the commitment of the players to the moves made (the impossibility of reversing an initiated move), the decisive element being precisely the actual presence of an "intrinsic pay-off" attached to the move played (Goffman, *Strategic Interaction*, 114–15).

[6] Goffman, *Strategic Interaction*, 120; furthermore, it is not really necessary to subscribe to the image of action that this sequencing suggests—an image, to tell the truth, overly decisionist—to arrive at the same conclusion as to the limited role of communication in interactions involving a strong strategic interaction component.

other's actions, the *expressive* aspect of the other's behavior, and an evaluation of the "objective" options available to him. It is in this respect that the tight game, as an ideal-type, helps us to grasp why, in strategic interaction, communication between the actors is, at best, only residual.[7]

Elements of Imperfection

However, what makes the distinction between tight and loose games relevant for the analysis of extended interdependence is not only this opposition between strategic interaction and processes of communication. Its interest also, and perhaps mainly, lies in the fact that, in some respects, fluid conjunctures tend to place the protagonists of the confrontations in situations close to tight game contexts. But this is only true *in some respects*, and it would no doubt be more rigorous—and more fruitful—to see in the forms of interdependence that emerge with the conjunctural desectorization of social space a particular type of game which I will call *imperfect tight game,* even if its imperfections distinguish it just as much from the loose game as from the tight game.

The first element of imperfection derives from the actual framework of the interaction, and here some "hard facts" must be borne in mind. First of all, this framework cannot be conceived, as in the ideal-type of the tight game, as a place where all the protagonists of the interaction are caught up in relationships of immediate physical proximity with one another. The imperfect tight game is not something like a generalized face-to-face interaction, in which each individual actor becomes interdependent, as regards his fate, with each of the other individual actors (this kind of interaction context, on the scale of the complex societies we are interested in, is hard to imagine, except as *pure methodological fiction*).[8] In the same way, there is no reason to believe that the enlargement of the confrontation space characterizing fluid conjunctures can uniformly constrain all the confrontation protagonists to play (i.e. to make a move). Alongside the *sense of urgency* and the *"now or never"* feelings[9], that can be observed especially at moments of derailment (*dérapage*), phenomena of tactical inhibition may, in such contexts, as I have already suggested, become a major component of the "style" or "climate" of the confrontation (and may easily coexist with a widely shared sense of urgency).

---

[7]Goffman, *Strategic Interaction*, 99, 101 and, above all, 143–4.

[8]As we shall see later, this does not prevent, in fluid contexts, relationships where everything is played out "face-to-face" from creeping into social relations from which, in routine conjunctures, they were institutionally absent. This phenomenon of course must not be confused with the fictional configuration of interaction mentioned above.

[9]On the outburst of these strange collective feelings, aptly captured by Pareto's famous *O ora mai piu* (now or never) on the eve of the March on Rome, see Linz, "Time and Regime Change," 7–8.

These remarks suggest that the differences between tight game and contexts of extended tactical interdependence do not simply relate to a change of scale. In fact, interactions *at a distance,* as encountered in the second case, do not obey the same "laws" as interactions of physical proximity. This is particularly true of the relationships between moves and their outcomes, which in the case of extended interdependence, lose much of their direct or "tight" character, at least for those actors who are not involved in a *local* context of direct physical interdependence.

As regards the moves exchanged, this means that, in cases of interdependence developing on a multisectoral scale, the actors are not all, uniformly and at the same time, forced by their own situational contexts to make only direct moves. One of the components of the particular climates characterizing critical conjunctures consists precisely in the *co-occurrence* of direct and of mediated moves. The analysis of crisis processes never attaches sufficient importance to the fact that, returning to the example of the Paris riots of February 6, 1934, the physical confrontations occurred at the very moment of the discussion in the Chamber of Deputies of the conservative deputies' interpellations and protests, and of the vote of confidence in his government demanded by Daladier.

This means that, while it is no doubt useful to partly retain the schema of the tight game in order to grasp certain important aspects of extended interdependence, this can only be done, strictly speaking, by conceiving spaces where direct moves are reciprocated as more or less *unstable islands of tight game*, located in an environment where genuinely physical interdependence between the interaction protagonists is much less present. In other words, the desectorization of social space and the emergence of extended interdependence can certainly not be equated with any generalization, in all the sectors undergoing multisectoral mobilizations, of the features characterizing the tight game. However, for this reason, the links which, in the tight game, connect moves to their outcomes are transformed and the crucial element of this transformation lies in the articulation of the tight-game islands with their surrounding environment.

This is clearly visible in the features specifying the kind of *loosening* at work in contexts of extended interdependence. For this cannot be described as a loosening of the tight game, at least not in the technical sense that Goffman gives the term and as clarified above. As a matter of fact, the operation of an institutional filter hardly may account for the mediation between moves and outcomes. This precisely because of the transformations experienced by the sectors impacted by multisectoral mobilizations (that is to the changes in their state). In other words, we simply cannot attribute the effectiveness of institutional moves—even if, as we know, this effectiveness is fluctuating—to the stability and the hold of sectoral logics. In these critical situations, the filter of an enforcement agency tends no longer to interpose itself between moves and outcomes with the same thickness, the same degree of objectification of social relations. And it no longer enjoys the same autonomy as in routine conjunctures, it is less able to impose on the actors its own definitions of situations, its own rules of the game and its own repertoire of feasible moves. In short, the "loosening" (now seen in a quite different light) concerns mainly *the state of the institutional filters* .

In these conditions, is it still possible to speak of a type of loosening characterizing situations of extended interdependence, and if so, what does this loosening consist of? To answer this question, I must introduce into the analysis, at least as regards tight-game islands, a supplementary element: the distinction between the *local* outcome of a move and its *extended* one. The local outcome will certainly have an "intrinsic link" with the move made, but only in this specific sense: in the tight-game islands, the interaction will come close to what the notion of tight game tries to capture. In such local contexts—and here the previously cited cases of the February 6, 1934, confrontations or the May 1958 seizure of the *Gouvernement général* building in Algiers are pertinent—it is the specifically physical features of the situation which will impose themselves on the local protagonists and will tend to force them to "play," to participate in the game, on pain of—locally again—disappearing as actors.

My point is that the effects of a given move, and its effectiveness, cannot be reduced to this purely local outcome. Actually, in contexts of extended interdependence, the effectiveness of moves will tend to be the product of the insertion of each given move and its direct outcome into the *diachronic* chaining of the other moves exchanged and their possible local outcomes. It is precisely here that we can identify the loosening element specific to contexts of extended interdependence, that is the element distancing the move from its outcome, the positive or negative payoff it procures for the actor. Or, if one prefers, something like a retranslation process. It is also here that the difference of extended interdependence contexts from routine conjunctures becomes clearly visible, provided, of course, that we accept the previously suggested approximate equivalency between the latter and loose-game contexts. While in routine conjunctures the effectiveness of the moves exchanged tends to depend on sectoral logics and on the definitions of situations these logics carry, in fluid conjunctures their effectiveness derives, on the analytical level, from a more complex process. It is a process which involves not only a direct confrontation between resources and lines of action that are usually—that is in routine conjunctures—compartmentalized, segregated from one another, but, above all, where the actors' moves will tend to be interpreted and evaluated *in relation to each other*, much more with regard to their temporal order than to sectoral logics.

This is obviously the origin of some tactical problems faced by actors in critical conjunctures. I have already mentioned one of these problems, that of the control by the actors over the meaning and impact of their own moves.

The difficulties they face in this respect, along with structural uncertainty, are one of the main factors of the caution they often display in these situations. This caution is discernible, first, in the surprising infrequency of *irreversible* moves[10]—as shown, for example, by the fact that in the French May 1958 crisis, the government camp made no irreversible move until the investiture of General de Gaulle, the tacit bargaining with the Algiers military leaders on a legalistic definition of the situation offering us a typical illustration of tactical moves that avoid being irreversible (but deprive their actors of the advantage of appearing to their adversaries to have "burnt their boats"). In another vein, it can also be seen in the *tactical paralysis* which, during the French 1968 events, seems to have gripped the "student movement" on the days of May 29 and 30, though this moment was perceived by all protagonists as a decisive one. It can be found again in the no less surprising features assumed, in such contexts, by certain charismatic strategies, like those of De Gaulle in 1958 or of Mendès France in 1968, an issue which will be developed in more detail later.

A second type of problem, quite close to the above, relates to how the "retranslation" process peculiar to the imperfect tight game affects the *credibility* of the acts, messages, threats, or promises that these convey.[11] A substantialist reflex might lead the scholar to look for the mainsprings of this credibility in the "intrinsic character" of performative speech-acts, the "illocutionary power" of discourses or in the personal qualities of the actor, for example his "charisma." However, to understand how this retranslation works, we must be more prudent, and pay at least equal attention to the *structures of plausibility*—I borrow this notion from Berger and Luckmann[12]—of moves within their temporal chaining. Thus, to draw on a much-commented example, the threat that De Gaulle's radio broadcast of May 30, 1968, intended to convey owed its credibility perhaps at least as much to the *halo effect* of other moves—De Gaulle's disappearance, his meeting with French military chiefs in Germany, the deployment of tanks around Paris, or the pro-government demonstration that followed (in which the broadcast appeared to play a tacit coordinating role)—as it did to its undeniable rhetorical character as an "appeal-speech" (*discours-appel*).[13] Similarly, the failure of the May 24 broadcast cannot solely be imputed to its hybrid aspect,

---

[10]That is *commitments*, in the sense that Schelling gives to this notion, see *Strategy of Conflict*, 121–3.

[11]On the notion of credibility, see especially Schelling, *Strategy of Conflict*, chapters 4 and 5, and Goffman, *Strategic Interaction*, 102–13.

[12]Berger and Luckmann, *Social Construction*, 174–5.

[13]On the distinction between *discours-appels* and *discours-bilans*, see Jean-Marie Cotteretand and René Moreau, *Le Vocabulaire du général de Gaulle* (Paris: Presses de Sciences Po, 1969), 17–37—though this does not analyze the broadcasts of May 24 and 30, 1968.

neither a "taking-stock speech" (*discours-bilan*) nor really an "appeal."[14] Its unfortunate[15] character also owes much to the sequence of moves surrounding it, in particular: (a) its fortuitous coincidence with the rebound of the movement, as materialized by what was, without doubt, the most vigorous, the most violent, of all the demonstrations during the May "events"; (b) the kind of "solution" it proposed (the referendum, whose acceptability was, as we shall see later, very weak—a point on which the broadcasts of May 24 and May 30 differ radically); (c) the start of a parallel, but also, de facto, competing, negotiation on another type of solution, in the "social" domain.

Another implication of all this is that, while extended interdependence is easily checked by first examining intersectoral relations and the changes these relations experience in fluid conjunctures (including, in particular, the opening-up of sectoral arenas), in no way can it be reduced to this. As a matter of fact, it possesses dimensions that are inseparable from the calculations and, more generally, from the *interpretative activity* of the actors. In other words, as regards the extended outcome of reciprocal moves, it is impossible to accept Goffman's distinction between, on the one hand, the assessment of the situation made by the protagonists in the confrontation, and on the other hand, an enforcement system producing outcomes, but remaining entirely external to the assessments and interpretive activity of the actors. *In imperfect tight game contexts, assessment is part of the enforcement system* and, contrary to what Goffman seems to believe, is not to be found exclusively *upstream* from the lines of action deployed by the protagonists of the interaction.[16]

---

[14]See, for example, Dansette, *Mai 1968*, 226 et seq.; Jean-Raymond Tournoux, *Le mois de Mai du Général* (Paris: Plon, 1969), 143-51; Jean Touchard, *Le Gaullisme, 1940-1969* (Paris: Seuil, 1978); see the text of the broadcasts of May 24 and 30 in *L'Année politique 1968,* 379 and 381.

[15]On the social conditions of unfortunate statements, see John L. Austin, *How to do Things with Words* (Oxford: Oxford University Press, 1972).

[16]Which also means that, in the imperfect tight game, we are dealing with a kind of "structure" determining the effectiveness of lines of action that is much more complex than those characterizing the other two types of actors' interdependence. This may be analyzed, though this is still a simplification, as a *double articulation* of the moves exchanged, with each move, each line of action being shaped simultaneously on two levels. The first is the one I have just described, the chaining of moves in which a given line of action takes place. This is the level where the outcomes of moves are determined. The processes that constitute it disqualify all substantialist conceptions of what makes resources and different lines of action effective. However—and this makes analysis complex—it seems that, at the same time, what happens locally in the islands of tight game also matters. The point concerns, so to speak, the special role of moves located in these tight game islands and of their local outcomes. To account more precisely for this role requires us to come back to structural uncertainty, one of the core components of fluid conjunctures. Indeed, in such conjunctures, actors, as we remember, tend to be deprived of reference points, tools for assessing situations, indices linked to sectoral logics. That is why their perceptions, expectations, and calculations can hardly ignore the immediate physical dimension, the *materiality* of the exchange of moves and their local outcomes. These present themselves as as focal points forcefully attracting the actors' interpretative activity, and we shall see later that this conjunctural weight of situational focal points in the defining of situations is

Only this can explain the *disproportion*, frequently observed in critical conjunctures, between the very limited physical content of certain moves and the magnitude of their effects, not only on the actors' perceptions, but, above all, on their tactical behavior, on the definition of the alliances to be sought, and even on what objectives they should pursue and on what is at stake in the confrontation. This "retranslation" is remarkably evident, to take an elementary example, in the episode—actually quite a minor one in physical terms—of the "landings" in Corsica during the 1958 French crisis, on May 24 (in fact, a local military coup). These landings undoubtedly represent a turning point in the confrontation, in the sense that from this moment on it becomes impossible to sustain the legalistic definition of the situation which, as already seen, the Pflimlin government had— with some difficulty, and more or less tacitly—been negotiating with the military command in Algiers since May 13. This is also one of the major factors explaining why these rather strange moves that are *provocations*—strange at least as regards the social conditions which favor their success—may occasionally prove effective: these moves always rely on this kind of amplification process in the interpretation of acts that, most often, have only a very tiny physical dimension.[17] But, having said this, it should also be stressed that, beyond the possibility of disproportionate outcomes, the fact remains that the "laws" governing this kind of "retranslation" are not easily mastered by these moves authors: if, actually, successful provocations seem relatively rare in critical conjunctures, it is also because—on account of this same "retranslation" process—these moves run serious risks of not working out in the way their authors intend (as we already know, the difficulty of controlling the effects of our own tactical acts is one of the general properties of extended interdependence contexts).

Marks, Moves, and Symbolic Politics

More generally, we find the same features in the emergence of *markers* which, in critical conjunctures, become bound to the situations and impose themselves on the actors' perceptions and calculations as defining elements of these situations. The range of these processes is very broad, from the direction the confrontation is evolving (e.g., toward its escalation or decline) to the offensive or defensive

---

a major property of fluid conjunctures. This means however that, since this special role also relates to the actors' interpretive activity, the effectiveness of direct moves and their local outcomes cannot be equated with their strictly physical "content," that is, with gains and losses in terms of the resources deployed and with the coercive control they might afford.

[17]See Gary Marx, "Thoughts on a Neglected Category of Social Movement Participant: The Agent Provocateur and the Informant," *American Journal of Sociology* 80, no. 2 (1974): 402–29, which does not directly address, however, the issue of the social conditions for the success of these moves.

posture of its protagonists. But these processes may also relate to the very existence of actors as discrete social entities, as collective actors or as parties who "count" in the confrontation, that is, whom the other protagonists must take into account. In this way, the analysis of the processes through which the markers are produced takes us into a singular and still little-known empirical field, that a particular approach in political sociology has sought to open up under the heading of "symbolic politics" (a label which seems above all to address reciprocal relationships between, on the one hand, the tactics deployed in political confrontations and contests and, on the other, the representations, symbols, or cognitive resources of the actors involved).[18] In this regard, I will limit myself in the following pages to single out some of the implications of the enforcement system specific to contexts of extended interdependence.

Escalations and Escalation Ladders

Let me begin with an example that seems transparent enough at first sight—the aforementioned case of conflict escalation processes in political crisis situations. The conception of these processes by contemporary authors more or less explicitly involves a combination of two distinct elements. The first consists of a hierarchical ordering of steps or thresholds, all of them organized in the form of a ladder according to their intensity, severity, or degree of resort to coercive resources, and each of these steps corresponding to specific lines of action or to the implementation of particular institutional technologies.[19] The second element is the idea of escalation as the *ascent of the ladder*, whatever, on the other hand, the authors' assumptions about what is the "motor" driving this ascent and how the latter is performed.[20]

---

[18]Murray Edelman, *The Symbolic Uses of Politics* (Urbana: University of Illinois Press, 1964); *Politics as Symbolic Action* (Chicago: Markham, 1971); *Political Language. Words that Succeed and Policies that Fail* (New York: Academic Press, 1977).

[19]The reference model for this conception of escalation remains, despite its focus (namely, escalation of international conflicts in the nuclear age), the work by Herman Kahn, *On Escalation. Metaphors and Scenarios* (New York: Praeger, 1965). This conception is also present in most of the objectivist systematizations through which jurists try to picture the dynamics of institutional conflicts; see, for a good example of this, Olivier Duhamel, "La Constitution de la Ve République et l'alternance," *Pouvoirs*, no. 1 (1977): 47–71.

[20]Quite often scholars tend to locate this motor—as concerns both internal and international conflicts—in the interplay of the conflict protagonists' reciprocal perceptions (especially in the possible effects of *misperceptions*) and also, interestingly enough, in the internal competitive dynamics affecting each collective protagonist, for example the dynamics around the "hawk/dove" divide, a kind of hypothesis which may lead to the idea of "objective complicity," on each side, between the hawks (or doves, indeed), and to the recognition that the motor of the escalation may therefore not lie in the overt or official issues, objectives, motives, or interests of the conflict (see in particular Murray Edelman, "Escalation and Ritualization of Political Conflict," *American Behavioral Scientist* 13 (September–December 1969): 231–45.

This traditional conception of escalation, at least as regards situations of extended interdependence, has a fundamental flaw: it attributes to escalation ladders a reality and role which they cannot possibly—and actually do not—have. Let me emphasize straightaway that it is not enough, in order to make the image of escalation processes more acceptable, to point out that in these processes the ascent of the ladder may be anything but steady or regular, and even that actual ladder-steps may be skipped, that in the ascent there are pauses, hesitations, or movements up-and-down.[21] For this still leaves us prisoners of the misleading idea that there is indeed a ladder structuring processes of escalation.

There is no such thing. First, because the steps, rungs, or thresholds, which appear in real processes, *do not necessarily preexist* the confrontations and are usually no more than results or emerging effects of these confrontations, taking significance as steps for the actors only in relation to the particular temporal chaining of reciprocal moves. For example, if the May 24, 1958, "landings" in Corsica are interpreted in terms of escalation, it is not because of their intensity, of the violence deployed, or their lethality. They have this effect, beyond what was said above (they result in the collapse of the fiction of legality), through the simple fact that the "landings" clearly *embody* a geographical extension, they indicate a direction (Corsica is between Algeria and metropolitan France), and they objectify a boost of the conflict. Their role is thus comparable to that played, in the "events" of May 1968, by the Paris demonstrations of May 24, much more violent no doubt, but whose escalation-step value derives much less from this violence than from the fact that they too embody an extension, the striking and much-commented passage of the street demonstrations from the left to the right bank of the Seine, along with, as we already know, a rebound of the movement.

What is true for each step is also true, a fortiori, for the escalation ladders as a whole. In contexts of extended interdependence, the successful imposition of an image of the situation as a "rise to the extremes" *does not imply* that the specific step reached at a given moment in the confrontation can be located on a preconstructed escalation ladder. Rather, it is markers of the kind just mentioned which, by emerging within in a particular sequence of moves, lend credibility to *threats* of escalation (which means these threats make sense for the actors only in relation to the moves played). If the threat represented by "Operation Resurrection" in May 1958—which was supposed to include parachuting troops into Paris—had, for the actors, the image of a rise to the extremes, then this was because it rode on the back of the expectations produced by the earlier

---

[21]A point which H. Kahn well understands (*On Escalation*, chapter 2). See also, on internal confrontations, Philip B. Scranton, "Escalation: A Comparative Study of Three Social Movements and the Process of Conflict Development" (PhD. diss., University of Pennsylvania, 1975), 5–9 and 65–7, an attempt to identify a "developmental structure" of escalation processes, that is, in other words, their natural history.

"landing" in Corsica. This means that escalation ladders, when they emerge as representations of the confrontation dynamics, are produced by the same processes, the same exchanges of moves, as their individual steps. This also has a further implication: it enables the analysis of escalation processes to shift away from the construction by the scholar of an *artifact*, that is, an *objectivist* hierarchization of actual or possible moves in terms of their severity, toward the exploration of the much less-ordered processes from which emerge certain types of representations like images of escalation, their structures of plausibility, and the markers around which these structures take shape.[22]

In fact, the crystallizations of such representations—precisely because of their dependence on temporal chainings of moves—are extremely precarious. That is why, for example, at least in periods of high political fluidity, imposing an image of escalation is for the actors who have a conjunctural interest in doing so, a very difficult tactical maneuver to accomplish. This, to refer to a negative case, is one of the main reasons why the French military putsch of April 1961, having thus failed to imprint the situation with the mark of escalation, collapsed by itself, without really having experienced any decisive defeat in the military sense.[23] An excellent example in the opposite sense—albeit a limit case—is provided by the period, during the Italian crisis of 1919–22, immediately preceding the March on Rome, which saw the Fascist squads, in successive waves, "conquer" town after town and region after region, and thus gradually impose the image of an irresistible territorial advance.[24]

The Marks of Existence

The difficulties encountered by actors in trying to master the tactics of marking are of course not confined to escalation processes alone. Similar observations

---

[22] It is interesting to note that the tactics of setting up a hierarchical organization of moves—something the actors frequently envisage—tend to occur with some efficiency mainly in situations characterized by a *deflation* of political fluidity, as, for example, in the case of the remarkable *normalization maneuver* which, during the French 1968 "events," followed the turning point of May 30 and whose markers took the form of successive "takeovers" by the public forces of a series of the "movement" symbols, namely the automobile factories at Flins and Sochaux (which at that moment experienced the painful final stages of the strikes), and, later, the Odéon theater and the Sorbonne in Paris. It is significant that the "takeover" of these last two "symbolic sites" took place practically without violence (we know that this "takeover," ordered by General de Gaulle immediately after his return from Romania on May 19, was blocked for an appreciable period of time by the combined resistance of the Paris police prefect Grimaud, and the prime minister Pompidou; see Maurice Grimaud, *En mai, fais ce qu'il te plaît* (Paris: Stock, 1977), 194, 208–15.

[23] See, for example, Viansson-Ponté, *Histoire de la République gaullienne*, vol. 1, 359 et seq.; Field and Hudnut, *L'Algérie, de Gaulle et l'armée*, 182 et seq.

[24] The best account of this process remains Angelo Tasca, *The Rise of Italian Fascism, 1918-1922* (London: Methuen & Co, 1938).

can be made about other types of situation, some of which have considerable relevance for the argument of this book. A prime example is the problems facing critical processes protagonists when they try to assert their *positions*, or even their very *existence*. In many tactical configurations that emerge in contexts of extended interdependence, this may, in fact, require very high costs. In this respect, one of the most significant types of configuration is provided by contexts where a *high density of direct moves* can be observed. Here are two salient and contrasting examples: first, the large-scale occupations of industrial factories and premises during the French strikes of May–June 1936 and especially those of May–June 1968 (in the latter case, the Confédération Générale du Travail (CGT) leadership sought to achieve what I will call a *saturation effect*); second, the "exploits" and "punitive expeditions" of the Fascists, especially in late 1920 and early 1921 (over this short period, in the Po Valley alone, more than 270 such expeditions were recorded, targeting in particular 73 People's Houses and Labour Chambers, almost 150 cooperatives and peasant leagues premises, and those of 29 socialist or communist organizations).[25] Frequently, however, to assert position or existence involving such a massive resort to direct moves represents a course of action which is not available to all the protagonists, and which, as we already know, clearly carries serious risks of producing effects (or extended outcomes) that escape control.

As remarkably illustrated by those that occurred, during the French 1968 crisis, in the week between May 24 and May 30, it is in this way that we should interpret the subtle ballet of demonstrations that define the contours of the different actors, of their alliances, and of the diverse strategies deployed.[26] With a much higher level of violence, a similar phenomenon is easily evidenced by the Paris demonstrations and riots of February 6, 1934, and the days that followed. Here, the case of the Communist Party is particularly conclusive: having participated, through its war veterans association, the Association Républicaine des Anciens

---

[25]Tasca, *Rise of Italian Fascism*, 120; these figures, based on some Fascist party internal records, are far from exhaustive.

[26]Here are some telling examples. On May 24, 1968, the CGT organized marches that were entirely separate from the "student" demonstration, and which broke up when the latter began. On May 27, the student Mouvement du 22 mars (or at least its dominant faction) separated itself from the rest of the "student movement" by not participating in the Charléty rally, in response to which the CGT, precisely to distance itself from the "Mendès France operation" (on this operation, see Chapter 6, "Charismatic strategies"), organized its own demonstration on May 29. This demonstration was joined by the dominant elements of the radical "Action committees," which, for their part, had also participated in the Charléty rally, once again in order to distinguish themselves from the Mendès France operation, which was associated with Charléty (but this was not the case with leadership of the UNEF [Union Nationale des Etudiants de France, French Students National Union], which had also been at Charléty). The extreme Right also organized several demonstrations, even before May 30, all of them on the right bank of the Seine, see René Chiroux, *L'Extrême Droite sous la Ve République* (Paris: LGDJ, 1974), 168–73.

Combattants (ARAC), in the right-wing riots of February 6, it subsequently felt forced in the following days to "rectify," again in the street (and this was costly), the confusion produced by its ambiguous involvement.[27]

Despite appearances, these problems of marking out positions and identities are not so very different from those that face governments, a special type of actor, when they too, in critical conjunctures, have to assert their "existence." The case of a government being unable to impose this sort of marker on the situation—as with the Pflimlin government in the French May 1958 crisis—is one of the most important factors in the possible emergence, in such contexts, of the perception of a *political vacuum* (which the potential resignation of the government could only reinforce, by further objectifying it).[28]

As a final word on the kind of effects produced by enforcement systems characterizing contexts of enlarged interdependence, I would like, without exploring here the implications or difficulties it entails, to suggest an additional connection. It concerns the relationship between, on the one hand, the particular role of direct moves in the processes analyzed above and, on the other, the street "theatrics" and "symbolisms" staged by fascist organizations in the interwar period, features which have particularly intrigued historians of fascisms, especially German fascism. Contrary to what these authors often believe, the ostentation of the displays of force, parades, *adunate*, and so on, the deployments of uniforms and flags, may well not merely represent the surface, the froth or residue of supposedly much "deeper" or more "fundamental" social phenomena.[29] To be more precise, I think that the use of what must be analyzed as a set of *rudimentary technologies of objectification* of certain social relationships, *identities*, or groups (a kind of phenomena that the catch-all thematic of "political symbolism" is incapable of even identifying) is not entirely unrelated to the place occupied, in the activity of definition of the situations in contexts of extended interdependence, by the tactics of marking. I should add that this perspective is not incompatible with the fact that in certain cases—notably those I have just

---

[27]Berstein, *Le 6 février 1934*, 158 and 235–45; Max Beloff, "The Sixth of February," in *The Decline of the Third Republic*, ed. J. Joll (London: Chatto and Windus, 1959), 9–35 . See also, on the demonstrations organized by the Communist Party and the communist-led Confédération Générale du Travail Unitaire (CGTU, United General Confederation of Labor) on February 9 and on those of February 12, Antoine Prost, "Les manifestations du 12 février 1934 en province," *Le Mouvement social*, no. 54 (January–March 1966): 7–27.

[28]See, in the wake of the works of Karl Bracher on the rise of national-socialism, Linz, *Crisis, Breakdown, and Reequilibration*, 4, 66, 78–9 and 81; however, as I have already said, this author sees "power vacuum" only as a particular phase in one of the historical sequences supposed to be typical of crises in democratic systems (in his perspective, this "power vacuum" seems to correspond more or less to the same phenomenon that he has called the "narrowing of the political arena," which I will discuss in detail later).

[29]On this point, see Dominique Pelassy, "Le Rôle des signes dans la dictature. Etude sur la symbolique nationale-socialiste" (PhD diss., Institut d'Études Politiques, Paris, 1975).

mentioned—these rudimentary technologies may survive (especially by becoming heavily institutionalized) in the more routine conjunctures that follow the crises in which they appeared. But it requires us, on the other hand, constantly to bear in mind that the principles governing the effectiveness of these technologies, and indeed their "functions"—at least if the hypothesis I propose here is correct— may well not be exactly the same in different conjunctures (a consideration that works on "political symbolism," in particular in the case of Nazism, do not really seem to take on board). This also means, just to underline the point, that there is good reason to suspect that this kind of phenomenon is not exclusively a feature peculiar to Nazi Germany, its culture, or even to the specific "political style" of fascist enterprises, though it is true that the latter, at least between the two World Wars, demonstrated unusual savoir faire and inventiveness in this domain.

Competitions for the Definition of Reality

Taken together, these observations show how much the emergence of definitions of situations that structure the perceptions and calculations of actors, and, more generally their practical experience, owes many of its key characteristics to the enforcement system operating in contexts of extended interdependence. Let me now subject the processes of this emergence to closer scrutiny.

Perceptions and Definitions

A few words first on the notion of "definition of the situation" and the way it is commonly used in contemporary social sciences, for this usage can lead to misunderstandings that are easily avoidable. The difficulties derive precisely from the fact that the scholar usually appeals to this notion to refer first to the content of the representations and perceptions of individual actors (or social entities he likens to individual actors) and, in parallel to this, but less systematically, to the way in which these representations and perceptions shape the actors' behavior and thereby contribute to the production of social reality.

The problem is that this focus, however justified, on the causal impact of idealities on the way definitions work, often has the effect of obscuring what is crucial for the perspective developed here, namely the moves, the tactics, the *activity of definition* itself, or, more generally, the diverse processes whereby definitions of situations emerge, impose themselves on actors, or collapse.

As a result, in the conventional uses from which I depart, it is primarily the representations of the *decision-makers* that are highlighted, with the researcher limiting himself to the simple description of how the leader(s) of *one* particular political entity perceive(s) the situation with which she or he is (they are) confronted)—for example, to refer to an influential work, the perception of the threat and the attendant risks, of the time available to act, and of the degree of awareness or anticipation of the crisis.[30] Consequently, often without even being conscious of it, we will tend to conceive the definition of the situation as a *cognitive* and *unilateral* fact, specific to one single actor or, at best, to a homogeneous category of actors. And, in that way, we will also tend to neglect especially the *interactions* between several actors or several distinct social entities, and thus neglect what may be at stake, as regards definitions of situation, in these interactions.

Now, neglect of the interactions evidently has some damaging consequences. Ironically, its drawbacks are particularly salient in those very areas where this conception of the definition of situation might deliver some interesting hypotheses and results, such as, for example, when it suggests that situations may well not be identical for different protagonists of a confrontation, that is to say, they may not be defined *unilaterally* in the same way by these protagonists—it is an aspect of what Schütz calls "multiple realities."[31] For, beyond this—in any event useful—recognition that several definitions of the same given "objective" reality *may possibly* coexist, the common uses of the notion of definition of the situation exhibit the serious flaw not only of ignoring the *confrontations* which set several definitions of the same situation against each other, and the contests where the issue may be the imposition of one particular definition (which could indeed become dominant if one of the protagonists should succeed), but also, and this is absolutely vital for understanding contexts of extended interdependence, of being unable to identify the *interdependence between several distinct definitions*, and between the individual fates of these definitions. To return to the elementary example of the "landings" in Corsica, this simply means that when an actor manages to define the situation in such a way as to appear to be *on the offensive*, as was the case of the Algiers camp with the formation of a Comité de salut public (Committee of public safety) in Corsica on May 24, 1958, the emergence of this definition cannot help but have an effect on other definitions

---

[30]Charles F. Hermann, "International Crisis as a Situational Variable," in *International Politics and Foreign Policy*, ed. James N. Rosenau (New York: The Free Press, 1969), 411; the author revealingly combines these three "variables" in order to describe several types of *decision-making situations* in international relations. On the influence of this conceptualization on the analysis of internal crises, see especially Martin Jänicke, "Die Analyse des politischen Systems aus der Krisenperspektive," in *Politische Systemkrisen,* ed. M. Jänicke (Cologne: Kieperheuer und Witsch, 1973), 33–4, and Knuth Dohse, "Das politische System in der Krise: Modell einer revolutionären Situation," *Politische Vierteljahresschrift* 12, no. 4 (1971): 555–78. Note that Hermann himself explicitly refused to limit the application of his conceptualization to international crises alone, see in particular Charles F. Hermann, "Some Consequences of Crisis Which Limit the Viability of Organizations," *Administrative Science Quarterly* 8, no. 1 (1963): 61–82.

[31]Alfred Schutz, "On Multiple Realities," in *Collected Papers* (La Haye: Nijhoff, 1962), vol. 1, 207–59.

of the situation that the other crisis protagonists may have developed for their own sake.

Finally, conventional uses of the notion of definition of situation lead to a perception of the tactical activity of the interaction protagonists as behaviors resulting from *previously* elaborated definitions, in other words as *consequences* of these definitions. In that perspective, tactical activity always follows on behind the representations and perceptions of actors; it originates in them. And it is only in this very narrow (and, indeed, improper) sense that this perspective makes reference to what Merton calls Thomas's theorem, whose classic formulation is as follows: "If men define situations as real, they are real in their consequences."[32] Now, while, of course, there is no question of denying the effects that the representations of actors have on "reality"—a reality of which these representations themselves are an integral part—it remains that, as soon as we draw away from a perspective which limits the definition of the situation solely to the unilateral perceptions and representations of individual actors, it becomes necessary also to abandon the mechanistic schema which conceives the relationship between definition of the situation and nonideational tactical activity solely in *sequential* terms, as the latter being *unequivocally determined* by the former.

To sum up, it seems to me much more productive to shift the focus of the analysis directly onto all the social processes whereby definitions of situations are elaborated, negotiated, and emerge, if only because this occurs in confrontations which are never purely ideational and which go well beyond the unilateral cognitive activity of their protagonists, and because the definitions of situation usually produce, for these protagonists, very uneven benefits. For this same reason, we can no longer view definitions of situations as immutable facts unequivocally governing behaviors. So we should try to single out the complex reciprocal determinations operating between definitions and behaviors—whereby the definitions themselves become vulnerable to the moves exchanged—are shaped by these moves, or, rather, are subjected to their "laws."

---

[32] Robert K. Merton, *Social Theory and Social Structure* (Chicago: Free Press of Glencoe, 1949). It may be worth remembering here the insightful warnings formulated by William Thomas, for whom analyses based on the definition of situations should never neglect what he calls "the factual elements of the situation" and focus solely on representations or on "subjective" situations, see in particular his "The Definition of the Situation," in *Symbolic Interaction*, ed. J. G. Manis and B. N. Meltzer (Boston: Allyn and Bacon, 1972), 331–6, and William I. Thomas and Dorothy S. Thomas, "Situations Defined as Real are Real in Their Consequences" [1928], in *Social Psychology through Symbolic Interaction*, ed. G. P. Stone and H. A. Farberman (Waltham: Xeros, 1970), 162–74; see also Peter McHugh, *Defining the Situation. The Organization of Meaning in Social Interaction* (Indianapolis: Bobbs-Merril, 1968), 7–20.

The Role of Situational Focal Points

This issue clarified, let me further explore a property I have already mentioned, all too briefly, namely the particular *attraction* exerted in fluid conjunctures by situational focal points. On such occasions, these focal points represent, for the actors of crises, both points where their expectations converge, and points fixing their interpretations, assessments, and perceptions.[33] It is around these focal points that effective definitions of situations take shape, those which, even if only for a short time, impose themselves on actors' calculations and on their tactical activity. These situational focal points may take forms as diverse as the markers evoked earlier, "cultural" facts, events and even, as we shall see, individuals and institutional procedures (whose effectiveness will depend more on their conjunctural quality as focal points than on the hold of their routine social logic). Their *situational* character requires clarification. Let me distinguish between two different types. First, the focal points that visibly stand out from the *concrete details of the situation*; this refers to mechanisms similar to the emergence of marks analyzed above, or, more generally, to those of the selection of "good forms" highlighted by *Gestalt* psychology. Second, we also find the *situational working* of focal points rooted in the *cultural* systems of a given society or a given social group, an ideal-typical example being provided by the uses, during the Iranian Revolution of 1978–79, of the calendars, rites, and martyrology of Shi'a Islam.[34]

This particular attraction of focal points must be related to the conditions of structural uncertainty characterizing critical conjunctures, that is the collapse of the efficiency of the instruments routinely used to evaluate and interpret situations.

---

[33] On the working of focal points in social interactions, see especially Schelling, *Strategy of Conflict*, 73–4 and 90–115. Note that Schelling himself points out the convergence of his own reflections with the insights of *Gestalt* psychology regarding the perception of physical forms.

[34] "The duration of religious mourning spontaneously defined the rhythm of the uprising. There was no need for speech. At the end of each uprising people prepared for another, forty days later. In the meantime, the *rendez-vous* for less important rallies would be on the third and the seventh day. Thus the fortieth day meant, for everybody, gathering, commemoration, continuation of the struggle, a day of mourning and anger," Berhang (collective pseydonym), *Iran, le maillon faible* (Paris: Maspero, 1976), 333. For some observations congruent with my own analysis, see Theda Skocpol, "Rentier State and Shi'a Islam in the Iranian Revolution," *Theory and Society* 11, no. 3 (1982): 274. It is also to this situational game that we should refer what Smelser calls *precipitating factors*, which, in his view, contribute to the emergence of "collective behaviors"; however, in the perspective I outline here, this means that such factors, at least in critical conjunctures, would *directly* work as components of the *cognitive structuring* of situations, and not merely *via* "generalized beliefs" which, according to Smelser, they help to shape; on cognitive structuring, see Neil J. Smelser, "Collective Behavior and Conflict. Theoretical Issues of Scope and Problems," *The Sociological Quarterly* 5, no. 2 (1964): 120, and Michel Dobry, "Variation d'emprise sociale et dynamique des représentations: remarques sur une hypothèse de Neil Smelser," in *Analyse de l'idéologie*, ed. G. Duprat (Paris: Galilée, 1980), tome. 1, 213–14.

Deprived of the reference marks, assessment tools, clues or indices which, in routine contexts, are provided by sectoral logics, the actors' calculations depend much more, in contexts of extended interdependence, on the emergence of such focal points in the exchange of moves itself (let me note here in passing that if situational focal points thus appear as the results of a dynamics that emancipates itself from the conditions of its birth, in turn they may contribute to this emancipation).

It is this kind of dependence on focal points, or rather its scale, that constitutes the core of the hypothesis outlined above. This is why this hypothesis *does not assume there must be any common* interest—even tacit or circumstantial— between the confrontation protagonists for them to experience the attraction of these focal points. Which also means that this dependence does not necessarily go hand in hand with some tacit coordination or cooperation. Moreover, the attraction of focal points may even, in such contexts, impose itself on the calculations and definitions of situations of actors who conceive their conjunctural interests as involving the denial of any "common language" or areas of agreement with their adversaries. A focal point may constrain their calculations, even when its emergence or persistence quite clearly carries for them massively negative implications, which they are precisely trying to evade through their tactical activity, for example by attempting to eliminate this focal point as saliency, as an unavoidable element of definition of the situation.[35] In this respect, the way situational focal points operate constitutes one of the major and distinctive features of extended interdependence contexts.

Finally, just as this operation of the focal points does not presuppose that, in every case, we are dealing with a conflict driven by "mixed" motives or dynamics, neither does it necessarily depend on the actual presence of problems of communication between the protagonists of the confrontation. Certainly such problems often arise in the exchanges of moves: for example, open, visible communication between adversaries—when they feel the need—is not always an easy matter. Which means, in particular, that this communication is not easy to publicize to your own side, to your own constituency (as in the situation, during the 1958 crisis, of the Pflimlin government and of the Socialist leaders in their negotiations with de Gaulle, or, in May 1968, that of the CGT and Parti Communiste Français (PCF) leaders in their contacts with the government, all

---

[35]Actually, when he refers to the notion of focal point or saliency, Schelling is basically thinking of "mixed motives" conflicts. He thus has difficulty in separating the operation of focal points from the presence in the interaction of an element of cooperation or *tacit coordination* between the confrontation protagonists; on that issue, see, for example, this particularly telling passage: "Even when one rational player realizes that the configuration of these details discriminates against him, he may also rationally recognize that he has no recourse—that the other player will rationally expect him to submit to the discipline of the suggestions that emanate from the game's concrete details and will take actions that, on pain of mutual damage, assume that he will co-operate" (Schelling, *Strategy of Conflict*, 108).

of them were forced to try, without always succeeding, to keep some of their bargaining activities secret, those they deemed essential). But this is not, in any way, the mainspring of the attraction exercised by focal points. Whatever the role of communication in contexts analyzed here, the effective factors explaining how focal points work at these times refer mainly to the properties of structural uncertainty already discussed, which are not primarily, in any sense, made up of communication, that is of intentional exchanges of information. This seemingly chimes with some of the conclusions that Goffman sought to outline through the methodological autonomization of strategic interaction as an empirical domain quite distinct from that of communication processes.

Variations in the Size of Definitional Activity

My final observation concerns a property that is analytically distinct from the one I have just discussed. It still relates to definitions of situations that emerge in contexts of extended interdependence, but this time considered in terms of the *size of activity* that social actors allocate in various ways to the shaping or fabrication of these definitions. Let me go to the heart of the matter. Its first aspect is that this volume of activity is liable to experience *conjunctural variations*. This simply means that we should never overlook the decisive fact that—depending on the conjuncture or the context of interaction—definitions of situations are not uniformly and at all times available to actors. While, in routine conjunctures, sectoral logics provide them with a significant stock of ready-made definitions, saving them the trouble of having to build definitions through their own activity, in other contexts, and especially in critical conjunctures, the very emergence of these definitions requires from the actors a genuine work of *reconstruction of the social world*, that is a specific investment or cost.[36] In short, in fluid conjunctures, where sectoral logics lose their hold, we should expect a significant increase in the volume of definitional activity. This increase may be detected, for example, in the *tests of position*, whereby the confrontation protagonists attempt, sometimes at great cost, to situate themselves and to situate others[37]; or in the extent of

---

[36]This reconstruction must not be confused with some other phenomena which may be linked to it, but which, despite appearances, actually play a much more marginal role in crisis processes. I refer to what happens in the cases of some "great" political crises, namely the more or less generalized recasting of *technical measurement tools* (like "weights and measures," the currency, the calendar) and the institutionalization of such changes (see in particular Béjin, "Crises des valeurs," 40). These phenomena, which often occur at the end of confrontations and which aim above all to mark a break with a previous social order, represent a kind of *symbolic or ceremonial repeat* of more extended, less-institutionalized, and less-controlled social processes, which these phenomena may sometimes conceal behind their own spectacular afterglow.

[37]On tests of position, see *supra*, Chapter 3. These tests may sometimes take the form of an genuine "on the spot" *political experiment,* as in the case of the Hamburg insurrection of 1923 when,

deliberations and the emergence, frequent in these contexts, of deliberative bodies or "organs"[38]; or, more indirectly, in what then becomes the object of the deliberations and in the issues that, in these conjunctures, seem to be within the scope of the actors tactical activity.

In this regard, it is probably the realm of *bargaining* and negotiation that represents the most impressive and fruitful empirical field. This is so, primarily, because of their overwhelming presence, their role in the unfolding of confrontations, the social locations where they take place, and the actors who take part in them. All this immediately brings to mind a series of major negotiations which, like Matignon in June 1936 or Grenelle in May 1968, have special standing for those involved in these historic episodes, an image no doubt reinforced at the time by the way they were staged or dramatized. However, this image requires substantial correction, not so much because these negotiations, which I shall term "central," were not important—they were, even if only because they were perceived as such by the crisis protagonists—but because this image obscures the full extent of the bargaining processes occurring in such contexts, and the actual place held by these central negotiations. This can be confirmed by switching focus away from central negotiations toward bargainings occurring *inside* collective actors and even inside "apparatuses" themselves. An excellent illustration may be found in the elimination—the diffuse sidelining—of the referendum that General de Gaulle had announced in his radio broadcast of May 24, 1968, as a solution to the crisis. It is true, of course, that the proposal was greeted with extreme and undisguised hostility in the ranks of the parliamentary Left Opposition and the student movement.[39] But the point is that this hostility was not the only factor undermining the "acceptability" of this attempted solution,

---

according to the most plausible accounts of this historical episode, certain elements of the Communist International seem to have tried to assess the fighting spirit—the "combativeness"—of the German workers' movement (see especially Neuberg, *Armed Insurrection*).

[38]. It is worth noting that this is often true even in the most "hardened" social sectors, namely the military ones. The emergence of such "organs" may in these cases sometimes consist in the conjunctural transformation of the "functions" usually performed by social ngathering places tied specifically to military life, such as clubs, *alumni*, recreational and sporting associations; see, for example, Antonio C. Peixoto, "Le Clube militar et les affrontements au sein des forces armées (1945–1964)," in *Les Partis militaires au Brésil*, ed. A. Rouquié et al. (Paris: Presses de Sciences Po, 1980), 65–104.

[39]The tone was set by Pierre Mendès France—"plebiscites are not to be discussed, they are to be fought." This marked a break with his previous strategy which, as we shall see, had involved silence and prudence. The referendum was denounced by the principal forces of the Left—including the PCF—but not without ambiguity, for the denunciation was accompanied by the call for a "No" vote (that is a de facto acceptation of the referendum), an ambiguity criticized by the leaders of the student movement. This public denunciation of the procedure went well beyond the ranks of the left opposition, as witnessed by the stance of the centrists representatives, especially the parliamentary Progrès et Démocracie Moderne (PDM) group, and of the reputedly "moderate" unions like Force Ouvrière, or the National Federation of Students of France (FNEF), a rival right-wing student organization to the UNEF (see the texts of these position statements in *Le Monde,* May 26–27 and 28, 1968).

nor, perhaps, the most decisive one, at least as regards its fate. Another powerful factor in its elimination is to be found in the *multiplicity of micro-bargainings* that took place inside the diverse administrative departments involved (or believing themselves to be involved) in the implementation of the referendum procedure, and also within the governmental team itself. Remarkably, these micro-bargainings all converged toward the same "conclusion," namely that it would be logistically impossible, or extremely risky, to conduct the ballot, thereby reflecting an inertia which, like all *self-fulfilling prophecies*, had the virtue of producing the anticipated outcome. As evidenced by numerous accounts, this genuine *imposition of the definition of what is probable* seriously undermined relations between Prime Minister Pompidou and President de Gaulle (it is true, as we know, that the faction around the prime minister was at the same time floating a very different solution, namely a central negotiation with the trade-union confederations and, beyond that, with the Communist Party—although the two solutions were not, *a priori*, entirely incompatible).[40] At least in this particular respect (the way that the referendum was eliminated), this case comes close to some other configurations of bargainings internal to "apparatuses," for instance to the previously mentioned episode of the resistance displayed in several sectors of the state "machine" immediately after the Paris riots of February 6, 1934. This resistance, which in the same way took the form of a definition of *what was probable* (in this case a dramatized vision of an uncontainable escalation of violent "disorders") and emerged from rather similar bargainings, led to the resignation of the Daladier cabinet, despite its investiture by a comfortable parliamentary majority the evening before.[41] Of course, not all internal bargainings necessarily appear so dispersed or diffuse, and some may come close to relatively "structured" configurations, that is to say, negotiations respecting preestablished ground rules. But, even in such cases, "respect for the rules" will itself tend to become one of the issues at stake in the bargaining process.

Here let me open a parenthesis, in the hope of avoiding some misunderstandings. In the present discussion, I have mainly focused on those bargaining processes that best illustrate and explain the strictly tactical problems which confront political crisis protagonists. However, the scale of bargaining processes in contexts of extended interdependence is not confined to such

---

[40]See, among others, the accounts of Michel Jobert, *Mémoires d' avenir* (Paris: Grasset, 1974), 48–9 and Balladur, *L'Arbre de mai*, 291, both close collaborators to Pompidou; see also Dansette, *Mai 1968*, 294–6. For the perceptions of other members of the government, see the account of Christian Foucher (the minister of interior during the "events" of May 1968), *Au service du général de Gaulle* (Paris: Plon1971), 261–2.

[41]On this expectation of escalation, clearly fuelled by alarmist reports from the police services, see Berstein, *Le 6 février 1934*, 206–10, especially Daladier's testimony given to the parliamentary commission of enquiry on the causes of the 6 February events) and Beloff, "The Sixth of February," 28–9.

cases: in reality, bargaining, and, far beyond it, the activity of defining situations, tends to pervade *all social relationships* in sites affected by multisectoral mobilizations. Understood this way, the scale of bargaining processes invites a reinterpretation of a frequently observed phenomenon, one which Michel Crozier has attempted to theorize, namely how, during the crises experienced by French society, social relations are rapidly transformed into *face-to-face* relationships, in marked contrast to their ordinary aspect. The nub of Crozier's argument clearly manifests its culturalist foundation (and bias): members of French society have supposedly internalized, through the socialization processes to which they have been exposed, a very special cultural pattern (or, more specifically, a pattern of authority relationships). Along with a universalist and absolutist "conception of authority," one of the basic traits of that pattern is their "fear of face-to-face" relationships, their "horror" of direct personal relations.[42] Now, according to Crozier, in times of "crisis" (crisis being regarded as French society's characteristic "mode of change"), things become radically different. Somewhat strangely, for this observation is scarcely compatible, in logical terms, with Crozier's culturalist interpretation,[43] this horror of the face-to-face suddenly gives way to its *opposite*: interactions take then the form of direct, personal, face-to-face relations. The problem is that this last observation is correct.

I will leave aside the issue of whether it makes any sense to characterize the behavior of all members of French society by a single cultural trait, the alleged "horror" of personal relationships—which, as if by magic, also characterizes, in Crozier's perspective, modern bureaucratic organizations.[44] In contrast, the sudden shift to "face-to-face" relationships in crisis conjunctures is of major

---

[42]See Crozier, *The Bureaucratic Phenomenon*. Regarding the fear of the face-to-face, Crozier's argument draws largely on Jesse Pitts's analysis of traditional values in French society, especially those resulting from modes of socialization in bourgeois families, in school, and in what the latter supposedly engenders, the "peer group" as *delinquent community* (for a detailed presentation of these analyses, see Jesse R. Pitts, "Continuité et changement au sein de la France bourgeoise," *A la recherche de la France*, ed. S. Hoffmann et al. (Paris: Seuil, 1963), 267–341. Surprisingly, those who pretend to explain the whole of French political life by these cultural traits have never tried seriously— whether at a theoretical or observational level—to identify through which agencies these traits could have marked every component of French society (which is anyway utterly improbable).

[43]Hence, the fluctuations and hesitations in the diverse attempts to formulate this property: the shift toward "direct human relationships" in times of crisis is attributed either to the principle of *le "bon plaisir"*—the conception of authority as absolute—and to "indispensable cooperation without which the organization could not survive" (Crozier, *Bureaucratic Phenomenon*) or to a huge "delirium" or frenzy of inversion, a "festival of the face-to-face" representing a dream of "total, spontaneous" communication and expression (see, this time on the May 1968 "events," Michel Crozier, *The Stalled Society* (New-York: Viking Press [1st French ed., 1970]). Schonfeld, who was aware of this difficulty, proposed a more elaborate explanatory model, but substituted for "horror of the face-to-face" another cultural feature, *the fear of risk* (i.e., fear of uncertainty and ambiguity), whose peculiarity to France is, it will be readily admitted, extremely dubious; see William R. Schonfeld, *Obedience and Revolt. French Behaviour Towards Authority* (Beverly Hills: Sage, 1976), 181–2.

[44]Crozier, *Bureaucratic Phenomenon*, chapter 9.

interest, not only because it basically corroborates the analyses I have been developing but also because these analyses, in their turn, shed light on at least some of the mainsprings of this phenomenon. In particular, the shift to face-to-face relations actually constitutes one of the observable manifestations of a key characteristic of extended interdependence contexts, namely the sheer scale of bargaining activities and, more generally, of activities involving situation-definition. The shift thus very often corresponds to what is experienced by individuals located in highly objectified social spheres (those where internal relationships are highly impersonal) as "exigencies of the situation": the "necessity"—at least when they try to bring institutional mechanisms into play (they may equally "choose" not to do so)—to put themselves on the line, to pay a high personal price (*payer de sa personne*), for instance, by taking the time to negotiate, *in person*, with individuals who are "normally" their subordinates, over issues which in routine circumstances are taken for granted, including to negotiate the very principles of their own authority. It is easy enough to find evidence of this in their timetable of activities, encounters with the "rank-and-file," direct contacts short-circuiting the hierarchy, or "doing the rounds" of the canteens—in contexts of fluidity, this is one of the most significant tactical options.[45] While there are many other bargaining configurations which produce face-to-face dealings in places where they rarely occur in routine conjunctures (for instance, the "necessity" to put oneself on the line may be encountered in "external" bargainings, that is, those entirely outside hierarchical chains of command[46]), it is very clear that, contrary to a frequent and naive idealization of the "face-to-face," the shift to direct personal relations does not necessarily represent, for the protagonists, a "return" to interactions supposedly more "genuine," more "authentic," more

---

[45]This does not prevent the actors concerned from often having the impression that they are innovating, changing the "style of action" or expanding their tactical repertoire; for example, Jules Moch, on May 19, 1958, the day of De Gaulle's press conference: "I take an initiative: though Minister of the Interior for only two days, I have been known to many of the most senior veterans in these units (police and gendarmerie) since 1947–48. I decide to go and visit as many of them as possible (. . .). Between 13.30 and the opening of the press conference, I drive at great speed from the ministry . . . to the Élysée, to the Assembly, arriving four minutes before de Gaulle, and to the units guarding the Palais d'Orsay. Everywhere I say a few words and receive a friendly, even a warm welcome: the officers have to contain their men to avoid excessive displays of support and to maintain a semblance of military discipline," Jules Moch, *Une si longue vie* (Paris: Robert Laffont, 1976), 525.

[46]In particular when it involves using bluffs or threats in order to influence the perceptions and calculations of adversaries on an individualized basis: "On the 24th Mr. Périllier (Prefect of the Haute-Garonne) announced by decree the dissolution of the *de facto* group calling itself the 'Comité républicain de salut public de Toulouse' [Republican Committee of Public Safety]. Rather than opting for police interrogations or house searches authorised by the minister, he considered it more diplomatic to invite the principal members of the committee individually to his office (. . .). He informed each of his visitors that the Comité de salut public had been banned and that he would regretfully have to take repressive measures if the Comité nonetheless tried to continue its activity," Jean-Paul Buffelan, *Le Complot du 13 mai 1958 dans le Sud-Ouest* (Paris: LGDJ, 1966), 119–20.

"human," or even just more agreeable. Last but not the least: this is also one of the reasons why, contrary to what the culturalist interpretation of French political life would have us believe, these types of shift to face-to-face relations are likely to occur whenever we find contexts close to extended interdependence, and this is true whatever the cultural features specific, or deemed specific, to the social systems concerned.

Having clarified this matter, let me now close the parenthesis and stress that, despite the great variety of their particular configurations, the extension of bargainings in critical conjunctures tends to confront protagonists with problems resulting precisely from *the ambiguity of the bargaining boundaries*. In other words, in contexts of extended interdependence, it is not easy for them to *confine the game* within clear limits. In these conditions, we should expect that a specific activity—very often the doubling-up of negotiations through the addition of other parallel bargainings, possibly using other channels—may well be intended to delimit both the participants and the issues at stake. Alongside this diffusion of bargainings—a process that certainly impacts even central negotiations (as we can see with the Grenelle talks in May 1968, which were permanently "structured" by a sort of "private" bargaining between the prime minister's faction and the CGT leadership, superimposed onto the overt negotiations)—attempts to confine the game, that is, to restrict access to it, may also assume a more coercive character, as can be seen, for example, in the tremendous efforts of the Algiers military leaders, during the 1958 crisis, as they sought, sometimes quite brutally, to keep away from Algiers the right-wing politicians from metropolitan France who had rushed there.[47]

But the diffusion of bargaining processes also has another aspect: in contrast to the difficulties it presents to the actors, it also affords them access to some very interesting tactical maneuvers. One of the most typical consists precisely in *playing on this diffusion*, taking advantage of it, one party informing the other protagonists in a bargaining that it risks losing control, both over its own camp and over its own moves. This was, in May 1958, one of the preferred maneuvers of the military chiefs in Algiers in their lengthy bargaining with the Pflimlin government.[48] It is worth noting that the government significantly deprived itself

---

[47]Cf. Philip Williams, *Wars, Plots and Scandals in Post-War France* (Cambridge: Cambridge University Press, 1970), 146–7; Tournoux, *Secrets d' Etat*, 261–2; thus, the pro-Gaullist activists J.-B. Biaggi and A. Griotteray were expelled, followed a little later by the ex-Poujadist ones, including J.-M. Le Pen, and the Poujadist deputy Berthommier. Apparently the military chiefs in Algiers even tried to persuade Jacques Soustelle, close to General de Gaulle, not to come to Algiers.

[48]Tournoux, *Secrets d' Etat*, 264–5 and 308.

of this same tactical option when it then refrained from, even if tacitly, seeking occasional support from the Communist Party.[49]

Finally, this diffuse character of the bargaining processes also comes from some of their modalities, namely from their tacit dimension or components. In fact, we already know the main ingredients of this—the information conveyed expressively by the moves exchanged, the operation of focal points and markers, and so on—and there is scarcely any need to dwell on them. I should nonetheless emphasize two points. First, the presence of tacit components in bargaining processes warns us, when considering their importance in contexts of extended interdependence, against focusing solely on negotiations which claim to be such (whether open or covert). As a matter of fact, such negotiations, as they unfold, are always permeated with elements of tacit bargaining. Second, I should point out that, as regards this tacit dimension, the distinction between what is *intentional* activity and what is not, is, for the present discussion, only of secondary importance. Hence, in spite of their manifestly intentional character, moves such as the deployment of tanks at the gates of Paris during the derailment phase of the May 1968 crisis[50] or during the August 1953 strikes should be regarded here as elements of tacit bargaining. In the same vein, it makes little difference what were the "real motives" behind De Gaulle's trip to Baden-Baden during this same 1968 crisis—whether, implausibly, despite what many commentators say, it was a masterful piece of theater, entirely stage-managed and controlled by De Gaulle, or whether it resulted from his psychological and physical collapse—the only relevant point being its meaning as a threat (a tacit one) which emerged and imposed itself through the chaining of moves within which this very distinctive move took place.

---

[49]On the rejection of the "hardline" option, advocated for a while by Jules Moch, which, whatever he said later, did indeed involve such a tacit alliance, see Tournoux, *Secrets d'Etat*, 268 et seq.

[50]Cf. the account given by Jacques Chirac of Georges Pompidou's role during the crisis: "Leave nothing to chance. So it was the day after Charléty, when he took upon himself, and upon himself alone, the responsibility of deploying tank units at the gates of Paris: on May 29 the CGT, which had strayed from the trade-union front, marched from Bastille square to Saint-Lazare railway station, to the very fringes of the Élysée Palace. Pompidou wanted them to know, along with the Communist Party—and they knew about it straight away—that the army was there" (Jacques Chirac, "Georges Pompidou en Mai 1968," *Le Monde*, May 30, 1978); see also on this point Grimaud, *En mai fais ce qu'il te plait*, 252–3, 281–4, and Georges Pompidou, *Pour rétablir une vérité* (Paris: Flammarion, 1982), 186.

Chapter 6
Some Typical Emergent Effects

I would like now to build on these reflections by addressing some of the tactical recipes which political actors frequently turn to in critical conjunctures. Whether it be, the use of preexisting constitutional procedures, the co-optation of "disloyal" oppositions or the recourse to the "strong man" or "providential leader," the possible efficacy of such "solutions" can only be understood if they are seen as emerging effects shaped by all the traits characterizing configurations of extended interdependence.

Institutional Solutions

Given the perspective developed here, the occurrence, in numerous situations of high political fluidity, of what I shall call institutional solutions may seem likely to attract objections, and will certainly appear somewhat paradoxical. For these solutions emerge in contexts where sectoral logics—and all the institutional procedures, definitions of situations, and routines that make up these logics—have lost their hold over the actors. They thus occur precisely when their success seems least likely, in the sense that we see institutionalized social relationships apparently working quite effectively in conjunctures where we might on the contrary expect their efficiency to be seriously reduced. We can observe this kind of solution emerging in the French crises of 1934 and 1958, with the appointment as Premier of Doumergue and De Gaulle, respectively (this is, of course, a simplification, since the structure of these two solutions is more complex),[1] as well as in the French crisis of 1968, with the dissolution of the National Assembly. In these three cases, the recourse to preexisting institutional procedures resulted in stabilizing the "nature" or the "value" of the resources and lines of action deployed. That is to say, in significantly *reducing the fluidity* of the situation. Another distinguishing feature of these solutions was that they tended to impose on the protagonists issues and stakes which *channelled* their tactics, calculations, and expectations (at least the short-term ones) toward certain official and "legitimate" institutional sites. And, as a matter of fact, in each of these cases the implementation of the solution was visibly followed by a "normalization," that is, a rapid *resectorization* of the political conflict,[2] even though it is worth noting that some of the crises "resolved" in this way may—like that of 1934, and even more that of 1958— subsequently experience serious twists and turns.

Let me come now to the question at hand, namely how to identify the driving forces behind the occurrence and possible effectiveness of this type of solution. The answer lies in the properties discussed in the previous chapter, that is, in the ways in which bargaining processes work and, more generally, in the conjunctural increase in the volume of activity devoted to the definition of situations. It is quite simply a matter of acknowledging that these solutions are *negotiated* ones, that is, that they constitute points of agreement occurring in the bargaining processes observable during the historical episodes referred to above. This has the first advantage of saving us from having to look for an explanation in the performance of some mysterious institutional force deemed inherent to the procedures concerned (rather like the illocutionary power often credited to speeches), or from having to attribute everything to the intervention of some providential leader, as we will see later.

Regarding in particular the solution of 1958, the answer I have just outlined may seem, at first sight, rather banal. After all, no historian (not even any of the protagonists of this crisis) could fail to recognize that De Gaulle's investiture represented a compromise—this was abundantly clear in the very composition of his cabinet—and in this respect the same could be said of the solution of

---

[1] While the decisive element in the solution of 1934 was the resignation of the Daladier government, the 1958 solution should be analyzed as a veritable "package" of reciprocal commitments and concessions, devised as interdependent, and which involved on the one hand issues brought on by the confrontation—including, indeed, the appointment of General de Gaulle—and on the other the constitutional issues toward which De Gaulle steered the outcome of the crisis, and, above all, the conspicuous procedures implementing these commitments.

[2] The channeling of this normalization toward a distinctly "political" site is what constitutes the main difference between these solutions and certain others, like those occurring in the 1936 or 1953 episodes, which nonetheless strongly resemble institutional solutions, as regards the social conditions of their success.

1934.[3] However, this was certainly not true of other cases, like that of the 1968 dissolution, which should suffice to underline just how vital it is to take into account the *tacit* dimension of the bargaining processes. Thus, for example, it is not even certain that all the observers of the May 1968 events have fully understood the role played, in the watershed moment of 30 May, by the resort to dissolution, in the sense that they failed to grasp in what way dissolution did indeed represent a solution, and, at the same time, De Gaulle did effectively "hit the nail on the head," *in spite of* his own perception of the situation and the tactics he was favoring until the very last moment.

However, the essential point is thrown into sharp relief by a comparison between the May 24 and May 30 solutions, their respective acceptability and trajectory. In addition to what has already been said in the previous chapter, the limited acceptability of the referendum proposed by De Gaulle in the May 24 broadcast was attributable, not just to the "bad reputation" of this procedure, but even more to the fact that the prospect of the referendum offered nothing very precise or tangible to the forces of the opposition. The expectations of possible mutual gains that it raised were, for the parties involved, too unequal and, above all, too vague and uncertain (De Gaulle's resignation if the vote was lost? What would be the substance of the questions put to the electorate? How would they be formulated?). In short, the referendum *put too little on the table*, which everybody realized immediately, not least, as we already know, within the government camp itself.

It was very different with the 1968 dissolution of the National Assembly. A key indicator is that numerous opposition leaders had explicitly called for dissolution in the days before its announcement, openly contrasting its "fairness" with the alleged "manipulative" character of the referendum procedure.[4] Dissolution—

---

[3] The Doumergue cabinet was distinctive in bringing together on the one hand the leaders of the Right—notably André Tardieu and Louis Marin—a Right which might have hoped at that point to eliminate the results of the 1932 legislative elections, and on the other hand the Radicals, who had in fact been the clear target of the January–February crisis. Herriot and Tardieu were "Ministers of State"—the higher protocolary distinction among the members of the government, alongside seven former *Présidents du Conseil* (Prime Ministers), together with Marechal Pétain at the Ministry of War; on the resemblance with the Poincaré cabinet of 1926, see also the remarks of François Goguel, *La Politique des partis sous la III e République* (Paris: Seuil, 1946), 489–91. The entry of the Radicals into this *"Union nationale"* coalition— those Radicals who favored it preferred to call it a government of "truce"—was approved (in contrast to what happened in 1926) by an explicit motion of the Cadillac Committee (an ad hoc meeting of the leadership of the party and the members of its two parliamentary groups), even if the party leadership would struggle to justify once again having surrendered to the demands of those who had just lost a general election; see Serge Berstein, *Histoire du Parti radical*, tome 2, *Crise du radicalisme*, 1926–1939 (Paris: Presses de Sciences Po, 1982), 289 et seq.

[4] Dissolution was invoked, in fact, as early as May 22 in the debate on the vote of no confidence (*motion de censure*) in the National Assembly, notably in the interventions by Gaston Defferre and François Mitterrand, and in that of Robert Ballanger on behalf of the Communist deputies. It would be raised again, more vigorously, in the days that followed (see, for example, François Mitterrand's

that is, legislative elections—was, unlike the referendum, accepted almost instantaneously, notably (and very ostentatiously) by the Communist Party, while the extra-parliamentary Left proclaimed its hostility, but reluctantly anticipated that the elections would take place.[5] If this high level of acceptability was also due, as has already been suggested, to other factors such as the *credibility* of the threat contained in the May 30 broadcast, it would be wrong to ignore what allowed it to become an attractive focal point, a possible point of agreement between several of the actors who "matter," that is, the actors with which everybody has to "count." The appeal of the solution was such that each of these protagonists was able to assume that the payoffs attached to it were acceptable to those adversaries with whom they might expect to establish both competitive and cooperative relations—at least as regards the issue of the *limitation of the conflict* (before dissolution intervened, the same was true of the prospect of De Gaulle's possible resignation). Besides, this solution also had the advantage of affording these actors an anticipation of its high acceptability, thus exempting them from the need to engage in open or even tacit consultation with their adversaries-partners. The dissolution of the National Assembly thus exemplifies the type of focal point where expectations converge, because it offers opponents a chance—here I use the indigenous terminology—to "win," or at least share, power through a possible success in the parliamentary elections. As a matter of fact, in the period preceding the dissolution, everything suggested that these same opponents were entirely justified in their optimistic expectations regarding the possible results of such elections.[6] Above all, however, this solution also offered the various "legitimate" actors of the political game the opportunity of *saving face*, which is always absolutely vital in their multiple internal bargaining processes.

Furthermore, once the move had been played, that is once the dissolution had been enacted (by the way, this was one of the very rare irreversible moves

---

speech on May 26 during a demonstration at Château-Chinon, in *Le Monde,* May 28, 1968). In his declaration on May 28, François Mitterrand envisaged having recourse to legislative elections only after the designation of a new President of the Republic, that is, following the prior departure of General de Gaulle, and in the interim the formation of a provisional government to manage affairs. This radicalization should be seen as one of the effects produced by the strikers' rejection of the Grenelle agreements (the text of Mitterrand's May 28 declaration may be found in *L'Année politique 1968*, 380). Finally, it is worth noting the proposition made by Jacques Maroselli, Radical deputy for the Haute-Saône, for the collective resignation of the noncommunist—Left deputies (*Le Monde,* May 23, 1968). This proposal does not seem to have found any support among the latter.

[5]Dansette, *Mai 1968*, 328 and seq.; significantly, the calls to action issued by some sections of the student movement do not seem anywhere to have led to any serious attempts to obstruct the electoral process (Dansette, *Mai 1968*, 342).

[6]In this respect, it should also be remembered that the opposition had only narrowly failed to win the legislative elections of March 1967 and the outgoing majority had only survived thanks to votes from the overseas territories, where it won fourteen of the seventeen seats.

played during this historical episode), this solution forced the "legitimate" political personnel and those connected to them to determine their tactical orientations within a very short time span. Either participate in the elections, thereby, whether they liked it or not, contributing to the normalization of the situation by channeling mobilizations into this particular institutional site, in other words contributing to the *resectorization of the conflict*. Or refuse to "play the game," boycott the elections, thereby giving up any possible benefits that might accrue from the elections if these actually took place, and, above all, running the risk of an escalation and of assuming its costs.

A close examination of the path of the solution entirely corroborates these observations. For one thing, this again brings us back to the internal bargainings within the government camp: once the other two discussed solutions (the referendum and the Grenelle accords) were eliminated, the dissolution of the Assembly constituted the major focal point in the preoccupations and calculations of a very large section of the government camp, especially, though not only, in the prime minister's entourage.[7] In the derailment (*dérapage*) phase of the crisis—starting, as we know, on May 24—the pressure exerted by these actors in favor of dissolution was empirically indistinguishable from the elimination of the referendum option. Even at the moment of *denouement*, all the accounts agree on this point, Georges Pompidou obtained the presidential signature on the dissolution decree only by resorting to an ultimate threat of resignation, faced by a General de Gaulle who, even at this point, seemed no nearer to understanding the significance of this tactical act than he had been in the preceding days.[8]

However, there are other factors in this path which matter as much, if not more, than these internal bargaining processes. First, of course, the elimination of the other solutions, which we do not need to revisit. Second, the impact of the protagonists' tactical activity on the way the diverse focal points operate and exercise "attraction." Here we touch on a fundamental issue. In the protagonists' perceptions, expectations, and calculations, before the move (the dissolution) had been played, *several* other focal points—ranging from the resignation of De Gaulle to the formation of a Mendès France government—*competed* with the solution that actually prevailed. My point is that the elimination of these competing focal points resulted not only from the occurrence of the solution itself but also from the specific modalities of that occurrence, notably its insertion into the temporal chaining of other moves and countermoves (where the dissolution "changed

---

[7]Cf. Dansette, *Mai 1968*, 294–5, 305, 309–10 (especially as regards the "address" to the president of the Republic drawn up by the leaders of the two parliamentary majority groups after their meeting with Georges Pompidou on 29 May) and 320–1; see also Tournoux, *Le Mois de mai du général*, 254–66 and 279–80).

[8]Cf. above all the account of Bernard Tricot in *L'Entourage de De Gaulle*, ed. G. Pilleul (Paris: Plon, 1979), 318–23, as well as Pompidou, *Pour rétablir une vérité*, 192–5.

sides," so to speak). It is hard not to see here another aspect of the emancipation (or autonomization) dynamics characterizing the processes analyzed in this book. But what we see above all is that the *realization* (in the strictest sense of the word) of this solution has the unsurprising effect of *narrowing the range of what is possible* (that is, of playable moves) and thereby—because it is then operating as an objectified definition of the situation—the effect of constraining the assessments and tactics of all the actors.

This leads to a final observation: nothing of this is genuinely specific to the May 1968 institutional solution. Tacit bargainings, as well as the constraining effects of solutions, once they occur, can also be observed in cases where the solutions have a much more overtly transactional character. The same goes for the operation of focal points, a classic instance of which is worth noting. It involves a familiar phenomenon: in the 1934 and 1958 crises, from the very outset both Doumergue and De Gaulle, irrespective of any personal action or strategy on their part, already represented excellent—in terms of effectiveness—points of convergence for expectations, even if, in 1934, the solution materialized much more rapidly than in May 1958.[9] And even if, in both cases, the venerable notion of charisma loses some of its charm (but I will return to this later).

The same is also true of the dynamics of the bargaining processes underlying the emergence of these solutions. Their emancipation from the initial conditions of the confrontation is strikingly visible in that the actual solutions occurring in critical conjunctures may frequently, as is clearly the case of the 1958 solution, be located well outside the range of solutions that were initially regarded as acceptable by the major protagonists. In other words, in contrast to the assumptions of standard conceptions of bargaining processes, these solutions may emerge *outside the contractual zones*[10] of the latter—at least, as these

---

[9] The Doumergue "saliency" is of special analytical interest in that it benefited from the *precedent* of 1926, an episode in which Gaston Doumergue had played a very active role when he himself was president of the Republic; on this point, see especially Jean-Noël Jeanneney, *Leçon d'histoire pour une gauche au pouvoir. La faillite du Cartel, 1924–1926* (Paris: Seuil, 1977), 129 et seq. President Albert Lebrun had indeed been thinking for some time about this type of solution and had already quite openly "sounded out" Doumergue a few days earlier, after the resignation of the Chautemps government. Doumergue had, on this first occasion, prevaricated, protesting his advanced age (Berstein, *Le 6 février 1934*, 96; see also, as evidence of the degree of convergence between the main leaders of the parliamentary Right on this point, upstream of the *journée* of February 6, the declarations of Tardieu, Barthou and L. Marin in *Le Temps*, January 29, 1934, and the same paper's editorial of January 30, 1934). The perceived *approximate homology* between the situations of 1926 and 1934 is a key factor in the situational revaluation of the specific *political capital* that Doumergue benefited from because of his past.

[10] The contractual zone is where we should find all the outcomes that are jointly acceptable to all the participating parties. Its construction by the scholar always depends on his knowing, or being able to determine, the respective "utilities" of the parties, or, in the case of so-called convergence theories, at least their initial "utilities; see, for example, John G. Cross, "A Theory of the Bargaining Process," *American Economic Review* 55, no. 1–2 (1965): 67–94; Alan Coddington, *Theories of Bargaining*

appear to the observer before the crises, for what is perceived as negotiable or nonnegotiable is subject to very significant fluctuations, linked no doubt to the specific properties of contexts of extended interdependence, and to the autonomous dynamics of critical processes involving multisectoral mobilizations.

Is There Something Like a Prevalence of the Hidden?

Close to the issue just discussed is the assumption, advanced by Linz, of a "narrowing of the political arena" in the critical phases of, at least, certain types of political crisis.[11] Indeed, at first sight, this idea, as with the aforementioned case of institutional solutions, might seem to contradict, head-on this time, the theoretical schema developed in the present work. That alone, of course, would be reason enough to give it some attention. However, once the assumption is closely scrutinized, its interest for the analysis of critical processes clearly goes well beyond any challenge it might pose to my own arguments, for it concerns certain key aspects of extended interdependence. In fact, Linz links this image of the political arena narrowing to another idea, equally incompatible with my own hypotheses: namely that, in these situations, secret negotiations and, more generally, covert or "invisible" moves and maneuvers are especially effective. Thus, such an assumption gives us the opportunity to conduct a *critical test* of the theoretical perspective I outline here on two separate fronts.

In Linz's view, the narrowing of the political arena is supposed to occur, at least in principle, in the most acute moments (or phases) of crisis processes experienced by democratic regimes.[12] More precisely, in one of the branching points he attributes to the historical sequences of these processes,[13] when, confronted with several alternatives, some of the "leading actors" of such regimes attempt to make overtures to the "disloyal" (or, possibly, "semi-loyal") opposition, that is, the opposition which more or less openly contests the

---

Process (London: Allen and Unwin, 1968); Oran R. Young, *Bargaining, Formal Theories of Negotiation* (Urbana: University of Illinois Press, 1975), especially 131–44 and 403 et seq.

[11]Linz, *Crisis, Breakdown, and Reequilibration*.

[12]Only in principle, because several of the historical episodes to which Linz's research group sought to apply this approach clearly do not match the "pure" cases of co-optation of a disloyal opposition, as evidenced for example, by the Chilean crisis of 1971–73, during which the main co-optations attempted by President Allende and his government were co-optation of what Linz calls "neutral powers," especially the military; see Arturo Valenzuela, "Chile," in *The Breakdown of Democratic Regimes*, ed. Juan J. Linz and Alfred Stepan (Baltimore and London: Johns Hopkins University Press, 1978), vol. 4, 91, 97 et 105.

[13]This indeed corresponds to a particular form—a tree-shape variant—of the "natural history" fallacy (see Chapter 2).

institutional arrangements as well as the very foundations of the regime.[14] This, Linz correctly insists, is one of the key mechanisms of "legal revolutions," that is, ruptures which—in terms of their formal legality,[15] sometimes very loosely defined—occur within the continuing institutional framework of the regime that is disappearing. The French crisis of May 1958 offers an atypical illustration of this mechanism, atypical because the regime that resulted from the crisis was a democratic one. More typical in this respect were the Italian and German cases with the co-optation, the "legal" accession to power, of Mussolini and Hitler, and it is clearly these cases that have directly inspired Linz's sequential scheme.[16] According to Linz, the narrowing of the political arena involves the operation of several distinct components or factors. First of all, the *secrecy* of the negotiations which take place in such crisis contexts between the leaders of the regime and their adversaries, the former often believing themselves capable of limiting the influence, or even of entirely controlling their future partners. The reason for this secrecy, says Linz, is that the co-optation of a disloyal opposition is a delicate operation—if discovered, it could fail. To explore whether the operation is feasible requires its protagonists, in each of the camps involved, to be able to go against the wishes of their own supporters, that is to neutralize or short-circuit them.[17] Hence, in these critical phases, the atmosphere of suspicion that pervades the world of professional politics. Hence also the fact that many of the officials and parliamentarians of the pro-government parties—those who, at least publicly, support the regime—feel themselves *out of the political game* and see their political weight seriously reduced. Hence, finally, the significant increase in the fragmentation of political parties, a process which in fact started in earlier phases of the crisis. In contrast to this marginalization of a sizeable fraction of the professional politicians, certain "intermediaries," more or less external to traditional politics, come to play an important role in the game, especially in

---

[14] Whatever the relevance (or analytical utility) of a typology of oppositions in democratic regimes according to their degree of loyalty to democratic ground rules—here Linz applies very demanding standards (see the criteria of loyalty that he lists (Linz, *Crisis, Breakdown, and Reequilibration*, 36–7)—this kind of approach always runs the risk of substantializing the dynamics of different political forces on the sole basis of their *ideological pronouncements*, when even minimal attention would lead the scholar to identify an extreme tactical ambivalence, especially in contacts, exchanges, and collusive practices with forces that are openly hostile to these regimes; it is worth noting that this ambivalence concerns first and foremost the leaders of these regimes themselves when they feel threatened (as in the case, for example, of certain leaders of the SFIO, the prime minister and the president of the Republic in May 1958).

[15] As, for example, in the case of the transition, in 1958, between the Constitutions of the French Fourth and Fifth Republics.

[16] Linz, *Crisis, Breakdown, and Reequilibration*, 75–80; for an application of this schema to the French crisis of May 1958, see Steven F. Cohn, "Loss of Legitimacy and the Breakdown of Democratic Regimes: The Case of the Fourth Republic" (PhD diss., Columbia University, 1976).

[17] Linz, *Crisis, Breakdown, and Reequilibration*, 78.

the co-optation bargaining. Another feature of the narrowing process lies in what Linz calls the rise of "neutral powers" (without doubt an unnecessarily normative term, borrowed from Carl Schmitt)—the army, senior civil servants, or even, in parliamentary systems, the head of state.[18] This rise of neutral powers is hard to distinguish sometimes from the action of certain "interest groups" (employers' organizations, churches, trade unions, but also the army, this time as a specific interest group) which the author seems to see as the fourth component of the narrowing process.[19] However, says Linz, as co-optation of the disloyal opposition becomes an increasing possibility, these diverse interest groups will tend to distance themselves from the institutions and leaders of the regime, if only to safeguard their own organizational future. All these processes combine, in this perspective, to shift the political process from the parliamentary to another arena, *invisible* and of considerably *reduced* size, where the decisive negotiations are conducted *in secret*. One last feature: the important role played by small groups of individuals, "coteries," "camarillas" (etc.), which according to Linz explains why, in such contexts, the interpretation of the events in terms of conspiracy enjoys such wide currency.[20] All in all, for Linz the narrowing of the political arena is clearly based on an opposition between, on the one hand, the efficiency he claims for covert and tightly confined bargaining processes, where co-optation is actually negotiated, and on the other hand the supposedly much reduced weight of open moves and, more generally, of visible tactical activities, the hidden arena thus constituting a kind of *over-determining* level for the confrontation as a whole. This is, I think, a highly debatable vision of the historical episodes that Linz had in mind when advancing his assumption.

Much of the problem can, however, be dispelled quite easily. That indeed was one of the purposes of the above brief inventory of the narrowing idea's components. Actually, it is far from certain that the choice of the term "narrowing" to cover all the different processes Linz subsumes under this heading was altogether a happy one. The multisectoral location of bargaining processes, the role played in them by interest groups and "neutral powers," rather seem to suggest an extension of the political arena or, more precisely, its *opening up*, its de-compartmentalization. In the French May 1958 episode, as Linz is aware, the bargainings systematically breach the frontiers of the legitimate political arena. First, no doubt, because the co-optation was that of an extra-parliamentary leader, as, *at that moment*, General de Gaulle actually was. But, above all, because of the direct and visible intervention in the game—and in

---

[18]Linz, *Crisis, Breakdown, and Reequilibration*, 70; on all these points, Linz's perspective is in fact very close to Poulantzas's analysis of the processes of "fascisization" in Italy and in Germany (see Poulantzas, *Fascism and Dictatorship*).

[19]Linz, *Crisis, Breakdown, and Reequilibration*, 53.

[20]Linz, *Crisis, Breakdown, and Reequilibration*, 76.

the bargaining processes—of actors like the army chiefs in Algiers and, indeed, the military hierarchy and all the upper echelons of the coercive sectors of the "state apparatus" with which the Pflimlin government had been negotiating incessantly since the early days of the crisis (which gave these bargaining processes a triangular appearance—quite misleadingly, for reasons soon to be explained). The same is also true of more typical cases of co-optation of a disloyal opposition. Let me take the example of the 1922 Italian crisis. It would be somewhat hasty to see Mussolini's investiture—because, in particular, of the organizational deficiencies of the March on Rome which historians of this episode love to dwell on[21]—simply as the work of a parliamentary arena reduced to a few of its more manipulative leaders (Giolitti, Salandra, or Nitti). To dispel this image, it suffices to recall the overall configuration of bargaining processes which took place in this phase of the Italian crisis: the secret negotiations with parliamentary leaders were not necessarily any more important than those that involved, in diverse forms, often quite visible, a variety of other protagonists—not only the army, employer organizations, the church hierarchy (and even, directly, the Vatican), the Crown, but also, for instance, war veteran associations and trade unions gathered under the "protection" of d'Annunzio, that is, actors who were for the most part entirely *external to the parliamentary arena.*[22] In other words, there is nothing in these components of "narrowing"—other than the term itself—that would contradict the perspective developed in the chapters above on the dynamics of multisectoral mobilizations or the specific features of extended tactical interdependence.

It is much the same the so-called marginalization experienced, in such circumstances, by part of the traditional "political class." This marginalization is best clarified when it is referred to the effects of the conjunctural desectorization of social space. Indeed, in the *relational perspective* outlined in the present work, it is almost inconceivable that the internal relationships and resource distribution in the sectors impacted by multisectoral mobilizations could have any chance at all of remaining entirely intact. But the problem for the social sciences resides in the fact that, there is no means of predicting *in general*, that is, for every historical case, how, within a given sector, the "cards will be redealt." This is why the possible marginalization of a section of professional politicians in conjunctures involving multisectoral mobilizations—especially in the "co-optation processes"— does not necessarily have the characteristics portrayed by Linz. This can easily be verified by examining the *internal bargainings* affecting different collective actors during some of these episodes. In the case of the French 1958 crisis, it

---

[21]For example, Tasca, *Rise of Italian Fascism;* Ernest Nolte, *Three Faces of Fascism: Action Française, Italian Fascism, National Socialism* (London: Weidenfeld and Nicolson, 1965).

[22]Tasca, *Rise of Italian Fascism*, 284–96.

is no doubt commonplace to point out the importance of the internal debates of the Socialist parliamentary group, whose stance seems to have been crucial in determining the very possibility of an institutional solution, namely the investiture of General de Gaulle (this, along with other similar bargaining processes, totally rules out the image of a triangular negotiation involving exclusively the leaders of the regime, the Algiers military chiefs and De Gaulle).[23] Thus, it is difficult to accept the idea of parliamentarians being radically sidelined like so much "lobby fodder," even though closer analysis of these internal negotiations would also reveal the effects of de-objectification processes affecting internal ground rules in the SFIO and the socialist group in the Assembly, rules which indeed become, in this period, a specific issue in bargaining and tactical maneuvers.[24] Moreover this also means, on a more general level, that the possible "marginalization" of the *underdogs* and middle ranks of the "political class" depends in the end on the details in the chaining of the played moves. Would the scholar have seen this marginalization quite in the same way if by chance the socialist group had succeeded in blocking the possibility of De Gaulle's "legal" access to power? However reluctant one might be to engage in this kind of counterfactual argument, it nonetheless intimates that the characteristics of marginalization are much more nebulous and fluctuating than Linz suggests.

It still remains for us to consider the most delicate part of the "narrowing" hypothesis. This mainly concerns the conjunctural role of secret negotiations in episodes involving the co-optation of a disloyal opposition. Let me say straightaway that this role is certainly not as important as Linz claims. This for one main reason: it is hard to see how this kind of negotiation and its supposed effectiveness should somehow avoid being subject to the fundamental properties characterizing contexts of extended tactical interdependence. Of course, the actors involved in attempting to co-opt a disloyal opposition do have recourse to covert bargaining (this is evident in the nocturnal meetings between De

---

[23] For example, Cohn, *Loss of Legitimacy*, 386–8 and 397–404.

[24] While, on May 27, it was the deputies and the executive committee (*comité de direction*) of the SFIO who openly disclaimed the initiatives of some of its leaders who sought a compromise with De Gaulle (especially Guy Mollet), by adopting (112 votes to 3 with one abstention) a text strongly opposed to De Gaulle's investiture, it would be a joint meeting of the groups from both parliamentary assemblies which, thanks to the vote of the senators, allowed the leaders to win socialist backing by a slender majority (*L'Année politique 1958*, 64 and 68); but, above all, at this meeting on May 31, according to the account of Jules Moch, "Georges Guille wound up (the discussion) by winning approval for a free vote, which astonished me. For this has only happened three times, in 1920 (during the split), in 1944 (at Vichy) and in 1954 (on the European Defense Community). There was even to be a free choice whether to participate in a future government. An indicative vote produced these unorthodox decisions: out of the 151 present (deputies, senators, members of the executive committee), 77 voted in favor of the investiture and 74 against. Among the deputies who voted, 50 were against (as opposed to 117 and 62 in the two previous votes) and 41 were for (as opposed to 3, then 29)"; see Moch, *Une si longue vie*, 43.

Gaulle and the regime leaders in May 1958, as well as in the aforementioned meetings between Mussolini on the one hand and Giolitti, Salandra, and Nitti on the other). But is this enough to "validate" the narrowing hypothesis? It would mean ignoring the fact that, in critical conjunctures, covert and noncovert bargaining processes tend to become interdependent. And above all that, in these conjunctures, *the invisible does not enjoy any particular causal advantage*. Promises, threats, commitments, even secret ones, are interpreted in the light of other moves and other forms of bargaining, whether visible or tacit—the latter, as we have already seen, conveying information which is all the more credible for being largely unintentional, uncontrolled, and therefore expressive. It is this bargaining structure that reveals the social conditions of possibility and efficiency of moves which consist in actually *violating secrecy*, as in the case of the famous communiqué of May 27, 1958, in which De Gaulle, after his secret night meeting with Pflimlin (and in breach of their explicit, secret, reciprocal commitments), unveiled the very existence of these negotiations with the regime's leaders, thereby giving these same negotiations a decisive twist.[25]

Finally, it is this same bargaining structure which allows us to understand why a tactical move like the "landings" in Corsica was able to radically transform, through its expressive content, the representations of all the actors, and this despite the intentions of some protagonists (in the government camp, but also among the Algiers military chiefs) and their attachment to the legalistic definition of the situation that had hitherto been negotiated. For this reason, the "landings" in Corsica may usefully be compared with the March on Rome. From the moment the march visibly began (with the equally visible nonintervention of the army, the decision to implement a state of siege having been revoked),[26] and whatever the moods and the hesitations of Mussolini, it actually determined *perceptions of what was probable*[27]—hence the curious "lack of drama," the sense that the events were a foregone conclusion—so that the secret negotiations with the leaders of the regime suddenly appeared quite devoid of any substance.[28]

---

[25]. It is, furthermore, necessary to stress the importance of the fact that some of the main issues at stake in these exchanges between De Gaulle and the regime leaders were precisely about *public* and *visible* gestures—at stake because, so to speak, of their *expressive value*—which these leaders wished to impose on him, especially as regards the "ritual" of parliamentary investiture. One of the major concessions that De Gaulle agreed to during the course of the crisis, a concession which was certainly much more costly than he was willing to acknowledge in his own account, was to accept, "with reasonably good grace," demands which he had firmly rebuffed at the beginning of the crisis; see Charles de Gaulle, *Mémoires d"Espoir*, vol. 1 *Le Renouveau, 1958–1962* (Paris: Plon, 1970), 32.

[26] On the first phase of the March on Rome, see Tasca, *Rise of Italian Fascism*, chap. X.

[27] Here lies the main reason why this "comedy," this "march that never was" (were not the same things said of the Corsican "landings" in May 1958?), actually weighed much more heavily than the fascist leaders believed, and indeed more than historians of this episode are willing to admit (including Tasca).

[28] Tasca, *Rise of Italian Fascism*, regarding the formula of a Salandra-Mussolini government.

Thus, not only is it mistaken to conceive covert bargaining processes in these contexts as a sort of overdetermining level in the overall tactical game, but, furthermore, the above observations also lead to the conclusion that the "narrowing" assumption grossly overstates the importance, in the development of these processes, of central negotiations—those which, even when covert, have intentionally and explicitly, at least for the negotiators, co-optation as the issue at stake.

If the prominence of central negotiations is in this way deceptive for both analysts and actors, it nonetheless permits us to glimpse a residual element of the "narrowing" assumption, and way in which it might be possible to partially reformulate it—but only very partially. This consists in taking seriously that some of the central negotiations in episodes of co-optation may become the *focus of attention* for all protagonists of the crisis (look, for example, at the bargaining processes that followed the resignations of the Pflimlin government in the French case and of the Facta government in the Italian one). Such phenomena, which actually are not taken into account or analyzed by Linz, can only be understood through both the working of situational focal points and the processes which, via the exchanges of moves, govern the emergence and the pervasiveness of these points. Here lie the roots of the impression, or image, of something like a "narrowing of the political arena" which *might well* impose itself on the perceptions of most protagonists in the kind of situation discussed here (where, in addition, as with the resignations of the Pflimlin and Facta cabinets, we find *objectifications* of a "power vacuum"). In sum, this is why the analysis of critical processes would no doubt benefit by making connections between, on the one hand, the processes that the "narrowing" hypothesis addresses, but without being able to understand them, and on the other, the issue of the emergence of "charismatic leaders" in crisis contexts, even though, as we shall see, at least in the cases that interest us, this emergence is not solely due to these leaders serving as focal points.

Charismatic Strategies: De Gaulle and Mendès France

In the pages that follow, I shall focus on just one very limited aspect of the phenomena referred to by what, since Weber, has become the accepted meaning[29] of the notion of charisma.[30] More precisely, I will focus only on some

---

[29]See in particular Weber, *Economy and Society* [1921] and *On Charisma and Institution Building*, texts selected by Shmuel N. Eisenstadt (Chicago: The University of Chicago Press, 1968).
[30]I shall, therefore, be leaving aside most of the very numerous, and serious, problems raised by the whole set of works that Weber's definitions and conceptualization have inspired as regards the study

of the mainsprings of charismatic strategies observable in conjunctures of high political fluidity, "charismatic strategies" being understood here in the specific sense of the pursuit, on behalf of a given individual, of the *social "confirmation" or "validation" of his charismatic qualifications*. Or, to use a more secular formulation, of his personal capacity to offer an exit, an outlet, a solution to the crisis in which he intervenes. This was indeed the case both in May 1958 of De Gaulle and in May 1968 of Mendès France, the implementation of a charismatic strategy thus being a quite separate issue from that of the actual outcome of the confrontations in which these "candidates for charisma" emerged, that is to say, separate from the issue of their possible access to power.

This line of approach to charismatic phenomena is not entirely new. A whole sociological tradition has focused on what may be called the construction of charisma (*travail charismatique*), highlighting the "extraordinary" qualities of the gestures, behaviors and speeches whereby the charismatic leader—here scholars most usually have in mind the figure of the prophet[31]—acquires a hold over his worshippers, disciples, or followers. Though this tradition insists, quite rightly, on the *transactional nature* of the relationship between the charismatic leader and his adherents, what makes this approach inadequate for my purposes is that—following some of Weber's lines of analysis—it restricts this work of charisma "confirmation" or "validation" to the strictly *personal performances* of the charismatic leader. Now, taking into account the properties that characterize contexts of extended interdependence allows us to identify processes of validation of charismatic qualifications that are very different from those envisioned by this sociological tradition, that is, processes where validation is certainly not dependent solely on the personal exertions of the candidate for charisma. These processes thus imply a significant revision of current conceptions of charismatic strategies and, indeed, of the very content of "charisma."

Let me further clarify the perspective that this brings us to. The limitations of the traditional view of charisma construction derive from its failure to recognize the *retranslations* and the *distance* which the enforcement system characterizing the imperfect tight game interposes between the actors' moves and their

---

of the issues that the notion of charisma seeks to capture; see especially: Claude Ake, "Charismatic Legitimation and Political Integration," *Comparative Studies in Society and History* 9 (October 1966): 1–13; Peter M. Blau, "Critical Remarks on Weber's Theory of Authority," *American Political Science Review* 57 (June 1963): 305–16; James V. Downton, *Rebel Leadership. Commitment and Charisma in the Revolutionary Process* (New York: The Free Press, 1973), 372 et seq.; Robin Theobald, "The Role of Charisma in the Development of Social Movements," *Archives de Sciences Sociales des Religions* 49 (January–March 1980): 83–100; Paul Veyne, *Bread and Circuses: Historical Sociology and Political Pluralism* (London: The Penguin Press, 1990 [1st French ed., 1976]); Peter Worsley, *The Trumpet Shall Sound. A Study of "Cargo" Cults in Melanesia* (New York: Schocken Books, 1968 [2nd ed. augmented]), IX–LXIX and 266–72.

[31]See, among others, Bourdieu, "La théorie de la religion selon Max Weber" and "Genèse et structure du champ religieux."

extended outcomes—that is, here, the "validation" of charismatic qualifications. In other words, we need to relate this validation to the processes whereby specific plausibility structures develop around focal points and markers as these emerge in the exchanges of moves. In this respect, the validation of charismatic qualifications does not differ significantly from the processes which—still in critical conjunctures—produce or affect the credibility of speeches, the crystallization of images of escalation or "political vacuum," or the attraction of an institutional solution. Thus, in this perspective, the validation of charismatic qualifications may be conceived as an *emerging effect* relatively autonomous from both the personal tactical activity of the charismatic leader and the direct results of that activity.

This is precisely why charismatic enterprises such as those of De Gaulle in 1958 and of Mendès France ten years later are of crucial interest. The two enterprises first have in common one component of their plausibility structures, as already discussed above: both De Gaulle and Mendès France represent, respectively in May 1958 and May 1968, a situational focal point constraining the expectations of these historical episodes protagonists. My argument is that this component, per se, has nothing to do with the possible personal "charisma"—in the most banal sense of the word—of these eminent political figures. Of course, behind the occurrence of this phenomenon we can certainly find what is distinctive about the *political capital* of each of these two candidates for charisma. But there is every reason to think that the relevant features of this political capital—the features that allowed them to function as situational focal points—are not to be found in what many are tempted, in an essentialist mode, to see as the mechanical effects of *erratic, disrupted, or uneven biographical trajectories*.[32] Such features may, in contrast, be identified much more convincingly in the way this political capital may enable the crisis protagonists— at least the protagonists caught up in the dynamics of a mixed motive game—to anticipate the *acceptability* of these figures to significant sections of the parties placed, during these periods, in *conjuncturally offensive positions* (it is worth noting that significantly Mendès France disappears as a situational focal point after the turning point of May 30, 1968).

It would no doubt be a quite difficult operation to ascertain, for example, how far the success of General de Gaulle in 1958 could be imputed as a whole to the fact he represented a situational focal point. But it would be hard to

---

[32]It is difficult to find, in the ups and downs of public careers like those of De Gaulle or Mendès France (or, even more, Clemenceau or Pétain) any clear indicators of their marginality or their predisposition to "charisma" or "heroic leadership"—on this basis, there would certainly be a large number of serious candidates for charismatic status (see, *contra*, Stanley S. Hoffmann, "Heroic Leadership: The Case of Modern France," in *Political Leadership in Industrial Societies*, ed. L. J. Edinger (New York: John Wiley and Sons, 1967), 127–8.

deny that, in the course of the May 1958 "events," this weighed, and weighed heavily, in the validation of his charismatic qualifications. The public calls for De Gaulle emanating from actors who were neither his followers nor his political allies[33]—but this is arguably even more striking with the case of Mendès France in 1968[34]—were certainly not issued from any belief in his "extraordinary gifts" (to use Weber's terminology), nor even in the power of his oratory, but, more mundanely, from the simple *calculation*, that is to say, as we have seen above, the quite reasonable fear that, without a compromise negotiated on the basis of this particular focal point, the situation might skid out of control toward issues and outcomes that were even less predictable and, above all, much more costly. There is, in fact, nothing particularly irrational about any of this; and, similarly, the "link" which the operation of the focal point creates between the crisis protagonists has strictly nothing in common with the relationships which, according to Weber, develop between the charismatic leader and the "emotional community" of his disciples—though, of course, this certainly does not mean that this kind of phenomena will never develop around such leaders.

The key point, however, concerns the modalities whereby this kind of political capital is, as it were, *realized*, that is how it is deployed in the game, and it is in relation to this issue that the two cases considered here present configurations of validation or confirmation of charismatic qualification that are very different from those suggested by Weber. At first sight, what is the underpinning of General de Gaulle's charismatic enterprise seems beyond admissible doubt.[35] A well-established tradition locates it in the distinctive features of his "personal message," in the "magic" of his oratory, in his distant and haughty "style," and so on. Or, more precisely, in the "encounter" of these factors with "circumstances": thus, when in May 1958 the "crisis occurs, when the issue at stake is nothing less than France's survival as a nation, then the particular message of De Gaulle— that France must restore its *grandeur* by saving its singularity (*personnalité*)—

---

[33]To begin with the most striking example, General Salan at the Algiers Forum, then, on May 21 and 22, well before the "political class" swung round, Georges Bidault and Antoine Pinay (*L'Année politique 1958*, 62).

[34]An initial wave of appeals, especially from the centrist leaders like Pierre Abelin, secretary general of the Centre Démocrate (Democratic Centre, a centrist and Christian democratic party) around May 18 and 19, was followed by a larger second wave where, alongside the centrists (Jean Lecanuet), we also find figures from considerably more conservative circles such as Alfred Fabre-Luce or Jacques Isorni, cf. Alain Pellet, "Pierre Mendès France et les événements de mai et juin 1968" (Master diss., Université de Paris, Faculté de droit, 1979), 50–2.

[35]See, for example: Inge Hoffmann and Stanley Hoffmann, *De Gaulle, artiste de la politique* (Paris: Seuil, 1973); Ronald Ingelhart and Avram Hochstein, "Alignment and Dealignment of the Electorate in France and the United States," *Comparative Political Studies* 5 (October 1972): 356 et seq.; Linz, *Crisis, Breakdown, and Reequilibration*, 86; Viansson-Ponté, *Histoire de la République gaullienne*, vol. 1, 100.

strikes the most sensitive chord."[36] It is factors such as these that are supposed to explain his tactical successes. And it is defective performance and flaws in the message—as we have seen with the May 1968 case—that are supposed to explain De Gaulle's failures[37] (parenthetically, this is also where we can find one of the sources, perhaps the source *par excellence*, of the naive frenzy with which social scientists have made the internal analysis of the message, in its various forms, their preferred method of study). It would not be helpful to go into detail about the different variants of this kind of interpretation: they all fail to pick up a phenomenon which, in the framework of Weberian conceptions of charisma, is difficult to describe, or even perceive. Namely this: during *this period* of the May 1958 crisis (i.e., up until the resignation of the Pflimlin cabinet), the validation of charismatic qualifications drew the bulk of its weight and of its "social reality" from actors other than the candidate for charisma himself, and also other than his supporters or followers. In this respect, not enough attention has been paid to the reserve, the prudence, the circumspection that, at the level of his visible activities, governed the tactical behavior of General de Gaulle in May 1958, and to his relative, but nonetheless quite remarkable *silence*. Certainly, in his covert activity, as we have seen, De Gaulle made considerable personal efforts. But in public he spoke very little. The reputedly "decisive" acts amount in reality to two communiqués, those of May 15 and 27, both very brief, from a written text of course, and, as all the evidence suggests, composed with meticulous care, with cautious balance, with much calculation. As to the press conference of May 19, this was a curious exercise in seduction, whose moderation sought to reassure, to balance the effects of the May 15 communiqué, to repair the damage of what De Gaulle himself seems to have seen, *at that moment*, on May 19, as a *faux pas* or, at least, an imprudence—an inevitable one perhaps.

Furthermore, rather than some supposed "oratorical magic,"[38] what drives the validation of charismatic qualifications should be sought in the visible links,

---

[36]Hoffmann and Hoffman, *De Gaulle*, 74–5.

[37]A typical example: "During the crisis of May-June 1968, De Gaulle's charisma at first *evaporated* so rapidly that his fall seemed inevitable to many people"; then, as regards his success: "It was May 24. Six days later the charisma was *resuscitated* and chaos was overcome" (Hoffmann and Hoffmann, *De Gaulle*, 96 and 100, emphasis by MD).

[38]There is reason to suspect that the observer would be more cautious in attributing such potency to the personal performances of the candidate if, as Robert C. Tucker remarks, he was not tempted by the retrospective illusion which tends to project onto the period preceding his access to power the use the "leader" makes of institutional resources once he is in power (Robert C. Tucker, "The Theory of Charismatic Leadership," *Daedalus* 97, no. 3 (summer 1968): especially 738–42). I should add that, very often, this same illusion also works in the opposite direction, in the sense that because of a "lack of success" a whole series of other phenomena, no less "charismatic," cease to interest the historian (Jacques Soustelle in 1958, Daniel Cohn-Bendit in 1968). In the same vein, in order to avoid this sort of difficulty, it is evidently not enough to substitute the notion of "charisma" with other notions like "heroic leadership" or "crisis leadership"—thereby including political "leaders " in times of war or international crisis (Clemenceau, Pétain). Dennis Kavanagh wisely notes the extent to which an external crisis—

or even the mutual identification that emerged, in a tacit way, from the exchange of moves between De Gaulle on the one hand and the army officers and the Algiers movement on the other. Indeed, it is only with regard to these links that the May 15 communiqué—which, as we know, echoed the *"Vive De Gaulle"* blurted out that same day in Algiers by General Salan—may be described as a "decisive" singular move, despite the very negative reactions it provoked in the metropolitan "political class."[39] In this configuration of the validation of charismatic qualifications, in contrast to the prudence of the candidate for charisma, it is the Algiers camp (not without hesitation or ambiguity on the part of the military chiefs) that assumed the costs and the risks of the action, especially the ways through which De Gaulle's political capital imposed or realized itself (hence, later, the bitterness of some of those most closely involved in this endeavor).

In fact, what we are dealing with here is a kind of *indirect* charisma, a transactional one, based primarily on the *mutual calculations* of the different parties. In this sense, it is noteworthy that, in all the bargaining processes in which De Gaulle was involved during this crisis, the only issue on which he remained absolutely adamant throughout in the face of the regime leaders' demands was precisely his refusal to disavow the actions of the Algiers camp, that is disavow what was his real *charismatic base*.[40]

---

unlike contexts which bring out what Weber saw as the "revolutionary" dimensions of charisma—may leave the internal political game and the institutional framework almost entirely intact, which, it should be stressed, in the case of France was certainly not true in 1939 (of course, the situation was not the same in 1914); see Dennis A. Kavanagh, *Crisis, Charisma and British Political Leadership* (London: Sage, 1974), 36–7.

[39] Under the famous title *"Paroles malheureuses"* (unfortunate words), here is what Sirius (Hubert Beuve-Méry, the newspaper director) wrote in *Le Monde* on May 17: "Coming after the statements of General Salan who agreed to be presented to the Algiers crowd by an emissary of the *Comité de salut public* and referring only to the military chiefs around him and to General de Gaulle, the Paris proclamation could not help but be interpreted as an implicit endorsement of the Algiers revolt. The secession was thus confirmed and encouraged (. . .). General de Gaulle had to speak. And speaking as he did, he multiplied the risks and compromised the hopes of salvation that many, by force of necessity, had continued to place in him. We fear dark days ahead."

[40] This was already one of the three points raised by Guy Mollet in the public bargaining he conducted through the press from May 16 (the two other points being De Gaulle's recognition of the regular government and his respect for constitutional forms in the event of his investiture); Guy Mollet returned to it in his letter to De Gaulle dated May 25 as did Vincent Auriol in his letter of May 26 (*L'Année politique 1958*, 537–8). Finally, it also seems to have been the central issue in the meeting between De Gaulle and Pflimlin on the night of May 26—and the main subject of the disagreement that occasioned that meeting, see Tournoux, *Secrets d'Etat*, 288–9). Moreover, it would be charitable to detect in the text of the May 27 communiqué, as some of the "leaders of the regime" wished to believe and have others believe—thus making virtue of necessity—any actual sign of this disavowal (e.g., Tournoux, *Secrets d'Etat*, 299–300); it was "Operation Resurrection," planned for Paris in the days that followed, that was disavowed, albeit with nuances ("while taking account of circumstances"), the message thus, paradoxically, reinforcing the *credibility* that benefited the threat of this operation.

Broadly speaking, the Mendès France enterprise in 1968 was also, like that of De Gaulle in 1958, a configuration of indirect charisma. The two enterprises differed, however, in the nature of the personal work, the personal input or contribution they required from the candidates. The difference is all the more visible because everything was as if Mendès France had modeled his tactical behavior on that of De Gaulle ten years earlier. This is suggested by several apparently similar moves: for instance, the same recourse to communiqués (May 19, 1968), the same reluctance as regards public verbal performances, limited to the press statement of May 29, entirely read from a text, and two or three remarks made "in the heat of the moment" (notably concerning De Gaulle's announcement of the referendum on May 24) and subsequently regretted.[41] Finally, the same silences, widely noticed at the time: silence on May 14, in the National Assembly, during the debate on the university situation; silence on May 22, during the censure debate; silence again (I will come back to this later) at the Charléty rally on May 27.

The difference, on the other hand, lies in what at first sight might seem microscopic and trivial acts, a short series of *visible physical sorties*, "to be a witness" said Mendès France, in the unitary demonstration of May 13, again at the heart of the May 24 demonstrations, and finally his appearance at the Charléty rally (for which he was later severely criticized). These acts were, however, the most puzzling feature of Mendès France's *personal* input to the assertion of his charisma. In fact, unlike the conjunctural position of General de Gaulle in May 1958, Mendès France had no option but to undertake this charismatic work *directly by himself*. He did not have at his disposal a charismatic base that could perform the same role as that played by the military and the Algiers movement— despite the positions held by some activists of the Parti Socialiste Unifié (PSU, Unified Socialist Party, a small left-wing party, of which Mendès France was a member), in the student union UNEF and the SNESUP (an university teachers union).[42] In these conditions, his sorties, his public appearances should be analyzed as "functional equivalents," that is, as substitutes for what were the "load-bearing" moves in the charismatic strategy of General de Gaulle, that is, the appeals by generals Massu and Salan and the tacit identification they set in motion. In short, Mendès France was forced to put himself openly on the line. Thus, in his enterprise, the process of "validation" of charismatic qualifications was significantly different from the configuration I have described in the case of the 1958 crisis: if it too is indirect, if it too relies on the tactical activity of actors

---

[41] . Pellet, *Pierre Mendès France*, 44–5.
[42] Notably with Jacques Sauvageot, provisionally heading the UNEF, and, among others, Alain Geismar, from the leadership of SNESUP.

outside the emotional community of the candidate's partisans,[43] it can do so only by superimposing or grafting his physical presence onto the locations where the student movement is making its moves. Besides, it is highly probable that Mendès France tried, without much success, other less costly ways of validating his charismatic qualifications, as evidenced by his multiple attempts to obtain, if not appeals, then at least *public* encounters with the leaders of the "movement."[44] His resignation from the PSU on June 12, 1968, was his response to the "inertia" apparently displayed in this respect by part of the leadership of this political organization (around Marc Heurgon).[45]

Another indication of the tactical weight acquired by such physical displacements at these moments is provided by the curious but highly significant "misunderstanding" between Mendès France and François Mitterrand, the leader of the Fédération de la Gauche Démocrate et Socialiste (FGDS, Federation of the Democratic and Socialist Left, a conglomerate of left-wing noncommunist groups), concerning Mendès's act of "witnessing" on the ground on May 24, the two politicians having agreed—the day before, it seems—not to attend the demonstrations one without the other, an agreement which Mendès France thus appears to have breached.[46]

As can be seen, the perspective developed above allows us to identify, on a more general level, several serious blind spots in what has become a classic opposition in the analysis of charismatic phenomena: on the hand, the "external" social (pre)conditions of charisma (crises or wars, the despair, frustration or anxiety of particular social groups, the conductivity of certain institutional arrangements, etc.) and on the other hand, the personal qualities of the leader,

---

[43]In fact, an *Association de soutien à Pierre Mendès France* was formed on May 22, but does not seem to have been able to play a major role; it was not the same, however, with a quite sizeable grouping formed mainly around elements in the leaderships of the Confédération Française Démocratique du Travail (CFDT, French Democratic Confederation of Labour) and the PSU, that resulted in particular in a series of appeals to the former prime minister, the most spectacular of which was certainly that launched, during a press conference, by the leaders of the CFDT on May 29 (it was also this grouping which apparently attempted, with very little success at the time, to get Mendès France's name acclaimed at the Charléty rally); see Jean Lacouture, *Pierre Mendès France* (Paris: Seuil, 1981), especially 479–87, and, as a corrective to the over-complacent assessments of Mendès's reception at Charléty stadium, Labro, *Ce n'est qu'un début*, 196, as well as Bensaïd and Weber, *Mai 1968*, 184.

[44]Cf. Pellet, *Pierre Mendès France*, 42–6, who notes the ease with which Mendès managed to see the "student" leaders, Sauvageot in particular, "in private," and the reluctance encountered over any public meeting.

[45]"According to Mr. Mendès France, the leaders of the PSU have always striven to prevent any *meaningful contact* between the student leaders and himself; Mr. Heurgon, in particular, apparently did all he could to prevent Mr.Sauvageot from meeting him; Mr. Rocard replied that in fact the former Prime Minister spoke several times and at length with Mr. Sauvageot" (Pellet, *Pierre Mendès France*, 92, emphasis by MD).

[46]Pellet, *Pierre Mendès France*, 44; Lacouture, *Pierre Mendès France*, 476–9; or, for a slightly different version, Claude Estier, *Journal d'un fédéré. La fédération de la gauche au jour le jour, 1965 1969* (Paris: Fayard, 1970), 224.

qualities which are then dignified as an "efficient cause" or an "intervening variable" necessary for the crystallization, the actual appearance of charisma (the selected personal qualities will usually be specific psychological traits, idiosyncrasies of oral expression, "styles," or, as already mentioned, erratic or disrupted social trajectories).[47]

This analysis of De Gaulle's and Mendès France's charismatic strategies thus allows us to identify a field of phenomena and a type of explanation that are distinct both from the macro-sociological (pre)conditions of charisma—which, de facto, come very close to the etiological vision of crises—and from the "exceptional" qualities of charismatic leaders. This field of phenomena and type of explanation correspond to what, strictly speaking, should be seen as *situational charismas*, at least as regards the social mechanisms of the validation of charismatic qualifications.[48] While the observations presented above should not be taken as a challenge to the theory of charisma in its entirety—though admittedly, in this respect, it has been hard to disguise my skepticism—these observations have however some serious implications which, in my view, apply well beyond the frontiers of the specific historical cases examined above.

This also requires a series of conceptual shifts, of which I will offer just two examples. The first deals with a central feature of the less substantialist variants of the Weberian tradition, which see "charismatic appeal" as a transaction between the charismatic leader and his public(s), the leader's discourse revealing, expressing, rationalizing, or justifying something deemed *to preexist* in a more or less latent form in the dispositions, attitudes, or interests of a given social group or segment. However, the identification of indirect configurations of validation of charismatic qualifications obliges us, if not entirely to reverse the terms of the transaction, at least to perceive it, in contexts of enlarged interdependence, as more complex, often much less personal, certainly less controllable, and above all much more diverse in its pathways. Another broadly similar case of conceptual displacement concerns the famous "instability of charisma," which does not actually seem so very different from the volatility that, in critical conjunctures, tends to impact all definitions of situation.

Some may object that, in all this, the theoretical specificity of "charisma" risks evaporating entirely. From the perspective outlined in this book, there is nothing disturbing in that prospect.

---

[47]See in particular Ann R. Willner, *Charismatic Political Leadership: A Theory* (Princeton: Woodrow Wilson School of Public and International Affairs, "Research Monograph" 32, 1968).

[48]"Situational" is used here in its strict sense, *and not*, in the manner of Willner, to name some assumed (pre)conditions of charisma (*Charismatic Political Leadership*, 8).

Chapter 7
Regression Toward Habitus

According to one of the most widespread ideas in contemporary social sciences, crisis or critical periods are believed to open up to individuals wider ranges of choice than are available to them in routinized or stable contexts. The idea seems appealing. However, as we shall see in the following pages, this is not the whole story. In several ways, the hypothesis of regression toward habitus—of which I will sketch here only *a working outline*—challenges that kind of "liberating" vision of critical periods. As its very formulation suggests, the hypothesis pertains to the peculiar—even if only relative—inertia of the individual's dispositions resulting from his socialization process.[1]

Habitus, Habit, and "Creative Effervescence"

It might at first appear strange to relate the way individuals' behaviors and representations come up in critical conjunctures to something like the *habitus*, so close both in name and in meaning to the notion of habit. For, as we well know, nothing is so "unusual" *(inhabituel)* as behaviors in periods of "creative effervescence": all the accounts attest how "unexpected," how "extraordinary," how "incredible" they are. The individual in such situations "surprises himself"; he "discovers himself" (we have only to consider the ideal-typical example of

---
[1] The argument developed in this chapter takes as its starting point the conceptualization of the notion of habitus proposed by Pierre Bourdieu in his *Outline of a Theory of Practice*. However, the hypothesis of regression toward habitus does not suppose that habitus should be viewed as a coherent and integrated set of dispositions. On my own way of conceiving socialization processes, much closer to that of Erving Goffman, see Chapter 4.

the French May 1968 "events"), performs acts that would be unthinkable in ordinary times, and feels himself "driven" by external forces, which shatter daily routines and "burst the confines of his existence." The problem thus seems to be a serious one, and furthermore, it is easy enough to see in all this some of the phenomenal or perceptual bases of the recurrent attraction still exercised today by various psychological or psycho-sociological approaches focusing on crowds or masses.[2]

If this type of objection proves lacking in real substance, this is because the notion of habitus is devised precisely to capture not only the actors' reproduction, in their practice, of the social universes that have shaped them, but also, at the same time, their improvisation, their discovery "in the act" of novelty,[3] that is, the transformation of these universes. Let me clarify this point as briefly as possible. The notion of habitus is evidently not the only notion claiming to account for the relationships between the social world and individual behaviors and perceptions. At least in my view, what best distinguishes habitus from the rest of this family of notions is the emphasis it places on the schemas of perception, evaluation, and action which the individual internalizes or, more accurately, *incorporates* durably during his daily confrontation with the social world[4]—and which may be likened to the notion of "operation" in the work of Piaget.[5] This means that the various schemas or dispositions which constitute the habitus are at work precisely where more traditional conceptions of socialization invoke the learning or internalization of values and/or roles. Finally, just like the notion of attitude,[6] habitus cannot be directly observed: it always requires complex inference from the individual's biographical trajectory, from practices being trackable within the diverse sites of his primary or secondary socialization, or from the length of time

---

[2]For a representative example, see Serge Moscovici, *The Age of the Crowd: A Historical Treatise on Mass Psychology* (Cambridge: Cambridge University Press, 1985 [1st French ed., 1981]).

[3]See in particular Pierre Bourdieu, "Le mort saisit le vif. Les relations entre l'histoire réifiée et l'histoire incorporée," *Actes de la Recherche en Sciences Sociales*, no. 32–33 (April–June 1980): 194; but the idea is present from the very first systematic formulations of his conceptions (cf., for example, his "Postface" to Erwin Panofsky, *Architecture gothique et pensée scolastique* (Paris: Minuit, 1967), 83–4, where the habitus is conceived as a principle "which allows us to account for what was an unpredictably novel creation." Evidently, this is very far removed from the pure and simple mechanism of "reproduction" which some authors have, imprudently, attributed to it (e.g., François Bourricaud, "Contre le sociologisme: une critique et des propositions," *Revue Française de Sociologie* 16, supplément (1975): 590–1.

[4]Bourdieu, *Outline*, 87–95; see also Bourdieu, *The Logic of Practice*, 72–9.

[5]See Philippe Perrenoud, "De quelques apports piagetiens à une sociologie de la pratique," *Revue Européenne des Sciences Sociales* 4, no. 38–39 (1976): 451–70.

[6]At least in principle, because the lax usage made of this notion by social scientists leads them in many cases to directly equate attitudes with the opinions gathered by pollsters, and, by the same token, to effectively evade the task of reconstructing or specifying a "neuro-psychic state" which orients or predisposes to action.

he was exposed to these practices; or, for many authors, from his very behaviors and actions, which is not without raising some major difficulties.

However, as regards the objection under discussion, the most relevant issue is not related to this. In my view, it primarily concerns the dispositions' mobile or *transferable* character as regards the diverse situations encountered by the individual. The habitus, as suggested by Bourdieu, "operates," so to speak, through *practical substitutability* or *transferability* of a limited number of fundamental dispositions or schemas[7]—which, from my own perspective, and at least in highly differentiated societies, also means these should be conceived as heterogeneous. Because of this mobility, dispositions may generate behaviors, evaluations (assessments), and perceptions in social contexts which are not necessarily those where these very dispositions usually operate, nor, indeed, where they were originally internalized.

So invention, in this perspective, is neither the simple duplication of what has been internalized, nor the sudden and mysterious eruption, ex nihilo, of innovation. Here is perhaps what most clearly distinguishes the notion of habitus from the seemingly similar notion of attitude. For with the latter the generation of behaviors and opinions is usually thought of in a way that is simultaneously fixist and mechanistic. *Fixist*, because attitude tends then to be seen as *a* specific organized reaction to *a* specific object (foreigners, death penalty, the new government) or, more rarely, to *a* specific situation (a situation of risk, of competition, of insecurity).[8] Tellingly, the term "change of attitude" is frequently used when this reaction to a specific object changes. But *mechanistic* too, because the change of attitude is then attributed to external factors or variables—for example, huge morphological changes in society, education, or urbanization—thereby very often ignoring the processes through which internalized schemas or dispositions shape perceptions of and reactions to external transformations, and thus constitute a form of mediation governed by a *specific and relative inertia* with respect to these transformations (in my view it is precisely this inertia that constitutes the key component of the social autonomy—and the singularity—of each individual).

---

[7]Bourdieu, *Outline*, 83, and *Logic of Practice*, 94–5.
[8]For example, Gordon W. Allport, "Attitudes," in G. W. Allport, *A Handbook of Social Psychology* (Worcester: Clark University Press, 1935), 798–844 and "Attitudes in the History of Social Psychology," in *Attitudes*, ed. M. Jahoda M. and N. Warren (Harmondsworth: Penguin Books, 1966), 15–20.

Dispositions and Conjuncture

Therefore, it is easy to understand that the Bourdieusian analysis of the relationships between habitus and conjuncture has hitherto focused primarily on the question of how "appropriate," or not, a given disposition (or a given *habitus*) is to the social contexts in which it operates. A significant illustration of this is provided by Bourdieu's reflections—derived from Max Weber's religious sociology—on the conditions governing the success of prophetic speech, especially in the contrast he draws between the priest and the prophet: "Just as the priest is linked to the routine order, so the prophet is the man of crisis situations, when the established order totters and the whole future hangs in the balance."[9] What Bourdieu calls *hysteresis of habitus*—for instance, the possible misalignment *(décalage)* of habitus with the properties of a given crisis conjuncture—is perfectly exemplified in the systems of dispositions inculcated by the church as a bureaucratic institution, that is, an institution which has, on the one side, routinized, ritualized, and stabilized its work practices and its tools of religious struggle, and, on the other, has shaped its specialized personnel in the same way, thus making this personnel ill-equipped to compete, in extraordinary conjunctures, with the extraordinary speech and behavior of the prophet.

The general idea underpinning this approach is evident enough: social reproduction only occurs—and even then only tendentially—when "the conditions in which the habitus functions have remained identical, or similar, to the conditions in which it was constituted."[10] It is equally clear that this proposition has important implications for understanding the dynamics of social transformations, especially in those cases where dispositions are out of step and behaviors are "inappropriate" or mismatched as regards the "demands" of the situation, exposing their authors to negative sanctions and thus leading to a wide range of possible "adaptations," from simple resignation to outright revolt. Furthermore, I should add that nothing guarantees that we will never face conjunctures of such fluidity that even prophets cannot really find a foothold (see, for example, Daniel Cohn-Bendit in the course of the French May 1968 "events").

This is not the place to discuss the implications of this approach: its possible interest is obvious, phenomena of *hysteresis* being equally likely to manifest themselves as simple crises of *interaction*, in face-to-face relationships, as in macro-sociological phenomena like the "diffuse revolts" of social groups or even of whole generations.[11] Similarly I will not elaborate here, at least at a general level, on the fairly serious limitations and difficulties of this aspect of Bourdieu's

---

[9] Pierre Bourdieu, "Genèse et structure du champ religieux," 295–334.
[10] Bourdieu, *Logic of Practice*, 84.
[11] For example, Bourdieu, "Classement, déclassement, reclassement," 2–22.

thought, which relate, in my view, to the highly questionable, and specious, imagery about the unescapable virtues of the *"appropriateness"* of dispositions to situations. This common fallacy is in particular at work when Bourdieu refers to the "encounter" between a habitus and an "objective event," for instance with a "revolutionary" conjuncture. In a nutshell: "revolutionary" action (i.e., the "determined response" to this conjuncture) is only thought of as an effect of the encounter of the objective event with individuals already endowed with a specific type of disposition to constitute it as such—that is to say, as a "revolutionary" conjuncture.[12]

For, as a matter of fact, regression toward habitus involves a quite distinct dimension of the habitus-conjuncture relationship, a dimension which precisely tends to be obscured by the focus on the issue of the "appropriateness" of dispositions to the social contexts in which they operate. My argument is that, in "encounters" between habitus and situation, the ways dispositions (or habitus) work *are not necessarily homogeneous*. Of course, in my mind at least, dispositions tend to operate whatever the context confronting the individual and—this also contrasts with some Bourdieu's formulations—however "appropriate" or not these dispositions are to the "exigencies" of the situation. But nothing allows us to infer from all this that dispositions always have equal relevance or contribute in the same way to the generation of behaviors and perceptions: here we touch on something that is at the very foundation of the hypothesis of regression toward habitus, namely the fact that the amount of space, so to speak, provided by different contexts for the operation of dispositions may be subject to significant *conjunctural variations*. Nor, indeed, should we forget that dispositions *are not* the only determinants of behaviors and perceptions.

From the perspective developed here, what I will call *strong determination* of habitus is clearly related to the emergence of fluid conjunctures. The main mediating link is to be found in a factor which has been neglected until now in the analysis of critical processes: the *unequal inertia* of different types or species of "capital" (to use Bourdieu's terminology), some of them consisting in social relationships objectified in institutions, and some others in incorporated schemas of action and perception, that is, in internalized dispositions.[13] Now, one of the fundamental characteristics of the latter is that they are not exposed in a similar way to processes of loss of objectification which, in my view again, may affect both institutionalized social relationships and objectified representations

---

[12]On this point, see first the original French edition of Pierre Bourdieu's *Esquisse d"une théorie de la pratique* (Geneve and Paris: Droz, 1972), 185; despite a serious modification, the English translation (Bourdieu, *Outline,* 82–3), remains fully dependent on the logic of the appropriateness fallacy mentioned above.

[13]For example, Pierre Bourdieu, "Les trois états du capital culturel," *Actes de la recherche en sciences sociales* 30 (November 1979): 3–6.

of the social world. In other words, dispositions are not as vulnerable, *at least in the short term*. No doubt incorporated forms of "capital" (i.e., dispositions) may also be subject to conjunctural depreciation, for example as a result of being deployed in "inappropriate" contexts (the phenomena of hysteresis). But there is "depreciation" and "depreciation": as I have already suggested, even dispositions that are "objectively ill-adapted" to their operational contexts *still nonetheless continue to operate*, that is, to say, they continue, with greater or lesser potency, according precisely to the state of the objectification of the social world, to contribute to the generation of behaviors and representations.

That is why, even if the inertia of habitus might represent a kind of "survival of the past," "regression" should not be taken to mean either a transition to something *deeper* or more psychological in the order of determinations, or a return to a supposedly older, earlier, or, indeed, initial (*original*) state of the social system.[14] Institutions—and sadly what should be self-evident still requires frequent repetition—are *historical products*, just as dispositions or habitus are, and like them they are constantly, and indeed simultaneously, reshaped by social systems and actors' interactions. Together, through their necessary daily encounters, they constitute the "reality" of these systems (and, furthermore, it would be futile to try to establish, or even to postulate, at least in the complex systems I am dealing with in these pages, one "level" as somehow more "real" than another). Finally, both institutions and habitus, and this is the most important point for my argument, operate in these encounters with their own particular features, their uneven inertia, or, if preferred, their *specific vulnerabilities*.

I should add that, in my view, these propositions are not necessarily incompatible with the principles of the conceptions developed by Bourdieu. In fact, at least as regards the point under discussion, I see them as simple theoretical extensions of these principles. As a further indication of this, note that Bourdieu—although he expressed it rather summarily—envisaged, for any social system, the "regulation" of its different domains of practices by contrasting, on the one hand, those that seem to be "free," that is, where practices refer primarily to the habitus and its "automatic strategies," and, on the other hand, domains where practices refer to explicit ethical or legal norms backed by sanctions.[15] It matters little for my present point that Bourdieu's characterization of the so-called non-free domains—those enjoying institutional objectification—in terms of norms and sanctions alone, is far from being satisfactory, particularly because it is excessively narrow (for instance, it should include other kinds of objectification,

---

[14]For example, these imageries clearly haunt the analyses of political crises developed by Crozier and Friedberg, *Actors and Systems*.

[15]Bourdieu, *Esquisse*, 204 or *Outline*, 21 (and, for the case of societies which leave more or less space for the "automatisms" of the habitus, Bourdieu, *Logic of Practice*, 145).

besides norms and sanctions). For what interests me most about the above distinction is that it possibly suggests the idea that the "weight" of the habitus in the determination of behaviors and representations may vary according to social contexts. For this reason, the major change that needs to be made to Bourdieu's conceptions, at least as regards the point at issue, is essentially this (which, indeed, is far from negligible): to account for the generation of actors' behaviors and perceptions, we must grasp the different *states of objectification* experienced *by the same* institutionalized social relationships, *in the same* society, and thus identify the variations in the ways dispositions work or operate according to these different states, rather than thinking of them solely in terms of distinct domains of practice (supposedly "free" or "non-free," in the sense seen above), or possibly in terms of distinct societies characterized by contrasted levels of institutional differentiation.

Logics of Position, Logics of Dispositions, and Confidence in the Habitus

Taking these points on board, the hypothesis of regression toward habitus nonetheless raises some delicate issues at the level of observation. The main reason for this is that the institutional positions occupied by the actors as well as the latter conjunctural locations may become powerful sources of "blurring," making the most readily used research routines quite ineffective, even though, at the same time, the identification of these sources may help us to neutralize or circumvent their effects.

In this respect, one of the most difficult problems arises as soon as we try to discern to what extent observable behaviors derive from the institutional positions occupied by individuals, and to what extent they result from the operation of the individuals' dispositions. According to Bourdieu, what we are dealing with here is an *unconscious alignment* of positions and dispositions, a phenomenon which, in his view, should be seen as a "genuine operational principle of the institution."[16] This theoretical conclusion is pregnant with significant consequences. First, because it directs our attention toward, on the one hand, the social mechanisms whereby agents are *selected* and *inculcated* with dispositions perceived as "adapted" or "appropriate" to the institution, and, on the other hand, to the fact that internalized dispositions tend to determine, at least in routine conjunctures, the probability of access to particular types of

---

[16]Bourdieu, "Le mort saisit le vif," 11.

position (one inevitably thinks, to take a familiar example, of the educational streams and social filters that feed into the "schools of power" and the *Grands Corps* of senior civil servants in France, or, to take a radically different type of political system, that of the *nomenklatura* in the Soviet-type systems of Eastern Europe). The second implication is that it allows us to understand why it is misleading to think of the relationships between social actors and the institutional positions they hold in terms of "roles" that they "perform" or "play": these actors, when they occupy these positions, do so with precisely what they "are" (i.e., with the dispositions they are endowed with) and therefore they frequently transform, not always intentionally, the very content of these roles—which Bourdieu clearly admits.[17] Finally, the conclusion is important because, in contrast with some objectivist conceptions still in vogue, it allows us see the *actors' own contribution* to the operation of institutions, even when these are "apparatuses." This operation can never simply be reduced to a conscious submission of the actors to the "objective" or proclaimed goals of the institutions, and indeed it may even be perfectly compatible with the distance that actors may experience, and often even claim, in relation to these goals.

However, can we seriously, as Bourdieu suggests, deduce from all this, that, at least in the case of successful alignments of positions and dispositions, there is no way to discriminate, in terms of practices, between "what is caused by positions, and what is caused by dispositions imported by the agents in these positions"?[18] Clearly such a conclusion, even if it in no way undermines the hypothesis of strong determination of habitus, would somewhat hamper our capacity to draw anything at all from the empirical observation of critical processes.

First, it can surely be agreed—though this criticism of Bourdieu's conceptions is not really crucial for the point under discussion—that the mechanisms for "allocating" individuals across the diverse institutionalized positions in a complex social system are very unlikely to approach the level of perfection. In fact, one of the most powerful effects of the operation of organizations in routine conjunctures is precisely that of making actually compatible the behaviors of individuals shaped by dissimilar social trajectories and, for this reason, possibly endowed with heterogeneous dispositions (thus, for example, the coexistence of workers from rural and from urban backgrounds is certainly not an unusual social mix in "industrial" societies).

However, the core of my argument is that, even in the case of "successful" alignments, it is possible to identify, in critical conjunctures, the specific operation of dispositions. To begin, let us focus our attention on the *differential resistance*

---

[17]Bourdieu, "Classement, déclassement," 14–16.
[18]Bourdieu, "Le mort saisit le vif," 9.

of various types of institution and organization to conditions of political fluidity.[19] It is precisely from this point of view that we can consider the full sociological significance of some *technologies of organizational survival* and *tactics of "last resort."* These technologies and tactics draw on the credit which actors, through their practical knowledge—that is without fully understanding or mastering its principle (and indeed without needing to)—ascribe to something that may be seen as a sort of community of habitus or, more often, as a strong probability that certain individuals, groups, or segments of organizations will implement similar schemas of action and perception, even though these schemas may have been internalized in the course of radically different social trajectories. To take an extreme example, at the most critical, the most precarious moments of certain episodes of high political fluidity—especially when other institutions, even fully militarized ones, "buckle" or "dissolve"—the authorities often call on the services of cadets from military academies or "elite" troops (including sometimes, following a well-tried formula already mentioned above, ethnically stigmatized troops, for example "warrior" ethnic groups), and this recourse clearly cannot be explained solely by the supposed technical efficiency of such corps. This means that this kind of credit is also based on what the individuals concerned are *believed to "be,"* which admittedly does not necessarily work in favor of the established political order, and which furthermore is not exclusively a characteristic of societies that are "delayed" in their "political development."[20]

This kind of crisis recipe is, in fact, only an extreme example of a much more diverse series of technologies, all working on the basis of what I will call *confidence in the habitus*. Albeit on rather different empirical terrain from those just mentioned, an excellent illustration of this concerns the exercise by an institution or organization of what G. Lavau has called the "tribune function" (*fonction tribunitienne*).[21] In contexts of political fluidity, such an institution or organization may be confronted with the "problem" of channeling social movements toward institutional outcomes or solutions, as was the case, for example, of the French Communist Party during the strikes of 1936 or of 1968. According to Lavau,

---

[19]Which can be reinforced especially by the sector's "hardening" that may result from the implementation of crisis control technologies I examined in Chapter 4.

[20]As can be seen, to take the example of French crises, in the very unequal participation of different military units stationed in Algeria during the events of May 1958, and even more clearly during the military putsch of April 1961, cf., among others, Eliot A. Cohen, *Commandos and Politicians. Elite Military Units in Modern Democracies* (Cambridge, MA: Harvard University, "Harvard Studies in International Affairs" 40, 1978), 65–70.

[21]Georges Lavau, "Le parti communiste dans le système politique français," in *Le Communisme en France*, ed. F. Bon et al. (Paris: Presses de Sciences Po, 1969), 7–81, and "The PCF, the State and the Revolution: An Analysis of Party Policies, Communications, and Popular Culture," in *Communism in Italy and France,* ed. D. L. M. Blackmer and S. Tarrow (Princeton: Princeton University Press, 1975), 87–139.

this channeling is one of the crucial aspects of the "functional contribution" that these institutions or organizations—and here it would no doubt be preferable to speak of them having a tribune *posture* or *dynamics* rather than "function"[22]—may make to the survival of a political system. But, of course, it still needs to be achievable, and this is where confidence in the habitus allows us to perceive one of the conditions of the *tactical mobility* on which an efficient channeling strategy depends, as regards the social makeup or base of the tribune institution. If the Communist Party proved able, in several "explosive situations," as this author puts it, to "deflect revolutionary potentialities" or, at least, to contribute significantly to such a process, then this also was because its tactical mobility benefited from the massive and systematic effort devoted to inculcating and homogenizing dispositions across the membership of its "apparatus" and from all the multiple and converging procedures of selection and co-optation of its staff.[23] It is thus quite remarkable that in the course of the May 1968 crisis, with all its twists and turns, the PCF was able to accomplish with minimal cost—that is, without any serious and immediate split in its apparatus or central core—a series of sudden and spectacular tactical shifts (rapprochement with the student movement around May 10, a kind of "radicalization" after the rejection of the Grenelle agreements, and, of course, the immediate acceptance of the electoral solution). It should be added that, *mutatis mutandis*, similar analyses might be developed concerning the social mainsprings of the Polish Church's tactical activity in the successive crises in Poland since 1956, and especially that of 1980–81 (as shown, for example, by the reluctance of the Polish episcopate, and even its attempts at obstruction, at the time of the birth of the new Solidarnosc—trade union). At a more general level, one could safely enough advance the proposition that, for an organization with a tribune posture and dynamics, the less homogeneous it is in terms of the dispositions of its apparatus personnel, the more we can expect the organization, in critical conjunctures, to be ineffective as regards its tactical activities; or, in other words, the more the organization will be exposed to loss of control—both internal and external (i.e., vis-à-vis its social clientele)—in terms of the exercise of its "tribune function."

Let me give one more illustration: it is most likely that this same confidence in the habitus is also at work in the *institutional dissociation (dédoublement institutionnel)*—that is, the separation of certain components from the rest of a

---

[22]Less because of the unnecessary functionalist connotations carried by the expression "tribune function" than in order to avoid any temptation to *essentialize* the "nature" (even if conceived as a "dual" nature) of this type of organization or institution and to avoid the eternal debates as to whether their nature is "reformist" or "revolutionary"—both being indigenous categories clearly linked to substantialist visions of the social world.

[23]Cf. especially Annie Kriegel, *The French Communists: Profile of a People* (Chicago: University of Chicago Press [1st French ed., 1968]).

given institution or organization—which, in a number of political crises, as not only in Latin America in the 1970s (Argentina, Brazil, Uruguay) but also in France in 1960–61, constitute the "response" to contexts of fluidity devised by the top echelons of strategic sectors (coercive, but also administrative). The filtering of personnel, the selection of individuals conducted on these occasions (or which occur, so to speak, of their own, without the actors or observers being able to discern who is responsible) allow us to realize that these dissociations are not just about the possibility of evading the sectoral legitimate rules of the game and action repertoires. The point is that they rely on something like networks of elective affinities, most often informal (but which may also lean on clubs, alumni associations, and other forms of "society" grouping). When they reach significant proportions, these institutional dissociations tend to spill over the borders of the concerned institutions and may draw on personnel deemed "reliable"—as regards internalized dispositions—from spheres of activity only marginally related to the "legitimate" institutions (in this sparsely documented domain, think, for example, of the recruitment practices that appeared in France in parts of the coercive sectors during the 1960–62 period).[24]

Finally, the previous examples clearly show that the social mechanisms of confidence in the habitus do not necessarily require that the social trajectories and internalized dispositions of the actors involved in this type of interactions should be identical. They also indicate that these interactions tend to be facilitated in critical conjunctures by the mobility, the *transferability* of internalized dispositions. Thus, for instance, dispositions for covert activity acquired through careers in the criminal underworld may well "operate" effectively in a quite different domain of activity. This obviously constitutes another important source of the "blurring" effects identified earlier.

Actors' Conjunctural Location and the Emergence of Poles of Structuration

This is all the more significant when combined with the effects of the—often highly variable—conjunctural location of individuals endowed with similar dispositions (or habitus). Here lies the source of the impasses confronting what seems to represent an empirical ideal for substantialist approaches to the generation of behaviors and perceptions. This empirical ideal basically consists of matching up, *item by item*, on one side various "personality types," social or psychological

---

[24]Assemblée Nationale, *Rapport de la Commission d'enquête sur les activités du Service d'Action Civique* (Paris, 1982), vol. 1, esp. 181–93.

traits or disposition systems, and on the other side specific types of their supposed products, that is, opinions, attitudes, behaviors, not to mention literary works, social movements, or even events.

Now, adopting this "empirical" stance may lead, here more than elsewhere, to very serious errors. What I have in mind first are those arising from building typologies based on phenomenally heterogeneous products or outcomes, but which, as we have seen in Chapter 2, may well result from social processes that are either identical, or quite similar in composition (and *vice versa*, of course). But this kind of empirical stance also leads us to simply ignore or misconceive what behaviors and perceptions owe to the different conjunctural locations of the actors. As, for individuals (or groups, though these raise specific difficulties which I will leave aside here),[25] a given overall conjuncture will certainly not constitute the same contexts of direct interaction, with the same situational components. It will not present to them the same practical problems, challenges, dilemmas, or opportunities. Neither the incentives to act, nor the threats or pressures of the *immediate environment*, nor indeed the resources that may be personally and directly mobilized, should then be considered to be *a priori* identical or equivalent. This means that one can understand how internalized dispositions or schemas contribute to produce perceptions, assessments, calculations and behaviors only when individuals are put in the particular *immediate situations* they are actually facing, *i.e.* situations where the global trend-properties defining the overall conjuncture materialize through practical and tangible "games" and stakes. Which is also why having comparable dispositions only very rarely implies that behaviors, evaluations or attitudes in the same overall conjuncture will be similar. And what makes the analysis even more complex is that, in his own distinctive "encounter" with the event, the individual is also located by the stands he made in the course of the event, his commitments, possibly his defections, or, in other words, by his very *career in the crisis* itself (and in this respect, what appears at first sight to be extremely tiny deviations may result, in terms of consequences, in widely different locations).

These remarks cast considerable doubt on the "probative" value of procedures based on the substantialist empirical ideal and its mechanistic vision

---

[25] Including the following: (1) Because, in particular, of the weight of primary socialization in the formation of dispositions, it is impossible to postulate that, for any actual social group, there is such a thing as a community of habitus, or even that in every case the dispositions of individual members of different groups will necessarily also be radically different (cf. Paul Di Maggio, "Review Essay: On Pierre Bourdieu," *American Journal of Sociology* 84, no. 6 (1979), 1467–8); (2) above all, there is no guarantee that the fact that the members of a given group share the same dispositions should in all circumstances be a source or factor of *solidarity* between them: phenomena of breaking ranks or free-riding may well have their origins both in acquired dispositions and in the expectations these dispositions may engender as to the probable behaviors of those who are (or are supposed to be) sociologically similar.

of the correspondence between dispositions and the behaviors and perceptions produced by these dispositions. But these remarks also have a more "positive" side, in the sense that they clarify the role, in the production of behaviors and perceptions, of the conjunctural location of the actors—which in turn defines, besides those already mentioned, a series of observation sites fully relevant to the hypothesis of regression toward habitus.

Within the limits of this book, I will focus on just one of these sites, perhaps the most promising one for the analysis of critical processes. It concerns the possibility, opened up by the perspective developed above, of identifying a whole series of *phenomena of structuration* which are at work in this type of conjuncture and which feed on their dynamics.

More specifically, this may first concern the structuration of social groups themselves or, at least, of what should be seen as their *hard cores* or nucleuses, even if that means renouncing all visions that portray social groups as homogeneous entities. This was indeed one of the conclusions emerging from Luc Boltanski's analysis of the genesis in 1930s France of the group commonly known today as "*les cadres*," but whose "success" (the widespread acknowledgment within French society of the group's taken-for-granted "social reality") was certainly not assured before this period.[26] However, what is important for my own argument is something much more restricted than the history of this "success" and is focused solely on the social context of the group's birth. Boltanski attributes this birth to the political confrontations and crises of the 1934–38 period. Admittedly, as Boltanski stresses, the group's appearance at that time coincided with a multiplicity of projects springing from diverse zones of the political field, all seeking both to reassert the value of and to mobilize the "middle classes" (*classes moyennes*). Similarly, there is also no doubt that one of the purposes of these initiatives was to bring about a blurring of existing cleavages and, more specifically, a blurring of the increased sociopolitical polarization that followed the 1934 confrontations, by imposing a tripartite representation of the social world. However, once this is recognized, the fundamental issue remains to be grasped, namely how such initiatives were able to enjoy relative success, success achieved, what is more, by a hitherto unrecognized social group built around "trade-union" organizations. The fact that certain political strategists imagined and favored the emergence of a middle social bloc is obviously not enough to explain how such a phenomenon did, even partially, come into being. In the perspective I am developing here, the formation of what Boltanski tellingly calls a "pole of attraction" or "social attractor" around which the group took shape, that is, around which it objectified itself, must be related both to the strong determination of internalized dispositions characterizing

---

[26]Boltanski, *The Making of a Class.*

critical conjunctures, *and* to the specific *conjunctural location* of the individuals who would constitute this pole. In other words, two factors seemed to govern the crystallization of this social attractor. On the one hand, the similarity of the dispositions acquired by a relatively small population of engineers (and, remarkably, engineers from industry) in the course of career trajectories marked by the same *Grandes Ecoles*, by roughly similar social backgrounds, often by the same colleges (usually Jesuit), and, as regards the activists, by membership in the same professional organizations linked to *Action populaire* and to social catholicism. But also, on the other hand, the rather uncomfortable conjunctural location of these individuals during the 1936 strikes: industrial engineers found themselves, as their representatives put it, caught "between the anvil of the plutocracy and the hammer of the proletariat," that is, often abandoned and left to fend for themselves by the companies' top management, while at the same time isolated from the strikers, and even physically expelled by the latter from the occupied workplaces. This isolation, a direct by-product of the exchanges of moves and mobilizations, would henceforth combine with the effects of the establishment of new institutional arenas of employee representation—where the CGT acquired semi-official status, and where it was necessary to "make ones presence felt"—and would give the emergence of this "hard core" the shape of an engineers' union.[27] Ultimately, it was all these processes which would give "concrete reality" to strategic projects or ideologies which might otherwise easily have remained in the realm of pure social fantasy.[28]

We can first see here why, in contrast with substantialist conceptions about the engendering of behaviors and perceptions, the "syndical response" represented *at that time* by the formation of engineer unions should not be sought in imaginary dispositions or predispositions to union action, which empiricist approaches would not hesitate to detect (though some dispositional schemas, especially those acquired in militant activities linked to *Action populaire*, may well have played a significant role—especially thanks to their *mobility*). But it must also be emphasized that, in such cases, resorting exclusively to regressive, archeological, or genealogical approaches risks being counterproductive for any analysis of critical processes. After all, not every formation of a hard core necessarily results in *subsequent* social "success," in the way enjoyed by the *cadres*, that is also to say, it does not necessarily lead to the coalescence, around this nucleus, of other social segments which, even if they are less "pure," "make up the numbers." Nor indeed does it necessarily result in the institutional objectification of the social group formed in this manner. In other words, the range of "hard cores" emerging

---

[27]Boltanski, *The Making of a Class*.

[28]On strategic ideologies, see Pierre Ansart, "Idéologie stratégique et stratégie politique," *Cahiers Internationaux de Sociologie*, nouvelle série, no. 63 (July–December 1977): 223–42.

in contexts of political fluidity may well be much wider and much more diverse than we might be led to believe if we take "successes" of the groups as the starting point of our inquiry.

This is one of the reasons why we should also expect to find similar processes in the case of other social "objects" besides groups. That is, objects which apparently are as different from one another as, for example, *generations*, at least when these constitute themselves as entities endowed with some "social reality,"[29] surges of recruitment to political parties or trade unions, whose possible coincidence with political crises has already attracted the attention of political scientists,[30] or phenomena like the emergence of "intellectuals" as a political force in France at the time of the Dreyfus Affair,[31] or even like that sort of "structural" fatality which weighed heavily on the whole life of the Weimar regime, with the very peculiar political apprenticeship made by some segments of German youth though their engagement in the *Freikorps* after the 1914–18 war.[32]

As a matter of fact, the boundaries between these social objects are much more blurred than the preceding lines might suggest: thus, it is hard to ignore that the formation of the *Freikorps* was also a crucial element in structuring a "real" generation, and that the same applies to some of the "crisis" surges in recruitment.[33] But that is perhaps not the most important point. Though I cannot discuss the matter in detail here, it should be emphasized that the framework of such social entities is made of *several* poles of structuration (with the French

---

[29]Thus, these "real" generations should not be confused with the statistical and descriptive tools used in demography: age groups, cohorts, and so on.

[30]See, for example, for the waves of recruitement during various crises in France since 1934, Jacques Lagroye et al., *Les Militants politiques dans trois partis français* (Paris: Pedone, 1976); Sidney Tarrow and L. Lamonte Smith, "Crisis Recruitment and the Political Involment of Local Elites: Some Evidence from Italy and France," in *Elite Recruitment in Democratic Polities. Comparative Studies Across Nations*, ed. H. Eulau and M. M. Czudnowski (New York: Wiley, 1976), 205–37; and, for elements of a more general reflection on crisis recruitment, Lester G. Seligman, "Political Parties and the Recruitment of Political Leadership," in *Political Leadership in Industrialized Societies*, ed. L. J. Edinger (New York: Wiley, 1967), 306–7 and 313–14; Kenneth Prewitt, *The Recruitment of Political Leaders: A Study of Citizen-Politicians*. (Indianapolis: Bobbs-Merrill, 1970), 64–5, 72–4 and 93–5.

[31]Cf. esp. Christophe Charles, "Champ littéraire et champ du pouvoir: les écrivains et l'affaire Dreyfus," *Annales ESC* 32, no. 2 (March–April 1977): 240–64.

[32] . Rudolf Heberlé, *Social Movements* (New York: Appleton-Century-Crofts, 1951), 120; James M. Diehl, *Para-military Politics in Weimar Germany* (Bloomington: Indiana University Press, 1977), 23–115; Michael A. Ledeen, "The War as a Style of Life," in *The War Generation*, ed. S. Ward (New York: Kennikat, 1975).

[33]Recruitment curves based on synchronic cross-sections of party activists (e.g., based on responses collected from activists of a party at a given moment in time) have every chance of telling us as much about the "resistance" or "loyalty" of different recruitment waves—in other words, about certain forms of the presence of "real" generations–than about the actual size of these surges (see especially Lagroye et al., *Les militants politiques*, 34; and, on the different generations of Communist activists, Kriegel, *The French Communists*).

so-called generation of 1968, for example, it is easy enough to distinguish militant poles derived from the ranks of student movement organizations, or from activists in Christian youth organizations, and so on,[34] as well as a pole more rooted in *mondain* social worlds, each contributing to shape the emblems and "myths" of the generation—and this indeed is one of the sources of their irreducible ambiguity). I should add, as a final word on this, that the hypothesis presented in this chapter may help us to discern how we can give specific content to rather intuitive notions like "exposure to the event" or what Heberlé calls "decisive political experience,"[35] notions whereby scholars sometimes try to indicate the relationships between "founding events" and the emergence of the kind of social objects discussed above. Or, to put it another way, it allows us to be a little more specific about *what these "knots of events" are made of*.

---

[34]On the latter, see for example, Danièle Hervieu-Léger, *De la mission à la protestation. L'évolution des étudiants chrétiens en France (1965–1970)* (Paris: Cerf, 1973), 53–97.

[35]Or, to be precise, "decisive politically relevant experience," Heberlé, *Social Movements*, 122.

Chapter 8
Political Crises and Delegitimation Processes

This last chapter of this book takes us even further away from the directly tactical aspects of the situational logics characterizing critical conjunctures. It concerns the losses of legitimacy that take place in contexts of political fluidity. Certainly, it might seem unwise to address this kind of issue without additional precautions, for discussions on legitimizing beliefs and feelings or on typologies of forms of legitimacy are most often marked by a discouraging confusion—a confusion which it would be easy enough to show has been present ever since the very first formulations that took place in this empirical domain, that is, once again, the conceptualization outlined by Max Weber.[1]

However, it is not my purpose here to deal with this confusion, and my incursion into such a minefield has a much more modest objective, namely to identify some of the consequences of the theoretical perspective developed above for the analysis of delegitimation processes occurring in contexts of political fluidity, and thereby to dispel a little of the mystery that surrounds the omnipresence of these processes—all crises, notes Lucian Pye, are in a way crises of legitimacy.[2] More specifically, the purpose is to bring to light types of delegitimation process that standard approaches, mainly because of their etiological bias, are bound to

---

[1] See especially, besides Weber's own works, Reinhard Bendix, *Max Weber. An Intellectual Portrait* (London: Heinemann, 1960), part 3. The confusions to which I refer largely concern the inconsistencies in Weber's use of the notion of legitimacy—in particular, the oscillation between the claim to legitimacy, the principles sustaining justification of a regime, the anticipated effects of promises made by political authorities, self-justifications designed for the "fortunate" (the wealthy or the "dominants"), and, less frequently than generally admitted, belief by the dominated in the legitimacy of the domination they experience; cf., in particular, Joseph Bensman, "Max Weber's Concept of Legitimacy: An Evaluation," in *Conflict and Control. Challenge to Legitimacy of Modern Governments*, ed. A. J. Vidich and R. M. Glassman (London: Sage, 1979), 17–18.

[2] Lucian W. Pye, "The Legitimacy Crisis," in *Crises and Sequences in Political Development*, ed. L. Binder et al. (Princeton: Princeton University Press, 1971), 136–7.

overlook. Hence the advantage of starting with what seems the most coherent variant of these approaches, David Easton's ambitious conceptualization in which he aims to account for the social mechanisms constituting support to diverse "political objects."[3] This conceptualization not only incorporates most of the presuppositions and kinds of explanation at work in standard conceptions of delegitimation processes but also, as a result of its systematicity, helps reveal precisely why, in order to grasp the properties explored in the pages that follow, it will be necessary to depart from the explanatory schemas deployed by these conceptions.

The Standard Paradigm

In Easton's conceptualization, legitimacy and the problems it raises are mainly addressed by distinguishing the different forms of what he terms "diffuse support," supposedly enjoyed by any political system (or rather, as we shall see, by certain particular elements of that system). According to Easton, it is possible to obtain a high level of diffuse support or "goodwill" from the members of a political system by cultivating a deep feeling of legitimacy to the regime and the individuals who act in its name, or by invoking symbols of the "common interest," or by reinforcing the degree of identification between members and the political community.[4] In this discussion, I will leave aside the issue of the relationship between these three types of possible reaction to a deficit in diffuse support, and indeed the question of how they might be distinguished from one another at both analytical and empirical levels (a much more delicate operation than Easton seems to think). For my own argument, the only decisive point—and here Easton's perspective is fully representative of the vision provided by most contemporary authors—concerns the distinction, first, between *diffuse* support and *specific* support and, second, between several "objects" which may enjoy support (especially diffuse support) from members of a political system.

The basis of the first distinction lies in the impact of the political system's *outputs*—that is, of authoritative decisions allocating assets or goods, whether symbolic or material. Thus, in Easton's approach, between the *outputs* of a political system and the specific support—conceived as an *input* of this system—there is a causal link, a causal relationship operating mainly in the *short term*. This type of support is supposed to correlate directly to the specific satisfactions obtained

---

[3] Easton, *Systems Analysis*; see also David Easton, "A Re-Assessment of the Concept of Political Support," *British Journal of Political Science* 5, no. 4 (1975): 435–57, and "Theoretical Approaches to Political Support," *Canadian Journal of Political Science* 9, no. 3 (1976): 431–48.
[4] Easton, *Systems Analysis*, 276–7.

by the members of the political system, and generated by that system. These satisfactions, in turn, relate—at least in principle, Easton's conceptualization being sometimes rather hesitant on this point[5]—to demands (or wants) that have already been, or are expected to be, presented by the members of the system themselves, or in their name.[6] Therefore, specific support relates directly to the performances of the political system. It may be represented, using Easton's terminology, by a simple feedback loop (specific *output*–specific *input*).

However, Easton says, if a system had to rely exclusively on specific support from its members, in exchange for the advantages it affords them through its specific *outputs*, "it is doubtful that it could survive"—here is the very heart of his approach. And, at the empirical level, we can easily check how far political systems are capable—and usually they cannot do otherwise—of deferring these advantages, of not immediately satisfying all the demands addressed to them, and of requiring sacrifices from their members in this respect. Thus, the survival of these systems can only be explained by the existence of *reservoirs of support* that are independent of any short-term satisfaction of the demands made by the members of political systems, in other words independent of their daily *outputs*.[7] On the other hand, in the long term, the nonsatisfaction of specific demands seems likely to impair the reservoir of goodwill, just as—still in the long term—a flow of favorable *outputs* should, according to Easton, have every chance of increasing the volume of diffuse support enjoyed by a political system.[8]

The fact remains that, for Easton, besides durable exposure to a flow of favorable *outputs*, the main source of diffuse support is to be found in processes of socialization[9]—which, indeed, explains the orientation of his empirical research into political socialization.[10] Evidently, from this perspective, as in the case of exposure to *outputs* produced by the political system, the contrast between diffuse support and specific support seems firmly established (we already know that, according to Easton's vision, the production of specific support is assumed to entirely derive from the performances of political systems). Finally, it should be noted that this contrast directly concerns the political system's legitimacy,

---

[5]Easton, "Re-Assessment," 442.
[6]Easton, *Systems Analysis*, 268. It should be emphasized that, according to Easton, this applies even if we deviate, as he himself does, from utilitarian assumptions when explaining reactions of support or withdrawal of support by members of the system (cf. in particular: 409, note 6).
[7]Easton, *Systems Analysis*, 270–3.
[8]Easton, *Systems Analysis*, 275; see also "Theoretical Approaches," 440.
[9]Easton, *Systems Analysis*, 275; "Re-Assessment," 445–6 and 448 et seq.
[10]David Easton and Jack Dennis, *Children in the Political System: Origins of Political Legitimacy* (New York: McGraw-Hill, 1969).

which is seen by Easton as one of the two main dimensions (indeed, "the most important" one) of diffuse support, the other being *trust*.[11]

In short, in Easton's perspective, delegitimation processes are primarily conceived as particular forms of decrease in diffuse support and—not without occasional fleeting hesitations[12]—as *long-term evolutions*, with withdrawals of legitimacy reflecting a slow erosion of the feelings and beliefs that sustain the legitimacy of the regime or the authorities. They are thus supposed to be located *upstream* of the political crises they help to produce. In this respect, at the analytical level at least, two distinct paths seem to characterize these processes. First, the expectations of members of the political system may no longer, over an extended period, be met by a sufficient flow of advantages derived from the system's performances—that is, its *outputs*. Second, delegitimations may also be generated by the possible emergence of discrepancies between, on the one hand, the values inculcated in individuals during their socialization, and, on the other, either the overall functioning, the image, the apparent state of the regime, or the behavior, way of being, expressed values of the authorities (or their most visible representatives). This "paradigm," albeit with nuances and often with significant terminological differences, strongly permeates the vast majority, if not all, of the conceptions of delegitimation phenomena, even including Habermas' "critical theory."[13]

All this needs finally to be clarified from an angle that Easton now considers crucial. It concerns the identification of three distinct *objects* that may enjoy support from the members of a political system: the political community, the political regime, and the authorities, that is, the personnel occupying authority positions within the regime. The distinction is meant to reflect the substitution of a systemic perspective for the conceptions of Parsonian action theory, which, says Easton, fails to separate the issue question of legitimacy from the issue of competition between rival political orientations or lines (a form of what Eckstein and Gurr call the "liberal bias").[14] This means that these conceptions cannot, for this very reason, capture the operation and characteristics of political support—

---

[11] Easton, "Theoretical Approaches," 438; "Re-Assessment," 446–53; it is possible to see here a slight adjustment of Easton's conceptions in comparison with his earlier formulations referred to above.

[12] Easton, "Re-Assessment," 445.

[13] "A crisis of legitimacy is therefore to be predicted unless the system generates expectations which cannot be satisfied, either by available assets, or more generally by compensations that conform to the system," Jürgen Habermas, *Legitimation Crisis* (Cambridge: Polity, 1976 [1st German ed., 1973]), 74. The distinction proposed by Habermas between crisis of legitimation and crisis of motivation is in no way incompatible, quite the contrary, with the "paradigm" I am discussing here, the crisis of motivation clearly relating to the expectations, attitudes, and values—*the motivations*—inculcated by what this author calls the "socio-cultural system," and to the appropriateness of these motivations to the "needs" of the system (*Legitimation Crisis*, 74).

[14] Harry Eckstein and Ted R. Gurr, *Patterns of Authority: A Structural Basis for Political Enquiry* (New York: John Wiley and Sons 1975), 230–1.

and those of the beliefs and feelings of legitimacy as a particular form of diffuse support—we may observe in nondemocratic political systems, and indeed, more generally, in nonelectoral processes of legitimation.[15]

Beliefs sustaining legitimacy only concern two of these three objects of support: the regime and the authorities (the third object, the political community, being subject to another form of diffuse support, the identification of members of the system with this community). The "necessity" of this analytical distinction does not, however, imply an absence of interactions between beliefs legitimating the authorities and those concerning the regime: according to Easton, the case of the French crisis of May 1958 shows that the activity of the authorities, the legitimacy they were able to acquire—Easton is clearly thinking of De Gaulle—is capable of consolidating the legitimacy of the regime itself, even of largely creating it.

In this approach, the same would be equally true of processes of delegitimation: the loss of legitimacy of the American authorities (Nixon and his entourage) at the time of the Watergate scandal could easily have had repercussions for the legitimacy of the regime itself. The necessity of distinguishing the objects from one another derives simply from the fact that these types of interaction do not occur in every case, and the advantage of accepting the distinction is that it allows us, even when there is interference between the legitimacies conferred on these two political objects, to identify possible *time lags* between them, for instance with delegitimation of the regime following that of the authorities (or possibly vice versa). As for the distinction between diffuse and specific support, this perspective aims above all to allow for independent variations in these two distinct types of legitimacy, as well as in diffuse support.[16]

Let me recap the above. First of all, it is clear that, for Easton, legitimation and delegitimation processes and, more generally, the growth and erosion of diffuse support, are long-term phenomena, a feature distinguishing them from the fluctuations that may affect specific support. More specifically, phenomena of delegitimation are basically understood as factors contributing to the production of political crises (once again, an etiological perspective). A second idea inherent in Easton's whole approach, beyond the distinction between diffuse support and specific support, is the hypothesis that the level of diffuse support is crucial for the survival of political regimes and systems, whereas the same is not true of the level of specific support. Finally, there is a third, albeit less explicit, element, at least when this approach comes to dealing with the impact of diffuse support on the survival of political regimes—namely, a somewhat undifferentiated vision of reservoirs of diffuse support (at a pinch, just one per political system). This

---

[15]Easton, "Theoretical Approaches," 435–40.
[16]Easton, "Theoretical Approaches," 439–40.

remains the case even if, at the same time, Easton insists, as an antidote to the liberal bias he attributes to Parsons, on the plurality of vectors that convey diffuse support—a quite separate issue, of course.[17] Actually, it is clear that the analysis of delegitimation processes in critical conjunctures needs to examine all the above issues more closely.

Delegitimation Effects and Structural Legitimacy

I shall begin with the place of delegitimation phenomena in critical processes, which is not what standard approaches claim it to be and what Easton has so remarkably portrayed. Far from being exclusively located upstream from crises, at their source or origin, delegitimations also appear—provided we accept that we must distance ourselves from excessively narrow etiological approaches—as *products of mobilizations*, as results of their dynamics, and not only as the "causes" of some of these mobilizations or of the crises themselves. In other words, we need to reverse the logical and causal chain which, more or less explicitly, is assumed to link together these two orders of processes.

Let me be quite clear about this, however. When I stress that delegitimation processes may be *autonomous* and distinct from "withdrawals of legitimacy" assumed to represent significant determining factors in the emergence of political crises, or at least in some of them, I am in no sense suggesting that such withdrawals may never be observed in periods preceding episodes of high political fluidity. In many cases, like those of the French 1934 and 1958 crises for example, such delegitimations occurring upstream of political crises are hard to deny (even if their configuration and causal weight—as we shall see later—are much more complex than historians of these episodes suggest and even if it is very likely that they are not the only delegitimation processes impacting the trajectory of these crises). Nor would I wish to deny that, upstream of certain other political crises, there may well have been a low level of diffuse support or legitimacy, without, however, it being possible to identify a delegitimation process, in the strict sense of the term. Indeed, on occasions, political systems may well face very serious crises without having been able, upstream of these crises, to build up, whether on behalf of the regime or the authorities, reservoirs of diffuse support that could be considered—from Easton's perspective—as "sufficient" (the French crisis of 1947, as we shall see, strongly resembles this configuration).

---

[17]Easton, "Theoretical Approaches," 434–41.

That said, the only point I wish to establish at this stage is that, alongside those that may possibly (*and only possibly*) occur upstream of crises, delegitimation effects also emerge *in the course of* the crises themselves, as integral components of the latter. And then they appear not only in a different place than standard conceptions assume but also with a *tempo* and a *sensitivity* to the exchanges of moves that are more like what Easton sees as characterizing the fluctuations of specific support rather than the rhythm and short-term independence from *outputs* that he attributes to diffuse support erosion processes. As I have already suggested, these particular features directly relate to processes of de-objectification of social relationships resulting from the dynamics of multisectoral mobilizations. Evidently, the perspective I am outlining here requires, at a theoretical level, a series of serious reorganizations or transformations in the way the social sciences conceive the operation and the very stuff of legitimation, and, indeed, delegitimation processes occurring in complex political systems.

But it also requires, this time at an empirical level, finding a way to observe these autonomous processes of delegitimation (which I will call *induced* delegitimation effects of the first type) and, more particularly, a way to isolate them from withdrawals of legitimacy located upstream of critical conjunctures. Or, to be even more precise—and this will amount to a *critical test*, that is, a test for deciding between several competing theoretical perspectives—it means being able to identify one or more cases of crises where a significant and sudden delegitimation process can be detected in the actual course of the crisis, and this without any discernible loss of legitimacy occurring, as supposed in standard conceptions, upstream from the crisis.

Here is why the French "events" of May 1968 are of such interest for my argument. As a matter of fact, the massive delegitimation which suddenly struck both the authorities and the regime—and which, as I have already said, was part of a much wider and much more multifaceted process of de-objectification perfectly matches with the configuration just described.[18] Thus, if we choose to look at the indicators used by most social scientists—Easton included—to assess the level of legitimacy or diffuse support, we would search in vain for any trace,

---

[18]It is the combination of a culturalist bias—May 1968 as a simple duplication of the Paris Commune—with the fallacy which consists in interpreting the whole historical episode solely in terms of its outcomes (the victory of the outgoing majority at the June legislative elections), a type of retrospective illusion already discussed (see Chapter 2), that leads a number of overhasty observers to seriously underestimate the importance of these processes in the provinces. Available opinion polling data only allows us to conclude that there was a *delay* in de-objectification processes in the provinces as compared with Paris, and this only in the first two weeks of the crisis (see in particular *Sondages* 30, no. 2 (1968): 71–93); on the scale of "participation" in the events in the provinces, at least in towns with more than 50,000 inhabitants, see Philip E. Converse and Roger Pierce, "Basic Cleavages in French Politics and the Disorders of May and June 1968," paper at the 7th World Congress of Sociology, Varna (1970), which relies on investigations conducted after the "events" and focus primarily on participation in street demonstrations and strikes.

in the period preceding the crisis, of withdrawals of legitimacy that might have affected the reservoir of diffuse support enjoyed by the regime or the authorities. This is true, in particular, of the opinion poll indicators favored by virtually all the authors who tried to "apply" or check Easton's hypotheses at an empirical level.[19] Whatever the problems posed by the use of this type of data, and there is no need to recall them here,[20] the indisputable fact is that, without any exception, *all* the indicators point to the same conclusion. Whether it be the indicators of adhesion to the institutions of the Fifth Republic and the principles governing their operation,[21] or the indicators of global "satisfaction" with the authorities, for example the president of the Republic or the head of government,[22] much more difficult to handle than is generally thought (especially as concerns the issue

---

[19] It is impossible to mention them all here; the following are among the most typical: Paul R. Abramson and Ronald Inglehart, "The Development of Systemic Support in Four Western Democraties," *Comparative Political Studies* 2, no. 4 (1970): 419–42; Jack Dennis, "Support for the Institution of Elections by the Mass Public," *American Political Science Review* 64, no. 3 (1970): 819–35; Arthur H. Miller, "Political Issues and Trust in Government: 1964–1970," *American Political Science Review* 68 (September 1974): 951–72; Edward E. Muller and Thomas O. Jukam, "On the Meaning of Political support," *American Political Science Review* 71 (December 1977): 1561–95.

[20] It should be noted, however, that these problems, often difficult to solve, go well beyond those commonly raised by the unconditional devotees of this kind of approach—that is the representativeness of polling samples, the choice of *items*, the selection of statistical significance tests (etc.). The problems also concern what is most uncontrollable, often blind, in these procedures, notably the fact that they often produce nothing more than simple artifacts, so that we no longer know what we are measuring when we measure; or, to be more specific, in the domain that concerns the above discussion, the fact that the we pass automatically, most often without realizing it—or sometimes without wishing to—from statements about individuals' opinions to statements about their attitudes, seen as *predispositions to action*, and even to propositions about their actual behavior (sometimes coyly dressed up under the heading "potential," for example the "potential for protest," for "violence" or for "aggressive political action").

[21] For example, in the polls conducted by Institut Français d'Opinion Publique (IFOP), the proportion of replies in favor of an equal or greater role for the president, which was 53 percent in January 1967 (and of 45 percent in October 1962), rose in March 1968 to 60 percent; see IFOP, *Les Français et De Gaulle* (Paris: Plon, 1971), 105, and, as concerns the polls conducted between March 25 and 30, 1968, *Sondages* 33, no. 2 (1971): 17.

[22] About the "popularity index" of General de Gaulle (which, from January 1968 to the end of April, saw the number of "satisfied" rise from 53 percent to 61 percent; see in particular *Sondages* 30, no. 2 (1968): 9, and 16, for the prime minister). Equally significant are the responses to a question in a poll conducted by IFOP in the week from April 9 to 16, 1968, that is, two weeks before the "eruption" of the crisis: 67 percent of individuals polled considered that the return to power of General de Gaulle after May 13, 1958, "had been a good thing" and only 14 percent "a bad thing," with 19 percent not responding; another remarkable point in the distribution of responses is that those who declared themselves, in the same poll, to be electoral supporters of the Fédération de la gauche (FGDS, a conglomerate of noncommunist left-wing organizations led by François Mitterrand) regarded De Gaulle's return to power as "a good thing" in the ratio of 50 to only 25 percent taking the opposite view, and among self-declared Communist Party voters there was also a majority of 43 to 39 percent; see *Sondages* 30, no. 2 (1968): 11–12. These results may be compared to those of a poll in June 1958, just after De Gaulle's investiture, in which his return to power was considered "a very good thing," "a lesser evil," or a "very bad thing," respectively by 54, 26, and 9 percent of those polled; *Sondages* 20, no. 4 (1958): 3.

of distinguishing variations in diffuse support for the authorities from specific support), in every case it is impossible to detect any negative evolution upstream of the "May events." Furthermore, I should emphasize that this whole set of indicators had stabilized *durably* at a relatively high level, much higher, anyway, than that achieved by similar indicators under the Fourth Republic between 1946 and 1958.

This conclusion is also confirmed if, instead of opinion poll data, we resort to other types of indicator, for example the extent to which institutions were openly contested by the opposition forces. In fact, it is in the period preceding the May 1968 crisis that the opposition leaders—at least those who, right from its birth, had fought vigorously against the Fifth Republic (and had condemned it precisely as "illegitimate")—began quite openly to embrace the regime, adapting to what seemed increasingly inevitable, and indeed to what seemed to please their electorates.[23] This evolution, as has often been noted, would substantially modify their constitutional thinking and the ground rules of their alliances. In the end, far from being an admissible indicator of any delegimation of the regime or the authorities, the admittedly relative (and above all unexpected) success of the opposition—the Left opposition in particular—at the 1965 presidential election and at the 1967 legislative elections weighed at least as heavily, if not more, in the acceptance of these institutions, as the actual "constraints" of the political game which are usually supposed to have been its main factors (i.e., the two-ballot majority voting system and the election of the president of the Republic by universal suffrage).[24]

If the fact that we can thus find induced delegitimation effects, in a sort of pure state, is sufficient to shatter the empirical foundations of etiological perspectives (though we should not forget that these effects do not always appear with this degree of "purity"), it nonetheless remains to extract some of its theoretical implications. Of course, the key point lies in the link I have already established between induced delegitimation effects and de-objectification processes at work in fluid conjunctures, that is, in the understanding of such effects as particular forms of these processes.[25] This clearly implies that the argument developed here

---

[23]See, for example, Olivier Duhamel, *La Gauche et la Ve République* (Paris: PUF, 1980), esp. 254–5 and 336–42.

[24]To use these successes as "proof" of the delegitimation of the regime or the authorities is seriously to misinterpret them, and is analogous to the mistake (albeit a more openly objectivist one) which consists in underestimating the (actually impressive) scale of delegitimation processes at work in the course of the May 1968 "events" on the basis of the election results of June 15 and 23, 1968—results occurring, as we have already seen, in a conjuncture that was significantly transformed in relation to the one in which these processes first emerged.

[25]For reflections fairly congruent with my own perspective, see especially Berger and Luckmann, *Social Construction*, 110, who analyze processes of legitimation essentially as "second order" objectifications of meanings, "first order" objectifications being represented by the institutionalizations themselves.

is based on the premise that legitimacy and processes of legitimation in general have a very different "texture" (certainly richer and more complex) than that ascribed to them in the etiological paradigm. In other words, this means that they cannot be reduced to their *normative dimension*, that is, the appropriateness of the characteristics or operation of political institutions, and the visible behaviors or social attributes of the authorities, to the values or "legitimate" expectations resulting from durable and supposedly coherent learning processes (i.e., socialization processes).[26]

On reflection, all this entails a genuine reorientation in the analysis of legitimation processes. This reorientation should aim first at giving full credit, at least as regards complex social systems, to what might be seen, borrowing Luhmann's terminology, as their "procedural aspect." This means emphasizing that induced delegitimation effects largely relate to the *self-legitimation* produced and reproduced in and by the routinized operation of the large bureaucratic organizations that, in Luhmann's view, are characteristic of modern social systems[27] — indeed, in my own perspective, self-legitimation is inseparable, as regards routine conjunctures, from the objectification that sectoral logics enjoy and the social hold they exert. But, perhaps more importantly, the reorientation I outline here involves a *theoretical decoupling* of delegitimation processes from their normative dimension, so that it becomes possible to think of the former without the latter. For the recognition by members of a political system of the legitimacy—or the "appropriateness" or "suitability"[28]—of its institutions or of the authorities is not necessarily based on legitimate expectations inscribed in their "personal convictions" or, a fortiori, expressed by their "voluntary acceptance."[29] Finally, beyond this, the reorientation developed here aims at shifting the theoretical focus away from the diversity of principles and values underpinning claims to legitimacy—indeed, it is in this diversity that Weber's taxonomic approach is primarily anchored—toward the examination of what day by day

---

[26]For an excellent example of this theoretical logic being pushed to some of its extreme conclusions (animal learning processes as paradigm for the development of political legitimacy), Richard M. Merelman, "Learning and Legitimacy," *American Political Science Review* 60, no. 3 (September 1966): especially 549–52.

[27]Niklas Luhmann, *Legitimation durch Verfahren* (Darmstadt and Neuwied: Luchterhand, 1978 [1969]), especially 27–37. While it must be noted that Luhmann does not seem to have broken entirely, far from it, with the etiological paradigm (at least as regards delegitimation processes), it is not this (unnoticed) aspect of his conceptualization that has drawn objections from his critics, but rather the political philosophy that the latter attribute to him; see in particular Claus Mueller, *The Politics of Communication. A Study in the Political Sociology of Language, Socialization and Legitimation* (Oxford: Oxford University Press, 1973), 136–42, and Habermas, *Legitimation Crisis*.

[28]Cf. the definition of legitimacy proposed by Lipset, *Political Man*, 64, which is, in fact, not very different from Easton's ("The conviction on the part of the member that it is right and proper for him to accept and obey the authorities," see *Systems Analysis*, 278).

[29]Luhmann, *Legitimation*, 34.

contributes to *sustaining legitimacy* (to use a somewhat risky but apt phrase), that is toward some much more trivial and extra-normative social processes or "mechanisms."[30]

I should add that, in my view, all this is merely one specific face of a wider dimension, which might be called—I borrow here an expression of Easton's work, though using it in an entirely different way[31]—the "structural" dimension of legitimation processes (or "structural legitimacy") in social systems characterized by a multiplicity of differentiated and more or less autonomous sectors, an additional important feature of this structural dimension being the gains in objectification resulting from the collusive intersectoral relationships that such systems experience.

Crises in Collusive Transactions and the Political Economy of Consent

Thus the attention that should be attached, when dealing with delegitimation processes, to the social location of diffuse support or legitimacy and, more generally, to the varied configurations assumed, in complex social systems, by what might be called the political economy of consent (the expression comes from Luhmann).

In light of this, two issues seem to raise serious difficulties. The first involves the implications—both theoretical and empirical—of approaches conceiving reservoirs of diffuse support as homogeneous or undifferentiated entities, a view broadly endorsed by Easton. The second issue is about the contribution of legitimacy or of diffuse support to the survival of political regimes. Easton, it will be remembered, considered this contribution to be absolutely decisive—admittedly along with the overwhelming majority of social scientists. On both

---

[30]This is why, in addition to the issues I will address below (which concern the social distribution of reservoirs of diffuse support), the reorientation I propose needs to also take account of the *cognitive* dimension of legitimation processes; see also Berger and Luckmann, *Social Construction*, 111.

[31]Easton introduces the notion of "structural legitimacy" when trying to discriminate between three types of sources of legitimacy, which he supposes to be ideology, personal legitimacy, and finally structural legitimacy, the latter conceived as an "autonomous belief in the validity of the structure and norms of the regime," which Easton distinguishes from the underlying principles of a regime, that is, ideational (ideological) or moral principles to which the members of a system may also be attached). So "structural" legitimacy, as in the case of "personal" legitimacy, is defined by the *object* benefiting from the belief, and not by the way this legitimacy is produced. In Easton's perspective, this "structural" legitimacy is only a "source" when it comes to thinking about the autonomous effect of *beliefs* legitimating the structures, that is, to say, the fact that it can by "extension" (for all his denials, here Easton draws, by reversing it, on Weber's concept of "routinization of charisma") benefit the authorities, those who hold positions of authority (Easton, *Systems Analysis*, 286–8 and 298–301).

issues, Easton's theoretical construction and its attendant perspectives have been conclusively contested, but from a significantly different angle from the one I will adopt here. This series of objections has been largely based on the "discovery," in the 1970s, of phenomena embodying the decline in diffuse support or legitimacy of authorities and regimes in pluralist political systems, and, above all, the development of what were referred to as political attitudes of "cynicism" or "withdrawal," especially in the North American electorate. These phenomena, which many have been tempted to categorize under the tenuous heading of "political alienation," have proved to be trends or fluctuations that were, at least apparently, disconnected from any sort of destabilization of, or challenge to, political regimes, and were therefore seen as incompatible with the conceptions systematized by Easton.[32] By identifying several highly diverse types of public, they called into question the undifferentiated vision of reservoirs of diffuse support. In a remarkable in-depth study, Wright has thus distinguished, alongside the social segments characterized by attitudes of consent (*consenters*) and of dissidence (*dissenters*), publics defined by attitudes of neutrality or assent (*assenters*)—assent having its essential roots in the political *under-organization and under-representation of these publics, as well as their low proficiency* in what makes up political knowledge and their lack of interest in politics.[33] Indeed, the very scale of this phenomenon—the "assenting half"—seems quite incompatible with the idea that a sufficient, a "minimal" level of diffuse support or legitimacy is a necessary condition for the survival of regimes. Hence the reversal of Easton's perspective: far from having as its condition a sufficient level of diffuse support, the survival of regimes is more likely to depend on the existence of publics, social segments, groups, or reservoirs of *assenters*, and this would considerably reduce the explanatory power of legitimizing beliefs and feelings.

To a large extent, this conclusion seems acceptable. Especially since works like those of Wright tend also to suggest, even if it is far from being their major concern, that the only legitimating beliefs, the only reservoirs of diffuse support that are really indispensable to the survival of political regimes, are located in "elites" or *establishments*—then deemed "strategic" in this respect, for example the military or economic establishments.[34] In fact, this is not an entirely new idea. Albeit associated with conceptions which still give too much weight to the normative dimension of legitimacy, it has been expressed very clearly by

---

[32] See notably Jack Citrin, "Comment: The Political Relevance of Trust in Government," *American Political Science Review* 68, no. 3 (September 1974): 973–88, and above all James D. Wright, *The Dissent of the Governed, Alienation and Democracy in America* (New York: Academic Press), 1976, which includes an extensive discussion of the interpretations of these phenomena, at least as regards the United States.

[33] Wright, *Dissent of the Governed*, 267 et seq.

[34] Wright, *Dissent of the Governed*, 269.

Stinchcombe: "A power is legitimate to the degree that by the virtue of the doctrines and norms by which it is justified, the power holder can call upon sufficient other centers of power, as reserve in case of need, to make his power effective."[35] As Jean Leca points out, this definition has in common with Easton's conceptions that it rejects any opposition between legitimation as manipulation "from above" and legitimation as beliefs producing consent, or "legitimacy from below."[36] But at the same time I think it is possible to detect within it a crucial shift away from Easton's conceptions since the reservoirs of diffuse support or legitimacy are no longer seen as undifferentiated and unified entities.[37]

However, in my own perspective, this shift has a much more specific basis and a far-reaching significance. It refers primarily to the multisectoral structuration of complex social systems and to its consequences, in particular those concerning the objectification of each particular sector. To put it in another way, this means that in such systems the political economy of consent is never entirely independent of the intersectoral transactions occurring within them. And the point is that ignorance of the location of reservoirs of diffuse support in several differentiated sectors inevitably leads one entirely to disregard some important types of delegitimation effects—which, indeed, could also be termed "induced effects" in as far as they are (just like those analyzed above)—*products* of mobilizations and, of course, distinct from delegitimation processes occurring "upstream." The specific feature of these effects is that they tend to emerge and strengthen whenever mobilizations involve the crisis, erosion, or collapse of collusive transactions within intersectoral consolidation networks (e.g., within the "state machinery").

In view of the above, it becomes clear just how much, in critical conjunctures, the internal structure of delegitimation processes differs from what the standard paradigm describes. And how much more diverse and complex are the configurations these processes may assume.Thus, processes of this kind—the *induced effects of the second type*—do not always arise with the same intensity in all the crises that interest us here. They play only a relatively secondary role in the unfolding of the French May 1968 "events," where no major manifestations of the erosion or collapse of collusive transactions between the main strategic sectors, in particular between the militarized and the governmental sectors, took place (in fact, on the contrary, it was the very visibility of these transactions that

---

[35]Stinchcombe, *Constructing Social Theories*, 162.

[36]Jean Leca, "Réformes institutionnelles et légitimation du pouvoir au Maghreb," *Annuaire de l'Afrique du Nord* 16 (1977): 4.

[37]As Wright rightly observes (*Dissent of the Governed*, 67), if Easton does not entirely ignore this fragmentation (he does note the special role, in political exchanges, of "relevant members" or those who "count"), this has no impact on his analysis of diffuse support and its fluctuations (see Easton, *Systems Analysis*, in particular 222 and 229).

De Gaulle, whether deliberately or not, played on during the crisis derailment phase). These effects also constitute the most important feature contrasting, at least as regards delegitimation processes, the episodes of the French crisis of 1947 from that of 1958, even though the two cases share, upstream of the crisis, the characteristic—admittedly more acute in the second case than in the first—of a relatively low level of diffuse support for the regime (provided that, for the purposes of the discussion, we agree to conceive this support in global terms). It is, incidentally, this feature which precisely distinguishes both these cases from the 1968 "events." The crisis of 1958 represents a typical configuration of the collapse of the mutual recognitions that the sectors' consolidation is made up. This is not, on the other hand, the case of the 1947 episode, even if it is not necessarily an easy task to empirically discriminate between induced effects of the first and the second types, and even if—as we will soon see—the reason why collusive transactions remained intact in 1947 *is not* to be found exclusively, or even mainly, in the legitimizing beliefs or feelings of the agents located in the strategic sectors.

In actual fact, the evolution of reservoirs of diffuse support under the Fourth French Republic is much less understood than is generally believed. The only extensive study devoted to the subject, that of Steven Cohn, reached conclusions that were somewhat unexpected and rather different from those I have just outlined. Cohn's conclusions may be summarized as follows: the regime of the Fourth Republic enjoyed from the outset, including the year 1947, a relatively high level of legitimacy, with the main erosion in support located in the period 1949–52 (curiously, in my view, because this was not only a period of consolidation for the regime—which "held on" during the 1947–48 events—but also a period when the oppositional political forces began to decline or even crumble). After this erosion, the level of diffuse support is described by Cohn to have stabilized, and, only on the eve of the 1958 crisis, just before January, increased, albeit at a limited scale and intensity.[38] Interesting conclusions indeed, but rather fragile. Cohn's entire demonstration relies mainly on opinion poll data, without any attempt by the author to control or even corroborate them by other types of indicator or empirical material. The main sets of data leading Cohn to the above conclusions are twofold. The first is the evolution of the "satisfaction" ratings of successive heads of government, where Cohn, for unconvincing reasons, selects the highest rating and the rating at the beginning of each prime minister's term in office; this has the effect (among others) of leading him to overlook the phenomena of short-term erosion of support, their scales, and their rhythms. The second indicator is based on three surveys conducted respectively in October 1947, February 1952 and January 1958, which included questions about the regime of the Fourth Republic.

---

[38]Cohn, *Loss of Legitimacy*, 101.

The problem here was the obvious heterogeneity of the questions asked each time, so that the comparison of levels of regime "legitimacy" measured in this way is deprived of any significance (1947: "In your opinion, should the Constitution be revised?" and "Would you be pleased to see a center party emerging between the communists and the RPF?"; 1958: "If there was a military uprising, what would you do personally?"; finally, in 1952, the questions concerned the choice between reforms and revolution, and whether or not the respondent would approve a forcible seizure of power in "certain circumstances" by the party for which he votes). While, as far as this issue is concerned, there would be no point in looking any further at Cohn's work in detail, it is worth noting that, as regards the 1947 crisis, the combined use of these indicators had the effect of seriously *overestimating* the regime's reservoir of legitimacy. While, as far as this issue is concerned, there would be no point in looking any further at Cohn's work in detail, it is worth noting that, as regards the 1947 crisis, the combined use of these indicators had the effect of seriously *overestimating* the regime's reservoir of legitimacy. A merest glance at the birth conditions of the Fourth Republic, that is, at the difficult gestation of its Constitution, especially at the outcomes of the two referenda it required, should have been enough to alert the author to the huge distortions resulting from his indicators. The first referendum (May 5, 1946) gave a negative vote, an extremely rare result in procedures involving the popular ratification or legitimation of new constitutional arrangements following a radical constitutional break. The second one (October 13, 1946, on a substantially amended project) was adopted by a narrow majority of just over 53 percent.

Although in the case of the 1958 crisis, Cohn's conclusions are scarcely more convincing, they do nonetheless indicate that in this respect things are perhaps not so straightforward as historians of this episode suggest. In fact, most of the latter simply infer, in a circular way, that the institutions of the Fourth Republic had undergone a real and intense delegitimation process *upstream* of the crisis, this on the sole basis of the slowness and relative weakness of public manifestations of support *in the course of the crisis* itself. Thus, they not only fail to understand that this inference posits a dubious equation between beliefs and actual behaviors but also deprive themselves of any chance of detecting the actual emergence of an induced delegitimation process. In other words, Cohn's work, despite its deficiencies, has the virtue of revealing that until the eve of the 1958 crisis, until the very first visible signs (i.e., signs visible to the actors themselves) of a significant loosening in the routines of intersectoral consolidation, the data commonly used to measure the level of diffuse support (especially those that Cohn uses as his first indicator) were far from uniformly registering any dramatic fall.[39]

---

[39] Cohn, *Loss of legitimacy*, 97–8 and 137–8.

In other words, the identification of delegitimation effects resulting from crises in collusive transactions has, as its primary consequence, to call further into question the role of the social mechanisms invoked not only by homogenizing or undifferentiated views of reservoirs of diffuse support but also by approaches that localize the production of diffuse support exclusively in exchanges between the political system and its environment—especially, whatever Easton may think of this equation, in electoral mechanisms and in the opinion polling practices which now accompany them in most democratic political systems. While it may admittedly not be wrong to discern, in the latter, actual processes of legitimation of political regimes or authorities, it should nonetheless be emphasized that these processes are definitively *not the only ones* at work in this type of system, and, most importantly, that delegitimation processes occurring in critical conjunctures cannot be attributed solely to fluctuations affecting these mechanisms.

The identification of delegitimation processes resulting from breakdowns in collusive transactions has two further consequences. The first, consistent with the aforementioned analyses on the diversity of publics (*assenters, consenters, dissenters*), pertains to the link that Easton posits between the level of diffuse support and the survival of regimes. While, in this respect, it is important to avoid the trap of seeing crisis in collusive relationships as a *necessary*—or even a *sufficient*—condition for the collapse of a regime (a sort of reversion to the logic of the natural history approach), it is nonetheless true that a massive fall in the "global" level of diffuse support, in the sense defined above, such as we can observe in the French case of October–November 1947, does not necessarily mean that the regime cannot possibly survive.[40] In other words, crises in collusive transactions could well be, on occasions, just as, if not more, dangerous for the survival of regimes than declines in the global reservoirs of diffuse support below the level deemed "sufficient" or "minimal."[41] The other implication is of a quite different kind: if we accept all of the above, it also follows that democratic

---

[40] It is remarkable that the regime, on the one hand, faced as it was with Gaullist successes at the October municipal elections and the demand—provoked by this success—for the dissolution of the National Assembly (highly problematic in constitutional terms) and confronted simultaneously, on the other hand, by a powerful strike wave, was nonetheless able to undergo, and overcome, almost at the height of these strikes, a ministerial crisis caused by the resignation of the Ramadier government on 19 November (see, among others, Jean-Pierre Rioux, *La France de la Quatrième République*, vol. 1, *L'ardeur et la nécessité* (Paris: Seuil, 1980), 178–86); in opinion polls, the "popularity" of Ramadier fell from 50 percent "satisfied" in March 1947 to 19 percent in September, see *Sondages,* December 1, 1947: 242.

[41] In Easton's perspective—which in this respect is narrowly *etiological*—we have no way of knowing, even roughly, where sufficient or "minimal level" lies; in fact it is simply inferred from the survival of the regime. Conversely, the level will be deemed insufficient as soon as it becomes clear that the regime has collapsed. On this aspect of Easton's theoretical model, see Dobry, *Sociologie des crises politiques,* 56–60.

systems are not the only ones, far from it, whose political institutions or authorities are vulnerable to processes of delegitimation.

To bring this issue to a close, let us return to the complexity of delegitimations, as we can see when the analysis takes account of all aspects of the structural dimension of legitimation processes at work in highly differentiated systems. In this respect, three remarks will allow me to complete the above observations, and, more importantly, to indicate in which directions further exploration needs to be pursued.

The first is about the relationships which develop, in critical conjunctures, between, on the one hand, the mechanisms that standard approaches regard as constituting global reservoirs of diffuse support and, on the other hand, the gains, the added value in objectification and legitimation generated through the working of collusive transactions. I would simply wish to point out that these relationships can be very variable, the most interesting configurations seeming to lie in possible time lags between the two types of process. The case of the confrontations culminating in the French *putsch* of April 1961 is very illuminating in this respect, the massive success of the January referendum on Algerian self-determination (approved by 75 percent of voters) having acted as a powerful brake on the development of a very serious crisis of collusive transactions.

The second remark is perfectly in line with what I have just said. The issue at stake is that it should be borne in mind that—this time contrary to one of the main assumptions behind Stinchcombe's definition of legitimacy—legitimizing beliefs and feelings are not necessarily the exclusive, nor even the principal mainsprings of the preservation or persistence of collusive relationships between governmental sectors during at least some of the French crises examined above. Thus, in the case of the 1961 crisis, there is little doubt that the reason the referendum results worked in this direction (i.e., the preservation of these relationships) was because of their impact on the perceptions and assessments of *what was probable*, rather than through some reactivation of internalized values. And it is not even certain that the persistence of collusive relationships in 1947, which may seem quite surprising in retrospect, was not also largely the by-product of the peculiar configuration of cleavages experienced in this crisis, with the regime being attacked on two fronts simultaneously, and consequently large segments of the coercive sectors not openly switching to the Gaullist opposition for fear of weakening the regime as it faced the vigorous Communist offensive of autumn 1947.[42]

---

[42]For a clear indication of the occasionally alarmist perceptions of the situation in government circles, see President Vincent Auriol's account in his *Journal du septennat,* tome 1: *1947,* in particular 485 and 521.

This brings me to a final observation. If it is true that the political economy of consent at work in the 1947 and 1961 crises is best grasped—when we want to understand the relative persistence of collusive transactions during these historical episodes—more in terms of the *calculations* of *dissenters* or *assenters* than in terms of the legitimating beliefs and feelings of *consenters*, then the hypotheses of Wright referred to above require a quite significant amendment. It consists in that *assenters* may well originate not only from lower or dominated social groups but also among those located in the upper echelons of strategic sectors. For example, such was, and sometimes still is, the case in many democratic political systems, of significant segments of the army officer corps or even of senior civil servants—as reflected quite clearly in the openly nondemocratic values that, at least in certain periods, these social segments may espouse. The fact is that all of this is more general in scope and applies as well to collusive transactions at work in non-democratic systems.

Conclusion

"The value of all morbid states is that they reveal, as through a magnifying glass, certain conditions which, though normal, are difficult to see in the normal state." When I first sketched out the broad lines of the present work, I believed it might be possible to turn this passage from a posthumous fragment of Nietzsche — stripped of its underlying medical analogy — into a guiding principle for understanding political crisis processes.[1] In these phenomena, I then expected to discern the "moments of truth" *par excellence* of a society, the moments when its different components — social groups, institutions, organizations, generations, and, of course, individuals — would present to the outside observer not only their "innermost" features, their "secrets," their weaknesses, but also their most unsuspected resources, in a word their deepest "inner beings."

(1) I soon abandoned the idea that critical conjunctures might exhibit this kind of "clarity." Not that the idea was absurd, and some of the conclusions of this book even seem to point in this direction. For instance, contexts of political fluidity may indeed provide the best "experimental" conditions for observing the dispositions (or practical schemas) internalized by individuals, and particularly for observing the transferability of these dispositions. And, in a somewhat different vein, it could be said that it is only in periods when collusive transactions between different state sectors collapse that we are able to fully grasp their strategic role in the functioning of the "State." It would be easy enough to add further examples to the above, but that would be a pointless exercise. For there is no doubt that "facts" are no less *opaque* in fluid conjunctures than they are in routine action contexts. And, from the social sciences point of view, the very resistance of these

---

[1] I first discovered this passage in Geneviève Bianquis's French translation of *The Will to Power* (Friedrich Nietzsche, *La volonté de puissance* [Paris: Gallimard, vol. 1, 1937 (1901)], §533), and this precise wording fed my reflection. This is why the above passage is taken from Bianquis's text. I had not fully realized at that time how much *The Will to Power* was nothing other than a shameful and artificial montage. Fortunately, as can easily be checked, Bianquis's translation of the quoted passage perfectly corresponds to the text of the German edition by Colli and Montinari which restored the posthumous Nietzsche's fragments of in their original configuration (Friedrich Nietzsche, *Werke: Kristische Gesamtausgabe*, ed. par Giorgio Colli et Mazzino Montinari (Berlin: W. De Gruyter, 1967), vol. 14.

facts to investigation is, in the case of fluid conjunctures, so systematic and recurrent that, as we have had occasion to note, it is hard to ignore.

(2) Above all, to adopt Nietzsche's idea would be to overlook an essential achievement of this work, namely that the properties of critical states experienced by complex social systems cannot in any way be reduced to a "magnification," even a distorted one, of the features characterizing their routine states. What the continuity hypothesis enables us to grasp is precisely that these critical states correspond to distinctive structural configurations, *different* from the structural arrangements specifying routine periods. What is true of the "structures" is also true of the tactical dimension of crises, that is of the moves exchanged. These are subject, in terms of their effects or performance, to the "laws of transformation" at work in contexts of extended interdependence. Finally, this difference is even to be found in the calculations of the actors themselves. The individual is probably no more and no less rational in a fluid political context than in a "stable" one. It is simply that both what I have called structural uncertainty and the situational logics that govern the individual's assessments, perceptions, acts, commitments, and evasions mean that calculations are carried out in significantly different ways from those we find in contexts where the individual and the group rely on anticipation tools and reference points that are both familiar and institutionalized.

(3) Just as political crises are not primarily moments that magnify the "normal" features of the societies in which they occur, neither are they purely and simply moments of "historical repetition." Everyone knows the opening pages of Marx's *Eighteenth Brumaire*, and, of course, no-one would deny their considerable evocative power.[2] However, it would be wise not to overload Marx's observations with theoretical scope and meaning. The properties identified and analyzed in the present study provide insight into the reasons why his observations could only capture the "surface," so to speak, or, at best, only a limited aspect of the phenomena referred to by the image of "repetition." Where Marx's observations are indeed relevant for the understanding of critical processes is in the emphasis they place on the various poorly named forms of "survival of the past" which seem to lie at the very heart of social upheavals. In my view, one of these forms should be understood in terms of the "webs of meaning," the cognitive stocks on which actors are forced to draw when confronted by a conjuncture of structural uncertainty, where they are deprived of the routine means of anticipating and assessing situations. It may also be worth pointing out another aspect of "repetition," which, I believe, may be related to the tendency of regression toward the habitus that characterizes contexts of fluidity. To be more precise, the rather curious phenomena of *role-taking* (*investissements de rôles*), which can be observed in such contexts—thus, in the French May 1968 "events," one

---

[2] Karl Marx, *The Eighteenth Brumaire of Louis Bonaparte* (New York: International Publishers, 1883).

fancies himself as Tocqueville in 1848 and the other as Lenin in 1917—should be thought of, in the perspective developed in this book, as genuine *projective tests* bringing to light some of the processes involving the mobilization and transfer of an individual's dispositions or schemas of action and perception. But we should be wary of an overhasty universalization of Marx's observation. The assumption of roles from the past is most probably just one type of possible "response" by individuals to fluid situations; among other types of response, one of the most interesting for the present discussion is *self-personification*, where the individual adopts the role of himself (in the style: "I am De Gaulle, what would De Gaulle do in this sort of circumstances?"), a reflexive—and somewhat strained— relationship toward one's own identity, which gives the notion of "role" a rather unexpected place in the analysis of crisis contexts.[3]

(4) However, the main difficulty with the image of "repetition" (as indeed with the idea of crisis as a "moment of truth" of the society which experiences it, a "revelation" of the "deep reality" of this society) is that it leads us to ignore the *autonomy* of the dynamics of fluid conjunctures identified in this work—its emancipation from precisely what, in the etiological approaches, is supposedly located *upstream* of the crises themselves. We should expect to find this dynamics, even as a mere trend, irrespectively of the "causes," "motivations," or "determinants" specific to the competing mobilizations that are the core constituents of each particular case of crisis, provided these mobilizations emerge simultaneously in several sectors of the relevant societies.

(5) Furthermore, we should expect to find this dynamics in a range of phenomena going well beyond the historical episodes that we usually call "political crises." One of the major, perhaps the most important, implications of the theoretical perspective developed in the pages above is that it invites, and in fact requires, a *redefinition of the field of phenomena* that social scientists address. Many social processes which everyday language (and the scholarly works that espouse its demarcations) regards as distinct or different from one another actually involve the very same multisectoral mobilizations, the same collapses of collusive transactions, the same conjunctural transformations of intersectoral relationships that we find in what is called "political crises," whatever the specific outward form (*allure phénoménale*) of these processes. Such is the case, for example, of *strike waves* and the intervention of industrial

---

[3]A phenomenon which recalls the fine analyses that Goffman has made of self-personification in situations that are certainly more ordinary, but where "normal appearances" have collapsed. An individual faced with this type of situation may be led to "suddenly manipulate, in a conscious fashion, routines which had become automatic over time, unconscious, and as a result he has the impression that he is staging a play, a performance, a production"; see Goffman, *Relations in Public*.

conflicts in what Pizzorno calls "political exchange."[4] But it is also the case of phenomena that have been much less explored, like *political scandals*. These bizarre phenomena—which, for want of any real theoretical grip, social scientists have generally avoided addressing head-on, such as the great *"affaires"* which peppered the life of the French Third and Fourth Republics, and indeed that of the Fifth as well—can only be understood once we begin to discern behind (and, in a way, "within") the anecdotal, their multisectoral location. It has sometimes been observed that scandals emerge at the intersection points of money and power, with money bringing its pressure to bear at the exact point where "real authority" lies—this point varying according to the regime.[5] But there is no serious reason to believe that "scandals" only occur where money and power intersect. Thus, if I confine myself to mentioning just some of the "great" French scandals, like the *"Affaire des fiches"* (secret files, 1904), the *"Affaire des généraux"* (1949) or the *"Affaire des fuites"* (leaked documents, 1954), the "Ben Barka Affair" (1965) or that of the *Rainbow Warrior* (1985), all clearly concern "intrusions" other than those involving money (it is of course interesting also to note that the "intersection points" are often located in transactions between the different sectors that constitute the "state machinery"). However, beyond the "scandalous acts"—which in reality involve quite commonplace transgressions of sectoral norms and logics—it should be stressed that the destabilizing properties of so many scandals must be seen as directly related to the interferences of sectoral logics, and to intrusions or infringements that undermine the autonomy of the affected sectors, which the scandals simultaneously "reveal" and *realize*. In short, as directly related to *the multisectoral mobilizations which these scandals consist of*. Thus, it scarcely needs adding that certain more or less culturalist interpretations are entirely mistaken in claiming that French society, or its political system, has a peculiar "propensity" for scandals.[6] This propensity can indeed be systematically found in all systems characterized by multisectoral configurations—we have only to recall recent episodes in the political life of the United States, Italy, Japan, or Federal Germany, with their reputedly very contrasting (political) cultures. And, moreover, it is significant that, entirely in line with the perspective developed here, we can also observe such scandals in political struggles inside authoritarian systems as different from Western democracies as that of the USSR.

(6) For the dynamics identified in this book should be expected to emerge in every society whose "architecture of complexity" closely resembles multisectoral configurations. This raises one of the issues that this work has merely touched on

---

[4]Alessandro Pizzorno, "Political Exchange and Collective Identity in Industrial Conflict," in *The Resurgence of Class Conflict in Western Europe since 1968*, ed. C. Crouch and A. Pizzorno (Basingstoke: Macmillan, 1978), vol. 2, 277–98.

[5]René Rémond, "Scandales politiques et démocratie," *Etudes* 336, no. 6 (June 1972): 849–64.

[6]For example: Williams, *Wars, Plots and Scandals*, 3–16.

and which deserves to be addressed for its own sake: Are democratic systems the only ones that, in Smelser's terms, are "structurally conductive" for multisectoral mobilizations? Are these systems alone, in other words, in experiencing a multiplicity of sectors? It would, to say the least, be highly imprudent to reply in the affirmative to this question, and it might indeed be pointed out that the unfolding of the crises taking place in a number of contemporary authoritarian systems (e.g., the countries of Eastern and Central Europe) clearly display all of the features whereby I have characterized the dynamics involved in multisectoral mobilizations.

This is why the dividing line between political systems, the one that is relevant to the theoretical argument developed here, does not coincide with the distinction opposing democratic and nondemocratic systems. From this perspective, there is therefore no reason to think that democratic systems are, by their very "nature," more vulnerable than others.

Bibliography

This bibliography includes only a part of the works and materials that I actually used. All these works, but a few exceptions (namely the English translations of books I originally read in other languages), were published before January 1984, when I defended the doctoral dissertation this book is derived from.

Abramson, P. R. and R. Inglehart. "The Development of Systemic Support in Four Western Democracies." *Comparative Political Studies* 2, no. 4 (1970): 419–42.
Adam, G., F. Bon, J. Capdevielle, and R. Mouriaux. *L'Ouvrier français en 1970*. Paris: Presses de Sciences Po, 1970.
Adams, R. N. *Energy and Structure. A Theory of Social Power*. Austin: University of Texas Press, 1975.
Agassi, J. "Methodological individualism." In *Modes of Individualism and Collectivism*, edited by J. O'Neil, 185–212. London: Heinemann, 1973.
Akamatsu, P. *Meiji 1868. Révolution et contre-révolution au Japon*. Paris: Calmann-Lévy, 1968.
Ake, C. "Charismatic Legitimation and Political Integration." *Comparative Studies in Society and History* 9, no. 1 (October 1966): 1–13.
Alinsky, S. *Rules for Radicals*. New York: Random House, 1971.
Allison, G. T. *Essence of Decision, Explaining the Cuban Missile Crisis*. Boston: Little Brown, 1971.
Allison, G. T. and M. H. Halperin. "Bureaucratic Politics: A Paradigm and some Policy Implications." In *Theory and Policy in International Relations*, edited by R. Tanter and R. H. Ullman. Princeton: Princeton University Press, 1972.
Allport, G. W. "Attitudes." In *A Handbook of Social Psychology*, edited by G. W. Allport, 798–844. Worcester: Clark University Press, 1935.
Allport, G. W. "Attitudes in the History of Social Psychology." In *Attitudes*, edited by M. Jahoda and N. Warren, 15–20. Harmondsworth: Penguin Books, 1966.
Almond, G. A. "Determinacy, Choice, Stability, Chance: Some Thoughts on Contemporary Polemics in Political Theory." *Government and Opposition* 5, no. 1 (1969–1970): 22–40.
Almond, G. A. "Approaches to Developmental Causation." In *Crisis, Choice, and Change*, edited by G. A. Almond, S. C. Flanagan, and R. J. Mundt, 1–42. Boston: Little, Brown, 1973.
Almond, G. A., S. C. Flanagan, and R. J. Mundt, eds. *Crisis, Choice, and Change*. Boston: Little, Brown, 1973.
Ambler, J. S. *The French Army in Politics*. Columbus: Ohio State University Press, 1966.
Ansart, P. "Idéologie stratégique et stratégie politique." *Cahiers Internationaux de Sociologie* 63, nouvelle série (July–December 1977): 223–42.
Apter, D. E. *The Politics of Modernization*. Chicago: The University of Chicago Press, 1965.
Archibald, K., ed. *Strategic Interaction and Conflict*. Berkeley: University of California Press, 1966.

Aron, R. "Macht, power, puissance; prose démocratique ou poésie démoniaque?" In *Etudes politiques*, edited by R. Aron, 171–194. Paris: Gallimard, 1972.
Aron, R. *Clausewitz, Philosopher of War*. Translated by Christine Booker and Norma Stone. Englewood Cliffs: Prentice-Hall, 1985 [1st French ed., 1976].
Assemblée Nationale. *Rapport de la Commission d"enquête sur les activités du Service d'Action Civique*. Paris: Moreau, 1982.
Auriol, V. *Journal du septennat, 1947-1954*, volume 1, *1947*. Paris: Armand Colin, 1970.
Austin, J. L. *How to do Things with Words*. Oxford: Oxford University Press, 1962.
Aya, R. "Theories of Revolution Reconsidered. Contrasted Models of Collective Violence." *Theory and Society* 8, no. 1 (1979): 39–99.
Bachelard, G. *Le nouvel esprit scientifique*. Paris: Presses Universitaires de France, 1934.
Bachelard, G. *Le Rationalisme appliqué*. Paris: Presses Universitaires de France, 1966 [1949].
Bailey, F. G. *Stratagems and Spoils. A Social Anthropology of Politics*. Malden: Blackwell, 1969.
Balladur, E. *L'Arbre de mai*. Paris: Jullian, 1979.
Bauer, A. *Essai sur les révolutions*. Paris: Giard & Brière, 1908.
Baumgartner, T., W. Buckley, T. R. Burns, and P. Schuster. "Meta-Power and the Structuring of Social Hierarchies." In *Power and Control: Social Structures and Their Transformations*, edited by T. R. Burns and W. Buckley, 215–88. London: Sage, 1977.
Behrang [collective pseudonym]. *Iran, le maillon faible*. Paris: Maspero, 1976.
Béjin, A. "Crises des valeurs, crises de mesures." *Communications*, no. 25 (1976): 39–72.
Beloff, M. "The Sixth of February." In *The Decline of the Third Republic*, edited by J. Joll. London: Chatto and Windus, 1959.
Bendix, R. *Max Weber. An Intellectual Portrait*. London: Heinemann, 1960.
Bensaïd, D. and H. Weber. *Mai 1968: une répétition générale*. Paris: Maspero, 1968.
Bensman, J. "Max Weber's Concept of Legitimacy: An Evaluation." In *Conflict and Control. Challenge to Legitimacy of Modern Governments*, edited by A. J. Vidich and R. M. Glassman, 17–48. London: Sage, 1979.
Berger, P. E. and H. Kellner. "Arnold Gehlen and the Theory of Institutions." *Social Research* 32, no. 1 (1965): 110–15.
Berger, P. E. and S. Pullberg. "Reification and the Sociological Critique of Conciousness." *History and Theory* 4, no. 2 (1965): 196–211.
Berger, P. E. and T. Luckmann. *The Social Construction of Reality*. London: Penguin Books, 1971 [1966].
Berstein, S. *Le 6 février 1934*. Paris: Gallimard-Julliard, 1975.
Berstein, S. *Histoire du Parti radical*, tome 2, *Crise du radicalisme*, 1926-1939. Paris: Presses de Sciences Po, 1982.
Binder, L., et al. *Crises and Sequences in Political Development*. Princeton: Princeton University Press, 1971.
Blau, P. M. "Critical Remarks on Weber's Theory of Authority." *American Political Science Review* 57, no. 2 (June 1963): 305–16.
Boltanski, L. *The Making of a Class: Cadres in French Society*. Translated by Arthur Goldhamer. Cambridge: Cambridge University Press, 1987 [1st French ed., 1982].
Bonnel, V. E. "The Uses of Theory, Concepts and Comparison in Historical Sociology." *Comparative Studies in Society and History* 22, no. 2 (1980): 156–73.

Boudon, R. "Mai 68: Crise ou conflit, aliénation ou anomie?" *L'Année Sociologique* 19, third series (1968): 223–42.
Boudon, R. *The Unintended Consequences of Social Action*. London: Palgrave Macmillan, 1982 [1st French ed., 1977].
Bourdieu, P. "Postface." In Erwin Panofsky, *Architecture gothique et pensée scolastique*, 135–67. Paris: Minuit, 1967.
Bourdieu, P. "Genèse et structure du champ religieux." *Revue Française de Sociologie* 12, no. 3 (1971): 295–334.
Bourdieu, P. "Une interprétation de la théorie de la religion selon Max Weber." *Archives Européennes de sociologie* 12, no. 1 (1971): 3–21.
Bourdieu, P. "Les modes de domination." *Actes de la Recherche en Sciences Sociales*, no. 2–3 (June 1976): 122–32.
Bourdieu, P. "La production de la croyance: contribution à une économie des biens symboliques." *Actes de la Recherche en Sciences Sociales* 13 (1977): 3–43.
Bourdieu, P. *Outline of a Theory of Practice*. Translated by Richard Nice. Cambridge: Cambridge University Press, 1977 [1st French ed., 1972].
Bourdieu, P. "Classement, déclassement, reclassement." *Actes de la Recherche en Sciences Sociales* 24 (November 1978): 2–22.
Bourdieu, P. "Les trois états du capital culturel." *Actes de la Recherche en Sciences Sociales* 30 (November 1979): 3–6.
Bourdieu, P. "Le mort saisit le vif. Les relations entre l'histoire réifiée et l'histoire incorporée." *Actes de la Recherche en Sciences Sociales* 32–33 (April–June 1980): 3–14.
Bourdieu, P. *Questions de sociologie*. Paris: Minuit, 1980.
Bourdieu, P. *Distinction: Social Critique of the Judgement and of Taste.* Translated by Richard Nice. London: Routledge & Kegan Paul, 1984 [1st French ed., 1979].
Bourdieu, P. *The Logic of Practice*. Translated by Richard Nice. Stanford: Stanford University Press, 1990 [1st French ed., 1980].
Bourricaud, F. "Contre le sociologisme: une critique et des propositions." *Revue Française de Sociologie* 16, supplément (1975): 583–603.
Bracher, K. D. *The German Dictatorship. The Origins, Structure and Consequences of National Socialism*. Translated by Jean Steinberg. Hardmondsworth: Penguin Books, 1978 [1st ed. in German, 1969].
Braudel, F. "Histoire et sciences sociales: la longue durée." *Annales ESC* 13, no. 4 (October–December 1958): 725–53.
Braudel, F. "Histoire et sociologie." In *Traité de sociologie*, edited by Georges Gurvitch, 83–98. Paris: PUF, tome 1, 1960.
Brinton, C. *The Anatomy of Revolution*. New York: Vintage Books, 1965 [1938].
Buffelan, J. P. *Le complot du 13 mai 1958 dans le Sud-Ouest*. Paris: LGDJ, 1966.
Camus, G. *L'état de nécessité en démocratie*. Paris: LGDJ, 1965.
Certeau, M. de. *La prise de parole. Pour une nouvelle culture*. Paris: Desclée de Brouwer, 1968.
Charles, C. "Champ littéraire et champ du pouvoir: les écrivains et l'affaire Dreyfus." *Annales ESC* 32, no. 2 (March–April 1977): 240–64.
Chazel, F. "La mobilisation politique: problèmes et dimensions." *Revue Française de Science Politique* 25, no. 3 (1975): 502–16.
Chiroux, R. *L'Extrême Droite sous la Ve République*. Paris: LGDJ, 1974.
Citrin, J. "Comment: The Political Relevance of Trust in Government." *American Political Science Review* 68, no. 3 (September 1974): 973–88.
Coddington, A. *Theories of Bargaining Process*. London: Allen and Unwin, 1968.

Cohen, E. A. *Commandos and Politicians. Elite Military Units in Modern Democracies*. Cambridge, MA: Harvard University Press (Harvard Studies in International Affairs, no. 40), 1978.
Cohn, S. F. "Loss of Legitimacy and the Breakdown of Democratic Regimes: The Case of the Fourth Republic." PhD diss., Columbia University, 1976.
Cohn-Bendit, D. *Le Grand Bazar*. Paris: Denoël-Gonthier, 1978 [1975].
Coleman, J. S. *Community Conflict*. New York: The Free Press, 1957.
Coleman, J. S. "Race Relations and Social Change." In *Race and the Social Sciences*, edited by I. Katz and P. Gurin, 274–341. New York: Basic Books, 1969.
Collier, R. B. and D. Collier. *Shaping the Political Arena*. Princeton: Princeton University Press, 1991.
Converse, P. E. and R. Pierce. "Basic Cleavages in French Politics and the Disorders of May and June 1968." Paper at the 7th World Congress of Sociology, Varna, 1970.
Coser, L. *The Functions of Social Conflict*. New York: The Free Press, 1956.
Cotteret, J. M. and R. Moreau. *Le vocabulaire du général de Gaulle*. Paris: Presses de Sciences Po, 1969.
Cross, J. G. "A Theory of the Bargaining Process." *American Economic Review* 55, no. 1–2 (1965): 67–94.
Crozier, M. *The Bureaucratic Phenomenon*. Chicago: University of Chicago Press, 1964 [1st French ed., 1963].
Crozier, M. *The Stalled Society*. New-York: Viking Press, 1973 [1st French ed., 1970].
Crozier, M. and E. Friedberg. *Actors and Systems: the Politics of Collective Action*. Translated by Arthur Goldhamer. Chicago: The University of Chicago Press, 1980 [1st French ed., 1977].
Dahl, R. "Pluralism Revisted." *Comparative Politics* 10, no. 2 (January 1978): 191–203.
Dahrendorf, R. *Society and Democracy in Germany*. London: Weidenfeld and Nicolson, 1968.
Dansette, A. *Mai 1968*. Paris: Plon, 1971.
Das Gopta, J. "A Season of Caesars: Emergency Regimes and Development Politics in Asia." *Asian Survey* 18, no. 4 (1978): 315–49.
Davies, J. C. "Toward a Theory of Revolution." *American Sociological Review* 27, no. 1 (1962): 5–19.
Davies, J. C. "Comments." *American Sociological Review* 39, no. 4 (August 1974): 607–10.
Davies, J. C. "The J-Curve of Rising and Declining Satisfactions as a Cause of Revolution and Rebellion." In *Violence in America. Historical and Comparative Perspective*, edited by H. D. Graham and T. R. Gurr, 415–36. London: Sage, 1979.
Dennis, J. "Support for the Institution of Elections by the Mass Public." *American Political Science Review* 64, no. 3 (1970): 819–35.
Deutsch, K. W. "Social Mobilization and Political Development." *American Political Science Review* 55, no. 3 (1961): 493–514.
Deutsch, K. W. *The Nerves of Government: Models of Political Communication and Control*. New York: The Free Press, 1963.
Diehl, J. M. *Para-military Politics in Weimar Germany*. Bloomington: Indiana University Press, 1977.
Di Maggio, P. "Review Essay: On Pierre Bourdieu." *American Journal of Sociology* 84, no. 6 (1979): 1460–74.
Dobry, M. "Clausewitz et l' 'entre-deux', ou de quelques difficultés d'une recherche de paternité légitime." *Revue Française de Sociologie* 17, no. 4 (1976): 652–64.

Dobry, M. "Variation d'emprise sociale et dynamique des représentations: remarques sur une hypothèse de Neil Smelser." In *Analyse de l'idéologie*, edited by G. Duprat et al., vol. 1, 197–219. Paris: Galilée, 1980.
Dobry, M. "Mobilisations multisectorielles et dynamique des crises politiques. Un point de vue heuristique." *Revue Française de Sociologie* 24, no. 3 (1983): 395–419.
Dobry, M. "Éléments pour une théorie des conjonctures politiques fluides." Doctoral diss. (*Doctorat d'Etat*), Institut d'Etudes Politiques de Paris, 1984.
Dohse, K. "Das politische System in der Krise: Modell einer revolutionären Situation." *Politische Vierteljahresschrift* 12, no. 4 (1971): 555–78.
Downton, J. V., Jr. *Rebel Leadership. Commitment and Charisma in the Revolutionary Process*. New York: The Free Press, 1973.
Dubois, P. et al. *Grèves revendicatives ou grèves politiques. Acteurs, pratiques, sens du mouvement de mai*. Paris: Anthropos, 1971.
Duhamel, O. *La Gauche et la Ve République*. Paris: PUF, 1980.
Durkheim, E. *Suicide*. Translated by John. A. Spoulding and George Simpson. Glencoe: The Free Press, 1951 [1st French ed., 1897].
Easton, D. "A Re-Assessment of the Concept of Political Support." *British Journal of Political Science* 5, no. 4 (1975): 435–57.
Easton, D. "Theoretical Approaches to Political Support." *Canadian Journal of Political Science* 9, no. 3 (1976): 431–48.
Easton, D. *A Systems Analysis of Political Life*. Chicago: The University of Chicago Press, 1979 [1965].
Easton, D. and J. Dennis. *Children in the Political System: Origins of Political Legitimacy*. New York: McGraw-Hill, 1969.
Eckstein, H. "On the Etiology of Internal Wars." *History and Theory* 4, no. 2 (1965): 133–63.
Eckstein, H. *Division and Cohesion in Democracy. A Study of Norway*. Princeton: Princeton University Press, 1966.
Eckstein, H. *Support for Regimes, Theories and Tests*. Princeton: Princeton University Press, 1979, Center of International Studies, Research Monograph n° 44.
Eckstein, H. "Theoretical Approaches to Explaining Collective Political Violence." In *Handbook of Political Conflict, Theory and Research*, edited by T. R. Gurr, 135–66. New York: The Free Press, 1980.
Eckstein, H. and T. R. Gurr. *Patterns of Authority: A Structural Basis for Political Enquiry*. New York: John Wiley and Sons, 1975.
Edelman, M. *The Symbolic Uses of Politics*. Urbana: University of Illinois Press, 1964.
Edelman, M. "Escalation and Ritualization of Political Conflict." *American Behavioral Scientist* 13, no. 2 (September–December 1969): 231–45.
Edelman, M. *Politics as Symbolic Action*. Chicago: Markham, 1971.
Edelman, M. *Political Language. Words that Succeed and Policies that Fail*. New York: Academic Press, 1977.
Eidlin, F. H. *The Logic of "Normalization." The Soviet intervention in Czechoslovakia of 21 August 1968 and the Czechoslovak Response*. New York: Columbia University Press, 1980.
Eisenstadt, S. N. and R. Lemarchand, eds. *Political Clientelism, Patronage and Development*. London: Sage, 1981.
Enloe, C. H. *Ethnic Soldiers. State Security in a Divided Society*. Harmondsworth: Penguin Books, 1980.
Erikson, E. H. *Young Man Luther*. New York: Norton, 1958.
Erikson, E. H. *Gandhi's Truth*. New York: Norton, 1969.

Estier, C. *Journal d'un fédéré. La fédération de la gauche au jour le jour, 1965-1969.* Paris: Fayard, 1970.

Etzioni, A. *The Active Society, A Theory of Societal and Political Processes.* New York: The Free Press, 1968.

Farneti, P. "Social Conflict, Parliamentary Fragmentation, Institutional Shift, and the Rise of Fascism: Italy." In *The Breakdown of Democratic Regimes: Europe*, edited by J. J. Linz and A. Stepan, 3–33. Baltimore: The Johns Hopkins University Press, 1978.

Favre, P. "Nécessaire mais non suffisante: la sociologie des effets pervers de Raymond Boudon." *Revue Française de Science Politique* 30, no. 6 (1980): 1229–71.

Ferro, M. "La naissance du système bureaucratique en URSS." *Annales ESC* 31, no. 2 (1976): 243–67.

Field, J. A. and T. C. Hudnut. *L'Algérie, de Gaulle et l'armée.* Paris: Arthaud, 1975.

Fischer, M. M. J. *Iran, From Religious Dispute to Revolution.* Cambridge, MA: Harvard University Press, 1980.

Flanagan, S. C. "Models and Methods of Analysis." In *Crisis, Choice, and Change*, edited by G. A. Almond, S. C. Flanagan, and R. J. Mundt, 43–102. Boston: Little, Brown, 1973.

Fouchet, Ch. *Au service du général de Gaulle.* Paris: Plon, 1971.

Frémontier, J. *Renault: la forteresse ouvrière.* Paris: Seuil, 1975.

Gamson, W. A. *Power and Discontent.* Homewood: Dorsey Press, 1968.

Gaulle, Ch. de. *Mémoires d'Espoir*, tome 1 *Le Renouveau, 1958-1962.* Paris: Plon, 1970.

Geertz, C. *The Interpretation of Cultures.* New York: Basic Books, 1973.

Gehlen, A. *Man in the Age of Technology.* Translated by Patricia Lipscomb. New York: Columbia University Press, 1980.

Georgescu Roegen, N. *The Entropy Law and the Economic Process.* Cambridge, MA: Harvard University Press, 1971.

Girardet, R., ed. *La Crise militaire française, 1945-1962.* Paris: Presses de Sciences Po, 1964.

Goffman, E. *The Presentation of Self in Everyday Life.* New York: Doubleday Anchor Books, 1959 [1956].

Goffman, E. *Asylums: Essays on the Social Situation of Mental Patients and Other Inmates.* Chicago: Aldine, 1961.

Goffman, E. *Interaction Rituals: Essays on Face-to-face Behavior.* Chicago: Aldine, 1967.

Goffman, E. *Relations in Public. Micro Studies of the Public Ordrer.* New York: Basic Books, 1971.

Goffman, E. *Strategic Interaction.* Oxford: Basil Blackwell, 1979.

Goguel, F. *La Politique des partis sous la IIIe République.* Paris: Seuil, 1946.

Goldstone, J. A. "Theories of Revolution: The Third Generation." *World Politics* 32, no. 3 (1980): 425–53.

Gouldner, A. "Reciprocity and Autonomy in Functional Theory." In *Symposium on Sociological Theory*, edited by L. Gross, 241–70. Evanston: Row, Peterson, 1959.

Granovetter, M. "Threshold Models of Collective Behavior." *American Journal of Sociology* 83, no. 6 (1978): 1420–43.

Gras, A. *Sociologie des ruptures.* Paris: PUF, 1979.

Grew, R., ed. *Crises of Political Development in Europe and The United States.* Princeton: Princeton University Press, 1971.

Grimaud, M. *En mai, fais ce qu'il te plaît.* Paris: Stock, 1977.

Gurr, T. R. "A Causal Model of Civil Strife: A Comparative Analysis Using New Indices." *American Political Science Review* 62, no. 4 (1968): 1104–24.

Gurr, T. R. *Why Men Rebel*. Princeton: Princeton University Press, 1970.
Habermas, J. *Legitimation Crisis*. Translated by Thomas McCarthy. Cambridge: Polity, 1976 [1st German ed., 1973].
Halbwachs, M. *The Causes of Suicide*. London: Routledge and Paul Kegan, 1978 [1st French ed., 1930].
Heberlé, R. *Social Movements*. New York: Appleton-Century-Crofts, 1951.
Hempel, C. G. *Fundamentals of Concept Formation in Empirical Science*. Chicago: The University of Chicago Press, 1972 [1952].
Hermann, Ch. F. "Some Consequences of Crisis Which Limit the Viability of Organizations." *Administrative Science Quarterly* 8, no. 1 (1963): 61–82.
Hermann, Ch. F. "International Crisis as a Situational Variable." In *International Politics and Foreign Policy*, edited by J. N. Rosenau, 411–16. New York: The Free Press, 1969.
Hervieu-Léger, D. *De la mission à la protestation. L'évolution des étudiants chrétiens en France (1965-1970)*. Paris: Cerf, 1973.
Hirschman, A. O. *Exit, Voice and Loyalty*. Cambridge, MA: Harvard University Press, 1970.
Hoffmann, I. and S. Hoffmann. *De Gaulle, artiste de la politique*. Paris: Seuil, 1973.
Hoffmann, S. *Decline or Renewal? France Since the 1930's*. New York: Viking Press, 1974.
Huntington, S. P. *Political Order in Changing Societies*. New Haven: Yale University Press, 1976 [1968].
IFOP. *Les Français et De Gaulle*. Paris: Plon, 1971.
Ilchman, W. F. and N. T. Uphoff. *The Political Economy of Change*. Berkeley: University of California Press, 1969.
Ingelhart, R. and A. Hochstein. "Aligment and Dealignment of the Electorate in France and the United States." *Comparative Political Studies* 5, no. 3 (October 1972): 343–72.
Jänicke, M., ed. *Politische Systemkrisen*. Cologne: Kieperheuer und Witsch, 1973.
Janowitz, M. "Preface." In Lyford P. Edwards, *The Natural History of Revolution*, ix–xii. Chicago: University of Chicago Press, 1970 [1st ed., 1927].
Jeanneney, J. N. *Leçon d'histoire pour une gauche au pouvoir. La faillite du Cartel, 1924-1926*. Paris: Seuil, 1977.
Jervis, R. *The Logic of Images in International Relations*. Princeton: Princeton University Press, 1970.
Jervis, R. *Perception and Misperception in International Politics*. Princeton: Princeton University Press, 1976.
Johnson, Ch. *Revolution and the Social System*. Stanford: Hoover Institution Studies, 1964.
Johnson, Ch. *Revolutionary Change*. Boston: Little Brown, 1966.
Joxe, A. *Le Rempart social*. Paris: Galilée, 1979.
Kahn, H. *On Escalation. Metaphors and Scenarios*. New York: Praeger, 1974.
Kavanagh, D. A. *Crisis, Charisma and British Political Leadership*. London: Sage, 1974.
Killian, L. M. "The Significance of Multiple-Group Membership in Disaster." In *Group Dynamics*, edited by D. Cartwright and A. Zander, 249–56. Evanston: Row-Peterson, 1953.
Kriegel, A. *The French Communists: Profile of a People*. Translated by Elaine P. Halperin. Chicago: University of Chicago Press, 1972 [1st French ed., 1968].
Kuhn, T. S. *The Structure of Scientific Revolutions*. Chicago: University of Chicago Press, second edition enlarged, 1970 [1962].

Lacouture, J. *Pierre Mendès France*. Paris: Seuil, 1981.
La Gorce, P. M. de. *La république et son armée*. Paris: Fayard, 1963.
Lagroye, J., G. Lord, L. Mounier-Chazel, and J. Palard. *Les Militants politiques dans trois partis français*. Paris: Pedone, 1976.
Lakatos, I. "Falsification and the Methodology of Scientific Research Programmes." In *Criticism and the Growth of Knowledge*, edited by I. Lakatos and A. Musgrave, 91–196. Cambridge: Cambridge University Press, 1970.
Landé, C. "The Dyadic Basis of Clientelism." In *Friends, Followers and Factions: A Reader in Political Clientelism*, edited by S. W. Schmidt et al., 13–38. Berkeley: University of California Press, 1977.
Lavau, G. "Le parti communiste dans le système politique français." In *Le Communisme en France*, edited by F. Bon et al., 7–81. Paris: Presses de Sciences Po, 1969.
Lavau, G. "The PCF, the State and the Revolution: An Analysis of Party Policies, Communications, and Popular Culture." In *Communism in Italy and France*, edited by D. L. M. Blackmer and S. Tarrow, 87–139. Princeton: Princeton University Press, 1975.
Leca, J. "Pour une analyse comparative des systèmes politiques méditerranéens." *Revue Française de Science Politique* 27, no. 4–5 (1977): 557–81.
Leca, J. "Réformes institutionnelles et légitimation du pouvoir au Maghreb." *Annuaire de l'Afrique du Nord* 16 (1977): 3–13.
Ledeen, M. A. "The War as a Style of Life." In *The War Generation*, edited by S. Ward, 104–34. New York: Kennikat, 1975.
Lefranc, G. *Juin 1936*. Paris: Julliard, 1966.
Lehmbruch, G. "Consociational Democracy, Class Conflict and the New Corporatism." In *Trends Toward Corporatist Intermediation,* edited by P. C. Schmitter and G. Lehmbruch, 53–62. Beverly Hills, London: Sage, 1979.
Lenin, V. I. *Marxism and Insurrection*. Moscow: Progress Publishers, 1980 [1st Russian ed., 1917].
Lerner, D. *The Passing of Traditional Society*. New York: The Free Press, 1958.
Leroy, P. *L'organisation constitutionnelle et les crises*. Paris: LGDJ, 1966.
Le Roy Ladurie, E. "La crise et l'historien." *Communications*, no. 25 (1976): 19–33.
Levy, M. J. "Does it Matter if he is Naked? Bawled the Child." In *Contending Approaches to International Politics*, edited by K. Knorr and J. N. Rosenau, 87–109. Princeton: Princeton University Press, 1969.
Lévi-Strauss, C. *Tristes Tropiques*. Translated by John Russell. London: Penguin, 2011 [1st French ed., 1955].
Linz, J. J. "Time and Regime Change." Paper given at the Edinburgh Congress of the IPSA, August 1976.
Linz, J. J. *Crisis, Breakdown, and Reequilibration*. Baltimore and London: Johns Hopkins University Press, 1978.
Linz, J. J. and A. Stepan, eds. *The Breakdown of Democratic Regimes*, 4 vols. Baltimore and London: Johns Hopkins University Press, 1978.
Lipset, S. M. *Political Man*. Garden City: Doubleday, 1960.
Lora, G. *A History of the Bolivian Labour Movement, 1948-1971*. Cambridge: Cambridge University Press, 1977.
Luhmann, N. *Funktion und Folgen formaler Organisation*. Berlin: Duncker und Humblot, 1964.
Luhmann, N. *Legitimation durch Verfahren*. Darmstadt and Neuwied: Luchterhand, 1978 [1969].

Luhmann, N. "Temporalization of Complexity." In *Sociocybernetics. An Actor Oriented Social Systems Approach*, edited by R. F. Geyer and J. Van Der Zouwen, 95–111. Leiden: Nijhoff, 1978.

Luhmann, N. *The Differentiation of Society*. Translated by Stephen Holmes and Charles Larmore. New York: Columbia University Press, 1982 [most of the essays in this work were published in German in 1971].

Lussu, E. *Théorie de l'insurrection*. Paris: Maspero, 1971 [1936].

Malloy, J. M. *Bolivia: The Uncompleted Revolution*. Pittsburgh: University of Pittsburgh Press, 1970.

Malloy, J. M. and R. S. Thorn, eds. *Beyond the Revolution: Bolivia since 1952*. Pittsburgh: University of Pittsburgh Press, 1971.

Marx, G. "Thoughts on a Neglected Category of Social Movement Participant: The Agent Provocateur and the Informant." *American Journal of Sociology* 80, no. 2 (1974): 402–29.

Marx, K. *The Eighteenth Brumaire of Louis Bonaparte*. Translated by Daniel de Leon. New York: International Publishers, 1897 [1st ed. in German, 1852].

McCarthy, J. D. and M. N. Zald. "Resource Mobilization and Social Movements: A Partial Theory." *American Journal of Sociology* 82, no. 6 (1977): 1212–41.

McHugh, P. *Defining the Situation. The Organization of Meaning in Social Interaction*. Indianapolis: Bobbs-Merril, 1968.

Médard, J. F. "Le rapport de clientèle." *Revue Française de Science Politique* 26, no. 1 (February 1976): 103–31.

Merelman, R. M. "Learning and Legitimacy." *American Political Science Review* 60, no. 3 (September 1966): 541–61.

Merton, R. K. *Social Theory and Social Structure*. Chicago: Free Press of Glencoe, 1949.

Miller, A. H. "Political Issues and Trust in Government: 1964-1970." *American Political Science Review* 68, no. 3 (September 1974): 951–72.

Moch, J. *Une si longue vie*. Paris: Laffont, 1976.

Moore, B. *Social Origins of Dictatorship and Democracy: Lord and Peasant in the Making of the Modern World*. Boston: Beacon Press, 1966.

Moore, B. *Injustice. The Social Bases of Obedience and Revolt*. London and Basigstoke: Macmillan, 1978.

Morin, E., C. Lefort, and J. M. Coudray [C. Castoriadis]. *Mai 1968: la brèche*. Paris: Fayard, 1968.

Moscovici, S. *The Age of the Crowd: a Historical Treatise on Mass Psychology*. Translated by J. C. Whitehouse. Cambridge: Cambridge University Press, 1985 [1st French ed., 1981].

Mueller, C. *The Politics of Communication. A Study in the Political Sociology of Language, Socialization and Legitimation*. Oxford: Oxford University Press, 1973.

Muller, E. N. and T. O. Jukam. "On the Meaning of Political Support." *American Political Science Review* 71, no. 4 (December 1977): 1561–95.

Nadel, G. "The Logic of the *Anatomy of Revolution* with Reference to the Netherland Revolt." *Comparative Studies in Society and History* 2, no. 4 (1960): 473–84.

Nadel, S. F. *The Theory of Social Structure*. London: Cohen & West, 1957.

Nettl, J. P. *Political Mobilization*. London: Faber and Faber, 1967.

Neuberg, A. [Collective pseudonym]. *Armed Insurrection*. New York: St. Martin's Press, 1970 [1st French ed., 1931].

Nietzsche, F. *Werke: Kritische Gesamtausgabe*, vol. 14. Edited by G. Colli and M. Montinari. Berlin: W. De Gruyter, 1967.

Oberschall, A. *Social Conflict and Social Movements*. Englewood Cliffs: Prentice-Hall, 1973.
Olson, M. *The Logic of Collective Action*. Cambridge, MA: Harvard University Press, 1965.
Parodi, J. L. "Le 13 mai 1958: les Algériens d'origine européenne et la politique." Master diss., Institut d'études politiques de Paris, 1960.
Peixoto, A. C. "Le Clube militar et les affrontements au sein des forces armées (1945-1964)." In A. Rouquié et al., *Les Partis militaires au Brésil*, edited by A. Rouquié et al., 65–104. Paris: Presses de Sciences Po, 1980.
Pelassy, D. "Le rôle des signes dans la dictature. Étude sur la symbolique nationale-socialiste." PhD diss., Institut d'Études Politiques de Paris, 1975.
Pellet, A. "Pierre Mendès France et les événements de mai et juin 1968." Master diss., Université de Paris (Faculté de droit), 1979.
Perrenoud, Ph. "De quelques apports piagetiens à une sociologie de la pratique." *Revue Européenne des Sciences Sociales* 4, no. 38–39 (1976): 451–70.
Perrow, Ch. "The Sixties Observed." In *The Dynamics of Social Movements*, edited by M. N. Zald and J. D. McCarthy, 199–205. Cambridge: Winthrop, 1979.
Pilleul, G., ed. *L'Entourage de De Gaulle.* Paris: Plon, 1979.
Pizzorno, A. "Political Exchange and Collective Identity in Industrial Conflict." In *The Resurgence of Class Conflict in Western Europe since 1968*, edited by C. Crouch and A. Pizzorno, vol. 2, 277–98. Basingstoke: Macmillan, 1978.
Planchais, J. *Une histoire politique de l'armée.* Paris: Seuil, 1967.
Pompidou, G. *Pour rétablir une vérité.* Paris: Flammarion, 1982.
Popper, K. R. *Objective Knowledge: An Evolutionary Approach*. London: Oxford University Press, 1972.
Popper, K. R. "The Logic of the Social Sciences." In *The Positivist Dispute in German Sociology*, edited by T. W. Adorno et al., translated by Glen Adey and David Frysby, 87–104. London: Heinemann, 1976 [1st German ed., 1969].
Poulantzas, N. *Political Power and Social Classes*, translation editor Timothy O'Hagan. London: NLB, 1968 [1st French ed., 1968].
Poulantzas, N. *Fascism and Dictatorship: The Third International and the Problem of Fascism*. Translated by Judith White. London: Verso, 1974 [1st French ed., 1970].
Prewitt, K. *The Recruitment of Political Leaders: A Study of Citizen-Politicians*. Indianapolis: Bobbs-Merrill, 1970.
Prigogine, I. and I. Stengers. *Order out of Chaos: Man's New Dialogue with Nature*. Boulder: New Science Library, 1984 [1st ed. in French, 1979].
Prost, A. "Les manifestations du 12 février 1934 en province." *Le Mouvement Social*, no. 54 (January–March 1966): 6–27.
Prost, A. "Les grèves de juin 1936. Essai d'interprétation." In *Léon Blum, chef de gouvernement, 1936-1937*, edited by P. Renouvin and R. Rémond, 69–87. Paris: Armand Colin, 1967.
Przeworski, A. and H. Teune. *The Logic of Comparative Social Inquiry*. New York: John Wiley and Sons, 1970.
Pye, L. W. "The Legitimacy Crisis." In *Crises and Sequences in Political Development*, edited by L. Binder et al., 135–58. Princeton: Princeton University Press, 1971.
Racine, N. "L' Association des écrivains et artistes révolutionnaires (AEAR)." *Le Mouvement Social*, no. 34 (January–March 1966): 29–47.
Rémond, R. "Scandales politiques et démocratie." *Études* 336, no. 6 (June 1972): 849–64.
Rioux, J. P. *La France de la Quatrième République*, tome 1, *L'ardeur et la nécessité*. Paris: Seuil, 1980.

Rittberger, V. "Revolution and Pseudo-Democratization: The Formation of the Weimar Republic." In *Crisis, Choice, and Change,* edited by G. A. Almond, S. C. Flanagan, and R. J. Mundt, 285–391. Boston: Little, Brown, 1973.
Ross, G. *Workers and Communists in France. From Popular Front to Eurocommunism.* Berkeley: University of California Press, 1982.
Rossiter, C. *Constitutional Dictatorship. Crisis Government in the Modern Democracies.* New York: Harcourt Brace and World, 1963 [1948].
Rule, J. and C. Tilly. "1830 and the Unnatural History of Revolution." *Journal of Social Issues* 28, no. 1 (1972): 49–76.
Sartori, G. "Concept Misformation in Comparative Politics." *American Political Science Review* 64, no. 4 (1970): 1033–53.
Schelling, T. *The Strategy of Conflict.* Cambridge, MA: Harvard University Press, 1960.
Schmitter, Ph. C. "Still the Century of Corporatism." *Review of Politics* 36, no. 1 (1974): 85–131.
Schnapp, A. and P. Vidal-Naquet. *Journal de la commune étudiante.* Paris: Seuil, 1969.
Schonfeld, W. R. *Obedience and Revolt. French Behaviour Towards Authority.* Beverly Hills: Sage, 1976.
Schutz, A. "On Multiple Realities." In A. Schutz, *Collected Papers,* edited by Maurice Natanson, vol. 1, 207–59. The Hague: Martinus Nijhoff, 1962.
Scranton, Ph. B. "Escalation: A Comparative Study of Three Social Movements and the Process of Conflict Development." PhD diss., University of Pennsylvania, 1975.
Séguy, G. *Le mai de la CGT.* Paris: Julliard, 1972.
Seligman, L. G. "Political Parties and the Recruitement of Political Leadership." In *Political Leadership in Industrialized Societies,* edited by L. J. Edinger, 294–315. New York: Wiley, 1967.
Sérigny, A. de. *La Révolution du 13 mai.* Paris: Plon, 1958.
Skocpol, T. *States and Social Revolutions.* Cambridge: Cambridge University Press, 1979.
Skocpol, T. "Rentier State and Shi"a Islam in the Iranian Revolution." *Theory and Society* 11, no. 3 (1982): 265–83.
Skocpol, T. and M. Somers. "The Uses of Comparative History in Macrosocial Inquiry." *Comparative Studies in Society and History* 22, no. 2 (1980): 174–97.
Smelser, N. J. *Theory of Collective Behavior.* New York: The Free Press, 1962.
Smelser, N. J. "Theoretical Issues of Scope and Problems." *The Sociological Quarterly* 5, no. 2 (1964): 116–22.
Snyder, D. and C. Tilly. "Hardship and Collective Violence in France, 1830 to 1960." *American Sociological Review* 37, no. 5 (October 1972): 520–32.
Staniszkis, J. *Poland's Self-Limiting Revolution.* Edited by Jan T. Gross. Princeton: Princeton University Press, 1984 [1st French ed., 1982].
Starn, R. "Historians and Crisis." *Past and Present* 52, no. 1 (August 1971): 3–22.
Steinbruner, J. D. *The Cybernetic Theory of Decision.* Princeton: Princeton University Press, 1974.
Stinchcombe, A. L. *Constructing Social Theories.* New York: Harcourt Brace and World, 1968.
Tarrow, S. and L. Lamonte Smith. "Crisis Recruitment and the Political Involvement of Local Elites: Some Evidence from Italy and France." In *Elite Recruitment in Democratic Polities, Comparative Studies Across Nations,* edited by H. Eulau and M. M. Czudnowski, 205–37. New York: John Wiley and Sons, 1976.
Tasca, A. *The Rise of Italian Fascism, 1918-1922.* Translated by Peter and Dorothy Wait. London: Methuen, 1938.

Theobald, R. "The Role of Charisma in the Development of Social Movements." *Archives de Sciences Sociales des Religions* 49, no. 1 (January–March 1980): 83–100.
Thomas, W. I. "The Definition of the Situation." In *Symbolic Interaction*, edited by J. G. Manis and B. N. Meltzer, 331–26. Boston: Allyn and Bacon, 1972.
Thomas, W. I. and D. S. Thomas. "Situations Defined as Real are Real in Their Consequences" [1928]. In *Social Psychology Through Symbolic Interaction*, edited by G. P. Stone and H. A. Farberman, 162–74. Waltham: Xeros, 1970.
Tilly, C. *From Mobilization to Revolution*. Reading: Addison-Wesley, 1978.
Touchard, J. *Le Gaullisme, 1940-1969*. Paris: Seuil, 1978.
Touraine, A. *The May Movement: Revolt and Reform*. Translated by Leonard F. X. Mayhew. New York: Random House, 1971.
Tournoux, J. R. *Secrets d'Etat*. Paris: Union générale d'éditions, 1962 [1960].
Trimberger, E. K. *Revolution from Above. Military Bureaucrats and Development in Japan, Turkey, Egypt, and Peru*. New Brunswick: Transaction Books, 1978.
Trotsky, L. *Problems of Civil War*. Translated by A. L. Preston. New York: Pathfinder Press, 1970 [1st Russian ed., 1924].
Tucker, R. C. "The Theory of Charismatic Leadership." *Daedalus* 97, no. 3 (summer 1968): 731–56.
Valenzuela, A. *The Breakdown of Democratic Regimes. Chile*. Baltimore and London: Johns Hopkins University Press, 1978.
Veyne, P. *Writing History: Essay on Epistemology*. Translated by Moore-Rinvolucri. Manchester: Manchester University Press, 1984 [1st French ed., 1971].
Veyne, P. *Bread and Circuses: Historical Sociology and Political Pluralism*. Translated by Brian Pearce. London: Penguin, 1990 [1st French ed., 1976].
Viansson-Ponté, P. *Histoire de la République gaullienne*. Paris: Fayard, 1970.
Voisset, M. *L'article 16 de la Constitution du 4 octobre 1958*. Paris: LGDJ, 1969.
Weber, M. *On Charisma and Institution Building*, texts selected by Shmuel N. Eisenstadt. Chicago: University of Chicago Press, 1968.
Weber, M. *Economy and Society*. Edited by Guenther Roth and Claus Wittich. Berkeley and Los Angeles: University of California Press, 1978 [1968], 2 volumes.
White, J. "State Building and Modernization: The Meiji Restauration." In *Crisis, Choice, and Change,* edited by G. A. Almond, S. C. Flanagan, and R. J. Mundt, 499–559. Boston: Little, Brown, 1973.
Williams, P. *Wars, Plots and Scandals in Post-War France*. Cambridge: Cambridge University Press, 1970.
Williams, P. *La Vie politique sous la IVe République*. Paris: Colin, 1971.
Willner, A. R. *Charismatic Political Leadership: A Theory*. Princeton: Woodrow Wilson School of Public and International Affairs, 1968, "Research Monograph," 32.
Worsley, P. *The Trumpet Shall Sound. A Study of " Cargo " Cults in Melanesia*. New York: Schocken Books, 2nd ed. augmented, 1968.
Wright, J. D. *The Dissent of the Governed, Alienation and Democracy in America*. New York: Academic Press, 1976.
Wrong, D. H. *Power, Its Forms, Bases and Uses*. Oxford: Basil Blackwell, 1979.
Young, O. R. *Bargaining. Formal Theories of Negotiation*. Urbana: University of Illinois Press, 1975.
Zald, M. N. and M. A. Berger. "Social Movements in Organizations: Coup d'Etat, Insurgency, and Mass Movements." *American Journal of Sociology* 83, no. 4 (1978): 823–61.

Zald, M. N. and J. D. McCarthy, eds. *The Dynamics of Social Movements*. Cambridge: Winthrop, 1979.
Zolberg, A. R. "Moments of Madness." *Politics and Society* 2, no. 2 (winter 1972): 183–207.
Zimmermann, E. *Political Violence, Crises and Revolution. Theories and Research.* Cambridge: Schenkman, 1983.

Index of Authors

Abbott, A.   xxii, xxii nn.15–16
Abramson, P. R.   172 n.19
Adam, G.   80 n.10
Adams, R. N.   77 n.5
Adorno, T. W.   100 n.1
Agassi, J.   100 n.1
Aït-Aoudia, M.   xi n.3, xix n.12, xxii n.17
Akamatsu, P.   55 n.79
Ake, C.   140 n.30
Alinsky, S.   88 n.25
Allison, G. T.   70 n.30
Allport, G. W.   151 n.8
Almond, G. A.   17 n.39, 48, 48 nn.61–2, 49 n.63, 49 n.65, 50 n.69, 51 n.70, 55 n.78, 81 nn.12–13
Ambler, J. S.   14 n.32, 59 n.5
Ansart, P.   162 n.28
Apter, D. E.   5 n.7
Archibald, K.   7 n.14
Aron, R.   3 n.4, 8 n.17
Arthur, W. B.   xvi n.8
Auriol, V.   144 n.40, 182 n.42
Austin, J. L.   107 n.14
Aya, R.   25 n.3, 29 n.8

Bachelard, G.   25 n.1, 65 n.22
Bailey, F. G.   2n.1, 60 n.8, 71 n.32, 85 n.18
Balladur, E.   13 n.31, 121 n.40
Bauer, A.   36, 36 n.28, 37, 37 n.31
Bauman, Z.   60
Baumgartner, T.   60, 61 n.9
Béjin, A.   93 n.33, 119 n.36
Beloff, M.   113 n.27, 121 n.41
Bendix, R.   165 n.1
Bensaïd, D.   72 n.33, 80 n.10, 96 n.37, 146 n.43

Bensmann, J.   165 n.1
Berger, M. A.   10 n.24
Berger, P. L.   62 n.13, 63 n.17, 65 n.21, 86 n.19, 88 n.26, 106, 106 n.12, 173 n.25, 175 n.30
Berstein, S.   13 n.31, 14 n.32, 113 n.27, 121 n.41, 129 n.3, 132 n.9
Beuve-Méry, H.   144 n.39
Bianquis, G.   183 n.1
Binder, L.   48 n.61, 165 n.2
Blau, P. M.   140 n.30
Boltanski, L.   72 n.34, 90 n.29, 161, 161 n.26, 162 n.27
Bon, F.   80 n.10, 157 n.21
Boudon, R.   32, 32 n.15, 100 n.1
Bourdieu, P.   xiii n.4, xviii, xviii n.11, xix, 12 n.28, 32, 32 n.15, 57 n.1, 59–60, 59 n.6, 60 n.9, 63, 63 n.18, 93, 93 n.33, 94 n.34, 140 n.31, 149 n.1, 150 nn.3–4, 151, 151 n.7, 152, 152 nn.9–11, 153, 153 nn.12–13, 154, 154 n.15, 155, 156, 156 nn.16–18
Bourricaud, F.   150 n.3
Bracher, K. D.   53 n.74, 113 n.28
Braudel, F.   94–5 n.34
Brinton, C.   25 n.2, 33, 33 n.19, 34, 34 nn.20–4, 35–7, 37 n.30, 38, 38 n.33, 39, 39 n.39, 40, 40 n.40, 46 n.54, 54
Buckney, W.   60, 61 n.9
Buffelan, J.-P.   123 n.46
Burns, T. R.   60, 61 n.9

Camus, G.   97 n.38
Capdevielle, J.   80 n.10
Capoccia, G.   xvii n.9
Certeau, M. de   86 n.22

Index of Authors

Charles, C.   163 n.31
Chazel, F.   5 n.8
Chirac, J.   125 n.50
Chiroux, R.   112 n.27
Citrin, J.   176 n.32
Clausewitz, C. von,   xxiii, 3, 20
Coddington, A.   132–3 n.10
Cohen, E. A.   157 n.20
Cohen, L. J.   60 n.7
Cohn, S. F.   134 n.16, 137 n.23, 178, 178 n.38, 179, 179 n.39
Cohn-Bendit, D.   88 n.25
Coleman, J. S.   17 n.38, 69–70, 70 n.29
Colli, G.   183 n.1
Converse, P. E.   171 n.18
Corcuff, P.   xix n.12
Coser, L.   21 n.46, 31 n.11
Cotteret, J.-M.   106 n.13
Coudray, J.-M.   86 n.22
Cross, J. G.   132 n.10
Crozier, M.   60, 61 n.9, 87, 87 n.24, 122, 122 nn.42–4, 154 n.14

Dahl, R.   10 n.21
Dahrendorf, R.   21 n.46, 52 n.73
Dansette, A.   13 n.31, 107 n.14, 121 n.40, 130 n.5, 130 n.7
Das Gopta, J.   97 n.38
David, P. A.   xvi n.8
Davies, J. C.   29–32
Dennis, J   167 n.10, 172 n.19
Deutsch, K. W.   4, 4 n.6, 18, 18 n.41, 49
Diehl, J. M.   163 n.32
Di Maggio, P.   160 n.25
Dobry, M.   x nn.1–2, xiii n.5, xix n.12, xix n.14, xxii n.17, 3 n.4, 32 n.16, 42 n.43, 48 n.61, 53 n.75, 81–2 n.13, 96 n.36, 117 n.34, 180 n.41
Dohse, K.   115 n.30
Downton, J. V., Jr.   140 n.30
Dubois, P.   16 n.36, 80 n.10
Duhamel, O.   109 n.19, 173 n.23
Durkheim, E.   3 n.5, 86, 90 n.30

Easton, D.   32, 32 nn.16–17, 49 n.64, 66, 66 n.26, 79 n.8, 166 nn.3–4, 167 nn.5–10, 168–72, 174–7, 175 n.31, 177 n.37, 180, 180 n.41
Eckstein, H.   24 n.53, 25 n.3, 26, 26 n.5, 168, 168 n.14
Edelman, M. J.   109 n.18, 109 n.20
Edinger, L. J.   141, 163 n.30
Edwards, L. P.   33 n.18
Eidlin, F. H.   100 n.1
Eisenstadt, S. N.   62 n.14, 139 n.29
Enloe, C. H.   78 n.7
Erikson, E. H.   50
Estier, C.   146 n.46
Etzioni, A.   5, 5 nn.9–11, 6, 6 nn.12–13, 8n.17, 77 n.5

Favre, P.   100 n.1
Ferro, M.   55 n.81
Field, J. A.   14 n.32, 111 n.23
Fischer, M. M. J.   35 nn.25–7
Flanagan, S. C.   17 n.39, 48 nn.61–2, 49 n.70, 49 n.78, 49 nn.64–8, 81 nn.12–13
Fligstein, N. xiii n.4
Fouchet, C.   121 n.40
Frémontier, J.   83 n.14
Friedberg, E.   60, 61 n.9, 154 n.14

Gaïti, B.   xi n.3
Gamson, W. A.   2 n.1, 8 n.18
Gaulle, Ch. de   138
Geertz, C.   63 n.16
Gehlen, A.   86 n.19
Georgescu-Roegen, N.   77
Girardet, R.   59 n.5
Goffman, E.   xix, xix n.13, 7, 7 nn.14–15, 9 n.20, 66 n.25, 67 n.27, 68 n.27, 70 n.31, 90, 90 n.28, 100–2 nn.4–6, 103 n.7, 104, 107, 119, 149 n.1, 185
Goguel, F.   129 n.3
Goldstone, J. A.   26 n.3
Gorce, P. M. de la   14 n.32
Gouldner, A.   79 n.8
Granovetter, M.   12 n.29
Gras, A.   93 n.33
Grew, R.   48 n.61
Griffiths, F.   59–60 n.7

Grimaud, M.   111 n.22, 125 n.50
Gurr, T. R.   26 n.3, 29 n.7, 32 n.14, 168, 168 n.14

Habermas, J.   168, 168 n.13, 174 n.27
Halbwachs, M.   90 n.30
Halperin, M. H.   70 n.30
Hamon, H.   11 n.27
Handerson, L. J.   37 n.30
Heberlé, R.   163 n.32, 164 n.35
Hempel, C. G.   21 n.48
Hermann, C. F.   115 n.30
Hervieu-Léger, D.   164 n.34
Heurtin, J. P.   xxii n.17
Hirschman, A. O.   61, 61 n.11
Ho Chi Minh   48 n.60
Hochstein, A.   142 n.35
Hoffmann, I.   142 n.35, 143 n.36
Hoffmann, S.   83 n.14, 122, 141 n.32, 142 n.35, 143 n.36
Hudnut, T. C.   14 n.32, 111 n.23
Huntington, S. P.   39 n.38, 40, 64 n.19, 65 n.23

Ilchman, W. F.   2 n.1, 17 n.39, 18 n.40, 18 n.43, 19 n.44
Ingelhart, R.   142 n.35, 172 n.19

Jänicke, M.   115 n.30
Janowitz, M.   33 n.18
Jeanneney, J.-N.   132 n.9
Jervis, R.   8 n.16
Jobert, M.   121 n.40
Johnson, C. A.   47, 47 nn.57–8
Joll, J.   113 n.27
Joxe, A.   78 n.7
Jukam, T. O.   172 n.19

Kahn, H.   109 n.19, 110 n.21
Kavanagh, D. A.   49 n.65, 143–4 n.38
Kelemen, R. D.   xvii n.9
Kellner, H.   86 n.19
Killian, L. M.   90 n.29
Knöbl, W.   xxii, xxii nn.16–17
Kriegel, A.   158 n.23, 163 n.33
Kuhn, T. S.   3 n.3

Labro, P.   88 n.25
Lacouture, J.   146 n.43, 146 n.46

Lagroye, J.   163 n.30, 163 n.33
Lakatos, I.   xi
Landé, C.   62 n.14
Lavau, G.   157, 157 n.21
Leca, J.   177, 177 n.36
Ledeen, M. A.   163 n.32
Lefort, C.   86 n.22
Lefranc, G.   83 n.15
Lehmbruch, G.   68 n.28
Lemarchand, R.   62 n.14
Lemieux, C.   xix n.12
Lenin, V. I.   48 n.60
Lerner, D.   5 n.7, 49
Leroy, P.   97 n.38
Le Roy Ladurie, E.   46 n.55
Lévi-Strauss, C.   77 n.5
Levy, M. J., Jr.   81, 81 n.11
Linz, J. J.   42, 42 n.44, 42 n.46, 43, 43 nn.48–9, 44 n.51, 59 n.4, 75 n.2, 75 n.4, 93 n.32, 103 n.9, 104, 113 n.28, 133–7, 133 nn.11–12, 134 n.14, 134 nn.16–17, 135 nn.18–20, 139, 142 n.35
Lipset, S. M.   90 n.30, 174 n.28
Lora, G.   38 n.37
Lord, G.   163 n.30, 163 n.33
Lowit, T.   60
Luckmann, T.   62 n.13, 63 n.17, 88 n.26, 106, 106 n.12, 173 n.25, 175 n.30
Luhmann, N.   xiii n.4, 57 nn.1–2, 60, 66, 66 n.26, 76, 77 n.5, 90 n.29, 174, 174 n.27, 174 n.29, 175
Lussu, E.   48 n.60

McAdam, D.   xiii n.4
McCarthy, J. D.   2 n.1
Mahoney, J.   xvii n.9
Malloy, J. M.   38 nn.34–5, 38 nn.36–7
Martin-Criado, E.   xiii n.4
Marx, G.   108 n.17
Marx, K.   184, 184 n.2, 185
Maslow, A.   30 n.9
McHugh, P.   116 n.32
Médard, J.-F.   62 n.14
Merelman, R. M.   174 n.26
Merle, V.   90 n.28

Merton, R. K.   116, 116 n.32
Miller, A. H.   172 n.19
Moch, J.   123 n.45, 137 n.24
Montesquieu   65 n.24, 96
Montinari, M.   183 n.1
Moore, B., Jr.   10, 10 n.22, 39 n.39, 55 n.81
Moreau, R.   106 n.13
Morin, E.   86 n.22
Moscovici, S.   150 n.2
Mounier-Chazel, L.   163 n.30, 163 n.33
Mouriaux, R.   80 n.10
Mueller, C.   174 n.27
Muller, E. N.   172 n.19
Mundt, R. J.   17 n.39, 48 n.65, 48 n.70, 48 n.78, 48 nn.61–2, 81 n.12

Nadel, G.   38 n.32, 40 n.40, 45, 46 n.54
Nadel, S. F.   54, 54 n.76
Nettl, J. P.   5 n.7
Neuberg, A.   48 n.60
Nietzsche, F.   183, 183 n.1, 184

O'Donnel, G.   xix n.14
Oberschall, A.   2 n.1, 10 n.23
Olson, M.   10 n.23, 98 n.40

Palard, J.   163 n.30, 163 n.33
Panofsky, E.   150 n.1
Parodi, J.-L.   71 n.33
Parsons, T.   21, 47, 168, 170
Peixoto, A. C.   120 n.38
Pelassy, D.   113 n.29
Pellet, A.   142 n.34, 145 n.41, 146 nn.44–6
Perrenoud, P.   150 n.5
Perrow, C.   2 n.1
Piaget, J.   150
Pierce, R.   171 n.18
Pilleul, G.   131 n.8
Pizzorno, A.   186, 186 n.4
Planchais, J.   14 n.32, 59 n.5
Pompidou, G.   125 n.50, 131, 131 nn.7–8
Popper, K.   xxiii, 91 n.31, 99, 100, 100 n.1

Poulantzas, N.   42, 42 nn.45–6, 43, 43 n.50, 45, 45 n.53, 47, 47 n.59, 65 n.23, 135 n.18
Prewitt, K.   163 n.30
Prigogine, I.   78 n.6
Prost, A.   83 n.15, 113 n.27
Przeworski, A.   xix n.14, 22 n.49, 23 n.51
Pullberg, S.   65 n.21, 88 n.26
Pye, L. W.   165, 165 n.2

Racine, N.   11 n.27
Rapoport, A.   8 n.15
Rémond, R.   186 n.5
Rioux, J.-P.   180 n.40
Rittberger, V.   51, 51 nn.70–2, 54, 54 n.77
Roger, A.   xi n.3, xix n.12, xxii n.17
Ross, G.   83 n.14
Rossiter, C.   97 n.38
Rotman, P.   11 n.27
Rouquié, A.   120
Rule, J.   40 n.41

Sartori, G.   22, 22 n.50, 23, 23 n.52
Schelling, T.   xix, xix n.13, 7 nn.14–15, 9 n.19, 106 nn.10–11, 117 n.33, 118 n.35
Schmitt, C.   135
Schmitter, P. C.   xix n.14, 68 n.28
Schnapp, A.   96 n.37
Schonfeld, W. R.   122 n.43
Schuster, P.   60, 61 n.9
Schutz, A.   115, 115 n.31
Scranton, Ph. B.   110 n.21
Séguy, G.   83 n.14
Seligman, L. G.   163 n.30
Sérigny, A. de   84 n.16
Shapiro, J.-P.   60 n.7
Siméant-Germanos, J.   xi n.3
Skilling, H. G.   59–60 n.7
Skocpol, T.   39, 88, 88 n.27, 117 n.34
Smelser, N. J.   42 n.43, 117 n.34
Smith, L. L.   163 n.30
Snyder, D.   31 n.12
Staniszkis, J.   60 n.7, 75 n.3, 86 n.23
Starn, R.   46 n.56
Steinbruner, J. D.   84, 85 n.17
Stengers, I.   78 n.6

Stepan, A. 42, 42 n.44, 75 n.4, 133 n.12
Stinchcombe, A. L. 19 n.44, 177, 177 n.35

Tarrow, S. 163 n.30
Tasca, A. 111 n.24, 112 n.25, 136 nn.21–2, 138 nn.26–8
Teune, H. 22 n.49, 23 n.51
Theobald, R. 140 n.30
Thomas, D. S. 116 n.32
Thomas, W. I. 116, 116 n.32
Thorn, R. S. 38 n.34
Tilly, C. 2n.1, 10 n.23, 11, 11 nn.25–6, 12, 16, 16 n.37, 18, 31 n.12, 40 n.41, 54
Tocqueville, A. de 29
Touchard, J. 107 n.14
Toukhatchevsky, M. 48 n.60
Touraine, A. 16 n.36, 87–8, 88 n.25
Tournoux, J.-R. 13 n.31, 84 n.16, 107 n.14, 124 nn.47–8, 125 n.49, 131 n.7, 144 n.40
Tricot, B. 131 n.8
Trimberger, E. K. 39 n.39, 55 n.80
Trotsky, L. 48 n.60
Tucker, R. C. 143 n.38

Uphoff, N. T. 2 n.1, 17 n.39, 18, 18 n.40, 18 n.43, 19 n.44

Valenzuela, A. 133 n.12
Veyne, P. 36 n.29, 42, 42 n.42, 140 n.30
Viansson-Ponté, P. 84 n.16, 111 n.23
Vidal-Naquet, P. 96 n.37
Voisset, M. 98 n.39

Weber, H. 72 n.33, 80 n.10, 96 n.37
Weber, M. 58, 58 n.3, 60–1 n.9, 62, 62 n.12, 64, 64 n.20, 139–40 n.30, 139 n.29, 140, 142, 146 n.43, 152, 165, 165 n.1, 174, 175 n.31
White, J. 55 n.78
White, S. 60 n.7
Whitehead, L. xix n.14
Williams, P. 61 n.10, 124 n.47, 186 n.6
Willner, A. R. 147 nn.47–8
Wollenberg, E. 48 n.60
Worsley, P. 140 n.30
Wright, J. D. 176 nn.32–4, 177 n.37, 182
Wrong, D. H. 19 n.43

Young, O. R. 133 n.10

Zald, M. N. 2 n.1, 10 n.24
Zimmermann, E. 26 n.4
Zolberg, A. 86 n.21

Index of Notions

acceptability (of solutions)   107, 120–2, 129–30, 141
action   xxiii, 8, 9, 14, 56, 82–3, 87, 102, 168, *see also* activity; agency; expectations; calculations; move; motivations; purpose; teleology
   collective   xi, 2, 10, 72
   irrationality   2, 142, 184
   lines of action   7, 17, 71, 82–5, 88, 91, 99, 101, 105, 107, 109, 128
   rational   xx, 10, 118, 184
   repertories   10, 71, 123, 159
activity, *see* action; move
   interpretative   63, 107, 110, 117
   tactical   2–4, 6–10, 20, 56, 60, 62, 72, 91, 106, 108, 116–18, 120, 131, 135, 141, 155, 158
actor (or protagonist)   105, 151, 156, *see also* identity; dispositions; positions; resources; motivations; purpose; roles; socialization
   collective (and corporate)   xx, 19, 55–6, 71–2, 84, 98, 105, 109, 112–13 120–1, 131, 136–8
   precariousness of the collective actor   13–14, 72, 84, 96, 112
   that "matters"   109, 130
ad hoc hypotheses (*adhocism*)   91
agency and structures   xviii, 4, 46, 56, 78, 107, 123, 138, 153, 174–5, *see also* action; heroic illusion; objectivism
appropriateness (fallacy)   8, 81, 168, 174
   in Bourdieu   152–5
   in Popper   100

arena   69, 162, *see also* sector, "narrowing of the political arena"
   opening up of sectoral arenas   75–6, 135
   and sectors   69
assent, assenters   176, 182, *see also* legitimacy; support
assessment   7, 12, 18, 60, 89, 102, 118, 151, 160, 181, 184, *see also* definition of situation; calculations
   of resources 'value' or effectiveness (*see* value)
   of situation   76, 102
attentism, *see* "wait-and-see attitude"
attitude   150, 172, 176
   and habitus   150–1
attractor states   78
authoritarian system   xi, 66, 69, 186
   and democratic system   58–9, 66, 97, 179, 187
   and differentiation (complexity)   186
autonomy
   sectoral autonomy   20, 65–9, 71, 74, 92 (*see also* complexity)
   of the crisis dynamics (*see* emancipation from etiology)

bargaining (negotiation)   76, 84, 106–8, 120–5, 128–39, 144
   tacit   17, 106, 108, 125, 129–30, 132, 138
beliefs   83, 117, 157, 165, 168–9, 175–81
bifurcation (branching point, 'critical juncture'turning point)   xvi, xvii, 14, 43–4, 108, 111, 141, *see*

also natural history; tree-shape variants; historicism
boundaries
    of bargaining   124
    of mobilizations   16
    sectoral   66, 74–5, 135

calculability   xx, 82
calculations   xviii–xx   8, 10, 12–16, 50, 56, 60, 70, 76, 80–4, 89, 92, 97–8, 107, 128, 144, 182, 184, *see also* focal points; metric transparency
    escaping (spill out), defined   76
    rational calculation (*see* rational choice)
    sectoral capture of   60–1
    tools of calculation   xix–xx, xxiv, 12, 60, 76, 82–4, 107, 117–18, 184
'capital' (political or charismatic)   81, 132, 141, 142, 153–4
    realization   142, 144 (*see also* resources)
career   2, 87, 141, 159, 162
    career expectations   28, 64, 87
    in the crisis   160
categories (everyday), categorization   x, xv, 16, 17, 40–2, 63, 74, 185–6
causality   xiii, xxi–xxiv, 2, 12, 14, 26–8, 31–2, 36–41, 45, 46, 50, 53, 74, 114, 138, 166, 170, 185, *see also* contingency; etiological illusion; historicism; teleology
    causal configuration   1
    conjunctural causality   xxiv
    determinism   41, 50
    nomological regularities   23–4, 73–87, 99, 177, 185–6 (*see also* trend properties)
    small and big effects   41
charisma   16, 106, 112, 132, 139–47, *see also* solution; 'capital'
    charismatic base   142, 144–5
    charismatic strategies   106, 139–40, 147
    as focal point   132, 141
    indirect charisma   144–6
    situational charisma   147

social confirmation   140–7
traditional view of charisma   140, 142, 146
choice   46, 81, 149, *see also* heroic illusion; calculation; decision
    rational choice   xx, 10, 13, 46, 48–56, 81
cleavages   161, 181
    'dominated' and 'dominants'   10
collusive transactions   67–9, 177–81, 183, *see also* consolidation; legitimacy
    crises in   68, 87, 180, 185
communication   102–3, 118–19
    tacit   102
    vs. expression   103–4, 125, 138
comparison   22–4, 33–44, 54–5, 185–6, *see also* natural history; outcome; historicism
    impossibility of comparing   xxi, 37, 40, 52
complexity (social)   20, 57–72, *see also* differentiation
    complex societies   xii, 20–3, 57, 154, 156, 177, 181
    suspension of complexity   98
conductivity   72, 187
confidence in the habitus   157–8
conjuncture   xvi, 3, 8, 9, 20–1, 24, 45, 56, 61, 73–8, 89–91, 99, 152–3, 160, 161, *see also* fluidity; plasticity of structures
    critical and routine   xv, xx, 17, 18, 46, 47, 105, 119, 152, 183
    as particular state of 'structures'   xii, xvi, xxiv, 3–4, 11, 20, 64–5, 73–98, 103–5, 138, 183–7
consciousness   29, 47, 48, 63, 65, 79, 155–6, 185, *see also* purpose; teleology; heroic illusion
    becoming "class-conscious"   72
    "false consciousness"   65
consensus   9, 13, 61, 64, 72
consent, consenters   10, 176
consolidation   67, 85, 87, 179, *see also* collusive transactions; state; objectification
conspiracy (plot)   14

Index of Notions

context   3, 19, 82, 99, 103, 105, 154, 161
   international context   34, 49, 52, 82
contingency   xx, xxii–xxiii, 13, 40–2, *see also* outcomes; historicism
continuity hypothesis   xiii, 1–3, 19–20, 27, 183–5
   methodological dimension of   51–3, 56
control
   loss of control   105, 124, 142, 158 (*see also* derailment)
   of mobilizations   15, 16
   of the moves' meanings (or effects)   91, 105
   of resources   5–6
   of the situation   61
conversion   70
   of resources   5–6
   of variables   53
cooperation   9, 69–70
   tacit   118 (*see also* mixed motives game)
cooptation of 'disloyal opposition'   133–8
coordination, *see* tacit coordination
credibility   106, 130, 141, *see also* plausibility structures
crisis, *see* conjuncture; fluidity; desectorisation; collusive transactions
   crisis structures (*see* 'structures')
   as everyday-language category   41–2, 89, 185
   as process (or dynamics)   xii, 1, 9, 10, 20, 73–5, 79, 92–3, 119, 132–3, 136, 170, 171, 185–7
   provisional definition   1
   as transformation of "structures"   3, 16, 19–21, 56, 70, 73–87, 104, 184–5
critical juncture, *see* bifurcation
critical test, *see* refutability
culturalism (culturalist bias)   xi, xv, 86, 114, 122–4, 171, 186
culture   xv, 12, 13, 35, 68, 78, 117, *see also* focal points; meaning; culturalism

decision   46, 50, *see also* calculations; heroic illusion; choice
decisional analysis   xvii, 5, 46
definition of situation   82–3, 105, 107–10, 113–17
   as activity   114–16, 119–25, 128
   interdependence of definitions   115
   precariousness of definitions   118, 147
   sectoral definitions   118–19
delegitimation   24, 63, 87, 165–82, *see also* collusive transactions; de-objectification; legitimacy; support
   induced delegitimation processes: 171–175, 177–82
   tempo of delegitimation process   171
de-objectification process   xiv, 64, 85–8, 137, 153, 157, 171, 172, 175, 180–2
   art of de-objectification   87
   and values   168, 174, 181, 182
democratic systems   10, 42–4, 58–9, 67–8, 176, 180, 182, 186, *see also* authoritarian systems
   'vulnerability' of democracies   180, 186
derailment (of the crisis process)   8, 15, 82–4, 103, 125, 131, 178, *see also* etiological illusion; emancipation from etiology; control of the mobilization; causality
desectorization   xii, xv, 74–80, 92, 99, 103–4, 136, *see also* fluidity; conjuncture
differentiation (structural)   xv, xx, 1, 17, 20, 57–8, 67, 186–7, *see also* complexity; sectors; sectoral logics
   non-functionalist view of differentiation   xiii, 58, 60, 69
dispositions   xviii, 10, 149–56, 160–2, *see also* inertia of dispositions; habitus; confidence in the habitus
   'appropriateness' to the situation: 152–153 (*see also* appropriateness fallacy)

homogeneity/heterogeneity of
  individual's dispositions   89, 151
  and socialization   155–6
  strong determination of dispositions
    (see regression toward habitus)
  transferability of dispositions   151,
    159, 162, 183, 185
domination (modes of)   63, 67
dual (or multiple) power   34, 54–5

elites (strategic)   176, see also
  collusive transactions
emancipation (autonomization), see
  etiological illusion; crisis as
  process; causality
  of critical process from its
    etiology   xiii, xiv, xxiv, 9, 28, 118,
    132, 185
  of institutions (conjunctural)   74–5
emergent effect   110, 127–47,
  170–4, 177–9, see also solution;
  charisma
energy   77, 88
enforcement system   101–3, 114,
  140, see also outcome; game
entropy   77–8
escalation   109–11, 121, 131
essentialist fallacy (and/or
  substantialism)   x, 16–18, 41,
  107, 141, 159–60, 187
  vs. relation (see relational
    perspective)
etiological illusion   xiv, 26–32, 170–1,
  173–4, 180, 185, see also
  causality
  macro-sociological variant   32
exchange of moves   2, 8, 9, 15, 20,
  78, 102, 104–5, 116, 118, 139,
  144, 171, 184, see also strategic
  interaction
existence asserting   109, 111–14
expectations   xviii, 7, 28–32, 34,
  50, 60, 64, 71, 80, 107, 117,
  128–32, 141, 168, 174, 184, see
  also perceptions; calculations;
  the probable
explicandum (shift)   xxi, xxiii, 2–3,
  7–8, 12, 15, 19–20, 27, 33,
  41–2, 53, 57, 64–5, 73, 99–100,

114, 146, 154, 156, 174–5,
  177, 184, see also continuity
  hypothesis
expression (vs. communication), see
  communication

face to face interactions (or
  relations)   122–3, 152
fallacy of useless measurement, see
  measurement
feelings (and affects)   80–1, 103,
  165–6, 168, 178, 181–2
fluctuations of the 'value' of resources,
  see resources
fluidity   xx, 20, 53, 73–98, 103, 127,
  152, 157, 183–6, see also
  conjunctures; desectorisation;
  structural uncertainty; de-
  objectification
  defined   73, 74, 80, 85
  deflation of fluidity   111, 128
focal point   xx, 107, 117–19,
  130–2, 139, 141–2, see also
  calculations; perception;
  charisma; bargaining; solution
  cultural and situational   117
focus of attention   139
frustration   26, 28–32, see also
  etiological illusion; causality
function
  alleged 'functions' of sectors or
    fields   58–9
  'tribune' function   157–8
  of violence   39
functionalism   21, 60, 67, 69
  as a bias   60, 69
  structural-functionalism   47, 49,
    79, 96

game   2, 10, 14, 16, 20, 21, 45–6,
  55, 60, 69, 94, 101–7, 124,
  130, 135, 139, 144, 160, 173,
  see also rules of the game;
  cooperation
  'mixed motives' game   9, 118, 141
  game confined   124
  game theory   2, 8, 10, 84
  tight vs. loose game   102
  imperfect tight game   103–9, 141

generation   44, 163
group (social, or class)   2, 11, 13, 14, 21, 29, 34, 35, 44, 65, 69, 71–2, 84, 87, 113, 117, 146, 147, 152, 157, 159–64, 178, 182–4, *see also* collective actor
   ethnic groups   78
   interest groups   135
   poles of structuration   161–4

habitus   xviii, 149–63, *see also* dispositions; socialization; confidence in the habitus
   and creative effervescence   149
   and habits   149
   strong determination of dispositions (*see* regression toward habitus)
heroic illusion   xviii–xix, 44–56, 78, 81, *see also* choice; decision; causality; agency
historicism   xxii–xxiii   40–2, 44, *see also* outcome; teleology; retrospective illusion; history; natural history
historicity   xii, 13, 41, 58, 71, 154, 162, *see also* contingency
history, *see* contingency; causality; critical junctures; historicism; natural history; teleology; temporality
   the 'march of history'   xxiii, 40, 43, 66
   historical *intrigue*   30
homology
   'structural homology' between sectors or 'fields' (assumption)   59
   perceived homology between situations   132

identity   185
   collective actor's identity   72, 112–13
   individual's multiple identity   89–90
   subjective identity   88
   unidimensionalization   90
   universal identity marker   90
illocutionary force, *see* speech acts; plausibility; structures

illusion, *see* etiological illusion; heroic illusion; natural history
impersonality (of social relationships)   62, 85, 86, 123, *see also* objectification
conjunctural personalization (and personal activity)   123, 142–3, 147
inertia (of dispositions)   151, 153
information   18–19, 82, 102, 138, *see also* metric transparency; expression; visibility; resource 'value'; structural uncertainty
inhibition (tactical)   82, 106
institution   1, 7, 10, 12–14, 20, 46, 51, 53–4, 58, 64–6, 71, 75, 77, 100–1, 104–5, 127–32, 155, 159
   institutional position (*see* position)
   total institution   66, 90
institutional dissociation   158–60
institutionalization (and deinstitutionalization)   60, 64, 69, 71, 86, 95–7, 113, 119, 154–5, 173, 184, *see also* objectification
intensification dynamics (as sociological imagery)   73, *see also* violence; rise to the extremes
intention   xiii, 9, 14, 47, 79, 94, 119, 125, 138, *see also* purpose
interaction   63, 70–1, 90, 101, 115, 152, 160, *see also* calculation; enforcement system; game
   at a distance   104
   face-to-face   70–1, 86, 103, 122–3
   between resources *vs.* between actors   70, 79
   strategic interaction   xix, 7, 14, 100–1, 119
interdependence   60, 70, 71, 96, 99
   of definitions of situation (*see* definition of situation)
   extended interdependence   xiv, 90–1, 99–125, 133, 136, 140, 147, 184
   local (sectoral) interdependence   60

interest xx, 9, 14, 61, 71, 79, 100, 109, 111, 118, 147, 166, *see also* motives; purpose
   imputation of interest by the scholar 9
   sectoral interests 60, 66
issues (and stakes) 11, 14, 28, 41, 51, 54, 60, 71–2, 75–6, 94–5, 97, 108, 120, 124, 128, 138, 160
   control over issues 142, 148
   issues emancipation or mobility 75–6, 94, 108

legitimacy (and legitimation):16, 18, 24, 63, 68, 87, 98, 165–82, *see also* delegitimation; collusive transactions; diffuse support; feelings; values; socialization
   legitimacy and collusive transactions 175–82
   legitimacy as objectification 171–4
   legitimacy and sectoral logics 174
   'liberal bias' 168, 170
   normative view of legitimacy 174, 176–7
   self-legitimation 174
   standard 'paradigm' of legitimacy 166, 169
   'structural' 170, 175, 181
location (individuals' conjunctural location) 159–64
logics (social) 98
   of economic markets 18, 62
   forced loyalty 61
   specific sectoral logics xiii, 17–18, 58, 59, 67, 69, 74, 76, 80, 82, 86, 88–9, 96, 98, 99, 101–2, 105, 118–19, 127, 159, 174, 186
   'semi-loyal' and 'disloyal' opposition 43–4, 133
   situational logics xiii, xxiv, 20, 54, 59, 99–100, 105, 165, 184
loyalty 10, 11

marks (and markers) 12, 72, 90, 108–14, 117, 125, 141, *see also* definition of situation
materiality 101–2, 107, 108, 112–13, 116, 162
meaning 14–16, 41, 105, 125, 173, 184, *see also* taken for granted; objectification; definition of situation
   battles for meaning 16, 41
   imposition of meaning 16
   sectoral webs of meaning 63, 184
measurement (and measure) 4, 6, 18, 53, 77, 81–4, 172, 179, *see also* structural uncertainty; 'value'; metric transparency
   fallacy of useless measurement 81–2
   function of value measurement (of political resources) 18
   technical measurement tools 119
methodological individualism 100
metric transparency 19, *see also* information; measurement; 'value'
mobilization 4–5, 15, 32, 170, 185, *see also* 'resources mobilization'; approach; action
   centralist fallacy 11, 15
   dispersion of 14–16
   manipulative view of mobilizations 16
   mobilization and moves 7–12
   mobilization's 'take off' 11–13
   multisectoral mobilizations xiii, 15, 20, 59, 70, 73–6, 85, 93, 99, 104, 122, 136, 171, 177, 185–7
   'social' mobilization 4, 49
   strategic dimension of mobilizations 12–16
'moments of madness' 86
motives (and motivations) 9, 29–31, 125, 168, 185, *see also* purpose; intention; interest; etiological illusion; teleology
move xx, 7–15, 36, 56, 59, 94, 101, 143–6, *see also* exchange of moves; strategic interaction; threat
   covert (or hidden) move 133–8, 143
   defined 7

direct   101, 104, 112
irreversible move   108
mediated   101, 104
temporal chaining of moves
    104–5, 107, 110, 125, 131,
    137
visible move   145–6
multiple insertion, *see also* institutional
    position
of individuals   89–90
multi-positionality   72
of organizations   68
'multiple realities'   115
'narrowing of the political arena'
    (hypothesis)   133–9

natural history approach (illusion)   xxii,
    33–46, 110, *see also* historicism;
    bifurcations; heroic illusion
stages identification   40–3
tree shape variants   42–5
typical sequence of stages
    33–4
negotiation, *see* bargaining
'normalization' (of the situation)   97,
    111, 128, 131, *see also*
    resectorization; channeling
    tactics

objectification   60, 62–5, 68, 71,
    72, 85–7, 104, 154, 161,
    173–5, 177, 181, *see also*
    institutionalization; collusive
    transactions; de-objectification
differentials of objectification   98
technologies of objectification   64,
    113–14
objectivist fallacy (objectivism)   4–7,
    16–17, 47, 64, 94, 99, 109, 111,
    156, 173, *see also* reification;
    roles
outcome   xxii, xvi, 2, 40, 76, 84,
    101–7, 160–3, *see also* natural
    history; regressive method;
    retrospective illusion; historicism
extended/local   105–8
outcomes and contingency   41
thinking from outcomes (fallacy
    of)   xx–xxiii, 36, 40, 43, 162–3

perception(s)   xix, 3, 8, 14, 19, 20,
    52, 59, 63, 67, 70, 86, 97,
    107–9, 113, 114, 116, 117, 120,
    129–32, 138–9, 150, 153, 160,
    181, 184, *see also* definition
    of situation; focal points;
    expectations; the probable
'appropriateness' of
    perceptions   8, 83
'misperception'   8
personalization, *see* impersonality
plasticity of structures   xiii, xv, 57, 65,
    73–98, 185, *see also* crisis (as
    transformation of structures);
    desectorization
plausibility structures   106, 111, 141,
    see also credibility
position (institutional)   34, 59–61, 65,
    66, 155
and dispositions   155–8
power   8, 19, 177, 186, *see also* dual
    power; transformation of the
    social division of political labor
'neutral powers'   135
and 'political currencies'   18
power vacuum   43, 75, 78, 113,
    139, 141
practical problems or dilemmas   3, 15,
    82, 160
practical recipes   47, 97–8, 127, 156,
    158–9
probable (perception and definition of
    the probable)   10, 13, 19, 82,
    97, 121, 130, 132, 138, 160,
    173, 181
provocation   87, 108
purpose (aim)   3, 14, 48, 94, 99–100,
    156, 161, *see also* intention;
    interest; motivation; heroic illusion

reconstruction of the social world
    119
refutability, 'validation'   xi, 23–4, 79,
    91–8, 159–61, *see also* ad hoc
    hypothesis
critical test   23–4, 92, 133, 171
and observation   91–8
regression towards habitus   153–64,
    see also dispositions; socialization

regressive method xxi, 36–40, 162–3, *see also* natural history; outcome; historicism
reification xv, 16, 20, 47, 64, 85, *see also* objectivism
relational perspective x, 16–17, 19–20, 82, 84, 92, 94, 105, 115, 136, *see also* essentialist fallacy
'reliable personnel' (selection) 157, 159
representations 14, 29, 47, 61, 63, 109–10, 114, 116, 153, 161, *see also* meaning; perceptions; beliefs
repression 34, 35, 87, 123
resectorization 128, 131
resistance differentials (of institutions or organizations) 156–9
resources 2, 4–6, 8, 11, 49, 69–70, 160, *see also* measurement; fallacy of inutile measurement; capital; conversion
  coercive resources 19, 28, 108, 109
  fluctuations of the 'value' of resources, xx, 18, 51–2, 54, 75, 80–4, 91, 99
  imputation of resources' 'values' by the scholar 81–2
  resources allocation 166
  resources' effectiveness 81–2
  relational *vs.* essentialist view of resources 16
  manipulative view of resources 16–19
  modes of giving 'value' or 'weight' to resources 8
  social distribution of resources xv, 6, 10, 52, 60, 136
  transferability of 17
'resources mobilization' approach 2, 5, 12, 16–20, 69
retrospective illusion xxi, 43, 46, 171, *see also* outcomes; natural history; historicism
revolution 23–31, 33, 47
  as everyday-language category 41
  'legal revolution' 43, 134 (*see also* outcome; natural history; etiological illusion)
  'subjective' and 'objective' factors of revolution xix, 47–8 (*see also* heroic illusion)
rhythms (sectoral) 66, 92–7
  rhythms' 'synchronization' (as illusion) 93 (*see also* temporalities)
  ruptures in sectoral rhythms 94, 97
rise to the extremes, *see* violence; intensification; escalation
role 89, 150, 156, 184
  role distance 156
  role-taking 184–5
rules of the game 61, 97, 100, 102, 159, *see also* game; specific sectoral logics
  internal or sectoral 61, 76, 85, 97, 102, 159
  pragmatic *vs.* official xx, 60–1, 63, 71, 72, 75, 95
  pragmatic principle of non-interference 67–8

scandal (or 'affair')
  as multisectoral mobilization 186
secrecy, *see* moves, covert; 'narrowing of the political arena'; bargaining; visibility
  prevalence of the hidden (as illusion) 133–8
  sectoral 'codes of silence' 65
  violating secrecy 134, 138
sector xiii, 20, 57, 68, 93, 94, 136, 159, *see also* complexity; differentiation; desectorization; functionalism
  and arena 69–72
  coercive (militarized) sectors 78, 97–8, 120, 135–6, 157, 159, 181
  hardened sectors 98, 120
  political sectors 61–2, 68, 74–6, 94–6, 161
  and related notions ('action system', 'field') 60–1
  specific sectoral logics (*see* logics)
  strategic sectors 67, 159, 182
selection of historical 'facts' or 'events' xxi, 36, 41, 44,

51–2, *see also* 'regressive method'; outcome (thinking from outcome); retrodiction; natural history; teleology; bifurcations
selectivity (methodological) 24, 89
self-defeating prophecy xxiv, 23, 121
self-personification 185
self-reference 60, 76
simplification, *see also* desectorization
   of individual's life 90
   of social games and of social space 89, 98
situation xvii, xxiv, 7, 15, 54, 60–1, 76, 82–5, 87, 101–3, 112, 117, 151–3, 158, 184, *see also* definition of situation; interdependence; logics of situation
   face-to-face situation 103
   individual's immediate situation 160–3
   Olsonian situation 98
   'unstructured' or 'amorphous' situations 54, 84
social division of political labor (transformations of) xv, 32, 97–8
socialization 89, 122, 149–51, 156, 167–8, *see also* dispositions; habitus; roles
social movement 4, 10, 16, 31, 71, 157, 160, *see also* mobilization
solution 51, 45, 84, 107, 120, 121, 127–32, 137, 140, 141, *see also* charisma; emergent effect; focal point; bargaining
   institutional solution 127–33, 157–8
speech acts 107, 142–3
state 13, 89, 121, 136, 183, *see also* complexity; actor, collective; collusive transactions; sector, strategic
   as differentiated sectors 17, 67, 98
   as consolidation network 67
strategic interaction, *see* interaction
structural uncertainty xiv, xix, 80–5, 106, 107, 117, 119, 184, *see also* calculation; desectorization; derailment process

structures xv, xix, 3, 20, 46, 53–6, 64, 73, 75, 78, 80, 85, 89, 184, *see also* plasticity of structures; complexity; differentiation; heroic illusion; objectivist fallacy
   crisis structures 54–6, 154
   realism of the structures 65
   structures and agency (*see* agency)
subjectivism (fallacy), *see* heroic illusion; decision; choice; purpose
substantialism, *see* essentialist fallacy
substratum of errors 25
support (diffuse) 87, 166–9, 173, 176, *see also* assent; feelings; legitimacy
   and legitimacy 87, 166
   'minimal level of support' 168, 170, 176, 180
   objects of support 168–9
   vs. specific support 167, 173
   reservoirs of diffuse support 167, 169, 175–81
symbolic politics (approach) 109–13
system analysis 32, 66, 96, 166–70

tacit coordination 59, 104, 118
tactical mobility 158
tactics, *see* deterrence; escalation; threat provocation, technologies, practical recipes
   channeling tactics 128, 131, 157–8
   de-blocking 87
   disconnection tactics 95
   dissuasive 8
   insulation 135–6
   last resort 157
   locking 95
'taken for granted' 62, 85, 97, 123, 161
technologies (institutional) 95–8, 109, *see also* objectification, technologies of
   of 'change' preservation 65
   of crisis control 97–8
   of isolation 78–80
   of organizational survival 157
   of sectoral autonomization 66, 96
   of splitting the political risks 96

tectonics (social) 72
teleology 3, 9, 43
temporality, *see also* objectivist fallacy
    and long term (*longue durée*) xxi, 41, 77, 86, 94, 168–9
    short term xv, 3, 6, 87, 128, 131, 154, 166, 171
testability, *see* refutability
test of position 61, 76, 119, *see also* definition of situation; calculation, structural uncertainty
'Thomas theorem' 116
threat 8, 110, 125, 131, *see also* escalation; move
threshold
    chronological 51–3
    in escalation processes 109
    in mobilizations 12–13, 96–7
    objectivist view of thresholds 12, 109, 110
totalist fallacy 24, *see also* selectivity
transparency, *see* metric transparency; visibility

tree shape variants, *see* natural history
trend properties xiv, xxiv, 21–2, 74–6, 90–1, 160, 185

urgency (sense of) 103, 131
'value' (or 'weight') of resources, *see* resources

values (social) 14, 67, 150, 168, 174, 181–2
violence 20, 30–1, 73, 109–10, *see also* resources, coercive
    'functions' of violence (*see* functions)
    disappearance of the State's 'monopoly of violence' 38
    level of violence 73
    rise to the extremes of xiii, 73, 110, 121
    social organization of violence xv
visibility 64, 98, 135–6

'wait-and-see' attitude 13, 121